◆ İmirler

◆ Maşat Höyük

azköy

◆ Alişar Höyük

◆ Kültepe

ük

ük

◆ Zincirli

◆ Carchemish

Euphrates R.

Murat R.

URARTU

Lake
Van

◆ Malatya-Arslantepe

Habur R.

Tigris R.

◆ Ayanis

Lake
Urmia

◆ Hasanlu

ASSYRIA

◆ Khorsabad

◆ Nimrūd
Fort Shalmaneser

Euphrates R.

● Baghdad

N
W   E
S

0   50 100 150 200 mi

0   100 200 300 km

The Archaeology of Phrygian Gordion,

Royal City of Midas

Ellen L. Kohler at Gordion. Source: Gordion Archive, Penn Museum, image 175958.

GORDION SPECIAL STUDIES

GORDION EXCAVATIONS FINAL REPORTS

MUSEUM MONOGRAPH 136

GORDION SPECIAL STUDIES VII

The Archaeology of Phrygian Gordion, Royal City of Midas

C. Brian Rose, editor

UNIVERSITY OF PENNSYLVANIA MUSEUM OF ARCHAEOLOGY AND ANTHROPOLOGY

PHILADELPHIA

Financial support for this volume's publication was provided by the Penn Museum, the 1984 Foundation, the Provost's Research Fund of the University of Pennsylvania, and the George B. Storer Foundation.

ENDPAPERS: Map of the Near East and the eastern Mediterranean featuring sites mentioned in this volume. Drawing: Kimberly Leaman.

LIBRARY OF CONGRESS CATALOGING-IN-PUBLICATION DATA

The archaeology of Phrygian Gordion, royal city of Midas / edited by C. Brian Rose.
   p. cm.
Includes bibliographical references and index.
ISBN-13: 978-1-934536-48-3 (hardcover : acid-free paper)
ISBN-10: 1-934536-48-2 (hardcover : acid-free paper)
1. Gordion (Extinct city)—Antiquities. 2. Phrygians—Antiquities. 3. Excavations (Archaeology)—Turkey—Gordion (Extinct city) 4. Historic buildings—Turkey—Gordion (Extinct city) 5. Material culture—Turkey—Gordion (Extinct city) I. Rose, Charles Brian.
DS156.G6A74 2012
939'.26--dc23

2012024670

Published for the University of Pennsylvania Museum of Archaeology and Anthropology by the University of Pennsylvania Press.

Printed in the United States of America on acid-free paper.

Table of Contents

Figures

Tables

Acknowledgments

This volume is intended to supply the first comprehensive overview of Gordion during the Phrygian period and to highlight the most recent research on the site. The conference at which these papers were originally presented (The Archaeology of Phrygian Gordion, April 2007) was organized in honor of Ellen Kohler, who devoted her life to the excavation, study, and publication of Gordion. She died two years before this volume was published, and we therefore decided to dedicate it to her memory, in recognition of the wisdom and support that she provided to all of us.

A few months before this volume went to press, we also lost another friend and colleague from Gordion: Crawford Greenewalt, Jr., or "Greenie", as he was fondly known. Many of the most significant publications in Anatolian archaeology during the last half-century have been skillfully guided by Greenie's hand. One does not often find tangible evidence of the extent of that guidance in the publications themselves, because Greenie never allowed the full acknowledgment of his contributions to a book or article to appear; but he contributed years of his life to editing, supplementing, and improving the manuscripts that all of us were writing. In other words, we were able to mature as scholars because he was willing to use the enormous breadth of his knowledge and vision to bring our scholarship to a level that it would otherwise not have reached. We therefore respectfully dedicate this book to him as well, in memoriam, in recognition of his intellectual support and generosity of spirit.

Many people have played a valuable role in the production of this book. Charles Williams and Crawford Greenewalt Jr. were founts of information on all aspects of Gordion, and they championed the project at every stage of production. Gabriel Pizzorno, Gareth Darbyshire, and Kimberly Leaman prepared and organized the illustrations, and served as a perpetual source of support, along with Mary Voigt. Gareth Darbyshire devoted long hours to the preparation of the index, and Theodora Ashmead and Walda Metcalf helped substantially with the editing, as did Caitie Barrett and Michael Strother. Jennifer Quick prepared the manuscript for publication with her customary speed and expertise, while Jim Mathieu provided overall guidance for the Penn Museum Publications department. The comments from the two anonymous reviewers were enormously helpful.

It is a pleasure to acknowledge the financial support for the volume's publication from the Penn Museum, the 1984 Foundation, the Provost's Research Fund of the University of Pennsylvania, and the George B. Storer Foundation.

1

Introduction: The Archaeology of Phrygian Gordion

C. Brian Rose

Between the fall of the Hittite Kingdom and the creation of the Persian empire, there arose in central and southern Asia Minor a series of powerful states whose rulers occasionally claimed descent from the Hittite kings, and whose inhabitants spoke a variety of languages—Luwian, Aramaic, Lydian, and Phrygian, among others (Mellink 1992; Hawkins 2000; Bryce 2005:384). Fieldwork at several of the leading cities in these states began over 50 years ago, but within the last two decades they have yielded an astonishing series of new discoveries that have completely altered our understanding of early 1st millennium BC Anatolia, including the monumental fortification wall at Sardis, the Phrygian inscriptions of the palace entrance at Kerkenes, and the Kattamuwa stele from Zincirli, which speaks of a soul separate from the body (Dusinberre 2003:49–56; Draycott and Summers 2008; Wilford 2008).

Some of the most dramatic new discoveries have been made at Gordion, the Phrygian capital that controlled much of central Asia Minor for close to two centuries and interacted with empires and states both east and west, including Lydia, Greece, Assyria, Persia, and the Syro-Hittite realm of Tabal, among others. Excavations have been conducted at Gordion over the course of the last 60 years: between 1950 and 1974 by Rodney Young, and from 1988 to 2006 by Mary Voigt. Although for many years its topographical development was regarded as relatively well understood, a recently revised analysis of Gordion's chronology has transformed what had been interpreted as a Kimmerian attack of ca. 700 BC into a conflagration possibly related to new construction that occurred 100 years earlier (DeVries 2007, 2008, Voigt 2005, Rose and Darby-shire 2011). As a consequence, the chronology of Phrygian architecture, ceramics, and artifacts has changed dramatically, as has our understanding of the history and archaeology of central Anatolia during the Iron Age.

In spite of the economic and political importance of Gordion and Phrygian culture in general, both topics have consistently been omitted from courses in Old World archaeology, primarily because Gordion lies too far to the west for many Near Eastern archaeologists, and too far to the east for those in the Classical world. The lack of scholarly focus on Phrygia has begun to change only recently. Several new books and articles on Phrygian topography and religion have appeared within the last decade (Uçankus 2002; Berndt-Ersöz 2006; Sivas and Tüfekçi Sivas 2007; Sams 2011b; Voigt 2011; Roller 2011), and an overview of recent research at Gordion was published in 2005, under the title *The Archaeology of Midas and the Phrygians* (Kealhofer 2005). Only a few of the chapters in the latter volume focused on the Phrygian settlements, however, and there remained a need for a second volume that dealt more comprehensively with the changing topography of Gordion and its surroundings from the 10th century BC through the arrival of Alexander in 333. With this objective in mind, a conference on the Archaeology of Phrygian Gordion was held at the University of Pennsylvania in April 2007, with papers that spanned six centuries of Gordion's history and included talks on the regional exploitation of wood, flora, and fauna in antiquity, as well as the consistently fluctuating interaction between the site's inhabitants and the landscape.

We also wanted to highlight the techniques we have developed to present our vision of Phrygian Gordion to the public—both the conservation/reconstruction of the buildings themselves, and their graphic rendering on a multi-phase plan. We therefore included chapters on Gordion's new site management plan by **Frank Matero**, on landscape preservation by **Naomi Miller**, and on the reconstruction of the city plan by Gabriel Pizzorno and Gareth Darbyshire.[1] Nearly all of the papers delivered at the conference appear in these proceedings, and to them we have added an unpublished article on Midas and Delphi by the late Keith DeVries. The authors whose names are highlighted in bold in this Introduction have contributed chapters to the volume.

Rather than summarizing each of the talks in this chapter, I have opted to present an overview of the topographic development of Gordion, incorporating references to this volume's chapters within the larger narrative and linking the archaeological changes as much as possible to contemporary historical events in Anatolia and the Near East. During the last few decades the chronological designations for the Phrygian levels have changed—what began as "Persian" was reassigned to "Middle Phrygian," and two different but linked systems are now commonly used. One is periodic (Early, Middle, Late Phrygian) and derives from the Young excavations; the other is based on stratigraphy, with a YHSS prefix (Yassıhöyük Stratigraphic Sequence), and was formulated by Mary Voigt. The two systems with numerical dates for the Phrygian levels appear below:

Early Iron Age	YHSS 7
	11th c.–ca. 950 BC
Initial Early Phrygian	YHSS 6B
	ca. 950–900 BC
Early Phrygian	YHSS 6A
	ca. 900–800 BC
Early Phrygian Destruction	
	ca. 800 BC
Middle Phrygian	YHSS 5
	ca. 800–540 BC
Late Phrygian	YHSS 4
	ca. 540–330 BC

The beginning of the Early Phrygian Period is generally dated to the 10th century BC, although the Phrygians' ancestors appear to have arrived in central Anatolia from Thrace during the 12th century, at roughly the same time in which another Thracian group began to occupy the citadel of Troy (Sams 1988, 1994a; DeVries 1990:371–72, 390–91; Wittke 2004; Vassileva 2005a. For Troy, see Rose 2008). As Mary Voigt and Robert Henrickson have noted:

> There is no stratigraphic break to indicate a significant hiatus in settlement at Gordion after the fall of the Hittites, so that time alone cannot account for the observed changes in architecture, domestic features, ceramics, and animal remains between the Late Bronze and the Early Iron Age. The ceramic data do not support a gradual transition from the Late Bronze Age into the Early Iron Age. Instead, the archaeological evidence strongly suggests a population change at this time, rather than simply a shift in political and economic organization. (Henrickson and Voigt 1998:101)[2]

The Early Phrygian citadel and its surroundings looked very different from what one sees today. The settlement would probably have risen 5–9 m above the surrounding plain (vs. 13–16.5 m today), and the Sakarya River lay on the east side of the mound (as one can see in Fig. 3.2 of Ben Marsh's chapter), having traveled to the western side relatively recently, perhaps as late as the 19th century (Marsh 1997:23–26; 1999; 2005). We currently perceive the mound as having contained a unified settlement across the upper surface, and from the Hellenistic period onward that was true; but in the Early Phrygian period the mound was probably significantly smaller, with a high, fortified elite quarter at the east (the "Eastern Mound"), a low domestic quarter at the west, probably unfortified (the "Western Mound"), and a street that cut diagonally through them (foldout plan in back pocket) (Voigt et al. 1997:4–6).[3] The street was over 7 m wide and slightly over 2 m lower than the walking level in the Terrace Zone area, while its length, from one end of the mound to the other, would have been ca. 285 m (Fig. 1.1).

The citadel's central area, on the east side of the mound of Yassıhöyük, had reached its final form before the end of the 9th century and was divided

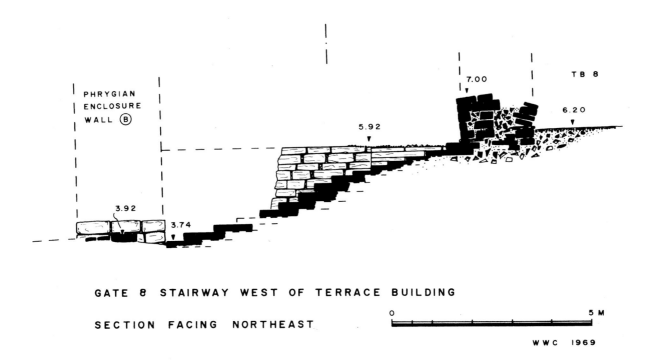

Fig. 1.1. South Enclosure walls. Section facing northwest. Drawing: W.W. Cummer. Source: Gordion Project, Penn Museum.

into two zones of very different function (Fig. 1.2) (DeVries 1990:373–77). A gate building probably decorated with carved stone orthostats was framed by two wings, one of which, at the north, was used for the storage of pithoi (Sams 1995, 2005; DeVries 1990:377).[4] The gate led to two courts (the "Outer," which was stone-paved, and the "Inner"), separated from each other by a wall that must have been over 4 m high judging by the breadth of its foundations. This was a quarter intended for the elite.

Although both courts were flanked by megarons, the Inner Court was much larger, with three times as many megarons. Reconstructing their original number is not easy since the remains are so lacunose; but the Middle Phrygian buildings are similar in number, size, and position to that of their predecessors. This fact, coupled with the foundations uncovered by Young, enables one to posit as many as 12 megarons in the Inner Court—vs. 4 in the outer one—with 4 on the western side and 8 on the eastern side, organized in two rows of 4 set opposite each other (cf. DeVries 1990:396) (foldout plan). A more precise discussion of the reconstruction method appears in the chapter by **Gabe Pizzorno** and **Gareth Darbyshire**, along with

a color phase plan that juxtaposes the Early and Middle Phrygian buildings. The 4 megarons in the Early Phrygian Outer Court, nearest the gate, appear to have had pebbled floors, with an unusually elaborate mosaic featuring polychromatic geometric designs in the main room of Megaron 2 (Salzmann 1982:4, 6–8, 78, 93–94 nos. 46–56; Megaron 2, Young 1958:143; Megarons 9, 12, Young 1964:288–90; Young 1965; Megaron 1, DeVries 1980a:37).[5]

Another zone of activity, on the southwest side of the citadel (the "Terrace Zone"), was devoted to industry. Although only 11 buildings here have been excavated, one can safely reconstruct two long rows of buildings—8 in each row positioned on either side of a 16 m wide court (foldout plan). The length of each building is close to twice its width, so each group of two represents a nearly perfect square, and the interior, at 21 x 11.50 m, encompasses approximately the same space as the megarons at Mycenae, Pylos, and Tiryns. Within the rooms was preserved an abundance of equipment for textile and grain processing, with some buildings containing between 500 and 600 loomweights (DeVries 1990:385–86; Burke 2005:71, fig. 6-2).[6]

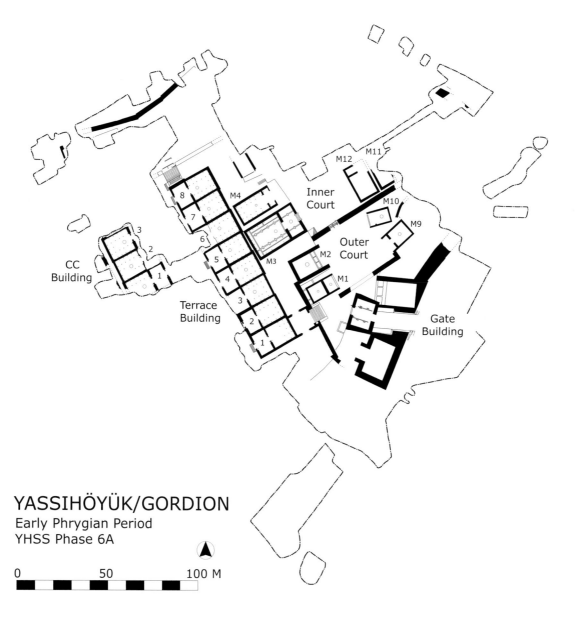

Fig. 1.2. Plan of the eastern side of the mound during the Early Phrygian period. Source: Gordion Project, Penn Museum.

Keith DeVries felt there was enough evidence to estimate the work force that would have handled this equipment on a regular basis, and made his calculations using the following method: 2 of the 8 buildings on the east side of the zone appear to have been used for storage, while the rest were intended for industrial activity. If one assumes the same situation at the west, then 12 would have been devoted to some aspect of production. Each one would have been large enough to house at least 25 people, almost certainly women; this would have meant a total of

300 workers in the zone if all of the buildings were in operation simultaneously (DeVries 1980a:40).

Primary access between the elite and industrial quarters appears, not surprisingly, to have been limited to one door on the inner side of the Gate Complex, with the backs of the industrial buildings facing the elite megarons at the east. Indeed, the highly restricted access routes between these districts suggest a society more tightly controlled than any other in Anatolia or the Near East. Although there was very likely a second city gate, careful coordination of traffic would have been essential, especially given the fact that workers would have continually exited to retrieve water from the Sakarya River since there were no wells or cisterns on the citadel (Young 1964:286).

Other than the elite objects discovered in Megaron 3, one receives a glimpse of aristocratic life in the citadel during this period from the "doodle stones," or incised drawings on the exterior of Megaron 2, analyzed here by **Lynn Roller**. These feature men, animals, and scenes that may refer to falconry, some of which may be linked to the Matar cult; they stand in stark contrast to the kind of activity that would have occurred in the industrial zone, with hundreds of women, probably slaves, providing the infrastructure for that lifestyle.

Until recently, the achievements of Early Phrygian Gordion were assumed to have occurred during the 8th century, but the radiocarbon and dendrochronological dates of seeds and wood found within the destruction level, coupled with the type and style of the associated artifacts and pottery, indicate a date of ca. 800 BC for the conflagration (Voigt 2005, DeVries 2007, 2008; DeVries in Rose and Darbyshire 2011). This discovery, in turn, allows us to situate Early Phrygian Gordion in a different historical context, set against the reigns of a series of powerful men: Assurnasirpal II and Shalmaneser III in Assyria, Sarduri I of Urartu in northeastern Anatolia, and Hiram I and Solomon in Phoenicia and Israel, respectively. We have no contemporary references to Gordion in the Assyrian texts, although the Muski—the Assyrian word for Phrygians—are mentioned in the Annals of Assurnasirpal II as having paid tribute to the king at the beginning of his reign (Wittke 2004).[7] In addition to tribute, there is good evidence for diplomatic and gift exchanges between these and other rulers, as evinced by the rock-cut relief of King Warpalawas at İvriz, near Konya. The ivory horse trappings in North Syrian style found in one of Gordion's Terrace Building units probably fall into a similar category (Young 1962a:166–67).[8]

The new chronology also demonstrates that Gordion's Early Phrygian architecture was even more innovative than had been previously thought: the site featured the earliest known stone megaron and akroterion in the Near East, dating to the initial Early Phrygian building phase in the 10th century

BC, as well as the earliest pebble mosaics, dated to the 9th century. The rows of workshops, over 100 m in length, were among the longest in Anatolia, second only to those in the Hittite capital at Hattuşas. The roofing systems are particularly noteworthy: the ceiling of Megaron 2 featured beams over 10 m in length with no internal supports, which is, as far as we know, a more daring feat of engineering than one would have found in roughly contemporary Assyrian palaces, including the throne room of Assurnasirpal II (884–859 BC) at Nimrud (Liebhart 1988). Such an achievement attests to an unusually high level of skill in architecture and carpentry, but it also led to extensive exploitation of the surrounding landscape. The latter subject is explored by **John Marston**, who has undertaken a comprehensive study of Gordion's utilization of specific wood types with an eye toward clarifying issues of ecology and landscape during the Phrygian period.

The amount of earth-moving that occurred during the Early Phrygian period would have been enormous, as one can judge from the monumental burial mounds, such as Tumulus W, or the tons of earth that separate the "Early Phrygian Building" in the elite quarter from Megaron 9, which stood above it. Moreover, the industrial buildings were constructed on a terrace that rose 2 m above the level of the Outer and Inner Courts, which would have necessitated the transport of over 20,000 m^3 of earth to the citadel. Nevertheless, even a project as extensive as the latter would have involved less earth than was necessary to build a medium-sized tumulus, and would have represented no significant challenge to a community accustomed to such ambitious building projects (DeVries 1990:373–74).[9]

An even more monumental public works project was still to come: toward the end of the 9th century, the rulers of Gordion planned for a major change in the appearance of the citadel—not in the number and general layout of the settlement's buildings (at least on the Eastern Mound), but in the height of the citadel itself, which would be raised 4–5 m above its Early Phrygian level. This involved the excavation and movement of over half a million cubic meters of clay—the same kind of herculean public works project that is foreshadowed in the construction of Tumulus W and would reappear 60 years later when Tumulus MM was created.

Preparations for the new project were already under way ca. 800 BC: the builders had blocked the access route between the Terrace Zone and the Outer Court, and had begun the process of laying rubble and clay fill in a partially dismantled Gate Complex, while adding new water facilities related to construction, as **Mary Voigt**'s chapter in this volume carefully demonstrates. Megaron 3 had been filled with a variety of luxury goods, many of which were found near the door and therefore perhaps placed here for storage during construction; most of the other megarons had been emptied of their contents,

although the buildings in the Terrace Zone still contained the equipment for weaving, grinding, and cooking that were in use there. It was at this time that a massive fire swept through the site during one of the summer months, with the flames probably fanned by winds from the north (DeVries 1980a:36; 1990:386).[10] The fire may, in fact, have been caused by construction-related activities, although summer fires in Anatolia were probably just as common then as they are now.

What is surprising, at first glance, is the complete absence of human skeletons within the destruc-

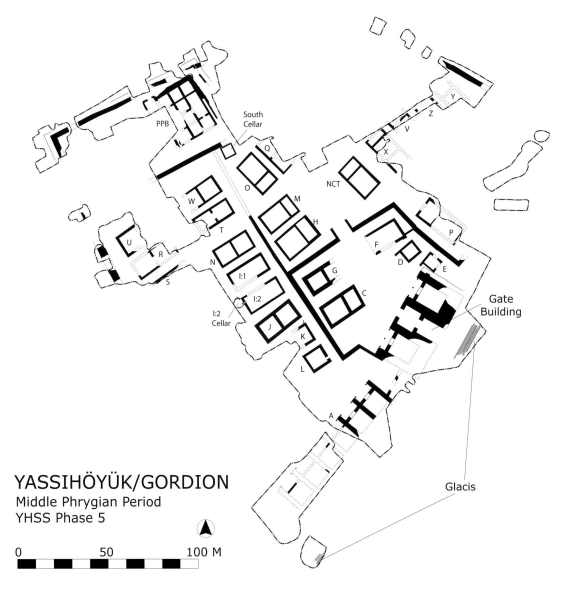

YASSIHÖYÜK/GORDION
Middle Phrygian Period
YHSS Phase 5

0   50   100 M

Fig. 1.3. Plan of the eastern side of the mound during the Middle Phrygian period. Source: Gordion Project, Penn Museum.

Fig. 1.4. The stone Glacis in front of the Gate Complex. Source: Gordion Project, Penn Museum.

tion level.[11] Moreover, items of value had not been retrieved from most buildings, and the 4–5 m of clay fill had been set over the destruction very soon after it had occurred.[12] Either no one was present on the citadel when the fire began, which seems impossible, or the residents had time to escape before the fire enveloped the citadel, which we should probably accept. This, of course, ties into the question of the number of city gates in operation at the end of the Early Phrygian period, and given the fact that the main gate was blocked before the fire started, the existence of a second city gate is virtually certain, as Mary Voigt argues in her chapter.

The redating of the destruction level has completely transformed our understanding of the material culture of Asia Minor in the late 9th century, as **Kenneth Sams** demonstrates in his chapter. Ceramics that were regarded as typologically backward in the old chronology can now be shown to have been innovative in form and decoration, just like the

architecture and city planning in evidence on the eastern side of the citadel. The earliest Phrygian inscriptions can now be placed ca. 800 BC or shortly thereafter, which means that they precede the oldest Greek inscriptions by at least a half-century (Rose and Darbyshire 2011; Sass 2005:146–52). Moreover, it is now clear that the destruction levels at Gordion and Hasanlu date to the same time, thereby supplying us with unusually detailed views of the public infrastructure in place ca. 800 BC at two key fortified citadels in central Anatolia and northwestern Iran (Dyson 1989).

During the new building program none of the earlier buildings was dismantled, and the Early Phrygian Gate Complex was actually used to support the foundations of its Middle Phrygian successor, which is why so many cracks are now visible in the masonry of the earlier structure (DeVries 1990:391–400). Other than the greater height of the new citadel, the layout of the constituent buildings was essen-

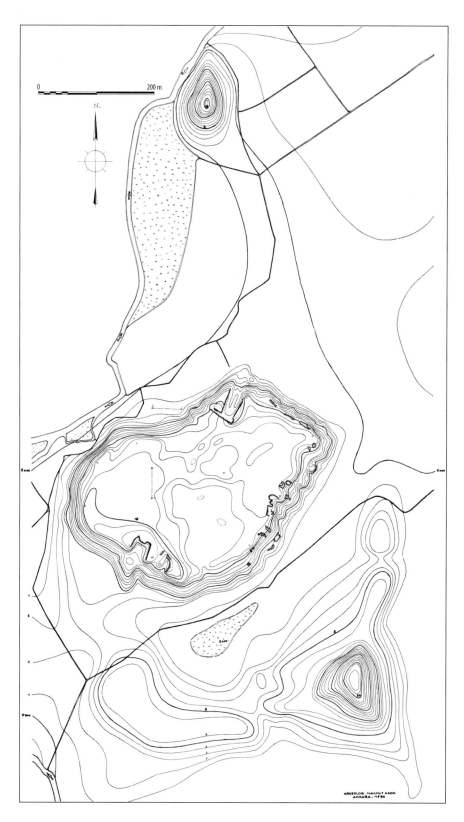

Fig. 1.5. Plan of the settlement with the forts of Kuş Tepe and Küçük Höyük. Source: Gordion Project, Penn Museum.

Fig. 1.6. Küçük Höyük during excavation. Source: Gordion Project, Penn Museum.

tially the same, although there were a few significant changes: the same number of Terrace Zone buildings were constructed, but they were shifted farther toward the new gate complex, and the vestibule of each building became much deeper so that it was essentially the same size as the main room (foldout plan). The buildings were also free-standing rather than components of a single conjoined row, presumably to hinder the spread of fire (Fig. 1.3).

The stepped Glacis of the new citadel was faced with sections of different colored stones, apparently from several different quarries (Fig. 1.4) (Voigt and Young 1999:205).[13] Although color had been a significant component of Early Phrygian architecture and its decoration, the choice of stone in this case may also have been intended to highlight the extent of the area under Phrygian control.[14] Such a manipulation of colored stone in architecture is also reminiscent of the alternating light and dark orthostat reliefs at Arslantepe/Malatya and Carchemish

during the same general period.

One completely new addition was Building A—a six-room complex constructed on the southeast side of the citadel adjacent to the Middle Phrygian Gate, which would have conveyed a sense of greater impregnability to the citadel's visitors. Although both the Eastern and Western Mounds were raised, the central street was not, which meant that it now lay ca. 7 m below the new occupation level within the Middle Phrygian citadel. The two mounds would consequently have seemed even higher than they actually were.

The new building program also included an outer fortification system that featured mud-brick walls at least 4 m high set on stone foundations 3.50 m thick, within a defensive ditch immediately in front of them.[15] Square towers were constructed at intervals of ca. 16 m, and the entire area under protection now reached nearly 500,000 m^2 (Figs. 1.6–1.9) (Sams 2010, Marsh 1999).[16] The walls were linked to forts constructed at the northern end (Kuş Tepe) and the southeast (Küçük Höyük) (Fig. 1.5). The latter mound was excavated by Machteld Mellink between 1956 and 1958, and revealed a mud-brick platform 12 m in height, at least 50 m long, and over 10 m wide, on top of which a four-story wood and mud-brick fortress had been constructed (Fig. 1.6) (Young 1957:324–25; 1958:140–41; Edwards 1959:264; Mellink 1959). The extent and position of these fortifications did not become clear until a program of magnetic prospection conducted between 2007 and 2009 revealed conclusively that the fortifications reached as far north as Kuş Tepe (Figs. 1.7, 1.8).

Such a dual system of defenses with inner and outer fortifications has a long history in ancient Near East, beginning at least as early as the 3rd millennium BC at Troy and continuing in the late Bronze and early Iron Age at Hattuşas, Kanesh, Zincirli, and Troy again in a different configuration (Jablonka 2006; for Troy, Rose 2008:409n55; for Hattusas, Seeher 2002; for Kanesh, Özgüç 1999; for Zincirli, Wartke 2005). The Trojan system also featured a defensive ditch, as did a relatively large number of settlements in Anatolia (Carchemish), Syria (Qatna, Ebla, Kadesh), and Palestine (Hazor, Lachish, Askelon), among others, so the presence of such a feature at Gordion is not unexpected (Bunimovitz 1992; Finkelstein 1992).[17]

The excavation of the fortification walls on either side of Küçük Höyük did not yield clear evidence for dating, but the earliest evidence for occupation within the Lower Town is Middle Phrygian (Voigt and Young 1999:211–15), and the following

Fig. 1.7. Magnetic prospection around the outer defensive walls. Photo: author.

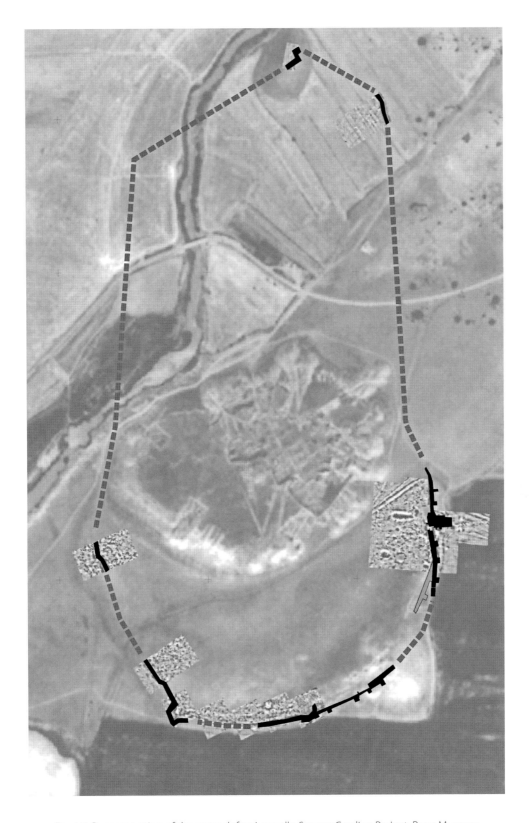

Fig. 1.8. Reconstruction of the outer defensive walls. Source: Gordion Project, Penn Museum.

sequence of construction activities seems logical. To raise the level of the citadel mounds, the work force used approximately 175,000 m³ of clay, and trace elements demonstrate that a substantial quantity of it came from the area adjacent to the Sakarya River (Voigt and Young 1999:203n6). In other words, there would have been a massive excavation along the river at the same spot in which the fortifications were built. It seems logical to assume that the digging for the foundations of the city wall yielded a substantial amount of the clay used to raise the level of the central part of the citadel, and that the two operations were part of a single building program. Such simultaneous construction of inner and outer fortifications was relatively common in Anatolia and the Near East in antiquity, both in the Bronze Age and in later periods. If the same situation prevailed here, which seems compelling, then we can date the construction of the outer fortifications to the early 8th century.[18]

The building program at the beginning of the Middle Phrygian period would therefore have been even more monumental than we have assumed.[19] Here too we should view such extensive building activity against the backdrop of an almost equally energetic campaign of city foundations and citadel constructions in eastern Anatolia (Urartu under Argishti I), the Upper Euphrates (Zincirli/Sam'al in North Syria), and Assyria (Nimrud under Assurnasirpal II). Each new construction would have highlighted the need for increasingly sophisticated defenses in the other areas.

It is worth noting that the population of Gordion increased significantly at this point, as surface survey and excavation have demonstrated, and with the coordinate increase in agricultural cultivation, more irrigation channels would have been cut, thereby furnishing additional clay for building activities in the citadel (Kealhofer 2005:148; Miller 2010). There is, of course, the question of how such a large population would have been fed, and many of the answers can fortunately be pulled from the site's plant and animals remains, as the work of Naomi Miller and Melinda Zeder has demonstrated (Miller, Zeder, and Arter 2009).

It may have been only at this time that substantial buildings began to be constructed in the Lower Town, in the area protected by the new fortification wall. In an area near Küçük Höyük Mary Voigt uncovered several Middle Phrygian buildings set on an artificial terrace well above the level of the plain—a development that is noteworthy in itself (Sams and Voigt 1995:375–76); Voigt et al. 1997:6–8). **Ben Marsh** shows in his chapter that alluviation from the Sakarya River increased significantly during the first half of the Middle Phrygian period, probably in large part due to the massive removal of clay along the river's course. Deforestation and grazing may also have played a role; but in any event, the periodic flooding that had begun to occur would have necessitated the construction of terraces for the new Lower Town structures, although the flooding would have been hindered by the new fortification walls.

New construction extended to the Western Mound as well: massive rubble foundations of Middle Phrygian date were excavated at the northwest corner of the Western Mound, possibly suggesting that a defensive wall now surrounded the public buildings and dwellings that appear to have existed there (Voigt and Young 1999:210–11; Voigt 2000:194). Further to the northwest lay the Outer Town, which was also the site of new occupation at this time, although excavation has revealed few of the houses that once punctuated the area (Voigt 2005:35). Combining all of the evidence for new building at Gordion during the 8th century allows us to reconstruct the following program: a 5 m rise in the heights of both Eastern and Western Mounds, with new monumental structures in both areas; the construction of an outer line of defense protected by a ditch and by forts at north and southeast; and the beginning of habitation in both the Lower and Outer Town, which were, in turn, linked by the stone-paved street that separated the Eastern and Western Mounds.[20]

It is only during this period of 8th century construction that we have evidence for the lives of two of Gordion's rulers—Gordias and Midas. Our information regarding the former is limited to the story of the knotted cornel bark attached to the ox-cart in which he had first entered the city; but Midas, reportedly his son, was an historical character whose career is described in contemporary writing (Roller 1983; Roller 1984; Mellink 1992:622–34; Sams 1995, DeVries 2008, Berndt-Ersöz 2008).[21] The Greek and Latin citations indicate that he mar-

Fig. 1.9. Tumuli on the Northeast Ridge, 1953. Source: Gordion Project, Penn Museum.

ried the daughter of the ruler of Aeolian Kyme and was the first non-Greek to have made a dedication at Delphi, specifically a wood and ivory throne that Herodotos saw in the Corinthian Treasury there.[22] A part of this may still exist: a statuette of an ivory lion-tamer in Phrygian style, probably dating to the late 8th century, was actually discovered near the Delphic Corinthian Treasury, and in this volume **Keith DeVries** attempts to link the statuette to the throne in question.

The most important references to Midas are in the Assyrian Annals, where he is referred to as Mita of Mushki, and these constitute our best historical sources for Phrygian military and diplomatic initiatives during the 8th century, most of which involved the Assyrians and the city-states in the Upper Euphrates/Taurus region. By the middle of the 8th century, many of these city-states were either independent or Urartian allies, having earlier been Assyrian vassals. With the advent in 745 of Tiglath-Pileser III, who launched a new war on Urartu, allegiances

shifted again, and several of the Syro-Hittite city-states sent tribute to the new king, such as Urik(ki) of Que (Cilicia) and Warpalawas of Tyana.[23]

This change in allegiance was also transitory: the Assyrian Annals indicate that during the last quarter of the 8th century Midas' support against the Assyrians was increasingly sought by cities in the Upper Euphrates region, including Pisiri of Carchemish, Ambaris, King of Tabal, and Kurti of Atuna.[24] Midas' prominence, however, clearly extended across a much wider area, as attested by the discovery in Tyana of a stone stele, probably basalt, that had been erected by Midas himself (Mellink 1979; Brixhe and Lejeune 1984:260–67, no. T2).[25] The presence of such a stele in Tyana is not surprising, since the king of the area, Warpalawas, was an ally of Midas, but the inscription is striking in that it was written in Phrygian even though Luwian was the primary language in the area.

By 709 Assyrian power had clearly forced Midas to reverse course: he sent tribute to Sargon II and sub-

Fig. 1.10. Wall fragments from the "Painted House." Reconstruction drawing: Piet de Jong. Source: Gordion Project, Penn Museum.

sophisticated fortifications. What is surprising, in light of Gordion's extensive interaction with North Syria, is the absence of sculptural representations of Gordias or Midas. During the 8th and 7th centuries, many of the Syro-Hittite city-states featured public stone statues of their kings, often 3 or 4 m high, while at Gordion none of the settlement's rulers appear to have been represented in sculpture or painting, and the same was true for Lydia.[26]

The primary mode of commemoration for the Phrygian kings lay in their tumuli, and in at least one case it looks as if a royal tumulus actually influenced the architecture of the citadel. This is Tumulus W, the oldest known burial mound at Gordion (mid-9th century), which was set on the highest point of a ridge to the northeast of the city. It looks as if the Early Phrygian Gate Complex was turned from its planned orientation so that both tumulus and gate were directly aligned (cf. Young 1962a:168). As Richard Liebhart has argued, it seems that a prominent individual at Gordion died while the gate was being constructed, which prompted the entrance to be modified so that anyone leaving the citadel would be directed toward the burial mound (Fig. 1.9).[27] During the Middle Phrygian rebuilding, the Gate was rotated approximately 30 degrees further toward the southeast, so that one now looked in the direction of the northernmost tumulus on the South Ridge upon exiting the citadel. Magnetic prospection reveals that this tumulus was never looted, and it should contain the tomb of an individual whose importance to the Middle Phrygian settlement was paramount.

Tumulus MM, which is the subject of four chapters in this volume, stands nearly twice the size of Tumulus W and can be seen from virtually every

sequently intercepted anti-Assyrian agents en route from Que to Urartu, ultimately turning them over to the Assyrian governor of Que (Mellink 1992:622). With so much military conflict and shifting allegiances, it is hardly surprising that Gordion and several of the neo-Hittite city-states constructed such corner of the site and its surroundings. Once regarded as the tomb of Midas himself, the dendrochronology points to a date ca. 740 BC for its construction, which suggests that the tomb was built by Midas at the beginning of his reign to honor his predecessor. The mound was nevertheless just as much a monument to Midas himself in that it was the largest tumulus in Asia Minor, and would remain so until the construction of the burial mound of the Lydian king Alyattes at Sardis nearly 200 years later (Hanfmann 1980:100–101).

Especially noteworthy is the technique used to construct the wooden tomb chamber within MM, which had to bear the weight of a 53 m high mound set above it, as **Richard Liebhart** has outlined in his chapter. It is this feat of engineering for which Midas should be remembered rather than the vast quantities of gold attached to him by later Greek and Latin authors. As has often been pointed out, not a single object of gold was discovered within the tomb chamber, nor are gold objects commonly found in excavations on the mound or in tumuli (for gold, DeVries 1990:382; for gold ring, rosette, Edwards 1959:265, 266; for gold and electrum fibulae and jewelry, Young 1962a:166; for furniture decoration, Young 1964:287; for gold foil, Voigt and Young 1999:211; for the tumuli, Kohler 1980; 1995:197). Yet as **Mary Ballard** notes in her chapter, we may be viewing the story of Midas' gold through the wrong lens. The shroud that covered the 60-year-old occupant of Tumulus MM featured an inorganic pigment called goethite that endowed the garment with a kind of golden appearance that may have been replicated in the textiles for which the Phrygians were famous.

Richard Liebhart's inspection of the chamber has also yielded an astonishing new discovery: it appears that some of the mourners at the funeral had their names inscribed on a wooden beam that was added to the roof at the conclusion of the ceremony (Sams 2010; Liebhart et al. n.d.). Most of this 9 m long beam cannot currently be viewed due to its location on the roof, but names appear on both ends of the beam, thereby suggesting that more of them were similarly inscribed, and one of those names also appears on a bronze bowl found by Young within the tomb chamber (Brixhe and Lejeune 1984:98–100, G-105). This practice, if interpreted correctly, differs little from that involving memorial books at modern funerals, but it was unique in antiquity as far as we know.

The menu of the funeral meal, which included barbecued goat or lamb, a lentil stew, and a wine-beer-mead punch, has been reconstructed by Patrick McGovern based on the residue in the vessels, while reconstructions of the extraordinary boxwood serving stands that held the various dishes are presented here by **Elizabeth Simpson**, who situates them within the context of woodworking at Gordion (for the meal, McGovern et al. 1999; for furniture, Simpson 2010). As **Maya Vassileva** notes, the Phrygians were equally famous for the fibulae and bronze belts that were found in large quantities in Tumulus MM and some of the other tumuli at Gordion. These fibulae have been found as far west as Athens and Olympia, while the belts, which occasionally featured incised geometric decoration, were imported by elite Greeks and dedicated in such high-profile sanctuaries as Delphi, Didyma, and Samos (Vassileva 2005b, 2007).

Strabo linked the end of Midas' life to the Kimmerian raids on Asia Minor ca. 700 BC, and most scholars found this relatively easy to accept as long as the destruction level of the site was dated to the same period (Strabo 1.3.21). The new chronology, however, has cast doubt not just on the circumstances of Midas' death, but also on the presence of the Kimmerians in this part of Anatolia (Ivantchik 2001; Berndt-Ersöz 2008:22–29). Certainly their strength during the late 8th and 7th century was formidable: the Urartian kingdoms were heavily damaged by Kimmerian raids in 714, and both Sargon II and the Lydian king Gyges reportedly died in combat with them in 705 and 654/2, respectively. There may in fact be some evidence for their attack on Gordion, although it is to be found in an extramural Middle Phrygian settlement northeast of the citadel. Excavation in this area, analyzed here by **Gunlög Anderson**, yielded a cemetery (the "Common Cemetery") above houses that appear to have been destroyed by an attack ca. 700. Although it is clear that the citadel was not seriously damaged by the Kimmerians, the outlying areas may have been.[28]

The 7th century evidentiary record at Gordion is not as full as that from the 9th and 8th centuries, but a significant amount of relevant material has been uncovered during both the Young and Voigt excavations, bringing new clarity to issues of local ceramic production and construction techniques as well as changes in agriculture and diet (Voigt et al. 1997, Voigt and Young 1999). The tumulus tradition continued, as did the wooden tomb chambers, but they now held both inhumation and cremation burials. If one examines five of those constructed between 650 and 600, one immediately notices the disappearance of the bronze belts and fibulae that had been so characteristic of the Phrygian elite during the 9th and 8th centuries, although gold objects now began to be included in the funeral assemblages (Kohler 1980, 1995). Thus far there is little evidence for contact with the Greek world during this period: only a small amount of imported pottery (Corinthian Late Geometric and Protocorinthian) has been uncovered, and only three amphoras, all of which date toward the end of the 7th century (DeVries 1980a, 1997, 2005, 2007, 2008).

At some point toward the end of the 7th century, Gordion's power began to diminish as that of Lydia grew, and Lydian influence is clearly detectable in Gordion's archaeological record throughout the first half of the 6th century (Mellink 1992:648–49). Electrum coins struck in Lydia were in use at the site ca. 600 BC or shortly thereafter, and the brightly colored figural and geometric architectural terracottas that begin to appear at Gordion in the early 6th century are probably in part a by-product of Lydian influence (Young 1964:283; for Lydian hoard, Bellinger 1968; Åkerström 1966:136–61; for architectural terracottas, Glendinning 2005). The fact that such substantial quantities of Lydian pottery have been found in the fort of Küçük Höyük may also suggest the presence of a Lydian garrison there (Young 1958:141). A visitor to Gordion from Lydian Sardis would undoubtedly have been struck by the large number of similarities between the two cities, as **Crawford Greenewalt** cleverly demonstrates in this volume.[29]

The influence of Phrygian culture on other areas of Asia Minor, however, was still pronounced: recent excavations at Kerkenes, nearly 250 km east of Gordion, have revealed a late 7th/early 6th century entrance to the palatial complex that features a Phrygian dedicatory inscription, while other areas of the site have produced an aniconic cult idol and bronzes in Phrygian style. At Midas City, nearly 100 km west of Gordion, a rock-cut monumental façade perhaps carved in the early 6th century was

dedicated to Midas, apparently as a kind of heroon, even though the area in question was now controlled by the Lydians (for Kerkenes, Draycott and Summers 2008; for Midas City, Berndt 2002).[30]

In the end, Gordion's sophisticated fortification system and its defenders folded in the face of the mid-6th century Persian attack: a large siege mound similar to the one at Cypriot Paphos is still preserved on the southeast side of Küçük Höyük, and hundreds of trilobate arrowheads discovered within the remains of the fort indicate overwhelming archery fire (Young 1957:324; Mellink 1959). Magnetometry and electric resistivity have also revealed the existence of a smaller siege mound against the northwest face of Kuş Tepe, which was reduced to an enormous pile of mud-brick as a consequence of the attack. Only two human skeletons were found in the remains of Küçük Höyük, but the casualties must have been high, as during the Persian attack on Lydian Sardis. With Gordion's two forts subdued, the Persians probably seized control of the city relatively quickly, and the compromised fortifications were never rebuilt.

Yet in this new phase of Persian control, generally referred to as Late Phrygian, the site continued to prosper, with notable new construction in several areas of the Eastern Mound during the late 6th/early 5th century (DeVries 1990:400).[31] These include the rebuilding of a massive megaron (Building C) and the addition of a small but extensively decorated structure at the northwest of the Gate Complex (for Building C, see Young 1955:8; Mellink 1980b:91). The latter featured polychromatic wall mosaics and painted processional friezes, probably related to cult, that provide our sole representations of Phrygian women at Gordion (Fig. 1.10) (Mellink 1980b).[32] More imposing was a radical addition to Building A (the "Mosaic Building"), the evidence for which **Brendan Burke** presents in this volume: the western end now featured a stone-paved court that led to a large room decorated with an elaborate pebble mosaic, and a colonnaded court with painted architectural elements at the south.

At some point in the late 5th or early 4th century the citadel buildings collapsed and began to be spoliated, although the precise chronology is not yet clear. Pharnabazos, the satrap of Hellespontine Phrygia, wintered at Gordion in 408 BC with a contingent of Athenians, which suggests a relatively high level of prominence still in place, but an earthquake may have occurred shortly thereafter, as well as an attack by the Spartan general Agesilaos in 395 BC.[33] Although the *Hellenica Oxyrhynchia* notes that the Spartan attack was unsuccessful, a profusion of arrowheads discovered by Young within and around the gate probably stems from that attack and stands as an indication of its severity (Young 1955:11).[34] By the same token, however, it also proves that the citadel's defenses were still functioning.

Several of the Middle Phrygian buildings had been robbed of stone before these events occurred, but the spoliation increased as the 4th century progressed, and the configuration of the mound was radically transformed (for those well underway by 500 BC, Voigt and Young 1999:202; for those of the mid-5th century, Edwards 1959:265).[35] Much of what had been the elite quarter was now devoted to metallurgical activities: a bronze foundry was constructed above the remains of the Painted House, and an ironworking complex was set up nearby (for bronze foundry, Young 1955:3, 10; for ironworking, Sams and Voigt 1990:79; 1991:460; Voigt and Young 1999:220, 224).[36] Yet none of this should be taken as evidence of a depressed economy. There is abundant evidence for the manufacture of alabaster, antler, and bone items, and the number of Greek imports actually increased at this time (Sams and Voigt 1990:79; Voigt, pers. comm. 2010). There also appears to have been a flourishing trade route in place between Gordion and the Black Sea site of Herakleia Pontike, as **Mark Lawall** demonstrates in this volume. Nevertheless, at the time of Alexander's arrival, one of the few prominent buildings still largely intact would have been the "Mosaic Building" adjacent to Building A, and this is perhaps the best candidate for the structure that would have held Gordias' ox-cart with the legendary knot.[37]

Until this point, the topography of the central part of the city had remained relatively stable, but this too would change in the early Hellenistic period: the central street that had divided the Eastern and Western Mounds was completely filled in, thereby creating a relatively level surface across the entire area that can still be seen today (DeVries 1990:400–401). Although this would have been a small-scale enterprise by comparison to some of the other public works projects at Gordion, it would still have involved the movement of nearly 14,000 m^3 of earth. The newly leveled area provided additional space for habitation, and houses were gradually built across it in the course of the Hellenistic period. The reasons for this leveling program were no doubt varied, but one may have been the shifting course of the Sakarya in the Lower Town, which probably made habitation there more difficult; another would have been the increased security that residence on the mound would have supplied, which is a phenomenon that occurred repeatedly at Troy as well.

Encapsulating all of these topographical changes in a single comprehensive plan is a daunting prospect, and the foldout color phase plan included at the back of this volume, influenced in part by Wilhelm Dörpfeld's plan of Troy, is still a work in progress that will change as new data become available. But this plan, together with the articles contained within this volume, will provide a new basis for assessing the evolving topography of Gordion during much of the 1st millennium BC, as well as the states and empires with which the Phrygian kingdom interacted.[38]

NOTES

1.1.   Two of the papers will hopefully be published separately in other publications: Melinda Zeder (*Diachronic Patterns of Animal Exploitation at Gordion*) and Robert Henrickson (*The Iron Age Beginnings of the Early Phrygian Ceramic Tradition*).

1.2.   The larger number of horse bones in the Early Iron Age levels may indicate that the new settlers brought horses with them (Zeder and Arter 1994:114). Genz (2003:185–88) has expressed reservations about the conclusions of Voigt and Henrickson.

1.3.   During the Middle Phrygian period, the street would have linked the "Outer Town" at the north to the "Lower Town" at the south, but there is no evidence for Early Phrygian occupation in either area. Early Phrygian levels were uncovered on the Western Mound in only one small sondage, so the nature of the settlement there is still very uncertain (Voigt and Young 1999:209).

1.4.   Three rows of pithoi were found in this wing at the time of excavation (Young 1956:260). For the orthostats, see Sams 1989; Orthmann 1971:31–33, 61–62, 220–21; Prayon 1987:48–52.

1.5.   The floor does not survive in Megaron 10, but all of the surrounding megarons had pebble floors, and this one would undoubtedly have followed suit. The floor in Megaron 9 featured red, white, yellow, and blue pebbles, so we should probably reconstruct a geometric design along the same lines as the one in Megaron 2, to which Megaron 9 was oriented.

1.6. In one of the CC (Clay-Cut) Terrace Building units, sifted barley lay on the floor, probably intended for beer production (DeVries 1990:386). The number of sheep bones in Early Phrygian levels represents an increase over those in Early Iron Age strata (Zeder and Arter 1994:113–14), but this is probably related more to meat consumption than wool production.

1.7. Although no images of rulers have been unearthed at the site, there are two objects retrieved from the destruction level that probably indicate how members of the Phrygian cavalry would have looked (Young 1960a:240; DeVries 1980a:47, figs. 7, 8). These include a wooden frieze with three warriors mounted on horses, probably part of a piece of furniture, as well as an ivory plaque of a single equestrian.

1.8. The distinctively Phrygian bronze belt worn by King Warpalawas in the İvriz relief may have been a gift from Midas (Mellink 1992:638), while the bronze situlae from Tumulus MM may have been offered to Midas' predecessor by the ruler of a region under Assyrian control (Young 1981:268). Hundreds of ivory plaques, some of which are very likely to have been gifts, were found in the palace at Samaria (Crowfoot and Crowfoot 1938), and Hiram I, king of Tyre, sent cedar trees to Solomon when he was building the Temple in Jerusalem (1 Kings 5:10).

1.9. I thank Ben Marsh and Mary Voigt for guidance regarding these estimates.

1.10. In the former article he mentions the discovery in Megaron 3 of 19 pits of cornelian cherries, a summer fruit that had apparently been consumed shortly before the fire. The buildings on the northeast side of the elite quarter were not burned, and the wind generally comes in from a northern direction, at least during the summer. The fire may therefore have started in the Inner Court and then moved with the wind in a western and southern direction toward the gate.

1.11. Only two cattle skeletons were found in the destruction level, in Building CC3, and they appear to have been slaughtered before the fire (DeVries 1990:386).

1.12. The fills in Megaron 4 were disturbed, and the building had clearly been searched for valuables after the fire (Young 1964:287).

1.13. The quarry sources changed completely between the Early and Middle Phrygian periods. Ryelite, a light igneous rock, was used for the upper part of the Early Phrygian Gate, presumably because it is lighter and would have been more suitable for an area of occasional seismic activity. There is no ryelite in Middle Phrygian architecture, although gypsum and andesite are used for the first time. I owe these observations to Frank Matero. The stone sources for Phrygian architecture were examined by William McClain in 1992, who determined that the volcanic and sedimentary stones came from Duatepe and Çile Dağ, respectively (Sams 1992:472–73).

1.14. This suggestion was proposed by Mary Voigt. The Early Phrygian architecture on the citadel was filled with color: the area between the gate complex and the "Post and Poros Building" was paved with red and white stones set in a checkerboard pattern (Sams and Voigt 1995:373); the Polychrome House featured walls of bright red and blue stone (Young 1956:260); and the first Early Phrygian circuit wall, which was connected to the Polychrome House, contained courses of white, red, and yellow (Young 1964:291). The wings of the gate were stuccoed but apparently unpainted (Young 1956:258).

1.15. The existence of the ditch is based on magnetic prospection conducted at the site in 2007 (Sams 2009).

1.16. The crescent shape of Küçük Höyük is the result of a Persian siege mound set up against the fort.

1.17. For advice on the Syrian and Palestinian examples, I thank J.P. Dessel and Jodi Magness.

1.18. This is not far from the reasoning proposed by G. Roger Edwards (1959:264), although he suggested an early 7th century construction date for the fortifications based on the generally accepted date of ca. 700 for the destruction level.

1.19. Mary Voigt's excavations had already demonstrated an increase in building activity during the Middle Phrygian period (Voigt et al. 1997; Voigt and Young 1999). With the magnetic prospection results attesting to the actual size of the outer fortifications, our estimate of the extent of that activity needs to be increased again.

1.20. Mellink's excavations revealed that there were several phases of construction in the Küçük Höyük area (Mellink 1959).

1.21. For the Classical sources, see Strabo 1.3.21; Aristotle Politics 1.3.16; Eusebius Chronicle 696 BC.

1.22. Herodotos 1.14 (ivory throne); Aristotle 611.37 (Rose); Pollux 9.83.

1.23. The historical sources for these events are conveniently summarized in Mellink 1992.

1.24. For possible royal gift exchange during the reign of Midas, see supra, note 1.8.

1.25. The Bayındır tumulus in Lycia contained a burial that included objects in Phrygian style, and this too was probably set up during the period when Midas ruled Gordion. For the contents, see Özgen and Öztürk 1996:27; for Bayındır, DeVries 2008:42–43.

1.26. For an overview of these statues, see Draycott and Summers 2008:17–21. Rulers regularly appeared in relief format in Near Eastern iconography, but the tradition of colossal statues in the round seems unique to the Upper Euphrates region, especially between the 9th and 7th centuries BC. The one example found thus far on the Anatolian plateau is at Kerkenes, dating to the early 6th century BC (Draycott and Summers 2008).

1.27. A full presentation of the evidence for the link between Tumulus W and the Early Phrygian Gate will appear in Liebhart et al. n.d.

1.28. Without additional evidence from the area linking the attack specifically to the Kimmerians, however, one can only speculate.

1.29. A puppy burial found in a late Middle Phrygian context on the Western Mound probably also indicates Lydian influence (Sams and Voigt 2004:196). For the tradition in Lydia, see Greenewalt 1978.

1.30. The polychromatic figural and geometric architectural terracottas from Pazarlı, near Çorum, constitute another example of continued Phrygian influence in the 6th century (Koşay 1941).

1.31. This included, in addition to the examples cited above, Building M (Edwards 1959:265); Building E (Young 1955:5), which featured a hearth constructed of well-cut red stone; Building X (Young 1955:5; DeVries 1990:396); and the "Yellow House" (Edwards 1959:266–67).

1.32. This building, generally referred to as "the Painted House," dates ca. 500–490 BC. The style of the paintings is similar in several respects to the frieze on the Polyxena sarcophagus from the Troad (Sevinç 1996).

1.33. Hellenica Oxyrhynchia 1.4; 21.6; Young (1955:6; 1962a:154) thought that the earthquake dated to the mid 5th century; DeVries (1990:400) to ca. 400. Building X (DeVries 1990:396) contained a bridle with ivory and bronze strips, similar to those from Persepolis. It therefore looks as if this structure functioned in part as a storage site for horse gear. For Agesilaos, see Bruce 1967:141–42.

1.34. A hoard of sigloi with a date range of 420–375 BC was almost certainly concealed at the time of the attack (DeVries 1990:400).

1.35. This was true also for the Lower Town, 500–480 BC (Voigt and Young 1999:214).

1.36. Access to the inner court was limited by a new wall set up near (but not blocking) the entrance pylon, ca. 475–450 BC (Edwards 1959:266).

1.37. Arrian (Anabasis 2.3) locates the cart and its knot in the Temple of Zeus at the time of Alexander's arrival at the site, but there is no evidence that temples per se existed at Gordion, other than (possibly) Megaron 2 during the Early Phrygian period (Mellink 1983).

1.38. For assistance during the preparation of this article, I thank Ken Sams, Mary Voigt, Andrea Berlin, Kathleen Lynch, Mark Lawall, Gabriel Pizzorno, Ben Marsh, Teddy Ashmead, and Gareth Darbyshire.

Mapping and the Landscape

2

Mapping Gordion

Gabriel H. Pizzorno and Gareth Darbyshire

Introduction

Six decades of archaeological investigation at Gordion have provided a wealth of information about ancient Anatolia, in particular regarding the Early and Middle Phrygian periods. However, with the ambitious scale of the project have come major challenges, chief among which is the recording of the spatial layout of the excavated remains: the mapping of Gordion.

The lack of accurate spatial representations of the site has consistently hindered the analysis and publication of the excavated material. A complete site map combining all excavated data was never produced, and little of the ancient architecture could be precisely located in a site-wide coordinate system. The seriousness of this situation is difficult to overestimate. Most of the records for the excavation trenches and their assemblages were ultimately linked to architectural features, many of which no longer survive. Consequently, the key data could not be located spatially with acceptable accuracy, either in absolute terms or relative to each other. The existence of specific problems associated with the mapping had long been known, and indeed some of the surveyors responsible for the maps and plans attempted remedies over the years, but no definitive solutions were ever found.

The situation reached a critical juncture in 2007, when two new initiatives required the accurate spatial referencing of Gordion's data. Brian Rose had just became co-director of the project and suggested that a phase plan of the Citadel Mound would improve the comprehension and presentation of the excavated remains. At the same time, the authors commenced the Digital Gordion project, the goal of which is to improve the accessibility and analysis of the Gordion

materials through the digitization of the archived records and the creation of an online research environment (Darbyshire and Pizzorno 2009b). It rapidly became clear that this new research environment would require an accurate spatial referencing component in order to fully integrate all the data.

The present chapter documents our research into the history of mapping at Gordion, outlines our understanding of the problems, and presents the strategy we have developed for rectifying the situation. If at times our evaluation of past work seems less than kind, it is only because a frank and in-depth investigation into the problems, their magnitude, and their root causes is an inescapable first step toward finding the best solution. To illustrate the potential of our approach, we include a provisional phase plan of the key architectural units excavated on the Citadel Mound from the Early, Middle, and Late Phrygian periods—the first such plan ever produced for the site (foldout in back pocket). We also include a new site map, customized to show the features relevant to our discussion (Fig. 2.1, see color insert). These are examples of the kind of select cartography that we can now generate from the Digital Gordion geo-spatial dataset.

Approaching the Problem

Earlier attempts to comprehend and resolve the mapping problems at Gordion were too narrowly focused and consequently failed to recognize their underlying causes. The few solutions that were formulated only addressed immediate concerns, without ever confronting the core set of problems that had created the situation in the first place. One of the greatest shortcomings of these earlier attempts was the restriction of their analytical scope solely to the maps and plans themselves. That is to say, the problems with the mapping were approached in a cartographic manner, focusing on the measuring and drawing of the plans but largely ignoring their content. In contrast, we have taken a holistic approach, one that, in addition to the cartographic aspects of the matter, also focuses on the content of the plans and the social milieu in which they were produced. Thus, while technical considerations remain a key component of our strategy, we have also taken into account other types of information: the archaeological evidence itself (structures, deposits, and artifacts); the site's topography; the operational context of the excavations (aims and methodology, personnel, organization, logistics, and scheduling); and technological details (the type, condition, and capabilities of the equipment used).

Our preliminary survey of the Gordion Archive for pertinent records included more than 2,000 maps and plans, together with ancillary materials such as excavation notebooks, surveyors' reports, and aerial and satellite imagery. Tracing and evaluating the development of mapping at Gordion over the course of 60 years is no easy task, in part because the project has outlived a number of those involved, but also because clear policies for documenting the survey work were never established. Where records exist, they are of uneven quality and scope, and the paucity of documentation means that our interpretations and working hypotheses inevitably carry some degree of speculation. Nevertheless, there is much to be learned from a series of short reports written by the surveyors themselves, and from the surveyors' logs that survive.[1] These, coupled with the maps, plans, and other documents (publications, notes, sketches, and correspondence), have allowed us to piece together a comprehensive history of mapping at Gordion.

Chronology of the Surveys and Mapping

The earliest archaeological excavations at Gordion were carried out in a single season by Gustav and Alfred Körte in 1900. Their published report includes a site map that is the first cartographic representation of Gordion's archaeology. The map presents key geographical features and trench locations, but only one of the trenches has a detailed plan in the publication (Körte and Körte 1904).

Following a hiatus of 50 years, archaeological investigations resumed in 1950 under the ægis of the University of Pennsylvania Museum of Archaeology and Anthropology (henceforth Penn Museum). The first excavation series, and the most extensive in terms of the area investigated, was directed by Rodney S. Young between 1950 and 1973.[2] Over 1,500 maps and plans were produced to document the results of the 17 seasons of digging.

The year 1974 saw only a limited survey season, directed by Keith DeVries. That autumn, Young was killed in a car accident and major excavations did not resume until 1988. In the intervening period, under the direction of DeVries and G. Kenneth Sams, work focused on the analysis of excavated material, particularly the tens of thousands of artifacts, and to a much smaller degree on the evaluation and conservation of excavated architecture (DeVries 1986, 1987a, 1988a). Surveying was only carried out in 1979 and 1980, as part of the architectural conservation program, and in 1987 in preparation for a renewed series of excavations.

Penn's second excavation series began in 1988, with Mary M. Voigt as field director, and lasted until 2006.[3] These excavations were much less extensive than Young's, but the recovery and recording of evidence was more detailed, and hundreds of maps and plans were generated. These years also witnessed a number of excavations and surveys carried out on behalf of Turkey's General Directorate for Cultural Properties and Museums. The Museum of Anatolian Civilizations, Ankara, excavated Mamaderesi Tumulus in 1988, under the direction of Melih Arslan, in cooperation with the Gordion Project (Arslan 1989, Temizsoy 1992, 1993, 1994), and in 1989 Tahsin Saatçi investigated the three Kızlarkayası tumuli (Saatçi and Kopar 1990, 1991). That same year, a general evaluation survey of Gordion's tumuli was conducted and the results plotted on the standard 1:5,000 Turkish cartographic series and on an unprojected schematic map (unpublished). Three more tumuli were dug by Remzi Yağcı in 1990 (Yağcı 1992). With the exception of thirteen small inspec-

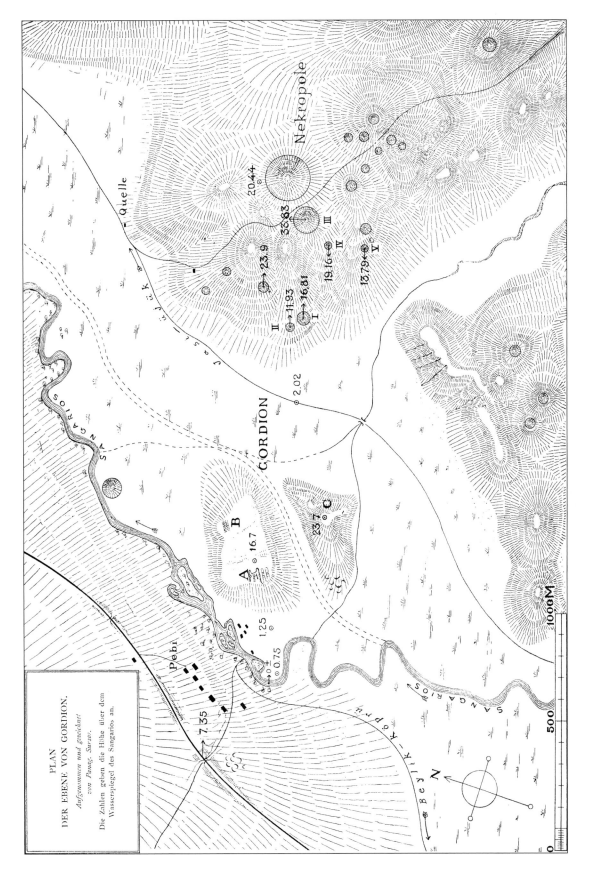

Fig. 2.2. The Körte map of Gordion, including the location of their excavation trenches on the Citadel Mound (A, B), in the Lower Town (C), and in five of the tumuli (I–V). Their vertical datum (0±) at the river Sakarya ("Sangarios") is marked directly southwest of the Citadel Mound. Also shown is the late Ottoman village of Bebi ("Pebi") and contemporary irrigation channels, springs, roads and tracks, and the railway line. Source: Körte and Körte 1904: Taf. 1.

tion trenches dug in selected areas of the site in 2007 (unpublished), no excavations have been conducted at Gordion since 2006.

As well as the excavations, other activities have generated spatial data. In 1987 and 1988 William Sumner conducted a survey of other sites in the area (the initial phase of the Gordion Regional Survey Project). The following year, a series of aerial photographs of the Citadel Mound and the Lower Town was taken by Wilson and Eleanor Myers using a balloon. In 1992 Andrew Goldman and Keith Dickey directed an intensive survey of the Outer Town, continued for another season by Goldman alone in 1995 (unpublished). A geomorphological study of Gordion and its environs was conducted by Ben Marsh between 1992 and 1995, and expanded for the Gordion Regional Survey Project directed by Lisa Kealhofer between 1996 and 2002 (Kealhofer 2005). Marsh's ongoing work has produced a number of important geomorphological and archaeological maps (Marsh 1997, 1999, 2005, and this volume). Another significant development has been the resumption, in 2007, of geophysical survey (unpublished geophysical investigations at Gordion had been conducted by E.K. Ralph in 1965). Ongoing work by Stefan Giese and Christian Hübner, of GGH GbR, has focused on the Citadel Mound, parts of the Lower and Outer Town zones, and on several of the tumuli. A second geophysics team, directed by Compton James Tucker and Joseph Nigro of the Goddard Space Flight Center, NASA, began work in 2009, focusing on the cemetery areas (Sams 2009:139–41; 2010:289–91; 2011a:462–64).

In 2008 a new survey of Middle Phrygian architecture on the Citadel Mound was initiated by Ömür Harmanşah of Brown University, and that same year a Penn team directed by Gabriel H. Pizzorno and William R. Fitts was on-site to resurvey as many extant fixed points as could be found. Most recently, in 2010, Gareth Darbyshire and John Hinchman carried out a new balloon aerial photographic survey of the Citadel Mound, Lower Town, and Northeast Ridge cemetery area. In addition, a differential Global Positioning System (dGPS) survey of the same areas, totalling more than 1,500 control points and including all extant visible architecture, was conducted by Darbyshire and Philip Sapirstein.

Mapping Gordion

The map produced by the Körte expedition of 1900 shows the contemporary relief, hydrology, vegetation, settlement, and transportation network, as well as the archaeological topography, trench locations, and elevations of selected points (Fig. 2.2). Although in many ways inaccurate, it constitutes a useful reference source for the late Ottoman landscape. Given the limitations of the Körte map and the absence of anything else that could be used, new cartography was essential at the beginning of the Penn project, and a number of basic site maps had to be produced during the first season.

Troubled Beginnings

In 1950, mapping work at Gordion was carried out by Mahmut Akok, an established Turkish archaeologist and illustrator; Edward B. Reed, a student from Princeton University; and Zihni Azım, who, like Akok, was an illustrator in Ankara. Although there are no accounts detailing the survey work that season, we have managed to reconstruct the essential sequence of events through a careful examination of the maps and plans that were produced (both draft and final versions), and the field notebooks and published reports (Young 1950, 1951).

Akok, who was the senior surveyor, spent only two weeks on-site collecting data (Young 1951:4), and produced three maps (the areas covered by these are indicated in Fig. 2.1). The first two, at a scale of 1:1,000, were based on his own survey of the areas excavated that season: the cluster of tumuli on the Northeast Ridge (1950-1; Fig. 2.3, see insert), and the Citadel Mound area, which also included the mounds of Kuş Tepe and Küçük Höyük (1950-80; Fig. 2.4, see insert).[4] The third, produced at a later date, is a 1:4,000 map of the entire site as it was then understood (1950-2; Fig. 2.5, see insert). Given the very limited time that Akok spent at Gordion, he could not have surveyed the whole area to produce the contouring on this map, and so it is likely that he also interpolated data from existing Turkish cartography (probably at 1:5,000 scale). This conjecture is supported by the fact that his survey stations are only marked on his two more detailed maps (1950-1 and 1950-80). The steps that Akok followed for his own survey can be deduced from a careful consideration of the survey stations, sight lines, and fixed points marked on his maps (Figs. 2.3 and 2.4).

Of particular interest is the 1:4,000 map (1950-2, Fig. 2.5), which shows grid intersection markers every 1,000 m. These suggest that Akok intended to create a grid system that would cover the entire site, with intervals at 1,000, 500, 100, 50, and 10 m, as reflected also by the later configuration of the grid over the Citadel Mound (Fig. 2.6, see insert). His first survey station had surely been placed on top of Tumulus MM, because this was the highest point in the area and the site of a Turkish geodetic marker. The use of this point as the survey's planimetric datum is also suggested by Akok's sight lines from there (as shown on map 1950-1; Fig. 2.3), and by its designation as a major grid intersection on map 1950-2 (Fig. 2.5). On the Citadel Mound, Akok established and measured four fixed points (A, B, C, and D), likely marked with temporary wooden stakes, and included them on his area map 1950-80 (Fig. 2.4). These were to serve as anchors for the implementation of the site grid over this area, with each pair of points (A-B and C-D) intended to define a baseline.

After Akok's departure, Reed used this survey as the basis for a detailed 1:500 map of the Citadel Mound, on which he recorded the positions of the four trenches dug there that season. There are two versions of this map in the Gordion Archive: a draft (1950-78) and an inked version (1950-77; Fig. 2.6). These are the first maps on which the site grid was fully rendered. The framework drawn by Reed is a square grid with intervals at 10 and 50 m. The minor intervals are designated by numbers along the west-east axis (1–65) and by letters along the north-south axis (A–ZZ). The origin of coordinates is ca. 200 m northwest of the Citadel Mound, across the Sakarya River. The bottom-right corner of the map was left ungridded in order to place an inset showing a map of the entire site (although in the event this was never added).[5] It is at this juncture that the first sign of trouble emerges: referring to Akok's fixed points A-D, Reed stated on the draft version of his map that the "stake layout here has been corrected from the inaccurate state shown on Mahmut's sunprint" (handwritten note on map 1950-78).[6]

A close examination of Akok's fixed points on his 1950-80 map does indeed show a problem. The east-west (A-B) and north-south (C-D) baselines are not perpendicular and are thus an inadequate foundation for a grid (Fig. 2.7, see insert). It is unclear whether the points had been erroneously marked on the ground, improperly measured, or incorrectly drawn on the map. Furthermore, they are off from the grid intersections they were supposed to represent in Akok's theoretical site grid discussed above. This is hardly surprising, since to connect the Citadel Mound survey with the planimetric datum would have required him to measure a length of 1,500 m (the distance between the first survey station on top of Tumulus MM and the first station he established on the Citadel Mound). The accurate measurement of such a long transect would have been very time consuming given the topography and the available equipment, and was very likely never carried out.

Reed's remedy, however, was hardly without issue. It is unclear as to what data he used for his corrections, especially since, by his own admission, he did not have access to Akok's site survey at the time (cf. note 2.5). Whatever the case, while drafting map 1950-78, Reed carried out a series of inexplicable actions that were to have long-lasting repercussions. He first redesignated the 2 m contour as the zero line. He then proceeded to alter the contour in the vicinity of fixed point B, redrawing the line so that it passed through the point itself, thus making B the new vertical datum (zero for elevations) at the Citadel Mound. He subsequently relabeled all the contours on the map, subtracting 2 m from the original elevations (Fig. 2.8, see insert).

Shortly after completing this map, Reed left the site and was succeeded by Azım, who focused on drawing the excavation plans. Most of the trench plans for the Citadel Mound from 1950 include some sort of reference to the site grid, but those for the six tumuli opened that season (and for the many dug in subsequent years) were not linked to it—at best, they were only approximately positioned on the site area maps produced by Akok (1950-1 and 1950-2; Figs. 2.3 and 2.5, respectively). This is particularly unfortunate since Akok's three maps do not match each other: the mismatch is immediately noticeable for features such as the irrigation canals, roads, and tracks, but it is also true for the contours describing the topography of the site (compare Figs. 2.3–2.5).

It would seem that Akok intended to use the same system of elevations as that employed by the Körte brothers, which took as its vertical datum the level of the Sakarya River.[7] Using the same origin point as for the planimetry (i.e., the top of Tumulus MM), Akok calculated the river's elevation above sea level and then used it as the vertical datum for his survey (Young et al. 1981, caption for fig. 1; Kohler 1995:2). He did not use this datum consistently, however, when preparing his maps.

In his general area map (1950-2; Fig. 2.5), the zero contour passes about 500 m north of the Citadel Mound and then heads north toward Yassıhöyük, not returning. By contrast, the Citadel Mound area map (1950-80; Fig. 2.4) has the same vertical datum, but the zero contour runs as far south as the area between the north end of Küçük Höyük and the eastern end of the Citadel Mound before turning east to disappear off the map. The area map of the Northeast Ridge (1950-1; Fig. 2.3) also has the same vertical datum, but the tracing of the zero contour is different from that of the general area map (1950-2; Fig. 2.5), for it runs much closer to Yassıhöyük and at one point even crosses the track that lies to the west of the village. An even more troubling attribute of this map is that contour lines are sometimes conflated, as for example with the 1 m line at the southern edge of the map, which becomes the 2 m line at the northern edge; these are not contours at all and consequently they render the entire series of intervals invalid (Fig. 2.3).[8] Lastly, as a result of Reed's adjustments, the 1:500 Citadel Mound map (1950-77; Fig. 2.6) has a different vertical datum, about 1.6 m higher, than that of the two area maps. In Reed's map the zero contour surrounds the base of the Citadel Mound, passing between it and Küçük Höyük before vanishing toward the west.

There are several likely reasons for the contour mismatches. As indicated above, Akok only surveyed two relatively small areas of the site (the end of the Northeast Ridge and the Citadel Mound); his other mapping data were presumably interpolated from already-existing maps. The need to combine these two disparate sources, compounded by the rush to produce the drawings, was probably the leading cause of errors. The immediate consequence was

that most of the elevations measured in the Citadel Mound trenches took as their reference the vertical datum of the detailed Citadel Mound map (1950-77; Fig. 2.6), while the elevations measured in other areas of the site were referenced to the vertical datum of the area maps (1950-2 and 1950-80; Figs. 2.4 and 2.5, respectively).

The four maps—the three area maps by Akok (1950-1, 1950-2, and 1950-80) and Reed's map of the Citadel Mound (1950-77)—remained the foundation of every map and plan drawn at Gordion over the next half-century. Almost a decade would pass before problems with the surveying began to be noticed. It did not help that the 1950 mapping staff did not return: the chief surveyor for 1951–1953 was Dorothy H. Cox, followed by Joseph S. Last from 1955–1962, with Cox returning in 1957.[9] However, the main reason that problems went unnoticed is that until 1958 Gordion's surveyors could avoid using the site grid. Their work in these years involved mapping either previously opened trenches, or extensions to these, which only required additions to existing plans; or mapping new trenches in tumuli, for which plans could be made without any use of the site's coordinate system.

Problems Become Apparent

In 1958 the opening of new trenches in previously unexcavated areas of the Citadel Mound, and the need to incorporate these into the site map, finally brought to light the problems with the spatial referencing. Using Akok's fixed points C and D as point of departure, Last built five new ones at the intersections of the gridlines to the east of them, in order to tie the new trenches to the site grid (Last 1958–59).[10] In the process, he compared the locations of the previously excavated trenches in the 1:500 general plans, referenced using the site grid, against their actual locations on the ground. In so doing, he found significant discrepancies that he tried to correct over the next few years by remeasuring the fixed points. He assumed that the root cause of the referencing problems was the way the trenches had been incorporated into the grid, rather than the grid itself. In the end, his efforts met with little success.

In 1963, perhaps in an attempt to address this situation, Mahmut Akok was brought back to Gordion. He apparently spent two months on-site, but no record of his activities remains. The other surveyor for that season was Charles K. Williams, who had previously worked with Last (Young 1964:279n1). Williams wrote a report that includes a description of some of the problems with the 1950 maps (1963). For the trenches on the west side of the Citadel Mound, he noted a discrepancy of more than 30 cm between points on the surface and those in the excavated levels. With regard to the Küçük Höyük, which had already witnessed several seasons of excavation, Williams reported that the mapped contours were inaccurate, and that the elevations did not conform with those on the Citadel Mound. As far as we can tell this was the first time that a concerted effort was made to understand and articulate some of the inconsistencies present in the site's maps.

Williams proposed a number of solutions including a full resurvey of the area and the rebuilding of the site grid. Unfortunately, none of his proposals seem to have been implemented, as the surveyors for the next two seasons, Aubrey Trik in 1965 and Joseph Shaw in 1967, focused once again on the mapping of features in existing trenches. The grid seems to have received little consideration from Trik and does not appear on any of his plans. Shaw, however, apparently tried to use it when he carried out a major update of the Citadel Mound trench plan (1967-1).[11] The fact that there are major problems with this plan suggests that Shaw was unaware of the fundamental issues besetting the site's spatial referencing system.[12]

The same focus on individual trenches continued in the next season, 1969, under Wilson W. Cummer. It was only in 1971, apparently, that he became aware of the problems with the referencing, when he was unable to tie his survey work to the site grid using several of the existing fixed points. Unable to find a solution, he decided to address the problem at the beginning of the next field season, in 1973. In his report for that year, he remarked that the accuracy of the Citadel Mound plans had deteriorated markedly since 1950, as demonstrated by the fact that he could neither correctly link his new trench plans to those from earlier seasons, nor accurately relate some of the older trench plans to each other. His efforts to resolve the situation were quickly abandoned because, in his own words, "…most of the old 1:100 plans do not show grid points or fixed points….We dropped

this job" (Cummer 1973). By the end of the season he estimated that the general degree of horizontal error on the Citadel Mound was at least 2 m. His own attempt to re-establish the site grid evidently did not meet with much success, since the problems of aligning the position of different trenches continued to be reported in later years. He did, however, produce a 1:500 Point Plan showing all the fixed points he could find and measure (1973-15).[13]

Surveying in the 1974 season was directed by John L. Miller. Upon arriving at Gordion, he checked the surveying instruments kept at the site, and reported serious problems with the transit, the wye level, and the tripods (Miller et al. 1974–2004:1–11). He concluded that the problems with the wye level could be mitigated by constant adjustments, but the transit was beyond salvage. Unfortunately, these warnings appear to have been ignored and the instruments continued to be used in later years.

Miller prepared a 1:4,000 map (1974-1) based on Akok's 1950 site area map (1950-2), on which he recorded the data from his survey of the Sakarya River channel, including twelve fixed points that he had set up along the banks (their locations were also recorded on a 1:1,000 scale map: 1974-2).[14] At the end of the season he candidly evaluated his own work: "this survey is appallingly inaccurate due to time limitations and instrument problems. Resurvey is urgently needed." Regarding Akok's survey he remarked that it was "not correct, hence [the need for] extensive fudging with [the] equally unreliable 1974 survey data and [the] resulting, highly approximate drawings" (Miller et al. 1974–2004:1–11). Clearly, by this point the magnitude of the mapping problems was impossible to ignore, but no immediate attempt was made to remedy the situation. The project was thrown into turmoil that year by Young's sudden death, and over the next decade only minimal fieldwork was carried out at Gordion. The only noteworthy surveying development during this period occurred in 1979, prompted by the need to record newly exposed walls of several Middle Phrygian structures on the Citadel Mound (Buildings P, Q, X, and Y). The project hired the architectural firm of Lightbody, Smith and Bell, who proceeded to survey the Citadel Mound for extant fixed points, managing to locate 11 in all.[15] They then attempted to rebuild the site grid using S26-S31 as the east-west base-line, finding in the process that the "survey grid appears to be incorrectly plotted—[it] should be shifted 1 m northerly"; but how they arrived at this conclusion is not specified in their notes (Miller et al. 1974–2004:12–26).

After a 13-year hiatus, major fieldwork was resumed at Gordion in 1988, under the direction of Mary M. Voigt. To prepare for this, she and Robert H. Dyson, Jr. (then the Penn Museum's director) conducted a preliminary reconnaissance in 1987, together with architect William C.S. Remsen, who prepared an assessment of the site's mapping corpus (1987). Remsen examined previous surveyors' reports, since he mentions those for 1963 (mistakenly assigned by him to 1967) and 1973. He also reviewed the surveying equipment stored on-site, warning that the wye level "has not been cleaned or adjusted in living memory and *should not* be used" (Remsen 1987, emphasis his). In addition to his report, he surveyed the limits of the previously excavated areas on the Citadel Mound and catalogued the visible fixed points, putting this information on a 1:500 map (1987-1). He also remeasured the points on Cummer's 1973 Point Plan, which, despite some discrepancies, he found to be generally accurate.[16]

These new measurements were used in the first of the new excavation seasons the following year, but the surveyor, Keith Dickey, noticed discrepancies between Remsen's elevations and his own. Uncertain as to the nature of the problem, Dickey decided to measure all the elevations for Voigt's operations relative to a single fixed point, M10 (see foldout), for which both sets of measurements concurred.

In 1992, Remsen returned to Gordion to carry out preparatory work for Voigt's excavations the next year. He established nine new permanent fixed points on the Citadel Mound (1992a–1992i), and he began the process of rebuilding the site grid, finishing it in 1993 (Remsen 1992, 1993). The reconstructed grid retained the original's spacing and orientation by using the extant fixed points and with the addition of at least one more (1993A). Remsen selected a new horizontal origin 2.5 km south and 2 km west of the Citadel Mound so as to avoid negative coordinates, and he established a new system of absolute elevations based on the Turkish geodetic marker on top of Küçük Höyük

(no. 1482, 701.59 m above mean sea level). For the 1994 season he planned to extend the grid westward to cover Voigt's Outer Town excavations, but this was never carried out.

Despite Remsen's efforts, problems with the site's referencing promptly re-emerged in the next three seasons (1995–1997), when surveyor Sean Gaukroger attempted to tie Voigt's operations in the northwestern sector of the Citadel Mound to the site grid. Gaukroger discovered discrepancies between his own survey and the earlier maps and plans, but he remained confident in the accuracy of his own work, though without explaining why (Gaukroger 1995).[17] His investigations into the inconsistencies were thwarted by problems with the theodolite kept on-site, for despite cleaning the instrument he was unable to fix the errors that occurred when measuring long distances. Another problem that he noticed when tying in Voigt's excavations was that the distance between S26 and S26N30 was only 29 m, not the 30 m it should have been. With regard to S26 he discovered that there were actually two fixed points in that general location, less than 1.5 m apart (marked as S26 and C on the phase plan, see foldout). After testing both of these against other known fixed points, he concluded that he and Remsen had not been using the same one, and that the point he himself had been using was the one that was true-to-grid.[18] Consequently he decided that it was the location of S26N30 that was erroneous, and he appears to have been satisfied with his results, though it remains unclear whether he ever corrected his measurements (Gaukroger 1996). No further work on the grid was done either in that season or in the next.

Following a hiatus between 1998 and 2000, Voigt resumed excavation on the western area of the Citadel Mound in 2001. The points set out by Gaukroger were used by Carrie Alblinger to lay out new trenches and take elevations, and an additional fixed point was built in the Citadel Mound's northwestern sector by William Collins (M.M. Voigt, pers. comm. January 12, 2010). Two other excavation projects were also carried out on the mound, directed by Brendan Burke (in 2001, 2002, 2005, and 2006) and Andrew Goldman (in 1997, 2004, and 2005), under Voigt's aegis. Although the mapping information for these seasons is limited, it does not appear that the grid was extensively used (Miller et al. 1974–2004:37–39).

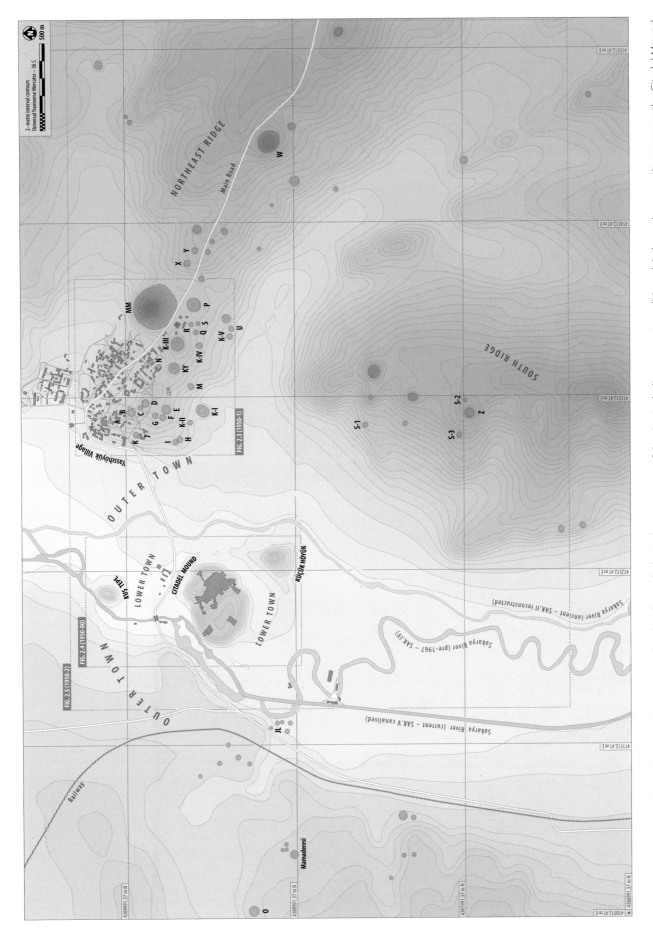

Fig. 2.1. New map of Gordion, showing select topographical and morphological components of the site, including: zones, tumuli (purple), the main excavation areas on the Citadel Mound (maroon), and the modern village of Yassıhöyük. The extents of the maps shown in Figures 2.3, 2.4, and 2.5 are also indicated. Source: G.H. Pizzorno and G. Darbyshire.

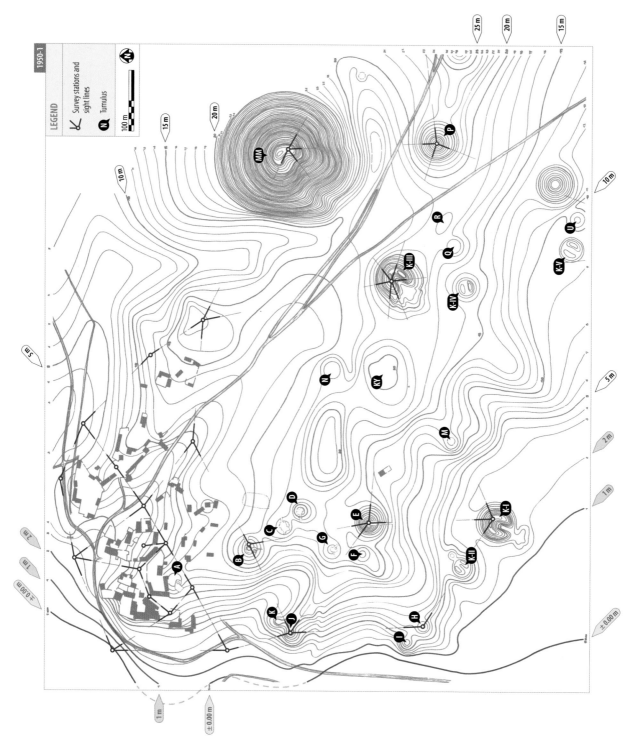

Fig. 2.3. Annotated version of Akok's map of the cluster of tumuli in the vicinity of the modern village of Yassıhöyük, on the Northeast Ridge (1950-1). The highlighted features are: the zero contour (red), the conflated 1 m / 2 m contour line (blue), and Akok's survey stations and sight lines. Compare with Figures 2.4, 2.5, and 2.6. Source: G.H. Pizzorno and G. Darbyshire.

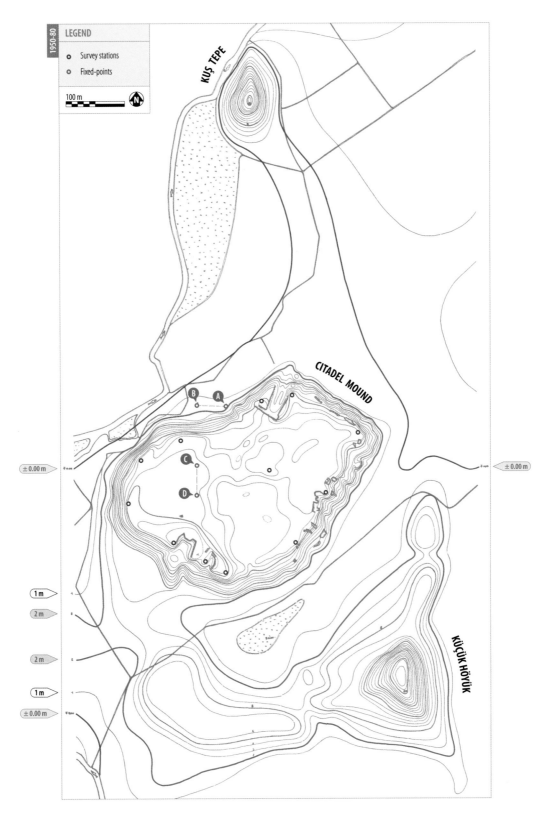

Fig. 2.4. Annotated version of Akok's map of the Citadel Mound, Kuş Tepe, and Küçük Höyük, prior to the 1950 excavations (1950-80). The highlighted features are: Akok's survey stations, his fixed points A–D, the zero contour (red), and the 2 m contour (blue). Compare with Figures 2.3, 2.5, and 2.6. Source: G.H. Pizzorno and G. Darbyshire.

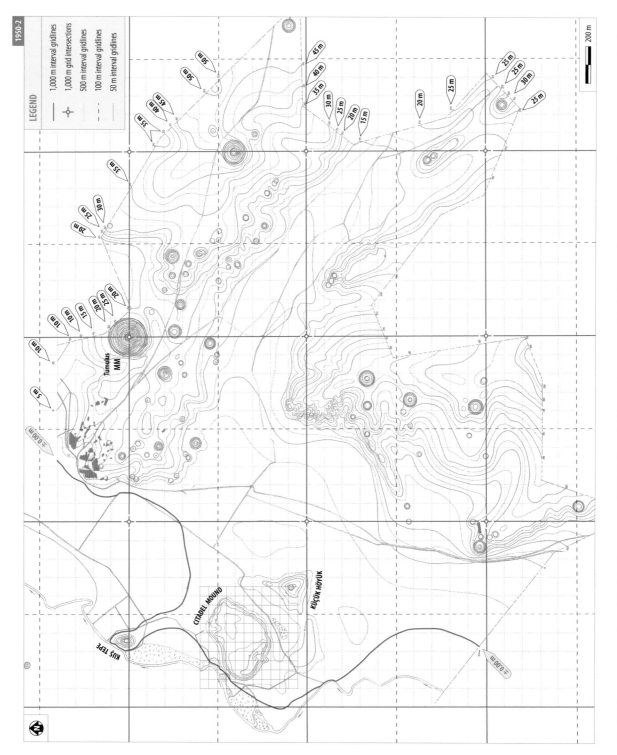

Fig. 2.5. Annotated version of Akok's site area map (1950-2). The highlighted features are his 1,000 m grid intersections, and the zero contour (red). Also included is a reconstruction of Akok's ideal site grid, with intervals of 1000, 500, 100, and, in the Citadel Mound area only, 50 m. Compare with Figures 2.3, 2.4, and 2.6. Source: G.H. Pizzorno and G. Darbyshire.

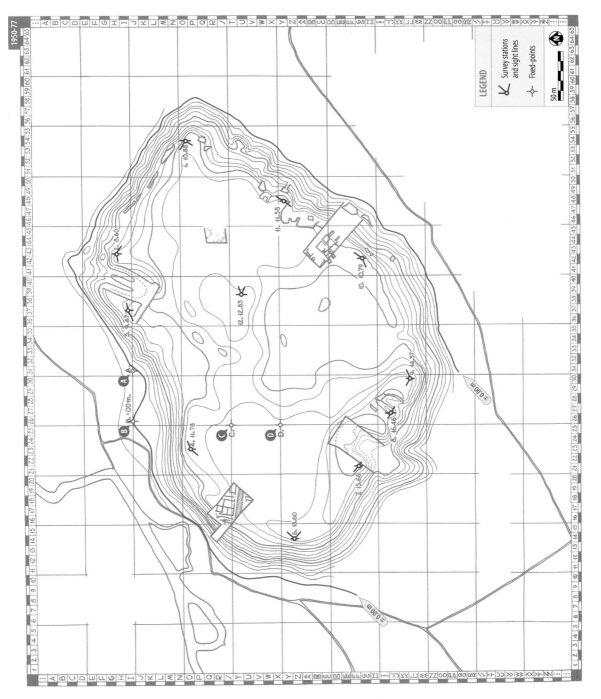

Fig. 2.6. Annotated version of Reed's inked map of the Citadel Mound (1950–77). The highlighted features are: Reed's new zero contour, formerly the 2 m contour (red); Akok's survey stations; and his fixed points A–D, as corrected by Reed. Compare with Figures 2.3, 2.4, and 2.5. Source: G.H. Pizzorno and G. Darbyshire.

Fig. 2.7. Annotated detail of map 1950-80 (cf. Fig. 2.4). The highlighted features are baselines AB and CD, and the 89-degree (i.e., not perpendicular) angle they form. Source: G.H. Pizzorno and G. Darbyshire.

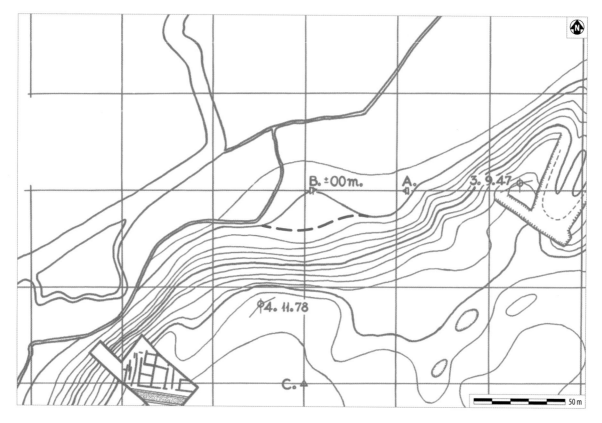

Fig. 2.8. Annotated detail of map 1950-77 (cf. Fig. 2.6), showing Reed's new zero line (formerly the 2 m contour) as redrawn to pass through fixed point B. The dashed blue line added to the original map indicates the tracing of the contour prior to Reed's alteration. Source: G.H. Pizzorno and G. Darbyshire.

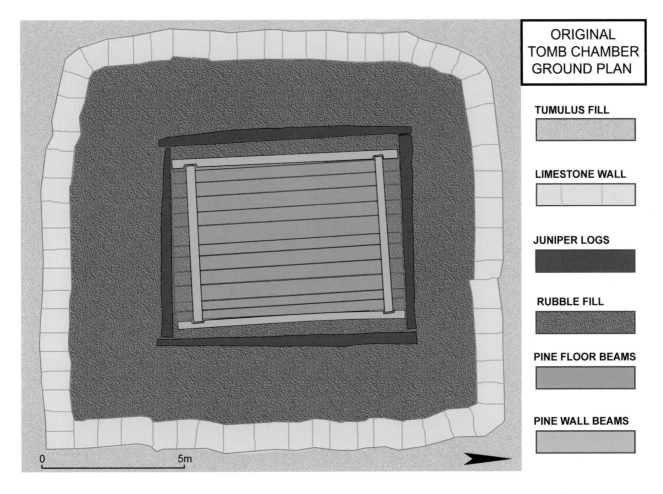

ORIGINAL TOMB CHAMBER GROUND PLAN

TUMULUS FILL

LIMESTONE WALL

JUNIPER LOGS

RUBBLE FILL

PINE FLOOR BEAMS

PINE WALL BEAMS

Fig. 9.11. Plan of the tomb chamber complex built to the level of the first wall beams. Drawing: R.F. Liebhart.

Fig. 11.1. Example of weaving found in 2003-Tx-1 similar to other Tumulus MM gold-colored tabby textile fragments. Photograph: M.W. Ballard.

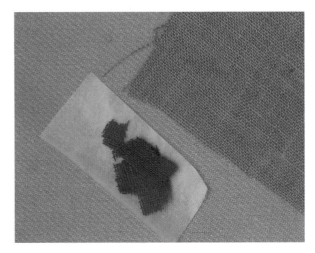

Fig. 11.3. A comparison of three goethite-coated materials. On glassine paper, small textile fragments 2003-Tx-1 from Tumulus MM. Beneath it, goethite film on polyester, and above it, goethite film on handkerchief-weight linen. Photograph: M.W. Ballard.

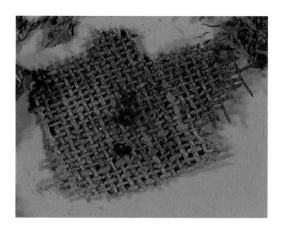

Fig. 11.7. Another of the 2003-Tx-11 fragments with an earthy green color. Photograph: M.W. Ballard.

Fig. 11.6. One of several 2003-Tx-11 textile fragments from the southeast corner of Tumulus MM. Photograph: M.W. Ballard.

Fig. 11.8. Two samples of modern goethite-coated linen overdyed with indigo are compared with copper-mordanted wool tied with cotton. Photograph: M.W. Ballard.

Evaluating the Problems and Their Underlying Causes

Over the last 60 years the Gordion project has produced thousands of maps and plans, including state drawings, working versions and sketches, and hundreds of plans in the field notebooks. It is no easy feat to track mapping developments with so many drawings, created over such a long period of time by so many different people. However, the most serious issue is the quality of the plans, not their quantity. Individual drawings might appear to be of a standard commensurate with that of similar, coeval projects. The real problem only becomes apparent when one moves away from the single trench and tries to piece together larger areas of the site into a coherent whole. It is the absence of referencing information on most of the Young-era plans that is the most serious difficulty we have yet uncovered. Unreferenced plans lack any spatial information that would allow them to be connected to any other plan: they are "floaters" that cannot be easily or accurately pinned to an actual location on the ground.

The Nature of the Problems

During excavation and surveying, the main spatial referencing tool would have been the site grid (by itself an abstraction), and its reification on the ground: the fixed points. The purpose of a site grid is indeed to tie all loci to one spatial frame of reference. Unfortunately, the Gordion grid was rarely used, probably because it was never comprehensively articulated on the ground. It was only actually marked in one area—the Citadel Mound—and even there it was never established accurately or in any reliably durable manner. For areas beyond the Citadel Mound—the Lower Town and Outer Town zones, and the cemeteries—the excavation and survey data were referenced by eye to nothing better than Akok's flawed area maps. Indeed, Edwards (formerly Gordion's associate field director) subsequently revealed in a letter to Dyson (then director of the Penn Museum): "In the main the trenches were laid out...I think, by and large, without much of any reference to a grid which, as far as I know, was purely honorary" (1984). This statement is also supported by Remsen, who noted in his 1987 report that one of the most challenging aspects of mapping at Gordion "was the casual use and abandonment of the original grid." In fact, the only plans which show the site grid were either those made during the 1950 season, or later ones directly based on them. References to fixed points are notably absent on the more detailed plans of post-1950 vintage. While periodic attempts were made by the surveyors to re-establish the grid (e.g., Last in 1958, Cummer in 1973, and Remsen in 1993), the results were never satisfactory, and the grid fell again into disuse soon afterward.

In general, the surveying of archaeological features seems to have been referenced to temporary markers and the baulks of individual trenches. The grid only appears to have troubled the surveying team when it absolutely demanded consideration, especially when new trenches were to be opened in previously unexcavated areas of the Citadel Mound. Extensions to existing trenches seem to have been mostly "eyed-in", as noted by Cummer, "added from year to year to the original trench plan without their being surveyed from fixed points and with no consideration for scarp erosion" (1973). The site grid's representation on the ground, flawed from the moment of inception, was never rigorously re-examined. Even the most comprehensive attempt at fixing the errors, in 1993, was far too limited in scope, with Remsen comprehending neither the grid's abstract model nor the full range of problems that plagued its implementation on the ground.

The problems with the horizontal component of the mapping are reflected and compounded in its vertical aspect. There is no evidence to indicate that there was ever in place a functional, site-wide referencing system for elevations. As discussed above, each of the site maps created in 1950, and used exclusively thereafter, had a different vertical datum. Even within specific areas of the site, where the elevations could have been kept consistent, major problems exist with the altimetry. In the case of the Citadel Mound, the problems created by Reed's arbitrary redefinition of the contouring and elevations were never fully addressed. Remsen's report reveals that an undocumented attempt was made some time between 1963 and 1987, by "persons unknown," to re-base the elevations of the Citadel Mound on the original Akok datum (1987). But the result seems to have been the introduction of yet more confusion, as the referencing was shifted from fixed points that had survived for years (e.g., point C')[19] to an assortment of ever-disappearing markers in the excavated areas (e.g., the TB series of fixed points).[20] The most comprehensive effort to unify the elevation system was again that of Remsen, who used the Turkish geodetic marker on top of Küçük Höyük (no. 1482) to tie the site's fixed points to a universal system of reference. Unfortunately, his assumption of internal consistency in the grid's implementation proved to be unfounded and, following the introduction of his new system in 1993, it was not long before problems began to be reported again (see discussion above). In addition, throughout the history of Penn's excavations at Gordion, there appears to have been persistent confusion among the surveyors with regard to the location and identity of the fixed points used for measuring elevations. Consequently, there is no unified, accurate altimetry for the Gordion Project's data. This state of affairs, when combined with the equally problematic planimetry, created a situation in which there was no reliable way to link features from different trenches, either vertically or horizontally.

A perfect illustration of how complicated matters became is the confusion surrounding fixed points C and S26, mentioned above. These two points are actually one and the same in the abstract site grid (the intersection of baselines S-T and 25-26), but they were somehow built twice on the ground in different locations, 1.5 m apart and with a vertical difference of 10 cm. This muddling had dire consequences, because the S26-S31 line was the one most frequently used as the basis for re-establishing the grid (such as when new fixed points were required). Thus, for example, in 1979, when Lightbody, Smith and Bell reinstituted the grid based on the S26-S31 line, they recorded that it was orientated 2° 42' west of magnetic north (Miller et al. 1974–2004:12–26). Yet in 1987, when Remsen re-established the grid using the same line, it was only 1° 45' west of magnetic north (Remsen 1987). This clearly indicates that they were each using a different point for their measurements, although both assumed that it was the true S26.[21] Consequently, the orientation of Lightbody, Smith and Bell's grid differs from Remsen's by almost a full degree. This might not seem much, but angular error increases with distance. Thus, for example, if we consider point N56 on the eastern edge of the Citadel Mound, its position in the

two grids differs by almost 5 m. How many times this kind of situation arose in the course of Gordion's excavations is anybody's guess.

Lastly, even if the problems with the referencing could be ignored, there still remains the fact that the 1950 site area maps were never revised to keep pace with developments and they soon became outdated. Until our own research began, they remained the principal means of presenting Gordion's spatial layout, even though none of them accurately shows the archaeological and topographical details of the site as these came to be understood. In particular, the large tract west of the Sakarya River was never presented in detail, despite the fact that it includes a significant portion of the Outer Town as well as tumuli, ancient roads, and other remains (compare Fig. 2.5 with Fig. 2.1, and with our annotated satellite image in Darbyshire and Pizzorno 2009a:14).[22] In addition, many of the tumuli on the northern and northeastern perimeters of the settled area were never surveyed, and there was never a map showing all of the excavation trenches in the various settlement zones (Citadel Mound, Lower Town, Outer Town), tumuli, and other cemeteries.

Underlying Causes

Based on our review, several key factors emerge from the web of causality responsible for Gordion's mapping problems. One of the most glaring is that the surveying equipment was not well maintained. As we have seen, Miller in 1974, Remsen in 1987, and Gaukroger in 1996 all pointed out that the project's equipment was dirty or mechanically faulty. An illuminating example is revealed in a letter by Edwards: "DHC [Dorothy H. Cox, surveyor for the 1957 season] was unable to show this on her plan [of Building M], that is what was exposed last year, because of measurements from a faulty tape, I understand" (1958:3). More than once, surveyors strongly recommended that the project should establish a formal equipment-maintenance policy but, as far as we can tell, this was never done. Faulty equipment would naturally have led to surveying errors that are now extremely difficult to identify.

Despite Remsen's assessment that "much excellent work has been done over the years" (1987), the limited skill and carelessness of some of the surveyors was a source of error, and from the very beginning of the project serious mistakes were made that were to have lasting consequences. These include a general lack of referencing on the maps and plans, and the occasional omission of scale and north arrow.

With regard to "north," it should be noted that inconsistency and imprecision in the designation of the cardinal points is widespread throughout the Gordion excavation corpus, and has continued to be a source of confusion. Besides the occasional use of magnetic north and, more rarely, true north, the excavators used two main orientation systems. In the Young excavations, the system for recording directions relied heavily on the use of "notebook north," sometimes called "notebook direction." Young arbitrarily selected true northeast to be used as north, so that, for example, the Phrygian megarons could be generally described as facing either north or south, whereas in fact they faced northeast or southwest. This system was used in Young's early publications, but starting with his 1968 report, magnetic north was employed. The Young excavation plans did not follow a consistent orientation, and there is usually no explicit indication of which "north" was being followed; in some cases north is not indicated on the drawings at all. In Voigt's excavations, the system employed was based on "dig east," which was marked as the point where the sun rises, and on "dig north," which was understood to be the general direction of the Sakarya River as seen from the Citadel Mound. Thus Voigt's "dig north" loosely corresponds to Young's west, or true northwest, so that the same megarons are described as facing east-west. The published plans from the Voigt excavations show magnetic north, which is also used in the accompanying written descriptions.

From the available documentation, it seems clear that it was the magnitude of the mapping tasks, in relation to the small number of personnel involved, that led to much of the confusion and many of the omissions and mistakes.[23] During the 1950 season, Akok was on-site for only two weeks, yet in that time he had to carry out two fundamental and substantial assignments: the creation of three site area maps, and the formulation and establishment of the site grid. Years later, Miller indicated in his 1974 report that time pressure was a major source of error in his own survey work. In addition to surveying, the mapping staff usually had to complete publication-ready plans in the field, and there was rarely enough time at the end of a season to review their work—neither on the ground nor on paper. To quote Cummer (1973:4):

> The worst aspect of our work was the "photo-finish," when we try to complete publication drawings within two days after digging stops. Inevitably mistakes are made and go unnoticed. There is no time for detail drawings and sections, no chance to study the structures for which we have spent three months and several thousand dollars to excavate. It would be more rewarding and more interesting for the staff to spend an extra two weeks together on the site, discussing the buildings and preparing careful drawings, rather than scattering and trying to piece work together later.

Some surveying staff also had other roles in the same season, such as trench supervisor or excavator, artifact illustrator, or architectural specialist, which in some cases may have distracted them from dealing with mapping issues as thoroughly as was required.

Young himself was also a factor. His determination to reach Iron Age levels meant that the remains of later periods were often not accorded the time and attention they deserved. The Hellenistic evidence suffered particularly as a consequence, with many buildings and associated artifacts being, at best, only rudimentarily mapped. As Edwards reported to Dyson: "(except in trenches I myself dug or supervised) so far as I know no [Hellenistic] levels were recorded and drawn by the architect. All others (still referring only to the upper levels) were, so far as I know, merely recorded in the notebooks" (1984). By contrast, the later excavations directed by Voigt placed equal weight on recording architectural, artifactual, and organic material of all periods.

Another problem was that continuity of mapping personnel does not seem to have been a high priority for the project. Less than half of them worked on-site consecutively for more than two seasons, and only Last worked as many as six.[24] As Remsen remarked in 1987, "much of the confusion seems to be due to the rapid turnover of architects at the site." He also highlighted another serious problem: the lack of documentation. The Gordion Project never established a policy for creating, maintaining, and storing a comprehensive, and comprehensible, corpus of mapping records, and surveyors' reports were produced only intermittently. Remsen singled out the lack of documentation for the location and identification of fixed points as being the major reason why many of the markers had been lost or misidentified over the years (1987).

What is surprising, given the obvious complexity of the site, is that there were so few attempts to address the mapping challenges at Gordion, despite the warning signals highlighted in the extant surveyors' reports.

Articulating a Solution

During our initial evaluation of the status of Gordion's mapping corpus, carried out in 2007, we developed a strategy built around two key goals. The first was to salvage as much spatial information as we could from all past mapping activities, to allow us to produce maps and plans of the earlier work that were as accurate as possible. We came to realize that this could only be done with a holistic approach, wherein all types of available data are weighted and combined while carefully considering their levels of accuracy. The second goal was to institute a new best-practice mapping framework, to ensure that all present and future work at the site is properly referenced.

To accomplish these goals, it was essential that we first establish an absolute referential framework to which all spatial data (past, present, and future) could be anchored. Thus we decided to use as our absolute reference the Universal Transverse Mercator coordinate system (UTM), which provides a standard, worldwide framework for specifying locations on the surface of the Earth, and is therefore impervious to the problems of a custom site grid.

We then undertook the exhaustive archival research necessary to acquire a detailed understanding of the history of mapping at Gordion. As part of this process we realized that not all the extant surveying documentation had been accessioned into the Gordion Archive. A detailed search located many stray items (including surveyors' notebooks, other documents, and working drawings) in the dig-house at Gordion, which we subsequently transferred to the Penn Museum.

We then proceeded to identify the original errors and their causes, and to reconstruct the sequence of events outlined above. Armed with this knowledge, we devised a fieldwork strategy to obtain accurate UTM coordinates for key features on-site, in order to guide the referencing of the original plans and maps. These features included fixed points used in the past, as well as extant architecture and excavation trenches.

Regarding the fixed points, many of these had long been considered lost. However, our research enabled us to locate many of them through the use of a predictive model that we tested on-site in 2008. Some of the markers were in fact still extant on the surface (although hardly visible), while others we had to unearth because they had been buried at different times in the past for a variety of reasons. By measuring their coordinates, we were at last able to produce a map of the key fixed points referenced to a single coordinate system (see foldout).

With regard to the visible architectural features and excavation trenches, the Penn 2010 balloon and dGPS survey served the dual purpose of providing us with a fully referenced map of extant architecture in key areas of the site, and over 1,500 control points to further improve the referencing of our imagery.

Resurvey alone is insufficient, however, since most of the excavated remains, and many of the trench outlines, no longer survive (the most obvious exception being the Early Phrygian Destruction Level). To address this issue we designed a Geographic Information System (GIS), centered on a series of "snapshots" comprised of aerial photographs and satellite images taken at different times over the last 60 years. These snapshots, when properly geo-referenced into the GIS, provide spatial cues for aligning the plans of trenches and structures from the excavations. This work began in late 2008, the basis for the geo-referencing being a QuickBird satellite image, which had been rectified using SRTM-30 data (Shuttle Radar Topography Mission) in partnership with NASA/Goddard Space Flight Center. In 2010 we enhanced the accuracy of the image by using the control points surveyed on-site with a dGPS unit, as noted above.[25] The rest of the available imagery, including Turkish aerial photographs from 1959 and the balloon photographs from 1989 and 2010, were then rectified against the QuickBird image.[26]

In 2009–2010, we used a University of Pennsylvania Research Foundation grant (URF), awarded to the authors in collaboration with Brian Rose and Philip Sapirstein, to create the Digital Gordion Mapping Project (DGMP). Under our supervision, a team of five Penn students scanned the original maps and plans, and these scans together with the drawings' metadata were systematized and integrated into a custom-built database. The team then used the GIS to reference the scans against features visible either in the current or in the legacy imagery, or against other maps and plans that had already been aligned. Once this work has been completed, vector maps and plans of the site will be constructed from the rectified data.

Phase Plan of the Phrygian Citadel

During the rectification of the imagery in 2008, we conducted a series of trials to establish the best workflow for processing the maps and plans. As part of this exercise, we carried out a preliminary referencing of many of the Citadel Mound drawings. The accuracy of the results was inevitably limited, since at that time we lacked not only the more precise spatial data but also the in-depth knowledge of the history of surveying at Gordion that we later came to acquire. Nevertheless, the results allowed us to generate far more accurate plans of the architecture than were hitherto available. Over the course of the following two years we developed the capability to map the key architectural phases in accurate relation to each other. Some of the results of this work are presented here as a large color foldout phase plan of the Citadel Mound. This particular format was suggested by Brian Rose, who wanted something similar to the phase plan of Troy published by Hueber and Riorden (1994). To be consonant with the chronological span covered by the present volume, the plan is restricted to the Early (YHSS 6), Middle (YHSS 5), and Late (YHSS 4) Phrygian periods, omitting the architectural data for the Early Bronze Age, the Early Iron Age, and Hellenistic, Roman, and later times.

The production of an archaeological phase plan is far more than a cartographical exercise. It involves a substantial amount of archaeological research and interpretation because mapping introduces a broad range of questions and problems, especially in terms of spatial and chronological relationships between different elements. Improving the accuracy of Gordion's spatial representations has forced us to re-evaluate many old issues, and deal with new ones that have arisen. In addressing them, we have necessarily had to return to all the primary sources—maps and plans, field notebooks, reports, and photographs—to verify and refine our interpretations.

This research has given us a clearer understanding of architectural relationships, leading to a number of important new archaeological interpretations, some of which are annotated on the plan. A good example is the Late Phrygian "Mosaic Building," a complex inserted into the southwestern corner of the citadel, on top of the demolished remains of Middle Phrygian Building A, and so-called because of its ornate pebble mosaic floors. For the first time, the structural components found in the many excavation trenches in this area have been accurately correlated and aligned. This remapping has indicated that a major wall of the Mosaic Building is actually coaxial with a more distant wall fragment whose identity had long been in doubt, allowing us to posit that the complex could have been much larger than previously assumed.

Our research has also enabled us to include architectural reconstructions in those areas of the Citadel Mound not yet explored by excavation. These reconstructions are an aid to appreciating spatial relationships, and also serve as a predictive tool for planning future excavations and geophysical surveys. They are feasible because of the regularity of the spatial patterning apparent in some of Gordion's architectural layouts, especially in the Early and Middle Phrygian periods. Although the final phase of Early Phrygian is the best preserved and currently the best understood, the Middle Phrygian layout is more extensively attested and its general similarity to the preceding Early Phrygian setup has allowed us to plausibly extrapolate the plans of both periods. Furthermore, while only relatively short stretches of the citadel enclosure's outer walls have been excavated, these are enough to indicate the general extent of the enceintes, and we have offered new reconstructions.

Besides the cartographical and archaeological issues of the phase plan, there are many design considerations that we have had to resolve. A great deal of thought has been given to appearance and presentation. We tested dozens of combinations of color schemes, line widths and typefaces, as well as other graphic elements. Throughout the design process, our primary goal was to maximize readability and usability. Given the great density of information on the plan, we wanted to ensure that the reader would not be overwhelmed by visual clutter. Quite often this meant having to emphasise one element of the plan over another. In some cases it was comparatively easy to decide which elements to prioritize. For example, placing the emphasis on excavated rather than extrapolated architecture was clearly preferable, and therefore actual excavated remains are represented on the plan with solid colors and lines while reconstructions are shown with semi-transparent colors and dashed lines.

A multi-phase plan presents particular design difficulties because of the great density of graphically overlapping information. A major issue was the selection of a color scheme to represent the architecture's diachronic dimension. Our intention was to make both phasing and periodization easy to comprehend. However, after exploring a variety of color schemes, we realized that the overall complexity made it impossible to emphasize both aspects equally. We therefore decided that architectural units spanning more than one phase would be best represented using color banding, which shows both the phase in which a structure was built (the broader bands) and its final phase (the narrower bands). Furthermore, to enhance the legibility of the banding, it made sense to maximize the contrast between the different phase colors. It also made sense to assign varieties of the same color to phases of the same period, to emphasize their relationship. Unfortunately, these individual color schemes did not work well together. On the one hand, the overly similar colors substantially reduced the contrast between the background and the banding, and thereby de-emphasized the phases. On the other hand, the widely differing colors dramatically increased the complexity of the presentation, and made the visual grouping of phases into periods an almost impossible task. Ultimately, we decided that it was preferable to emphasize the periods at the expense of the phases, since the former are the higher-level and more familiar analytical units at Gordion. Thus, all phases within a period share the

same hue but vary slightly in lightness and saturation. The intended effect of this color scheme is that the reader readily discerns the periods at a glance, while the phases only become apparent upon closer scrutiny. To follow the phase changes within a particular period is therefore a much more involved exercise, but we assume that anyone interested in such detail would naturally expect to encounter a greater deal of complexity.

Conclusions

The process of resolving the mapping problems at Gordion outlined in this chapter should be considered a work in progress. Even though significant advances have been made, there is still much to be done. Nevertheless, analyses such as the phase plan that accompanies this volume highlight the potential of our approach for addressing Gordion's mapping quandaries. We hope that the publication of the phase plan will facilitate the work of Gordion researchers by providing them with an improved visualization of the spatial, functional, and chronological complexities of the Phrygian architecture on the Citadel Mound. Furthermore, the methodologies we are continuing to develop may be applicable to other archaeological sites with similar analytical difficulties, making Gordion a model for reconstructing and managing archaeological cartography.

NOTES
2.1. Surveyors' reports were prepared for the 1963, 1973, 1987, 1992, and 1993 field seasons (Williams 1963; Cummer 1973; Remsen 1987, 1992, 1993). Surveyors' logs survive for the seasons of 1955, 1956, 1958, 1959, 1974, 1979, 1980, 1987, 1989, 1996, 1997, and 2004 (Last 1955–56, 1958–59; Miller et al. 1974–2004; Gaukroger 1995, 1996, 1997). Note that at Gordion, the surveyors were often trained as architects, and the terms surveyor and architect were used interchangeably.
2.2. Reports on the excavations can be found in: DeVries 1990; Edwards 1959, 1963; Kohler 1980, 1995; Young 1950, 1951, 1953, 1955, 1956, 1957, 1958, 1960, 1962a, 1964, 1966, 1968, and 1981.
2.3. Reports on the fieldwork can be found in: Sams 1992, 1994c, 1996, 2002, 2005b; Sams and Burke 2008; Sams, Burke and Goldman 2007; Sams and Goldman

2006; Sams and Voigt 1990, 1991, 1995, 1997, 1998, 1999, 2003, 2004; Voigt 1994; Voigt et al. 1997.

2.4. The numbers in parentheses after a map indicate the Gordion Archive identification number for that map. The first four digits indicate the year in which the map was produced; the number after the dash is a sequential number assigned for archival purposes, and does not necessarily indicate the chronological sequence in which the maps were produced. The full references for the maps and plans mentioned in the present chapter are:

1950-1: Gordion, General Plan of Site and Central Tumulus Area (1:1,000), by Mahmut Akok

1950-2: Gordion, Topographical Survey (1:4,000), by Mahmut Akok

1950-77: General Plan of Citadel Mound Showing 1950 Trenches (1:500), by Edward B. Reed

1950-78: General Plan of Citadel Mound Showing 1950 Trenches [draft] (1:500), by Edward B. Reed

1950-80: Survey of Citadel Mound Area (1:1,000), by Mahmut Akok

1967-1: Outline of Trenches on Citadel Mound (1:200), by Joseph W. Shaw

1973-15: Point Plan (1:500), by Wilson W. Cummer and Fritz Hemans

1974-1: Survey of Entire Site and Preliminary Reconnaissance of Ancient Road and Sangarios Crossing (1:4,000), by John L. Miller

1974-2: Survey of Citadel Mound and Preliminary Reconnaissance of Ancient Construction in Sakarya Channel (1:1,000), by John L. Miller

1979-1: Survey Control: Archaic Level (1:500), by Bruce Lightbody, Richard Smith, and Robert Bell

1987-1: Limits of Excavation (1:500), by William C.S. Remsen.

2.5. In an apologetic note added to the draft, Reed informed Young that the reason for the omission was because he had "no sun print or record of [the] whole area." This indicates that Akok did not leave all of his work at Gordion after he left the site—and indeed, his three extant maps are labeled "Ankara, 1950," though they made their way to the Gordion Archive soon afterward (map 1950-2 was published in Young 1950). It might also suggest inadequate communication between Reed, Akok, and Young, although the extent to which the surveyors overlapped on-site is unclear.

2.6. A "sunprint" is a facsimile of a drawing, produced

by chemical means. It was commonly used to create quick working copies of plans and maps.

2.7. The Körtes' vertical datum is indicated on their map at a point southwest of the Citadel Mound. See Fig. 2.2.

2.8. At its most basic, a contour is a line that connects points of the same elevation. In order to accurately represent terrain configurations to the naked eye, successive lines must show a fixed difference in elevation ("interval") between them. Thus, if the contour interval for a map is said to be 2 m and one is looking at the 6 m contour, the next lines up and down from it will be the 8 m and the 4 m contour respectively. If this basic principle does not apply, then the lines are not contours.

2.9. Dorothy Cox's work was very poorly documented, and in the absence of any surveying notes or reports it must be deduced from her drawings and from scattered references in later sources. The documentation for Last's work is rather better. His working drawings and two of his surveying notebooks are in the Gordion Archive (Last 1955–56, 1958–59). Unfortunately, the notebooks were mostly used as scratch paper, filled with calculations and lists of distances and elevations without a narrative, and so extracting information from them is a difficult task.

2.10. Points E and F were built along the same east-west line as point D (gridline X-Y), on the intersections with lines 30-31 and 35-36, respectively. Points G and H were built along the same east-west gridline as point C (gridline S-T), at the intersections with lines 30-31 and 35-36, respectively. Finally, point J was built at the intersection of gridline N-O with line 35-36 (see foldout).

2.11. His notes, while very incomplete, show that he set up fixed points G2, I, and K (see foldout).

2.12. The 1967 trench plan (and all trench plans based on it) is severely flawed, to the extent that the total area covered by the drawn trenches is almost 10% larger than the real area of excavation as measured on the ground.

2.13. Cummer's plan also renamed the fixed points: C became S26, and G, H, I, and K became S31, S36, S41, and N41, respectively. Cummer also plotted the points that he had added himself in previous seasons, including S31N30 and S26N30 (located not at grid intersections, but rather 30 m north of the S-T line on the 25-26 and 30-31 baselines, respectively), as well as fixed points N56 and WCW (see foldout).

2.14. The new fixed points were partly based on the Turkish geodetic marker on top of nearby Kuş Tepe, and were identified with a 2-digit year plus letter designation: 74A to L.

2.15. Of the 11, they could only identify 9: A, N41,

N56, G2, S26, S26N30, S31, S31N30, and WCW (see foldout). The points were plotted in schematic form on map 1979-1.

2.16. The discrepancies that Remsen found included the locations of the following fixed points: S26N30 (which was in fact 28.2 m due north of S26, rather than 30 m); N56 (3.2 m north of the east-west grid line, rather than on it); and N41 (15 m from the east-west grid line where it should have been). The discrepancy in the position of S26N30 (more than a meter south of its intended position, as also independently noted by Gaukroger in 1996) could account for Lightbody, Smith and Bell's suggestion in 1979 that the grid ought to be moved a meter northward.

2.17. The earlier drawings exhibited a slightly different north orientation compared with Gaukroger's, and their positions were shifted on the grid, both on the north-south and the east-west axes.

2.18. One of the points is marked by a round concrete installation featuring a bent iron rod aligned roughly east-west. Gaukroger believed this one to be S26 and true-to-grid. The other marker is a form-built concrete pylon, newer in appearance, with a nail in the top. Gaukroger erroneously believed that it had been built in 1979 (without explaining why) and he offered no indication as to its identity (1996).

2.19. It was probably at this time that a fixed point designated as C', located at the northwestern angle of the Middle Phrygian Gate Complex, began to be employed as vertical datum. It would continue to be used into the 1960s.

2.20. One of many examples of this state of affairs is a note written by Cummer in 1969, in which he states that his "elevations from M-3 [Megaron 3] point I (4.601) are regularly 0.14 m lower that those of A. Trik [in] 1965 and about 0.20 m higher than those of C. Williams [in] 1963."

2.21. The only other possible cause for the 57-minute arc discrepancy, barring surveyor's error, would be magnetic declination. This, however, is not the case, as the difference between the magnetic declination at Gordion in 1979 (3° 23' E of true north) and 1987 (3° 37' E of true north) is only 14 minutes.

2.22. The area west of the river was presumably omitted from the 1950 maps because it was, and still is, outside the Gordion Project's official zone of investigation (even though occasional rescue excavations have been permitted there by the authorities).

2.23. From information in the Gordion Archive we have reconstructed the list of mapping personnel who worked at the site, including at least 14 chief surveyors. The number of staff working at any one time was small: usually just a head surveyor, sometimes with one or two assistants.

2.24. The surveyors who spent three seasons or more at Gordion are Cox (1951–1953, 1957), Last (1955–1956, 1958–1962), Williams (1958, 1961, 1963), Cummer (1969, 1971, 1973, 1980), Remsen (1987, 1992–1994), and Gaukroger (1995–1997).

2.25. dGPS measurements are usually accurate to within 2 cm of the true global coordinate of a point.

2.26. This initial work could not have been accomplished without the help of Eileen Vote, to whom we are extremely grateful.

3

Reading Gordion Settlement History from Stream Sedimentation

Ben Marsh

All archaeological landscapes degrade over time, but the landscape at Gordion is unusual in the way that the site has been directly attacked by the river adjacent to it. The damage to the cultural landscape by the Sakarya River is an indirect result of the environmental damage done to the river and its basin by human activities. It was human agency that ultimately resulted in the erosion and burial of Gordion.

The human and natural landscapes in the region of Gordion have changed significantly since the Iron Age. Massive erosion in the uplands was initiated by early human landuse changes. That erosion cut into the hillsides, thinned soils, dried up streams and springs, and silted up the hydrological system. Sediment accumulated in the stream and river valleys, raising floodplains and burying topographic and artificial features. The overall effect of these changes on the archaeological record has been to hide or remove much of the evidence of complex patterns of landuse immediately around the Citadel Mound—structures, roads, city walls, gates, and earthworks.

Determining the river changes is important because it tells us about both the nature of human impact on the adjacent uplands as recorded in the local landscape processes, and also the ways in which the site has been altered since its abandonment. Knowledge of changes to the site is useful for reconstructing the ancient city, and therefore for interpreting its archaeology. Landscape changes tell us about the nature of human-induced degradation of the nearby landscapes, and therefore also about the timing and intensity of causative human activities. In the case of sedimentation at Gordion, the evidence suggests that the local area was far more conducive to settlement than other parts of the Sakarya watershed, and it was settled earlier. In fact, the productive early settlement in this region might be a factor in the initial establishment of the city at Gordion.

River-plain and lake sedimentation is one of the most important sources of evidence of settlement, landuse, and environmental change in ancient archaeological situations. Sediment provides a well-datable and more-or-less continuous record of local environmental and landuse history. River sediment yields information through the position and preservation of its contents—buried structures and artifacts—as well as from the sediment itself. Calculated sedimentation rates reveal the magnitude of environmental disruption in contributory watersheds; buried sediment texture tells of the rates of erosion and the character of earlier streams; and sediment color and geochemistry can disclose its changing source areas.

Anatolian archaeology has benefited for decades from analyses of stream behavior and sedimentation. The earliest serious work, since highly reinterpreted, is Vita-Finzi (1969); more nuanced recent work is typified by Boyer, Roberts, and Baird (2006). These works and others like them have documented a series of environmental disruption events—perhaps the best known of which is the Beyşehir Occupation Phase visible throughout central Anatolia, recording a distinct agricultural intensification beginning in the late Iron Age (Bottema and Woldring 1990).

The central presumption behind most sedimentation analyses is that streams respond to increased supplies of sediment by aggrading, and that the ma-

Fig. 3.1. Reconstruction of archaeological chronology onto a Sakarya River section, 1 km north of Citadel Mound. Illustration: author.

jor source of Holocene increases in stream sediment is anthropogenic erosion. Certainly climate changes are relevant influences on stream behavior, but the unequaled magnitude, long temporal extent, and great spatial continuity of near-simultaneous Holocene sedimentation events across the Mediterranean basin strongly argue that the bulk of these changes were caused by the relatively abrupt arrival of humans, who are known to affect streams through accelerated erosion associated with land clearance and plowing, lumbering, fire, fuel collection, and grazing.

The Environmental Situation of Gordion

The Citadel Mound at Gordion lies on the plain of the Sakarya River a short distance upstream from its confluence with the Porsuk. Although it is now chan-

nelized for flood control, in historic times the river was shallow, muddy, and meandering. The topography and soils near Gordion are generally typical of central Anatolia, with steep hills ringing the site at a distance of 5 to 15 km. The region is characterized by extensive, unproductive, marl-rich plateaus to the south, west and north, but an unusually rich zone of low-slope, basalt-based soils dominates the rolling plains immediately east of the site, continuing over low passes to extensive plains stretching toward Ankara. The higher edges of these plains, at the foot of the mountains, are well watered with springs and even perennial streams.

Sakarya River History at Gordion

Evidence of landscape alteration at Gordion is widely visible. Features of the present floodplain topography represent now-damaged walls and structures. Rubble, mud brick, and debris within the cut of the channeled river demonstrate previous positions of the river and the former geography of the city, as does the sediment and brick-wash found below the floodplain (Marsh 1999). The evidence from the river plain indicates that 3.5–5.2 m of sediment have accumulated since the Bronze Age (Fig. 3.1). Timing of the sedimentation indicates that river aggradation began by creating a thin layer of silt before the establishment of the Iron Age city at ca. 1500 BC. The early rate of accumulation was very slow, only one or two cm per century (Fig. 3.2). The sedimentation rate picked up significantly sometime in the period between 720 and 440 BC—finer resolution is precluded by a radiocarbon "plateau" during this era. Sedimentation has continued in the river since that time at about 15 cm per century, apparently without major fluctuation into the 20th century.

The sediment in the river came from its entire watershed, and affected the river for many kilome-

ters up- and downstream from Gordion. The effect of this aggradation on the city has been considerable. Major aggradation began while the city was occupied. Lower parts of the city, especially in the southern end, were apparently abandoned after the Phrygian period, even as the upper parts of the city were occupied for many centuries more. Some large bodies of artificial fill are found on the lower floodplain, and may represent flood-avoidance measures by the occupants.

Over the centuries, the river changes buried the Lower Town under several meters of silt, and the river removed or leveled sections of the city wall. The sedimentation finally shifted the position of the Sakarya River from the east side of the mound to its present position in the narrows to the west of the mound (Fig. 3.3). Considering the changes in detail, one can see the burial of the city from examining wall and building sections in the entrenched river, and from brick and other urban material found by

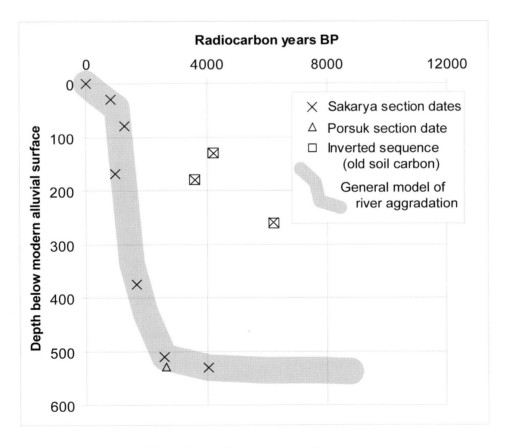

Fig. 3.2. Sakarya River sedimentation trends. Illustration: author.

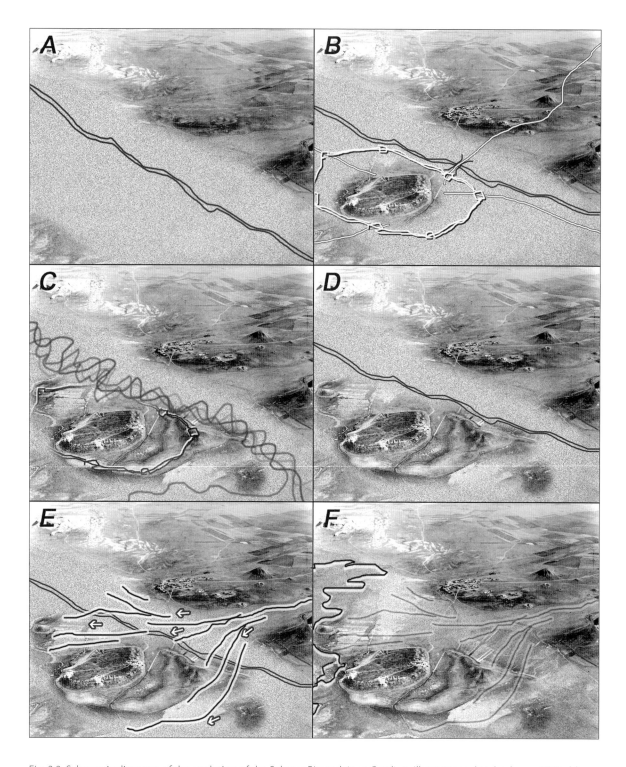

Fig. 3.3. Schematic diagrams of the evolution of the Sakarya River plain at Gordion. Illustrations sketched on a 1950 oblique air photo. A: Pre-human river plain of "Sakarya I" stream stage. B: Iron-age city (with walls, roads, and a bridge) beside "Sakarya II" stream stage. C: Meandering path of "Sakarya III" as it aggraded after the end of the Iron-Age. D: Late-stage Sakarya III, showing leveled and removed wall elements. E: Effect of "Red Fan" sedimentation from the Sülüklü Çay valley. F: "Sakarya IV" position after the stream shifted to the west of the mound, perhaps as recently as the 19th century. Illustration: author.

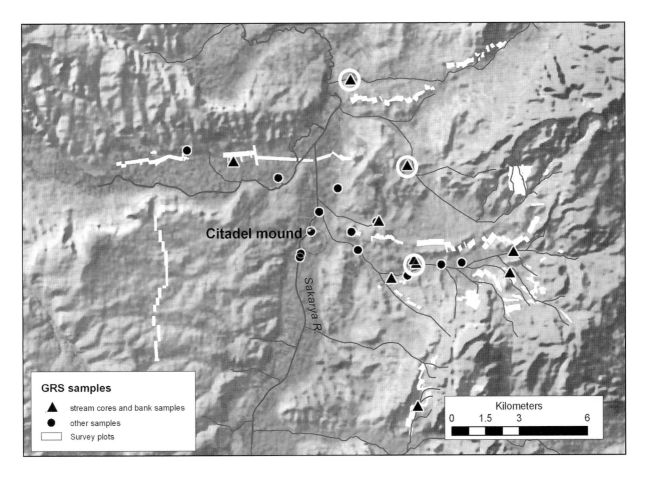

Fig. 3.4. Survey areas and sites of dated material within the Gordion Regional Survey. Illustration: author.

coring at depths to 4 m. As the river aggraded, the full energy of the stream would have been expended against the higher parts of the city wall, which had previously been above stream level. This caused erosion of the major city walls, especially immediately to the east of the Citadel Mound. As the river deposited sediment into its own channel, the middle of the floodplain was raised above the sides and the river's position became unstable. Sediment washing in from the stream called Sülüklü Çay, which enters the valley from the east at Gordion, eventually forced the river out of its earlier channel, and to a new streambed through the narrows on the west side of the mound. It remained in that position until the river was channelized in the 1960s.

The river chronology can be best structured around a sequence of stage names for the river as it aggraded. Sakarya I is the river before significant human influence, below the thin Bronze Age layer; Sa-

karya II is the river that flowed beside (to the east of) the Iron Age city; Sakarya III is the disturbed and aggrading river that attacked the walls of the city; Sakarya IV is the river after it shifted to the west of the mound; and Sakarya V is the present artificially entrenched river.

Additional recent stream research has been conducted in association with the Gordion Regional Survey (Kealhofer 2005). The survey sought, in part, to understand the relationship between the geography of smaller watersheds near Gordion and the regional landuse history. A component of that research has involved dating cores from a variety of small streams (Fig. 3.4). General preliminary results are presented here pending publication of the watershed analysis (Marsh and Kealhofer n.d.).

The clear chronological evidence is that small streams in the local watershed began to silt-in seriously about 2000 years before the river did, and the small stream sedimentation decreased markedly before the Sakarya began to silt in significantly. The overall pattern presented in Figure 3.5 shows an abrupt and significant surge of sedimentation in many small basins at 4000 RC years BP, which corresponds to 2550 BC (Early Bronze Age). The magnitude of sedimentation was apparently about 2 m in just a few centuries. This great surge gave way to a more gradual long-term rate of accumulation, about 5 cm per century. The entire major period of sedimentation in the local watershed happened at about the same time as the very earliest disturbance visible on the Sakarya floodplain, the subtle "paleosol" layer of over-bank sediment laid onto the surface on which the city was built. This event happened at least 1400 years before major sedimentation of the Sakarya River.

Analysis of the smaller streams at the scale of Figure 3.5 does not permit highly precise dating, in part because of the range of streams being considered at once. The dating sequences for many streams not presented here contain temporal inversions—old sediment above young. Two factors probably account for these apparent impossibilities. First, some samples collected from stream banks have anomalously young ages due to root intrusions. Second, a number of anomalously old samples appear to be products of the deposition of residual soil carbon from erosion and transport of the rich brown mollisols typical of this environment. The evidence of a fill sample from Tumulus P reveals that mollic surface soils manuported for mound-building in the Gordion region show AMS RC dates about 5000 years older than the time of their use. It is expected that stream deposits of equivalent soils would also be thousands of years younger than their RC dates.

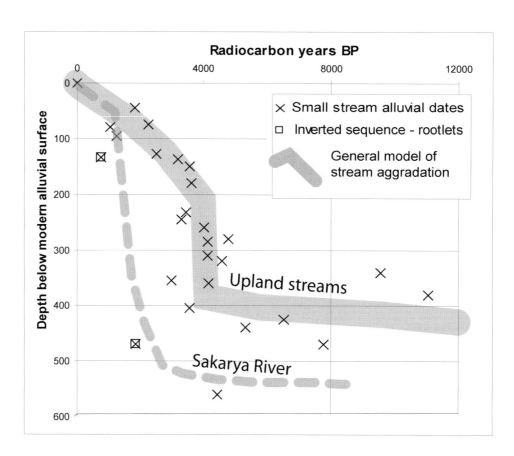

Fig. 3.5. Comparison timing of upland sedimentation in the local watersheds, with Sakarya River sedimentation. All upland stream dates—including those from watersheds of very different sizes—are combined for this highly schematic presentation. Illustration: author.

The Date of the Sakarya's Shift from East to West

The dating of the river's shift to the west side of the mound has not yet been precisely pinpointed. At the limits, it happened before the Körtes arrived in AD 1900, and after AD 1200, the latest radiocarbon dates of organic material from the pre-shift river sediment, coming from 25+ cm down the section. It may have been quite late, 18th or 19th century, judging by how little of the distinctive red post-shift sediment is deposited at the mound—only 5 cm in a 350 cm post-Bronze Age section—and by the fact that the river in its post-shift position still had the unstable and evolving profile typical of a young stream. One theory about the proximal cause of the shift is that artificial channels dug for irrigation or to run a mill invited the river to shift during flood to the shorter, steeper new route, which had been enabled by the long-term processes of river meandering and aggradation.

Discussion

It is a significant fact that the watershed adjacent to Gordion responded to human disturbance at very different times and rates than the entire Sakarya did. The local watersheds were disturbed much earlier than the river, and the local disturbance was decreasing by the time that the river began to be most affected. In fact, the local watersheds have now begun to recover from human disturbance: smaller streams are currently cutting down into their anthropogenic floodplains and seeking the level they had before humans arrived.

The differences in behavior between the Sakarya River and the smaller watersheds in the region of Gordion suggest that the latter area was densely occupied by humans well before the larger Sakarya basin was. The Sakarya River was affected much later by the massive changes in sediment load that occurred after humans removed vegetation from across its entire watershed. Trees were removed for timber, for fuel, and to open agricultural land; open land was maintained by grazing, plowing, or burning. The exposed soil was much more prone to erosion compared to its earlier state, and the load of sediment yielding to the streams increased substantially. As the stream load increased, sediment was deposited in the channels and on the floodplains, and the river rose up to affect the city. The Sakarya River was at first slightly altered in the Middle Bronze Age, and then responded rapidly during the Phrygian period and thereafter.

The same land use processes affected the local watersheds, and the streams responded in a similar way. But the local streams began to aggrade to a significant degree almost 2 millennia before the river. The much-earlier beginning of alluviation in the smaller streams reflects differences in the settlement timing in the area local to Gordion, compared to the larger Sakarya watershed. This evidence suggests that the local watersheds were extensively settled by the Early Bronze Age, while human activities did not significantly alter the entire Sakarya watershed until the Middle Iron Age (Middle Phrygian). The implication is that the area around Gordion—which is unusually fertile and well watered compared to the rest of west-central Anatolia—attracted settlement earlier than the surrounding region. The establishment of Gordion may have been preconditioned by the unusually dense Bronze Age settlement that preceded it in this place.

Acknowledgments

The Gordion Excavations supported this work over several seasons by providing housing, logistics, and colleagues. Lisa Kealhofer, through National Science Foundation Award #9903149, supported the fieldwork and dating behind the local stream sedimentation chronologies.

4

Reconstructing the Functional Use of Wood at Phrygian Gordion through Charcoal Analysis

John M. Marston

The site of Gordion is notable in world archaeology for the astonishing quantity and variety of wooden artifacts that survive from Phrygian burial contexts, including the tomb structure of Tumulus MM itself and the wooden furniture within (Liebhart and Johnson 2005; Simpson and Spirydowicz 1999). Wooden beams from the Tumulus MM structure and from the destruction level of the Phrygian citadel on the Citadel Mound have provided tree sections for radiocarbon and dendrochronological dating of the site and aided in the creation of an absolute chronology for the eastern Mediterranean (DeVries et al. 2003; Kuniholm 1996). Understanding the functional use of wood from settlement contexts at Gordion, however, is rarely as easy as finding preserved wooden artifacts in a tomb. Most wood, whether structural, fuel, or furniture, ends up as carbonized fragments strewn across the site. It is the goal of this chapter to use a contextual, stratigraphic analysis of those fragments of wood charcoal to understand how inhabitants of Phrygian Gordion utilized wood resources in their natural environment and chose particular wood types for a variety of functional uses.

Analytical Approaches to Archaeological Charcoal

Carbonized wood often makes up the largest percentage in botanical assemblages from archaeological contexts, due to its ubiquity, utility, and frequency of deliberate burning. Identification of archaeologi-

cal wood charcoal has a greater than 100-year-long history (see historical overviews in Asouti and Austin 2005; Pearsall 2000; Smart and Hoffman 1988), but the primary focus of the technique remains ecological interpretation. The identification of natural environmental change (Willcox 1999), human-induced deforestation (Miller 1985, 1991, 1999b), and local ecological interactions (Asouti 2003a, 2003b; Pearsall 1983) has proven the value of charcoal analysis to paleoenvironmental and ecological studies.

Previous analysis of Anatolian charcoal assemblages has focused on these environmental variables, including work done at Pınarbaşı (Asouti 2003b), Çatalhöyük (Asouti 2005, Asouti and Hather 2001), Cafer Höyük (Willcox 1991), Can Hasan (Willcox 1979), Aşvan (Willcox 1974), Troy (Shay, Anderson, and Shay 1982), and Gordion (Miller 1991, 1999b, 2007). Gordion has proved an excellent site for the investigation of human interaction with the natural environment due to the time depth of settlement, focus on local and regional settlement patterns (Kealhofer 2005), geomorphological survey (Marsh 1999, 2005), and ongoing ethnographic and ecological studies (Gürsan-Salzman 2005; Miller 1999a). The multiple accidental fires documented archaeologically at Gordion, in addition to the deliberate combustion of wood over thousands of years, have generated massive quantities of wood charcoal at the site. Since 1988, this charcoal has been systematically recovered and analyzed (Miller 1991, Sams and Voigt 1990).

While these previous studies have utilized wood charcoal to enhance our understanding of the paleoenvironmental conditions in Anatolia, little attention has yet been paid to behavioral implications of these remains. Some authors have made the distinction between deliberately and accidentally burned wood (e.g., Miller 1991), and even suggested that some wood species might be preferred for certain uses (Asouti 2003b:1200; Miller 1991:7). I argue here that in-depth analysis of the archaeological context of charcoal samples, combined with ecological interpretation of local wood species, provides stronger links between behavior and environment than have been previously suggested. In this contextual study of wood charcoal at Gordion I identify trends in wood use and consider their behavioral implications, making possible the testing of formal ecological models as a mechanism for explaining *why* people made certain decisions regarding wood use in the past.

Behavioral Models in Charcoal Analysis

Several scholars have considered the role of human preference in shaping archaeological charcoal assemblages, beginning in the 1940s (Godwin and Tansley 1941, Salisbury and Jane 1940). Human preference is generally seen as an additional source of unexplained variation that renders charcoal less suitable for paleoenvironmental reconstruction than other botanical remains, as reviewed most recently by Asouti and Austin (2005). Most arguments for or against the validity of charcoal as a paleoenvironmental marker are based on behavioral assumptions (Godwin and Tansley 1941), experimental observations (Chabal 1992), or ecological models for the comparison of archaeological and modern data sets (Smart and Hoffman 1988). The focus is still environmental reconstruction, and human preference remains problematic "noise" in the archaeological record.

A notable exception is the conceptual model of the relationship between environment and human activity proposed by Shackleton and Prins (1992). The authors consider the general assumption in charcoal studies of the "principle of least effort," that charcoal frequency directly tracks environmental presence with a one-to-one correspondence

(Shackleton and Prins 1992:632). They propose four different environmental circumstances reflecting different availability of preferred wood species and of dry versus green wood, and argue that under certain of these environments the assumption of the "principle of least effort" is valid, and in others it is not. Their conclusions are open-ended, and they suggest that no archaeological mechanism currently exists to differentiate between environmental availability and human preference in determining the composition of an archaeological charcoal assemblage. Following Ford (1979) and their own prior research, Shackleton and Prins suggest that ethnographic analogy is the only method for inferring the likelihood that certain wood species would be preferred or avoided.

An alternative approach to behavioral interpretation comes from the field of human behavioral ecology (HBE), which has been applied to archaeological problems with increasing frequency over the past 20 years (Bird and O'Connell 2006, Kennett and Winterhalder 2006, Winterhalder and Smith 2000). HBE is a discipline rooted in animal behavioral ecology and ethology, and originated in the 1970s as a tool to explain hunter-gatherer decision-making processes, mostly related to foraging (Winterhalder and Smith 1981). HBE is concerned with how and why decisions are made given a range of alternative activities. The "optimization assumption" states that behavior tends towards efficiency as the result of biological and cultural evolutionary processes (Foley 1985), leading to a variety of formal models for behavioral decision-making. The diet breadth, or prey choice, model states that foragers rank all available prey based on their post-encounter profitability, and that the proportion of different prey taken can be estimated based on their profitability, frequency, and handling time (Krebs and Davies 1981:52–57). This model has been implemented in a variety of paleoethnobotanical studies to interpret why certain food remains are more plentiful than others in the archaeological assemblage (Diehl and Waters 2006, Gremillion 1996, Piperno and Pearsall 1998, Winterhalder and Goland 1997), but has not yet been applied to the interpretation of archaeological wood charcoal.

The advantage of HBE models is that they are broadly applicable to human foraging for raw materials, whether plants, animals, stone (as discussed by Brantingham 2003), or wood, as I propose here. The diet breadth model posits that foragers rank their prey based on utility. Wood, however, has multiple uses, and the wood types that are best suited to construction may not be preferred for fuel. The application of such a model to an entire archaeological assemblage would produce misleading results if the assemblage includes wood brought in for more than one purpose, or if the use of the wood is mischaracterized. In order to distinguish between the functional uses of wood, one should first undertake a detailed contextual study of the charcoal remains under consideration and use other archaeological evidence to identify their original use context.

Phrygian Contexts Recently Excavated at Gordion

Excavations at Gordion since 1993 have focused on the Northwest, Southwest, and Southeast zones of the Citadel Mound, on the Lower Town, and the Outer Town (Fig. 4.1). Due to this focus, and the research goals of the director, most contexts excavated between 1993 and 2002 date to the Middle Phrygian and later periods (Voigt et al. 1997, Voigt and Young 1999). Stratigraphic analysis of all phases of excavation is not yet complete, so not all charcoal samples analyzed could be securely placed within a temporal phase or archaeological feature. Additionally, I have not yet completed the analysis of charcoal from the flotation

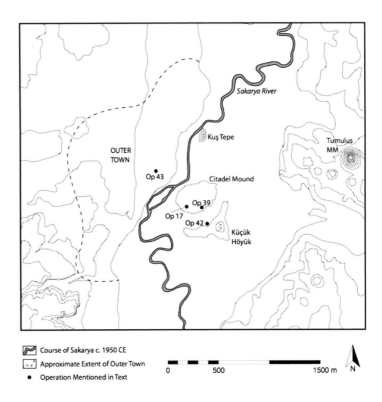

Fig. 4.1. Map of Gordion. Source: after Voigt and Young 1999:194.

samples taken systematically from most contexts, and so have only the results of the hand-picked charcoal samples, which are less numerous. Given these limitations, only five well-defined contexts with at least four separate charcoal samples date to the Middle and Late Phrygian periods, as shown below in Table 4.1.

Only charcoal fragments larger than 2 mm with at least one complete growth ring were identified. At least 10 pieces of charcoal were identified for each sample, and as many as 30 were identified if the sam-

Table 4.1. Middle and Late Phrygian contexts with ≥4 hand-picked charcoal samples.

Feature	Area of Site	Operation	Phase	# Samples	Total Wt.
Trash Deposit	SW Zone	17	Mid. Phrygian	11	225.21 g
Pithouse Fill	SW Zone	17	Late Phrygian	19	470.40 g
Mosaic Building Porch	SE Zone	39	Late Phrygian	8	245.74 g
RAKS SW Pit-structure	Lower Town	42	Late Phrygian	4	8.44 g
Large Pit	Outer Town	43	Late Phrygian	5	6.42 g

Table 4.2. Wood taxa identified from Middle and Late Phrygian contexts, 47 total samples.

Identified Taxon	Common Name	No. Samples	Ubiquity
Pinus sp.	Pine	32	0.68
Quercus sp.	Oak	27	0.57
Juniperus sp.	Juniper	18	0.38
Salicaceae	Willow, Poplar	9	0.19
Maloideae	Pear, Hawthorn, Apple	4	0.09
Prunus sp.	Plum, Peach, Almond, Apricot, Cherry	1	0.02

ple was large and heterogeneous. A 75x stereoscopic microscope was used for low-power examination, and an incident-light metallurgical microscope was employed at 100x-400x for examination of the tangential and radial sections of the wood charcoal. Methods of identification follow those outlined by Schweingruber (1990;, Schweingruber et al. 2006) and Miller (1991 Appendix I). Six types of wood were identified from the 47 samples analyzed from these contexts (Table 4.2). Most types are identified to genus, but the woods of willow and poplar are difficult to distinguish and are here grouped by family (Salicaceae), while the woods of several genera within the Maloideae (e.g.,

pear, apple, and hawthorn) are indistinguishable so are assigned to a single taxon (Schweingruber 1990).

The samples for each context were grouped by taxon, and their composition is shown by percentage of total charcoal weight (Fig. 4.2). This method of display is biased towards denser woods, such as oak, as they have a greater proportion of the total by weight than by volume. The significance of this bias is dependent on the use of the wood: while construction requires a certain volume of wood, combustion requires mass. As such, we might hypothesize that in construction contexts, light woods would be underrepresented and dense woods would be overrepre-

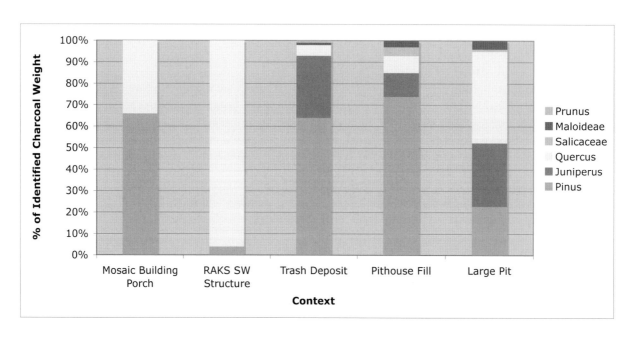

Fig. 4.2. Charcoal composition of Middle and Late Phrygian contexts, by percent total weight. Illustration: author.

sented, but combustion contexts would be relatively unbiased. I do not believe that this bias affects any of the results described below, due to the limited construction debris present.

Analysis of Contexts

These five contexts represent two different chronological phases, four areas of the site, domestic and public architecture, and both primary and secondary deposition. As such, any comparison between contexts is limited by these multiple degrees of freedom, and is merely suggestive of any broader site-wide relationships or patterns.

Public Architecture: The Late Phrygian Mosaic Building Porch

Excavations in 1995 exposed a previously unknown porch on the north side of the Late Phrygian Mosaic Building (Sams and Voigt 1997, Voigt and Young 1999), first discovered by Rodney Young in 1950 (Young 1951). This building is believed to have served as an administrative building for the Persian rulers of Gordion in the early 5th century BCE (Sams and Voigt 1997:479; Voigt and Young 1999:221). The porch was identified by the presence of four attached column bases at the approximate floor level of the Mosaic Building, as shown in Figure 4.3 (Sams and Voigt 1997:479–80).

The eight charcoal samples were distinguished as two stratigraphic units during excavation, one representing the collapse of the porch, and the other refuse piled atop the collapse. One sample, containing nearly all the pine charcoal, comes from the collapse level, while the other

seven samples, almost exclusively oak charcoal, were deposited atop the porch collapse. The distinction between the primary deposit of the porch and the secondary deposit of trash highlights the importance of careful stratigraphic excavation, such as practiced at Gordion, in distinguishing the use of different woods. This large quantity of pine amid bricky collapse likely represents the remains of a structural timber used in the porch or porch roof construction.

The use of pine to frame the roofs of large buildings at Gordion is not unique to the Late Phrygian period. The major public or elite building of the later Hellenistic phase during which Gordion was inhabited by Galatians shows a similar charcoal signature, with pine comprising roughly 80% of the total weight of charcoal recovered from that structure (Dandoy et al. 2002, Marston 2007). Two large buildings from the Early Phrygian (Terrace Building 2A) and the Hellenistic ("Abandoned Village" Structure) periods excavated in 1988–1989 also had 99% and 89% pine charcoal by weight, with small quantities of oak (Miller 1999b). Beams from other Early Phrygian structures were identified as pine by Kuniholm (1977), including Megarons 3,

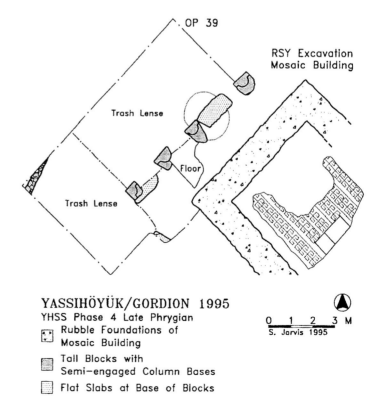

Fig. 4.3. Plan of Mosaic Building Porch in Op. 39. Source: after Sams and Voigt 1997:489.

4, and 5, and Clay Cut Building 3. The support beams for the Tumulus MM tomb chamber are also all pine, as are timbers from Tumulus P (Kuniholm 1977; Liebhart and Johnson 2005:191–92). Pine is a suitable wood for roofing a large building, due to its long, straight trunk and relatively compression-resistant fibers, especially in comparison to its weight (Liebhart 1988, Panshin and de Zeeuw 1970). Based on this analysis and comparative sample, I suggest that the porch of the Mosaic Building was roofed with pine.

Domestic Architecture: Lower Town Pit-Structure

The most characteristic type of Late Phrygian domestic architecture is the semi-subterranean building, or pit-structure. These structures are set as much as 1 m or more below grade, and are interpreted as storage rooms, cellars, and semi-subterranean houses (Voigt and Young 1999:223–33). These structures are typically roughly square in plan and range from 4 to 10 m on a side, with the larger structures subdivided by projecting walls (Voigt and Young 1999). Pit-structures have been excavated on the Citadel Mound and in the Lower Town, but the few Late Phrygian structures excavated in the Outer Town were all constructed at grade (Voigt and Young 1999:233–34). The RAKS SW structure from Operation 42 is one of a group of Late Phrygian pit-structures excavated in the Lower Town Area B (Fig. 4.4). It is one of the smallest of its type and is more likely to be a storage building or cellar than a dwelling area (Voigt and Young 1999:233).

The charcoal from the RAKS SW structure was recovered from several carbon streaks or possible hearths, and is more than 95% oak, with small quantities of pine. The preponderance of oak is not uncommon in domestic and industrial contexts from Gordion. Compared to the charcoal assemblages in five other domestic activity areas, dating to the Hellenistic, Roman, and Medieval phases, three of those were also more than half oak charcoal by weight. This pattern also held in a number of industrial contexts from the Hellenistic period (Marston 2007).

Based on phytogeographic data, Miller (1999b; 2010) has argued that oak would have grown within a few kilometers of Gordion in antiquity. This is probable, given the presence of a dense scrub forest of oak growing on hillsides within 20 km, and smaller groupings of oak trees within

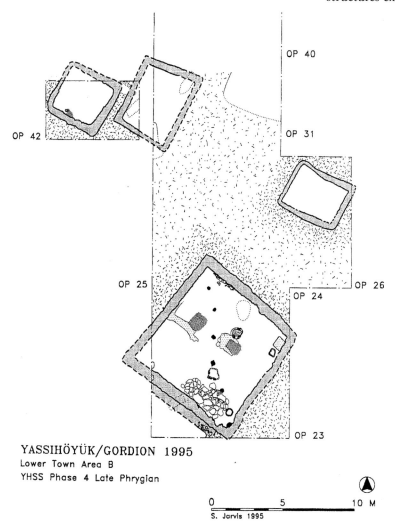

YASSIHÖYÜK/GORDION 1995
Lower Town Area B
YHSS Phase 4 Late Phrygian

0   5   10 M
S. Jarvis 1995

Fig. 4.4. Plan of Lower Town Area B, including RAKS SW Structure. Source: after Sams and Voigt 1997:487.

10 km of the site today. The "steppe forest" ecotype of Central Anatolia includes a significant oak component (Zohary 1973), and oak is the most abundant hardwood in the Gordion region. It is possible that oak was preferred as fuel wood in antiquity, due to its local abundance and high caloric (heat) value per unit weight (Marston 2009). This is consistent with the context of the charcoal samples from the RAKS SW structure, which suggests that the oak wood was deliberately burned. This charcoal likely represents secondary deposition of the remains of small fires in the area, but may also be the remains of *in situ* burning. This interpretation is consistent with the charcoal assemblages from other domestic contexts at Gordion.

Secondary Refuse Deposits: Southwest Citadel Mound and Outer Town

Operation 17 was the primary excavation unit in the southwestern area of the Citadel Mound excavated between 1993 and 1996. This operation was initiated as a deep sounding from the level of the Roman remains left by Rodney Young. It reached the earliest Middle Phrygian levels in 1996. Much of the 1996 season consisted of the excavation of a massive Middle Phrygian trash deposit that the excavators interpreted as clean-up of the surrounding area after widespread destruction during the Persian siege of the mid-6th century BCE (Sams and Voigt 1998:684–85; Voigt and Young 1999). This massive Middle Phrygian trash dump, and a later dump within an abandoned Late Phrygian pithouse, yielded large quantities of charcoal.

The Outer Town context in Operation 43 is a large, deep pit with a mud-brick lining along the top. This may represent a filled-in pit-structure or more likely another type of pit, possibly for storage. The samples were taken from several levels of the fill. The pit appears to date to the Late Phrygian period, when the extent of the Outer Town was at its greatest (Voigt 2002). There is no indication that any of its contents are related to its function; all appear to be secondary fill deposits.

All three contexts are remarkably heterogeneous compared to other contemporary assemblages from Gordion. Each contained five wood taxa and substantial amounts of juniper, which is increasingly rare after the Early Phrygian period (Miller 1999b). This heterogeneity, and the relatively small proportion of oak in these deposits, is characteristic of other secondary trash deposits from later periods at Gordion (Marston 2007). An interpretation of these deposits as representing a particular use context would be misleading, since these are clearly secondary deposits and represent a combination of many individual activities. Heterogeneity, however, may be useful as a marker of mixed deposits and a warning against contextual interpretation.

Context and Behavior at Gordion

Only two structures described here, the Late Phrygian Mosaic Building Porch and the RAKS SW Pit-structure, allowed for the reconstruction of original use contexts for their wood contents. The other three contexts appear to be secondary trash deposits, as recognized during excavation, although two of the three are contained within well-defined archaeological features. The marked disparity between the homogeneity of wood taxa in the porch and pit-structure and the heterogeneity of wood taxa in the secondary trash deposits suggests that the distinction of use context and secondary disposal context for wood charcoal may be possible from the charcoal assemblage itself.

The patterns observed here, though not statistically representative of any site-wide trends or behavioral regularities, allow for the construction of testable hypotheses that can be addressed with larger data sets. The application of models from human behavioral ecology has the potential to explain, on the basis of functional ecological variation between wood species, the noted differences between the Mosaic Building Porch's pine construction and the oak combustion that took place within the RAKS SW pit-structure. As the stratigraphic analysis of recent excavation seasons continues, the sample size for comparison will increase. Additionally, preliminary comparisons to later periods of occupation have supported the trends noticed above and more comprehensive site-wide analyses suggest that wood preference at Gordion is constrained by both functional needs and local forest ecology (Marston 2009).

As demonstrated by Miller (1999b; 2010), Zeder (Miller, Zeder, and Arter 2009), Marsh (2005), Kealhofer (2005), and Gürsan-Salzman (2005), the geomorphological and cultural landscapes of Gordion have changed dramatically throughout its history, and these changes continue today. The plant ecology of the Sakarya basin has shaped human subsistence patterns and the local economy for thousands of years, so any systematic interpretation of human behavior at Gordion requires an understanding of the regional ecology. This detailed contextual interpretation of plant remains from archaeological contexts is the first step towards understanding how people interacted with their environment, and how that environment shaped successive cultures at Gordion.

The Early Phrygian Citadel

Fig. 5.1. Excavation of Unit 3 of the CC Building, a part of the Destruction Level. Keith DeVries by wall at left. Source: Gordion Project, Penn Museum.

5

The New Chronology for Gordion and Phrygian Pottery

G. Kenneth Sams

The destruction of the Early Phrygian citadel at Gordion constitutes a major stratigraphic and cultural event for Iron Age Anatolia. When the citadel's monumental buildings burned to the ground, they were rich in contents that provide a vivid picture of Phrygian material culture at the time of the disaster (Sams 1994a:2–7; Figs. 1.2, 5.1). Thanks to recent chronological developments, we now can place the conflagration around 800 BC instead of 700, as had been long held, which means that the Destruction Level provides a picture of Phrygian life as it was by the end of the 9th, not the end of the 8th century (DeVries et al. 2003).

The pottery and artifacts from the Destruction Level occur in great quantity and with remarkable variety (Sams 1994a:187–92). Of the many goods left in the wake of the disaster, one may single out a set of ivory horse trappings of Syrian origin, perhaps the gift of some ruler to a nameless Phrygian one, and ivory inlay plaques that appear to be of local manufacture (Sams 1993:552). The Destruction Level and its great material wealth also serve as an important index, both for gauging the relative placement of outlying cultural deposits such as burial tumuli, and for judging internal material development, leading up to the disaster and subsequent to it.

Table 5.1 above summarizes select cultural events on both the old and new chronologies. The old ordering had presented a number of stratigraphic puzzles, in that the artifacts found in the Destruction Level seemed too early for the date that was traditionally assigned to them. Moreover, items found in Tumuli Koerte-III, P, and MM were either scarce or not to be found at all in the Destruction Level or in the earlier Early Phrygian stratigraphic sequence. Yet those same types were present, sometimes in relative abundance, in the New Citadel/Middle Phrygian contexts of the citadel, such as the South Cellar deposit (DeVries 2005:37–43). Certain types found in the Destruction Level, such as bronze fibulae, were regarded as typologically backward in comparison to goods from tumuli that supposedly pre-dated the destruction.

Table 5.1. Tumuli and cultural events at Gordion listed by old and new chronologies.

Old Chronology	New Chronology
Tumulus W (ca. 750)	Tumulus W (ca. 850)
Tumulus K-III (ca. 730)	Destruction Level (ca. 800)
Tumulus P (ca. 720)	Tumulus K-III (ca. 780)
Tumulus MM (ca. 700)	Tumulus P (ca. 770)
Destruction Level (ca. 700)	Tumulus MM (ca. 740)
Clay layer / New Citadel (7th century)	Clay layer / New Citadel (8th century)
South Cellar deposit (ca. 400)	South Cellar deposit (ca. 700)

5cm

Fig. 5.2. Side-spouted sieve jug in Brown-on-Buff Ware, from the Destruction Level (Gordion inventory P 1270). Source: Gordion Project, Penn Museum.

Even before the reality of the new C-14 datings, Keith DeVries, Mary Voigt, and the author had begun to consider whether the great destruction might in fact pre-date the tumuli in question. Our discussions prompted Voigt to submit samples from her excavations in the Destruction Level for radiocarbon dating, which ultimately led to the new chronology for that level. Soon after those astonishing results were received, we also got a new radiocarbon date for the felling of the juniper logs in Tumulus MM. The second column of the table shown above indicates how the key events in Gordion's history are now generally viewed, thanks to the Wiener Laboratory at Cornell University, but also in large part to the brilliant seriation studies of Keith DeVries (DeVries 2007). He was also largely responsible for letting us see that the important South Cellar deposit is basically an integral unit

dating to around 700, rather than its previously considered diachronic amalgam.

The new chronology removes many puzzles, especially in the case of pottery, as this chapter attempts to illustrate. A particularly elegant class of Phrygian painted pottery is Brown-on-Buff Ware, of which examples from Tumuli K-III and P are particularly well known (Sams 1994a:165–73). The ware includes several examples bearing linear animals executed in a consistent style of drafting (Sams 1974). On the old, low chronology, the painted figures were thought to have begun in the later 8th century. A single example, with small panels of animals, occurred in the Destruction Level, where the ware in general was rare (Fig. 5.2) (Sams 1994a:277, catalogue entry 832). Three more examples came from Tumuli K-III and P (Körte and Körte 1904:55, Abb. 18, Nr. 3; Taf. 2, Nr. 6; Taf. 3, Nr. 10. Young 1981: pls. 16–17,

TumP 55–57). Those from K-III, like the example from the Destruction Level, all have animals in a small-panel format; those from P, which is slightly later than K-III, bear larger panels of more finely detailed animals (Figs. 5.3, 5.4). The latter seemed a logical development from the smaller panels, yet it was puzzling that only a single, certain example of the linear animals was known from the erstwhile later Destruction Level, and that it had small panels.

More puzzling still was the fact that the majority of examples of the class in general, both with and without animals, came from contexts that postdated the laying of the great clay fill for the new, Middle Phrygian citadel. Included here are vessels that bear either small or large panels of animals (Figs. 5.5, 5.6), although most bear no animals at all (Fig. 5.7) (Sams 1994a:302–5, cat. nos. 1036–1064.). Also included in this general post-clay assemblage are enormous, stylistically related vessels that display large scenes of two or more figures on the shoulder and panels of single animals on the neck (Figs. 5.8–5.10) (Sams 1994a:305–8, cat. nos. 1065–1081). They are seemingly a development beyond that of the vessels with large figural panels from Tumulus P.

These contextually later examples were difficult to explain in terms of the former chronology, which assumed that the construction of the Middle Phrygian citadel did not begin until the 7th century or later. Yet under the new, high chronology, and with the Destruction Level pre-dating Tumuli K-III and P on typological grounds, the puzzling aspects of Brown-on-Buff ware and its stylistic circle find resolution.

The single example from the now ca. 800 Destruction Level becomes the earliest known exemplar of the figural group. Those from Tumuli K-III and P, now posterior to the Destruction Level by probably no more than a few decades, show, respectively, small and large animal panels, suggesting, as Rodney Young had already thought, that P is the later of the two burials, if only by a decade or so. The tumuli share a number of close material correspondences; both also find correspondences with the Destruction Level (Young 1981:269–70; Sams 1994a:193).

The chronology of the numerous post-clay examples, including the huge, stylistically related vessels, is aided by the fact that a sherd of the bona fide ware and two fragments of the huge class had been discarded in the ca. 700 South Cellar deposit. At the

Fig. 5.3. Large round-mouthed jug in Brown-on-Buff Ware from Tumulus P (Gordion inventory P 1455). Source: Gordion Project, Penn Museum.

same time, nothing resembling Brown-on-Buff ware or its stylistic circle is known from tumuli of the 7th century and later at Gordion.

The overall category may thus be viewed as having its origins in the 9th century, when examples are few: a side-spouted sieve jug from Tumulus W (Young 1981: pl. 92, G-I, TumW 61), now dating to around 850, and a handful of sherds from pre-destruction Phrygian contexts in the citadel (Sams 1994a:165, cat. nos. 114, 167, 385, 408). Examples continue to be scarce by the time of the Destruction Level at the end of the 9th century (Sams 1994a:165, cat. nos. 527, 832.). In the first half of the 8th century, however, Tumuli K-III and P show that the ware had a vogue in elite burials of the time, early in the Middle Phrygian period, although curiously the furnishers of Tumulus MM, now dated to ca. 740, had no interest in any variety of showy pottery. Yet, as the numerous post-clay examples indicate, the ware and its stylistic circle were to enjoy relative popularity among the living across the remaining 8th century and perhaps for a few decades beyond.

A parallel case occurs with dark-polished monochrome pottery. Again in Tumuli K-III and P, the presence of fine black-polished pottery was curious, since the intensity of the polish and the true black color are rare in the Early Phrygian sequence through the Destruction Level (Sams 1994a:35). Equally unusual, and for the same reason, were such relief treatments as crisp fluting, reeding, and modeled surfaces borne by a number of the vessels in question (Sams 1994a:121; Fig. 5.11). As with the linear animals, these traits may now be viewed as post-Early Phrygian, i.e., early Middle Phrygian developments of the 8th century.

Fine black-polished pottery is abundant in post-clay contexts of the Middle Phrygian New Citadel. In connection with it we also see relief treatments analogous to those already present in Tumuli K-III and P (Fig. 5.12). Numerous examples from the ca. 700 South Cellar deposit demonstrate that these developments accelerated across the 8th century (Young 1966: pl. 74, figs. 3-4; DeVries 2005:37–42 and fig. 4-4), while finds from later contexts indicate

Fig. 5.4. Detail of large round-mouthed jug in Brown-on-Buff Ware from Tumulus P (Gordion inventory P 1456). Source: Gordion Project, Penn Museum.

Fig. 5.5. Body sherd of a vessel in Brown-on-Buff ware from a post-clay context on the citadel; small animal panels (Gordion inventory P 3476). Source: Gordion Project, Penn Museum.

that such elegant black pottery continued to be produced at least into the 5th century.

The new, high chronology for the Destruction Level has ramifications that extend beyond Gordion and Phrygia. In terms of pottery, one case in point may serve as an illustration. A ceramic marker of Iron Age sites to the east of Gordion, in the Halys region and Tabal, is the style of vase painting generally referred to as Alişar IV (Sams 1978:231–33; Bossert 2000:46–51). Characterized primarily by silhouette animals and stick trees amidst concentric circles and other geometric designs, the style is relatively abundant at such sites as its namesake,

Fig. 5.6. Fragment of a jug in Brown-on-Buff Ware from a post-clay context on the citadel; large animal panels (Gordion inventory P 967a). Source: Gordion Project, Penn Museum.

Fig. 5.7. Bowl in Brown-on-Buff Ware from a post-clay context on the citadel (Gordion inventory P 2184). Source: Gordion Project, Penn Museum.

Boğazköy, Kültepe, and Maşat Höyük. Farther afield it is known from Arslantepe/Malatya and the Yunus cemetery at Carchemish in Syria. At Gordion the style is rare, with about a dozen examples known from the Young excavations, mostly from post-clay contexts (Sams 1994a:163). Yet three of the vessels represented come from the pre-destruction stratigraphic unit EPB V, dated now to around 850, while a fourth is from the unit EPB VII, among the latest of contexts that pre-date the Destruction Level

(Sams 1994a: catalogue entries 169–171 and 186, pls. 113 (top) and 161, color plate III (for one fragment of 186). From the Destruction Level itself, a krater with silhouette animals appears to be under the influence of the eastern style (Fig. 5.13) (Sams 1994a:162–63 and pl. 126, catalogue entry 932). Although the lower temporal limit for production of the style and its variants in the east remains unclear, the evidence from Gordion now indicates a beginning in the course of the 9th century. The point is

Fig. 5.8. Sherd from shoulder of a large vessel in the style of Brown-on-Buff Ware from a post-clay context on the citadel (Gordion inventory P 544g). Source: Gordion Project, Penn Museum.

worth making because much of past scholarship has tended to see the Iron Age in Central Anatolia as not really getting under way until around the year 800 (e.g., Akurgal 1955:120–23).

Although pottery has been the focus of the present chapter, the ramifications of the new, high chronology for Iron Age Gordion extend far beyond the activities of Phrygian and other Anatolian potters. In the Early Phrygian citadel, what had already been exceptional for the 8th century becomes even more striking in a context of the 9th. For example, the buildings of the destroyed citadel (Fig. 1.2) already constituted the premiere showcase for monumental architecture of the Iron Age in Central Anatolia. They may now be viewed as representing Phrygian architectural achievements of the 9th (not the 8th) century. With the former, lower date, the structures, especially the largest, Megaron 3, had been seen as generally contemporary with the rise of monumental architecture in the Greek world to the west. Now, however, these structures can be viewed as pre-dating

Fig. 5.9. Neck and rim sherds from one or more large vessels in the style of Brown-on-Buff Ware from post-clay contexts on the citadel (Gordion inventory P 544a-c). Source: Gordion Project, Penn Museum.

64

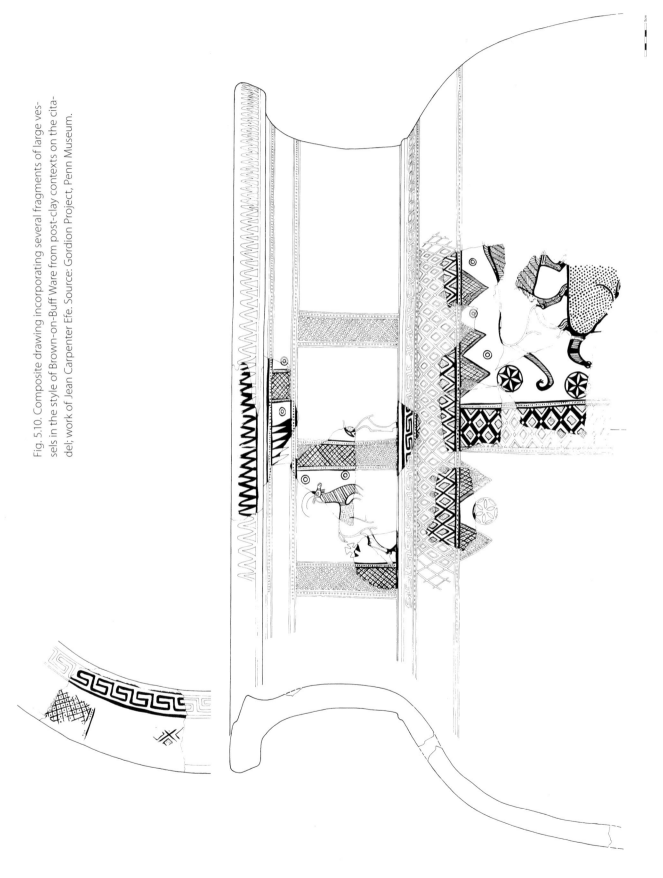

Fig. 5.10. Composite drawing incorporating several fragments of large vessels in the style of Brown-on-Buff Ware from post-clay contexts on the citadel; work of Jean Carpenter Efe. Source: Gordion Project, Penn Museum.

Fig. 5.11. Side-spouted sieve jug, black-polished with reeded decoration, from Tumulus P (Gordion inventory P 1432). Source: Gordion Project, Penn Museum.

Fig. 5.12. Side-spouted sieve jug, black-polished with reeded decoration, from a post-clay context on the citadel (Gordion inventory P 1248). Source: Gordion Project, Penn Museum.

the large-scale building movements in Greece by as much as a century. With that temporal distancing in mind, one might well wonder whether Phrygian monumental architecture had any influence on that of Greece. Another possible case in point is the stone roof crown or akroterion, which occurs in Phrygian architecture already in a phase that predates the buildings of the Destruction Level, i.e., now early

9th century if not earlier still (Sams 1994b:212–13). In like manner, the presence of patterned pebble mosaic floors, as best seen in the main room of Megaron 2, had been a remarkable phenomenon for erstwhile 8th-century Gordion (Young 1965). Now, as a developed art of the 9th century, the early patterned mosaics of Gordion stand fully unparalleled for their time and become all the more remarkable as distant precursors to those of later Greece.

As for Midas and the Kimmerians, long believed to be inextricably linked to the destruction of the Early Phrygian citadel (e.g., Sams 1994a:1), the archaeological picture is now less direct. The famous Phrygian king may well have played a role in the rebuilding of his capital's citadel (Sams 2005a:14–18), but nowhere in that great complex are there palpable signs of a destruction that might have been caused by the Kimmerians around 700.

Fig. 5.13. Krater painted in style of Ališar IV, from the Destruction Level (Gordion inventory P 3729). Source: Gordion Project, Penn Museum.

6

The Unfinished Project of the Gordion Early Phrygian Destruction Level

Mary M. Voigt

When visitors to Gordion approach the entrance to the Early Phrygian fortified area or citadel, they are often puzzled by a massive pile of stones that stands just inside the towering walls of the gateway (Figs. 6.1, 6.2). If they examine this pile, they find that it is a large tank or Drain Basin with finished stone blocks lining its interior, and remnants of a stone-lined channel lead down into it from the north where the Early Phrygian Palace Quarter lay, its buildings preserved by a great fire that took place around 800 BC (Figs. 1.2, 6.3). This drainage system, which would have blocked access into the citadel, also presented a significant puzzle to its excavator, Rodney S. Young. He encountered the basin in 1953, his third season of excavation at Gordion, and he initially thought that it might date to the same period as the Early Phrygian Gate Building (1955:15, fig. 26).

As he gained a better understanding of the archaeological remains inside the citadel walls, he assigned the basin's construction to the rebuilding of Gordion after the fire, or to what we now call the Middle Phrygian period (Young 1956:258, 260, fig. 38) (Figs. 1.3, 6.3). The area inside the Early Phrygian Gate Building continued to present stratigraphic and chronological problems for Young, and he eventually created an "interim period" *between* Gordion's destruction and reconstruction, in which he placed the drain system as well as other unspecified architectural anomalies (Young 1964:284; an oblique statement which was tied to the Drain Basin by DeVries 1990:n.28).

After Young's death, the puzzle began to be resolved. Keith DeVries, Young's successor as Gordion

Project Director, re-studied the Drain Basin while preparing a preliminary report on the 1969–1973 excavation seasons. On reading the excavation field records, DeVries found evidence that the Drain Basin (and thus the drainage system) was already in place at the time of the Early Phrygian destruction, and was actually one of a series of structural elements that he referred to collectively as the "unfinished final pre-destruction building project" (hereafter the Unfinished Project) (Fig. 6.4) (DeVries 1990:387–88, fig. 22).[1] This dating presented an interpretive challenge, since it was not compatible with the history of the site as constructed by Young and accepted by his colleagues after his death in 1974 (Young 1981). Young used the few references to Gordion in documentary sources to construct a chronological framework for the site (Voigt 2009). He attributed the Early Phrygian destruction to Kimmerian nomads who raided the countryside as they traveled across Anatolia from the east in the early 7th century BC. But if the Unfinished Project was begun shortly before 700 BC (as DeVries thought in 1990), why did the Phrygians choose a moment when they were in peril to start a construction project that had opened a primary entrance into their citadel to anyone who walked by?

Information gathered from excavations since 1988 has revised some of our ideas about the history of Gordion that are relevant to a consideration of the Unfinished Project. First, a deep stratigraphic sounding conducted in 1988–1989 indicated that only a brief period of time had elapsed between the fire and the beginning of the rebuilding process that resulted in Middle Phrygian Gordion, or Phase 5

Fig. 6.1. Air view from 1989 showing Young's Main Excavation Area on the eastern half of Yassıhöyük. Photo: Will and Eleanor Myers.

Fig. 6.2. The Early Phrygian/YHSS 6A Destruction Level Gate Passage with Drain Basin to right. Source: Gordion Project, Penn Museum.

in the Yassıhöyük Stratigraphic Sequence or YHSS (Voigt 1994:275; 2005) (Table 6.1). With any significant gap between destruction and reconstruction eliminated, the Unfinished Project appears in an entirely new light: it no longer represents a minor modification of the Early Phrygian/YHSS 6A Palace Quarter, aborted and abandoned at the time of the fire, but is instead the first stage of what became the Middle Phrygian/YHSS 5 construction project, a project that was interrupted but not much delayed by the fire. Second, radiocarbon and dendrochronological determinations showed that the fire took place around 800 BC (DeVries et al. 2003; Rose and Darbyshire 2011). The Middle Phrygian/YHSS 5 reconstruction therefore took place in the early 8th century BC, when the Phrygians were at the height of their political power and there was little risk in dismantling and rebuilding the fortification system.

Table 6.1. The Yassıhöyük Stratigraphic Sequence (YHSS).

YHSS Phase	Period Name	Approximate Dates
0	Modern	1920s
1	Medieval	10–15th c. AD
2	Roman	1st c. BCE–4th c. AD
3A	Later Hellenistic	260?–100 BC
3B	Early Hellenistic	330–?260 BC
4	Late Phrygian	540–330 BC
5	Middle Phrygian	after 800–540 BC
6A-B	Early Phrygian	900–800 BC
7	Early Iron Age	1100–900 BC
9-8	Late Bronze Age	1400–1200 BC
10	Middle Bronze Age	1600–1400 BC

This chapter reexamines the archaeological evidence related to the nature and scope of the Unfinished Project, a study that began in 1987 when I started my research at Gordion. The two goals of this chapter are, first, to provide more detailed information on the initiation of new construction within the Early Phrygian/YHSS 6A citadel as represented by the Unfinished Project, and second, to suggest some revisions of the plan of the Early Phrygian/YHSS 6A Palace Quarter before the Unfinished Project had begun.

By using Young's field notes along with published sources, DeVries and I were able to arrive at a picture of Early Phrygian/YHSS 6A Gordion at the time of the 800 BC fire that is quite different from Young's. The data are not perfect. Young records architecture and architectural levels, but stratigraphic observations are rare in his field notes. Nevertheless, the conclusions drawn here rest on Young's own records, which are viewed within a different chronological framework and with a somewhat different set of assumptions (see Voigt 2009 for discussion of these changes).

I have focused on evidence around and to the northwest of the Early Phrygian/YHSS 6A Gate Building, which consists of two large courts (North Court and South Court) on either side of a Gate Passage (Figs. 6.5, 6.6). At the west end of the Gate Passage, or the entrance into the Palace Quarter, is a small, lightly built structure of wood and stone that has two doorways in line with the Gate Passage. Referred to in Young's publications as the "Polychrome House," this small structure presumably had doors that could be closed, and thus is the actual "gate building," a function that it served from the time of its construction in YHSS 6B until it was torn down as part of the 6A Unfinished Project (Fig. 6.6). Because the term "Gate Building" has generally been used for the massive 6A stone structure (courts and passage), I have retained the name Polychrome House for what we might more properly call the "gate house." There are still uncertainties about the area to the northeast and southwest of the Gate Building that can only be resolved by a more comprehensive and detailed study of field records. Thus, what is presented here

Fig. 6.3. Standing structures of the Early Phrygian/YHSS 6A Destruction Level, with section showing red level (arrowed) and the overlying Middle Phrygian/YHSS 5 layer of fill with rubble foundations. Source: Gordion Project, Penn Museum

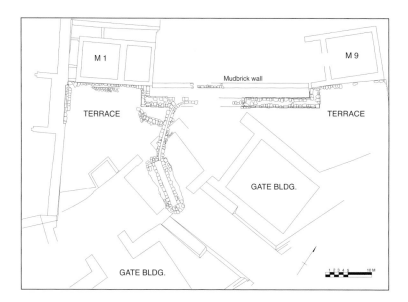

Fig. 6.4. DeVries' 1990 plan of the Unfinished Project. Source: Gordion Project, Penn Museum.

must be regarded as a preliminary rather than a final report on the Unfinished Project.

Components of the Unfinished Project

The excavated area of the Early Phrygian/YHSS 6A Palace Quarter can be described in terms of four major zones: (1) the Gate Building and area just inside it; (2) an Outer Court bordered on the northeast and southwest by large megarons; (3) an Inner Court bordered by at least four megarons; and (4) an elevated area (the TB Terrace) to the southwest of the Courts that supports two rows of buildings running northwest/southeast on either side of a broad street (Fig. 1.2). A fifth zone beyond the Terrace Buildings at the northwest was probably an open area at the time of the fire.[2] Construction projects were then underway in three and perhaps all four major zones. As DeVries described, elements of the Unfinished Project included a brick wall stretching between Megarons 1 and 9, high terraces located between the Early Phrygian/YHSS 6A Gate Building and the southernmost megarons, and a drainage system located inside the remains of the Polychrome House (PH) (DeVries 1990: fig. 22; Fig. 6.4). To this list we can now add the first phase of construction of at least one Middle Phrygian/YHSS 5 building (C) and the demolition or modification of Early Phry-

gian/YHSS 6A walls and pavements, including a stone wall that enclosed the southern end of the Outer Court, at least one wall of Megaron 9, the primary stairway leading from the Polychrome House up to the Terrace Buildings, and the removal of much of the stone pavement of the Outer Court (Figs. 6.5, 6.6). I will also argue that the demolition of parts of the Early Phrygian/YHSS 6A Gate Building, the related construction of a wall diagonally across the gateway,

Table 6.2. Names used for YHSS 6A architecture.

No.	Current Name	Names previously used
1	Brick Enclosure Wall	Brick Wall, Kerpiç Wall
2	Stone Enclosure Wall	Stone Wall, Archaic or Persian Wall, Mandra Wall
3	Stepped Terrace	Phrygian Terrace, stepped terrace, staircase terrace
	TB Terrace	Terrace
	Brick Barrier Wall	-
	Reception room TB Terrace	South Phrygian House
4	Building Proto-C	Rough Under-foundations of Early C
	Building C1	Early C
	Building C2	Later C, Building C
5	Shed	Shed
	Stone Deposit	-
6	Drain Basin	Grease pit
	Main Channel	Second Grease pit
	Side Drain	Side Drain
7	Eastern Terrace	-
9	Dam Wall	Dam Wall

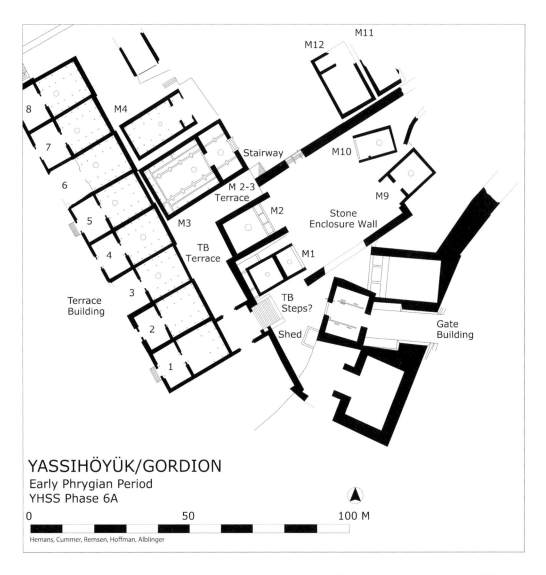

Fig. 6.5. Early Phrygian/YHSS 6A plan before the beginning of the Unfinished Project, with major buildings referred to in text. Source: Gordion Project, Penn Museum.

and the earliest filling of areas to the south of this diagonal wall were undertaken before the 6A fire of ca. 800 BC.

In the following discussion I will describe these elements or projects, moving from the area bordering the Outer Court toward the gateway. My focus will be on the Gate Building and areas to the north and northwest, all of which have been thoroughly researched using the relevant excavation notebooks and unpublished photographs. For the pre-fire construction and demolition project in the area to the northeast of the Gate Building I have relied on pub-

lished sources and some unpublished photographs, so a final interpretation of this area awaits a more complete examination of field records.

The Brick Enclosure Wall

The key to an understanding of what was happening at Gordion when the Palace Quarter caught fire is a brick wall that stretched between the southern walls of Megarons 1 and 9, effectively closing off the Outer Court from the area just inside the gate to the south (Young 1956: figs. 40, 38) (Figs. 6.5,

6.7, 6.8, 6.11, 6.17, 6.22) (For terminology used in this paper and earlier names see Table 2). The foundations of this Brick Enclosure Wall consisted of a single course of soft white "poros" stone cut into rectilinear slabs that were laid in two lines; on the slabs were set mud bricks 37 cm square and 9 cm thick, laid with 2.5 bricks across the width of the wall (RSY NBK 54, 1955:22–23).[3] The wall rested on a "very thin layer of gravelly fill with a hard surface"; this lens (which was probably kicked up from the gravel fill of terraces located in front of the Gate Building) covered a stone pavement that had been laid across the Outer Court at the beginning of the 9th century BC/YHSS 6A (RSY NBK 61, 1959:19; Young 1956:261). At its southwestern end, adjacent to Megaron 1, the Brick Enclosure wall had a preserved height of over 60 cm. A doorway ca. 2.20 m wide lay near this end of the wall. At the time of the fire, a line of small stones extended across most of the doorway,

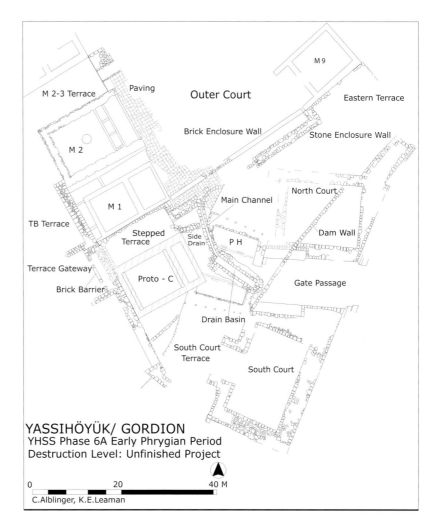

Fig. 6.6. Revised plan of Unfinished Project. Source: Gordion Project, Penn Museum.

leaving only a small gap to the southwest. DeVries suggested that the line of stones was a threshold (1990:388; Figs. 6.4, 6.5, 6.8); however, a lack of wear observed by Young (RSY NBK 54, 1955:34) casts doubt on DeVries's interpretation, and the stones may simply represent a temporary blocking of the doorway.[4]

The northwestern face of the Brick Enclosure Wall was heavily burnt at its western end, and burnt debris from Megaron 1 was found piled up against this face so that the wall necessarily dated before the Early Phrygian/YHSS 6A fire (Young 1956:261; 1962a:159; RSY NBK 54, 1955: 22–25, 34–37, 64–72, plan p. 39). DeVries described the wall as "makeshift," "flimsy," and "temporary" and considered it as an element in the Unfinished Project (1990:388). Al-

though I would characterize the Brick Enclosure Wall as more substantial than DeVries, it certainly appears to be temporary: the ends of the wall are neatly finished, leaving a gap between the wall and the adjacent megarons (Fig. 6.5). Thus, although it provided a solid barrier, demolition of the brick wall would have been relatively easy.

If we accept an interpretation of the Brick Enclosure Wall as temporary and recently built at the time of the fire, it then becomes a means of closing off the living areas to the north from the construction zone to the south, where the elements identified as part of the Unfinished Project lie. The Brick Enclosure Wall can therefore be seen as an ancient equivalent of the temporary wooden fences that surround modern construction sites.

Fig. 6.7. Mud-brick Enclosure Wall (right) and remnant of Stone Enclosure Wall (left) resting on Outer Court pavement; looking southwest. Joining (but not bonded with) the eastern end of the Stone Enclosure Wall (foreground) is the retaining wall of the Eastern Terrace. Source: Gordion Project, Penn Museum.

The Stone Enclosure Wall

A stone wall parallel to and just to the southeast of the Brick Enclosure Wall has been interpreted differently by Young and DeVries (Figs. 6.4, 6.5, 6.7, 6.8, 6.10). This Stone Wall is far more substantial than the Brick Wall, measuring up to 1.9 m in width, with foundations that were stepped out on both faces to reach a maximum width of 2.15 m (RSY NBK 61, 1959:19–20). When found, the

Stone Wall was relatively well preserved toward each end but nonexistent in what should have been its center. At its eastern end the Stone Wall has a short stub wall running northwest; the northeastern face and the northwestern face (which abuts Megaron 9) of this stub wall are smooth and preserved to a height of seven courses, but the southwestern "face" is irregular, representing what had been the interior of the wall (CKW NBK 86, 1961:97, plan 96) (Fig. 6.9a). Piled up against the smooth northeastern face of this stub was a deposit of gray clay that represents the fill of the Eastern Terrace (Fig. 6.9b; CKW NBK 86, 1961:90–91).

The western end of the Stone Enclosure Wall is preserved to a height of seven courses and also has a short stub wall running northwest which is not bonded into the main wall (Fig. 6.5). Here the end of the main wall and the outer or northeastern face of the stub wall are smooth, while the northwestern face, which retains the western Stepped Terrace, is rough. To the northeast of the stubwall, the main line of the Stone Enclosure Wall has been torn away with several blocks out of place (Fig. 6.10). Young described the western end of the stone wall as "built of miscellaneous blocks—hard limestone, red basalt, etc.—in large squarish stones, quite different from any masonry we have yet seen at the [Early] Phrygian level. But here as further to the [east] this wall was covered by clay and therefore belongs to the pre-clay [Early Phrygian] period"; he concludes that it "was a *mandra* or enclosure wall…presumably built to replace the *kerpiç* [brick] wall beside it" (RSY NBK 61, 1956:96, 97; RSY NBK 54, 1955:26–27, 54). From the beginning, then, Young considered the Stone Enclosure Wall to belong to the main phase of the Early Phrygian/YHSS 6A occupation, and believed its partial demolition to be contemporary with the laying of clay fill during the Middle Phrygian/YHSS 5 period.

Fig. 6.8. Brick Enclosure Wall from southeast with low blocking in doorway. Beyond and to the right, the Outer Court with preserved paving in front of Megaron 1, under excavation. At the west end of the Brick Enclosure, the rubble foundations of a later building can be seen cutting into the east end of the Stepped Terrace. Parallel to the Brick Enclosure Wall is the western stub of the Stone Enclosure Wall. In the foreground is the Main Drain Channel. Source: Gordion Project, Penn Museum.

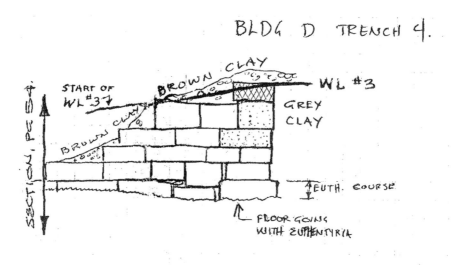

Fig. 6.9a (top). The finished wall face at the northeast end of the Stone Enclosure Wall with the retaining wall of the Eastern Terrace to the right. The fill against the smooth face of the Stone Enclosure Wall has been removed, exposing the uneven back of the Eastern Terrace retaining wall. Source: Gordion Project, Penn Museum.

Fig. 6.9b. Sketch elevation at the northeastern end of the Stone Enclosure Wall made by Charles K. Williams showing its differential preservation. The "grey clay" to the right represents the fill of the Eastern Terrace. Source: Gordion Project, Penn Museum.

DeVries, who described the stone masonry as "handsome" and "the most imposing known at the site" within the Early Phrygian/YHSS 6A period, saw the Stone Enclosure Wall as under construction at the time of the fire and included it within the Unfinished Project (1990:387, 388). Although he does not tell us why he decided that the wall's preserved state was a result of construction rather than demolition, it seems likely that he was influenced by the fact that at least some of its masonry is different from that typically found in the Early Phrygian/YHSS 6A buildings, and by an observation made by Charles K. Williams II, who excavated the eastern part of what was then called the "Persian Wall." Williams found a "large grey stone," similar to the other blocks used to construct the Stone Enclosure Wall, lying at an angle on a layer of clay above the wall stub, along its north face. Two faces

of this block were "pick finished," and he makes the following comment: "Apparently this block [was] in process of being trimmed for [the] Persian wall when plans changed" (CKW NBK 86, 1961:61, plan pp. 48–49).

Williams was undoubtedly correct, and we can now relate the disruption of the building process to the Early Phrygian/YHSS 6A fire, but the status of the Stone Enclosure Wall at that time must still be determined. There are several lines of evidence indicating that the incomplete state of the Stone Enclosure Wall was due to partial demolition rather than partial construction. First is the fact that the wall is best preserved at either end, where it had been incorporated as part of the retaining system for the Unfinished Project's Eastern and Stepped (western) terraces; at each end, smooth finished faces of the Stone Enclosure Wall supported terrace fills, a clear indication that the wall

Fig. 6.10. Building C1 and the Stepped Terrace from the northeast. The trench cut into the Stepped Terrace, along the north wall of C1, represents a cut for the foundations of Building C2. The east end of the Stepped Terrace is formed by the Stone Enclosure Wall and a blocked doorway between it and the south wall of Megaron 1 (right). Source: Gordion Project, Penn Museum.

was built before the terraces (Figs. 6.7, 6.9a, 6.10). If the Stone Enclosure Wall was not constructed before the Eastern and Stepped terraces were built, none of this masonry makes any sense. Second, beyond the line of the stub walls, the ends of the Stone Enclosure have been torn apart, leaving the jagged remains of what had been a well-bonded wall; I find these jagged faces impossible to interpret as parts of a wall under construction, but very easy to see as the robbed-out remains of walls that had changed in function from free-standing to retaining walls.

A third argument rests on a change in the style of masonry found at the east end of the Stepped Terrace. Whereas some of the blocks used to construct the Stone Enclosure Wall in this area are the soft white stone described as "poros" by Young (a kind of material characteristic of Early Phrygian/YHSS 6), the southwestern corner of the wall has the tumble that Young described as a miscellaneous collection of blocks (RSY NBK 61, 1956:96). There is a clear suggestion of a change of plan that apparently involved strengthening a wall that was already partially robbed. Finally, a few stones from the lowest course of the Stone Enclosure Wall were being incorporated into the drain of the Unfinished Project when the Unfinished Project was abandoned—again an observation that would not fit with a wall under construction (Figs. 6.10, 6.11).

The Stepped (Western) Terrace

The Stepped Terrace was almost as much of an enigma to Young as the drain system (Fig. 6.6). When excavating to the south of Megaron 1 he found a long and relatively narrow raised area that ran northeast and southwest at a height of 2.20 m above the Destruction Level surface. This Stepped Terrace was slightly higher than the older TB Terrace adjacent to the west, and was con-

Fig. 6.11. Foreground, the Brick Enclosure Wall with blocking to the left. Behind the Brick Wall and parallel to it is a discontinuous line of parallel blocks that represent the remains of the Stone Enclosure Wall; two of the blocks have been incorporated into the Main Drain Channel. See also Figure 6.8. Source: Gordion Project, Penn Museum.

Fig. 6.12. The western end of the Stepped Terrace during excavation. The high ashlar walls in the background are Building C2, set on a foundation course of wood that overlies Building C1. Three carefully laid stairs lead to the Stepped Terrace. The flat stones that form a rough lower course constitute part of the "wall" shown in this location on previous plans. The difference between the smooth surface of the TB2 Terrace (right) and the fill at the base of the Stepped Terrace stairway is clearly visible. Source: Gordion Project, Penn Museum.

nected to the latter by a series of three carefully laid steps with a broad course of flat stones at the base of the steps (Fig. 6.12). Lying on the steps and on the surface of the raised area to the east was burnt debris, unequivocal evidence for the construction of the Stepped Terrace before the fire (RSY NBK 44, 1957:47–49, 59).

Photographs of the Stepped Terrace after its southern edge had been partially cut away show that it was built up of layered clay fill. This fill was supported to the west by the TB Terrace, and to the north by a high stone retaining wall built adjacent to Megaron 1's southeastern wall, with clear evidence of the fire in both areas (DeVries 1990:388; RSY NBK 44, 1957:48–49). To the east the terrace fill was supported by the western end of the Stone Enclosure Wall and the short stub wall that linked the Stone Enclosure Wall to the northern retaining wall. No burning was found in this eastern area, but photographs show that this area had been disturbed by the foundations of a Middle Phrygian/YHSS 5 wall. To the south, the Stepped Terrace rested against nicely cut ashlar

Fig. 6.13. Relationship of Megaron 1 to the Stepped Terrace. The northern retaining wall of the Stepped Terrace is visible beyond the remains of the unevenly preserved south wall of Megaron 1. To the left, nearly abutting Megaron 1, is the western end of the Brick Enclosure Wall. Source: Gordion Project, Penn Museum.

blocks that Young interpreted as the foundations of Middle Phrygian/YHSS 5 Building C1 (Fig. 6.13). There was apparently no burning on Building C1, leaving us uncertain about the southern boundary of the Stepped Terrace.

The relationship of the Stepped Terrace to the older TB Terrace is another area where my interpretation differs from that of DeVries. To the west of the Stepped Terrace stairway is more evidence of the way in which the Phrygians blocked access into the construction zone. A short mud-brick wall set between narrow stone pylons (hereafter the Brick Barrier Wall) was built at the eastern entrance to a gate or reception room that led in turn to the Terrace Buildings, two facing rows of structures intended for food storage, food preparation, and textile production (Figs. 6.5, 6.6) (DeVries 1990:384–87; Burke 2005). The Brick Barrier Wall was heavily burned on both faces and thus was in place at the time of the fire.

Working from plans that were misleading, DeVries had thought that there was a substantial north-south wall in place parallel to the Stepped Terrace steps and immediately west of them (1990:388, fig. 22). An examination of field notes, photographs, and state plans made during excavation shows that what appears on most published plans as one face of this "wall" was instead a line of flat stones that look like foundations for the Stepped Terrace stairway (Figs. 6.5, 6.12). The TB Terrace "Reception Room" (which Young referred to as the South Phrygian House) had a good clay floor to the west of the Brick Barrier Wall, but photographs show that between the Brick Barrier Wall and the foundation course for the Stepped Terrace stairway the excavated "surface" is a mixed fill rather than a floor. Although seemingly a minor change in soil texture, the break between plaster floor and fill probably reflects the location of a stairway that once led from the area in-

Fig. 6.14. The east wall of Building C1, showing the deep rubble foundation of C2 cut into the clay fill to the east of Building C1. The smooth face of the cut into the clay is clearly visible to the right. In the foreground are the remains of the west end of the Polychrome House (right) and the Drain Channel (left). Source: Gordion Project, Penn Museum.

Fig. 6.15. The relationship between Building C1 and the drainage system of the Unfinished Project can be see here, with the rubble foundations of the east wall of C1 overlapping the Drain Basin and part of the Main Channel. The rubble foundations of Building C2 are also visible above the Main Channel. To the right are the remains of the eastern end of the Polychrome House. Source: Gordion Project, Penn Museum.

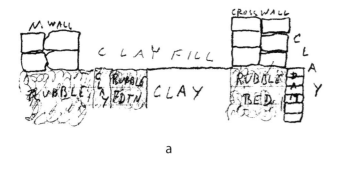

a

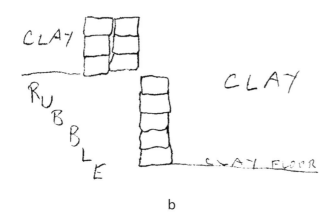

b

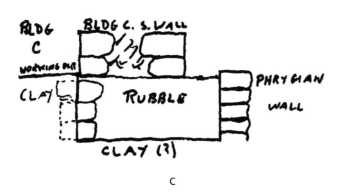

c

Fig. 6.16 a-c. In his field books, Rodney Young sketched the relationship of the "rough under foundations" to Building C1. In sketch Figure 6.16a he showed the difference in location between the east wall of C1 (which for Young was the "north wall") and the offset wall further to the west that represents Proto-C. Taken together, the sections show the working floor that runs over Proto-C and the clay floor at the base of its foundations. Also visible is the way in which the rubble foundations for the west and central walls are bounded by masonry "dam walls." Source: Gordion Project, Penn Museum.

side the Gate Building up to the TB Terrace (Fig. 6.6). The primary evidence for this reconstruction is a vertical face in the TB Terrace wall that appeared in the area where Young removed part of the southern edge of the Stepped Terrace (Fig. 6.18).

Although certainty depends on checking in the field, it seems highly likely that this edge represents one side of a stairway that was filled in and/or demolished when the Stepped Terrace was built. Such a stairway would have extended out beyond the TB Terrace's northeast face onto the Early Phrygian/YHSS 6A ground level to the south of Megaron 1, but no trace of stairs can be seen in photographs. One possibility is that the neatly cut blocks used to build the stairs to the Stepped Terrace represent a re-use of blocks from the older TB Terrace Stairway.

A good example of an Early Phrygian stairway was excavated next to the northwest wall of Terrace Building 8 (Fig. 1.2; DeVries 1990: figs 11, 13–15). In looking for a model for our reconstruction of the TB Terrace Stairway, Carrie Alblinger and I placed the TB 8 stairway in the gap in the TB Terrace wall where we thought the TB Terrace stairs would lie. The width of the TB 8 and hypothesized TB Terrace stairways were extremely close if not identical.

In addition to burnt debris on the Stepped Terrace, DeVries (1990:388) tells us that the northwest face of the Stepped Terrace retaining wall, which was built against the outer face of the southeastern wall of Megaron 1, was also burned. This face is not visible today, buried by fill placed above Megaron 1 in order to preserve its remains, but it could be seen until the early 1990s. DeVries' statement is presumably based on his examination of the standing remains of these walls, and perhaps on photographs where a blackened surface is clearly visible on the Stepped Terrace northern retaining wall in the area near the eastern end of Megaron 1 (Figs. 6.13, 6.17, 6.23). For the retaining wall to scorch, the southeastern brick wall of Megaron 1 must have been at least partially down at the time of the fire, but this can be attributed to its collapse during the fire rather than any demolition of the wall before the fire.

Building Proto-C

A series of superimposed structures that have collectively been referred to as "Building C" lies to the south of the Stepped Terrace (see Young 1955:6–8, figs. 8, 11, 13–14; 1958:142, fig. 1; 1960:233). Young defined two major rebuildings: Later C (hereafter Building C2), which was still in use during the Late Phrygian/YHSS 4 period; and Early C (hereafter Building C1), which has architectural details suggesting that it is one of the first Middle Phrygian/YHSS 5 buildings (Fig. 1.3). Building C2 was massive, larger than C1, with rubble foundations that were cut down into the clay fills that bordered C1 to the west, north, and east, thereby destroying much of the stratigraphic evidence that could help to relate

C1 to surrounding structures (Figs. 6.14, 6.15).

In an earlier version of this chapter, I had argued that C1 was a part of the Unfinished Project, primarily because the clay fill of the Stepped Terrace ran up against the foundations of its northern wall. Like Young (RSY NBK 78, 1959:145–46, 155), I assumed that there had to be something that created a southern edge to this terrace, but unlike Young I did not reject Building C1 as forming this edge. The difference in interpretation can be attributed primarily to the fact that Young had inserted a 150-year gap between the fire and the Middle Phrygian/YHSS 5 rebuilding, while I saw only a short time gap between the distinctive architectural styles of the Early/YHSS 6A and Middle Phrygian/YHSS 5 buildings based on stratigraphic data. I had also benefited from DeVries'

Fig. 6.17. View of the east end of the Stepped Terrace after the removal of Building Proto-C. In the foreground from right to left are the Brick Enclosure Wall with the stones blocking its doorway; the Stone Enclosure Wall with its unbonded northern segment; and the Side Drain, leading down from the Stepped Terrace and emptying into the Main Drain Channel. Note that the cover stones for the Side Drain are still in place, protected by the rubble foundations of Building C1. On the far left is the burned clay fill, visible as a rising surface against the TB Terrace Wall. The straight northern edge of the fill probably represents its juncture with the south wall of Building Proto-C. Source: Gordion Project, Penn Museum.

Fig. 6.18. View of the TB Terrace Wall with fired mud-plaster to the left and unfired plaster, protected by Building Proto-C, to the right. Below the fired plaster is a lump of fill that is fire-reddened on top, evidence that the fill was in place at the time of the fire. Source: Gordion Project, Penn Museum.

research, which identified a transitional (Early/Middle Phrygian) masonry style in the Eastern Terrace of the Unfinished Project. Thus, for me, having a building that was Middle Phrygian/YHSS 5 in style as part of the Early Phrygian/YHSS 6A Unfinished Project was not a great problem.

But there were two significant difficulties in considering C1 as part of the Unfinished Project: first, no evidence of burning on the wall adjacent to the Stepped Terrace had been reported; second, photographs show that the northeast or front wall and foundations of this building are uncomfortably close to the edge of the Unfinished Project's Drain Basin, and perhaps even project slightly over it. This overlap, visible on slides (Fig. 6.15), was pointed out to me by Charles Williams and was also emphasized by Young in his rejection of C1 as the southern retaining wall for the Stepped Terrace (RSY NBK 49 1955:89–90).

Architectural plans should have provided definitive evidence on the relationship between Building C1 and the Drain System, but attempts to locate C1 relative to the Early Phrygian buildings (including the Unfinished Project) proved frustrating. A resolution to the problem posed by Building C1 came from Young's preliminary reports and especially his field notes documenting the demolition of this structure. In his preliminary report on the 1959 season he notes an anomaly:

A change of plan during the construction of the building [C1] was suggested by the observation that the lowermost layers of the rubble bedding did not coincide with the line taken by the cross-wall between cella and pronaos above but lay farther out toward the [east]; evidently the *change in plan* involved a deepening of the pronaos. The filling inside the building was entirely of hard clay which yielded only irrelevant Hittite potsherds, and nothing was found that could help in dating the original construction of Building C. (Young 1960:233)

Young refers to these "lowermost layers of the rubble bedding" in his field records as the "rough under foundations" of Building C1, which I will call "base foundations." (RSY NBK 78, 1959:157ff).

The lightly built base foundation for the northwest-southeast wall that was never built (the "change in plan") lies parallel to but 2.6 m east of the base foundation for the cross-wall between the cella and pronaos/vestibule of Building C1 (RSY NBK 78, 1959:161–62). These two northwest-southeast base foundations are separated by a broad expanse of clay,

and a thin deposit of clay also lies to the east of the "abandoned" base foundation. Young's sketch sections show that the base foundations for the two short walls of the C1 cella are unusual in that the approximately 1.5-m-wide beds have neatly laid "dam walls"—lines of masonry that form the inner edge of the foundations, separating the rubble core from the clay fill under the floor of the cella of C1 (Fig. 6.16a-c) (RSY NBK 78, 1959:159).

The long walls for Proto-C are less well documented. Young says that he found a base foundation for the northwest wall of C1, which formed a corner with the base foundation of the southwest wall at the same point as the corresponding corner of Building C1 (RSY NBK 78, 1959:144); he also noted the presence of a southern base foundation (RSY NBK 80, 1959:142). Tying together these rubble base

Fig. 6.19. Southern end of the Drain Basin extending through the eastern wall of the Polychrome House. In the right foreground, a segment of the Dam Wall remains *in situ*. Inside the Drain Basin are blocks with ashy fill at the top. Extending partially over the eastern wall of the Drain Basin is a clay surface, which may be identified with the clay and wood capping observed by G. Roger Edwards. Source: Gordion Project, Penn Museum.

foundations were a clay "floor" or surface running beneath them, and a white "working floor" running immediately above them (Fig. 6.16c). While this working floor (the Gordion name for thin layers of white stone chips) is probably to be associated with the construction of Building C1, it does link all of the base foundations that Young noted (RSY NBK 80, 1959:141–43), and it establishes a break between Proto-C and C1. The absence of any trace of fire on top of the rough base foundations is potentially troubling, but this evidence would presumably have been erased when the construction of C1 began.

With the existence of the earliest phase of Building C or Proto-C documented, the next step is to establish a stratigraphic or architectural relationship between these foundations and the Stepped Terrace. This can be done by means of a small covered drain (the "Side Drain") that leads down from the southeast corner of the Stepped Terrace (Figs. 6.5, 6.7, 6.10, 6.17). When he first found the Side Drain in May 1959, Young considered its stratigraphic position, and he clearly states that "it must have been intended to drain the level of the Phrygian [Stepped] terrace" (RSY NBK 78, 1959:170). This relationship is also clear on photographs.

But as he continued to work to the north, he found that the Side Drain empties into the Unfinished Project's "Main Drain Channel," which he had already linked to a construction period after the fire (labeled "the abortion period"). As he continued to remove the remnants of Building C1 and Proto-C, he linked the Side Drain to C's "rough under foundations," and consequently regarded Proto-C as part of the Unfinished Project: "The small steep built drain which comes down from the stepped Phrygian Terrace at its NE corner *overlies* (barely) the [NE] corner of [the] early rough under foundation of Bldg C; and it is itself covered almost to its entire end by the actual built foundations of C1's NW corner. The lowest foundation of Bldg. C [i.e., Proto-C] thus seems to belong to the abortion period" (RSY NBK 80, 1959:143–44) (Fig. 6.10, 6.17). Although Young discusses and firmly rejects a link between any of the incarnations of Building C and the Early Phrygian/YHSS 6A Stepped Terrace (RSY NBK 80, 1959:141–42), his architectural observations tie together the Drain System, Proto-C, and the Stepped Terrace.

Once Proto-C had been removed, Young excavated to the south of it in the area bounded by the TB Terrace wall, a low terrace in front (northwest) of the South Court of the Gate Building, and a roughly built stone wall that ran between the South Court Terrace and the TB Terrace wall. To the east lay the drain system (Figs. 6.17, 6.18). In this constricted area, Young found traces of burning on top of a relatively low-lying layer of clay. His notebook entry is as follows:

> Continue to take out clay. But it may be Phrygian clay after all, not Persian…[H]ere in the clay as on the face of the [TB Terrace] wall we get many more traces of burning: the mud stucco is much blackened and the clay against the wall face at the level of the beam is reddened by fire and heat. This means that the clay was already there when the fire took place, and that the clay must presumably be Phrygian. We check at the west, at the end of the terrace floor [by?] the staircase and by digging back a little find that the pink burned clay is there also at the level of the beam. The beam itself, with wall blocks above and below and clay in front must have burned underground; but all the filling behind it is of rubble and this must have been plenty for vitrification. On K[üçük] H[öyük] we have seen plenty of examples of beams which have burned underground, and more examples may be cited from …the city mound. (RSY NBK 80, 1959:151–52)

Color photographs show not only the bright-red color of the TB Terrace wall facing toward the northwest, but also plain mud-colored plaster in the area between the TB Terrace wall "jog" and the south face of the Stepped Terrace (Fig. 6.18). The area with unfired plaster is precisely where the foundations that represented Building Proto-C lay before their removal.

At this point the evidence that Proto-C was built before the fire seems conclusive, but the strength of Young's assumptions about the architectural sequence prevented him from accepting his own data: "Evidently I was deceived by the way the rough under foundation of Bldg. C fitted into the clay: it looked as if both had been laid together…But since the clay in which it lay had been in place when the Phrygian city was destroyed, we must divorce clay

Fig. 6.20. The Drain Basin at the completion of excavation. Note that stones along the left (southwestern) side and at the south rounded end of the Basin have been removed, as have the blocks laid in its interior. Source: Gordion Project, Penn Museum.

and rough under foundation. The last must actually have been laid in a cut in the clay." (RSY NBK 80, 1959:152–53). Young's sketch sections of the "rough under foundations" show no evidence of a cut. Moreover, evidence collected in the 1988–89 Stratigraphic Sounding (see Voigt 2005, 2007; Voigt and Young 1999) as well as observations made by Young in his field notebooks show that for Middle Phrygian/YHSS 5 buildings that were constructed toward the beginning of this period, the clay fill was laid *with* the rubble, so that tongues of fill extend

inward between chunks of rubble (and into the walls of the Op 2 cellar) (Voigt 1994). Only very late Middle Phrygian/YHSS 5 structures had foundations cut into the fill, such as Building C2 or a wall attached to Building I:2 (Voigt 1994:274, pl. 27.7.2).

What did Proto-C look like? So far, no plans or photographs of the "rough under foundations" have been located in the Gordion Archives, but the evidence we do have indicates that Proto-C was smaller than Building C1 and had a very shallow pronaos or vestibule. The foundations for Proto-C's northeast wall lay well to the west of the Unfinished Project Drain System and seem to be aligned with the northeast end of the Stepped Terrace. It is logical to expect that the finished structure would have opened out onto a surface at the height of the Stepped Terrace. What we don't know is the level at which the foundations of Proto-C began, a point that is significant for two reasons. First, we would like to know how much clay fill had been laid in the area south of the Stepped Terrace before the fire. Second, if we are comparing the construction techniques used in the Unfinished Project with later YHSS 5 structures, some clay should lie between YHSS 6A surfaces and the base of the YHSS 5 foundations.

Young states that some clay lay beneath the "rough under foundations" but gives no measurements (RSY NBK 80, 1959:153). Young's sketch section shows all of the elements of Proto-C, with the working floor at the top of the foundations at the same level as the top of the TB Terrace (RSY NBK 44, 1957:157). Two years later, however, he says that the working floor meets the TB Terrace "at a level half-way up the fifth course (from the top)" of the TB Terrace (RSY NBK 80, 1959:141). Photographs show that both the line of stones at the juncture of the Stepped Terrace and TB Terrace (which I have interpreted as a foundation course for the Stepped Terrace Steps) and the top of the intact, unburned layer of mud plaster lie at approximately the fifth course of the TB Terrace wall (Fig. 6.18).

That the clay fill laid beneath Proto-C had some depth is suggested by two pieces of evidence. First, in his note concerning the Side Drain (RSY NBK 80, 1959:143-44), Young says that its channel "barely" overlaps the northeast corner of the rough under foundations of Proto-C. On Figure 6.20, bits of rubble can be seen beneath the Side Drain, ending perhaps 20 or 30 cm above the excavated surface; although the fill adjacent to the rubble bits rises to the west, this is probably part of the Stepped Terrace that has been partially cut away. Second, Young found upright stone slabs in the area beneath Proto-C (Fig. 6.18; see also below). These are said to have been embedded in clay and so were probably in the clay layer below Proto-C. Again, they appear to be 20–30 cm tall, giving at least an approximation of the depth of fill laid below the foundations that represent Proto-C.

The Area Between Building Proto-C and the South Court of the Gate Building

The clay fill to the south of Proto-C has already been established as having been laid before the fire. Three aspects of this fill deserve mention. First, the clay was laid over an earlier YHSS 6A building that Young referred to as the "Shed." The Shed was small and approximately rectangular with three very light walls 0.25 m thick that had white poros foundations; its fourth wall was formed by the edge of the terrace in front of the Gate Building South Court (Fig. 6.6). Fragments of unburned brick were found within the building, and a single course of green mud brick was found in place on the northwestern wall. Although the structure seems to have been quite flimsy, it had a pebble floor, and the "back" wall face (i.e., the South Court Terrace edge) had been covered with white plaster, decorated with a narrow band of red (RSY NBK 80, 1959:158–72). The history of this structure seems to have been complex, but its end can be dated by sherds of Phrygian Painted Ware found in the clay fill adjacent to the Shed; these sherds join with others from the fill around the Drain Basin in the Polychrome House (RSY NBK 80, 1959:167–68; see also Sams 1994a:14).

Second, a short stone wall preserved to a height of only two-three courses was found running between the TB Terrace wall and the point where the western wall of the Shed met the terrace in front of the South Court of the Early Phrygian/YHSS 6A Gate Building (Fig. 6.5). Young describes this lightly built wall as made of "large blocks, probably reused, roughly put together" and tells us that it was covered with the burned clay layer in this area (RSY NBK 80, 1959:166; 173–74). Although it is impossible to link the two architectural elements physically, it seems possible that this short wall was roughly contemporary with the Brick Enclosure Wall and was part of the plan to block access to the open storage areas of the Gate Building from the west. Standing at the time of the fire, but probably built earlier, was a short but apparently better-built wall that ran between the north end of the North Court of the Gate Building and the Stone Enclosure Wall (Figs. 6.6, 6.7), blocking access to the area in front of the gate from the east.

Fig. 6.21. The Eastern Terrace in 1993. Megaron 9 has been removed and is represented only by stone foundations underlying the retaining wall of the Eastern Terrace. Beyond the Terrace lies the YHSS 6A Gate Building South court, and resting on those walls, part of the YHSS 5 Gate Building, recognizable by its large ashlar blocks. In the background is the Küçük Höyük. Source: Gordion Project, Penn Museum.

The Drainage System in the Early Phrygian/YHSS 6A Gate

Set at the inner end of the Early Phrygian/YHSS 6A gateway was a large stone basin that was the end point of a drain system built as part of the Unfinished Project. This Drain Basin was fed by a Main Channel running down from the north, which was in turn fed by the small Side Drain leading from the Stepped Terrace (Figs. 6.5, 6.10, 6.11, 6.15, 6.17, 6.20). The Early Phrygian/YHSS 6B-A Gate House (the "Polychrome House," PH in Fig. 6.5) was partially demolished to build the Drain Basin, which lies over the foundations of both the inner (western) and outer (eastern) walls of the Polychrome House (Young 1956:258). In his field notes Young summarizes key aspects of the Basin (which he called "the Grease Pit") as follows:

This "grease pit" is built of blocks similar to these of the Phrygian gate, but apparently of blocks reused from it—the masonry is like the Phrygian, but it is also like the Persian dam wall…It is built inside-out, with good masonry faces toward the inside, rough ones to the outside. It can therefore have been intended only as an underground (or partly underground) structure for a level a meter or so higher than that of the Phrygian gateway. One suspects that it was an entirely underground structure, and that it is fully preserved. (RSY NBK 49, 1955:68–69)

The blocks placed along the sides of the Drain Basin were roughly piled, sloping down to the floor of the

Polychrome House (Figs. 6.19, 6.20). Although this rock fill is asymmetrical on published plans, with the eastern segment thicker than the western, photographs taken during excavation suggest that some of the Drain Basin's supporting rock fill was removed without planning in order to see aspects of the construction of the underlying Polychrome House.

The outer walls of the Drain Basin would have been concealed by fill that was laid inside the Polychrome House up to the top of its (preserved) outer walls. This fill had to have been in place before the flat course of stone that forms the top of the basin was laid (Fig. 6.19). The Drain Basin's interior was filled with more blocks, some of them neatly laid, that rested on an earthen floor, so it was apparently intended to serve as a French drain. At the northern end of the Drain Basin was an off-center aperture through which the drain was fed by its Main Channel. The latter was not completed when the Unfinished Project was abandoned, since its walls have gaps in the area of the Stone Enclosure Wall and no cover stones were found to match those on the Side Drain coming down from the Stepped Terrace (Fig. 6.20).

Young included this drain system as part of his "interim period" between the fire and the main pe-

Fig. 6.22. The Eastern Terrace retaining wall and Megaron 9 from the northeast. The full width of the Megaron 9 foundations is documented by the northern long wall to the right. Based on this evidence, the Eastern Terrace wall covers nearly half of the south wall of Megaron 9. In the background are the Brick Enclosure Wall, and in front of it, under the Outer Court paving, is the drain built at the start of YHSS 6A. Source: Gordion Project, Penn Museum.

Fig. 6.23. Megarons 2 and 1 with Outer Court paving preserved as a strip in front of the buildings. In the foreground is the thick Megaron 2-3 Enclosure Wall that had been covered by a layer of fill to form the Megaron 2-3 Terrace at the time of the fire. Source: Gordion Project, Penn Museum.

riod of Middle Phrygian/YHSS 5 construction, but DeVries established that the Drain Basin was in place before the fire, based on observations made by G. Roger Edwards, who dug this area in 1953 (DeVries 1990:388). Edwards reports a series of long cavities within a layer of clay that capped the Drain Basin. These cavities ran horizontally over the top of the basin, along its short axis. Two of the cavities were filled with charcoal, while the rest were simply hollows where wooden beams had decayed (GRE NBK 45, 1953:15–16; see also 49). Just above the cavities was a hard flat surface that lay at the same level as the preserved tops of the walls of the Polychrome House (RSY NBK 49, 1955:69–70). It was this surface that must have been in place at the time of the fire, but no evidence of burning on the clay fill was noted. This raises a question as to why timber used in the walls of the Polychrome House (also documented by hollows in the clay) were not burned

(Young 1956:258; RSY NBK 80, 1959:157). Some of the timber from inside the building may have been removed before it was filled, and any wood left in the foundations of the building would have been too deeply buried to be charred. Nevertheless, the presence of vertical hollows without charcoal in the terraces along the side walls of the Polychrome House is slightly troubling.

The Eastern Terrace

A high terrace with a retaining wall made of roughly cut squared blocks was constructed at the eastern end of the Stone Enclosure Wall (Figs. 6.5, 6.21, 6.22). While the front or northwest face of the Eastern Terrace retaining wall was relatively smooth, the back or southeast face that actually held back the terrace fill is very uneven—the usual form of retaining walls at Gordion (Young 1960:235). The western end of this terrace was formed by the eastern stub of the earlier Stone Enclosure wall, and the excavator, Charles Williams, records a thick layer of clean clay fill resting against the latter (CKW NBK 86, 1961:90–91) (Figs. 6.9a-b). In general the Eastern Terrace retaining wall is poorly built, with several areas in which consecutive courses of blocks are not bonded, perhaps because the area to the north of it was soon to be covered by more clay. Given the lack of bonding, the possibility that the retaining wall went through two stages, with a doorway between it and the Stone Enclosure Wall in the first stage, must at least be considered.

DeVries states unequivocally that the Eastern Terrace was built before the fire (1990:387, fig. 22), but he does not give evidence to supports this conclusion. This part of the Early Phrygian/YHSS 6A citadel did not burn, so evidence of fire could not have been used as a chronological marker (Sams 1994b:3; Young 1964:288–89).

I have not yet studied all of the relevant field records for the Eastern Terrace, but from a preliminary examination of plans and photographs, and accepting DeVries's inclusion of the Eastern Terrace as part of the Unfinished Project, I would suggest one amendment to his description of how it was built. Both photographs and plans show the Eastern Terrace wall resting on one edge of the foundations of the southeast wall of Megaron 9 (Fig. 6.22). DeVries states that the mud-brick superstructure of this Megaron 9 wall was "shaved" in order to accommodate the Eastern Terrace retaining wall (1990:387). If one takes into account that Megaron 9 was built at the very beginning of

Fig. 6.24. The Dam Wall was constructed of blocks removed from the Early Phrygian/YHSS 6A Gate Building. In this photo the north wall of the Gate Passage has been partially removed in front (north) of the Dam Wall as part of the Unfinished Project. A deep rubble deposit within the Gate Building North Court has already been removed through excavation, as has clay fill to the north of the Dam Wall within the Gate Passage. The Dam Wall, which dips down to a low point in the middle of the Gate Passage, is being cleared of a railway dike. Source: Gordion Project, Penn Museum.

Early Phrygian YHSS 6A, and was one of the oldest megarons around the Outer Court, a careful shaving and preservation of its walls during what was clearly a major remodeling project seems unlikely.[5] What we know about Phrygian construction practices suggests that the clay fill of the terrace was put in place simultaneously with the construction of the Eastern Terrace retaining wall. If Megaron 9 had still been in place, the mason would have had to have stood to the north of the retaining wall, working from its rough or back side. This scenario is highly unlikely.

It is far more plausible to suppose that at least the southeastern wall of Megaron 9 and perhaps the entire structure had already been demolished when the Eastern Terrace wall was built. When excavated, the walls of Megaron 9 had been leveled down to one or two courses, and its mosaic floor had been ripped out (Young 1964:289–90). Published photographs show that the height of the floor of Megaron 9 is well below that of the Outer Court Pavement (*contra* Young 1964:290), which was presumably put in at the same time that Megaron 9 was built. The base of the Eastern Terrace retaining wall rests at this level.

Construction and Demolition in the Outer and Inner Courts

The stone pavement that covered the Outer Court during YHSS 6A was missing over much of this area when it was excavated (Figs. 6.7, 6.8, 6.23; Young 1958: figs. 2, 6). The pavement, however, was preserved in a strip under the Brick Enclosure Wall, in the area between the Brick Wall and the dismantled Stone Enclosure Wall, and in a broad north-south strip bordering Megarons 1 and 2 (Fig. 6.7).

There are three pieces of evidence for removal of the paving before the fire—two direct and one indirect. First, a reddened burned area was observed on the surface on which the pavement had originally been laid in an area excavated in 1993. Although the patch was not large, it certainly was scorched clay and not some remnant of burned debris left from the Young years. Second, when Young excavated along the Brick Enclosure Wall in 1955 he found five paving blocks displaced: "They seem to have no purpose and to form no plan; but their position

indicates that at least some of the stone pavement had been ripped up before the fire" (RSY NBK 54, 1955:73–77). Third, the fact that relatively large stretches of pavement were left intact in front of Megarons 1 and 2 suggests that these buildings were still in use when pavement removal began. Megarons 1 and 2 were nearly, but not completely, empty at the time of the fire, presumably in preparation for the extension of the construction project into this area (Gareth Darbyshire, pers. comm. 2008). If these buildings had gone entirely out of use (i.e., after the fire), we would not expect later builders to leave perfectly good and accessible building material lying about. There was some burned debris on this pavement, presumably just abandoned when work resumed after the fire, but blocks without debris were also left in place (RSY NBK 54, 1955:sketch plan p. 39).

Not only is there evidence for demolition in the area of the Outer Court before the fire, but there are also two areas to the west of the courts in which the ground level had been raised. First, the area between Megarons 2 and 3 or Megaron 2-3 Terrace was raised to the level of the TB Terrace:

> [The TB Terrace was] extended by a long tongue [east]ward to the edge of the square, burying the stump of the enclosure wall between the two buildings, which had been demolished; at its [east] end a stone staircase was built to give access from the square to the higher level. In the latest phase of M 3, then, the original level remained only at its…front—the level of the open square, here a pebbled rather than a stone-paved surface. At the other three sides the base of the building had been buried outside to a depth of nearly 2 m by the piling in of rubble to make the terrace. (Young 1962a:164)

Once the Stepped Terrace had been built (filling in the older stairway to the TB Terrace), the Megaron 2-3 Terrace Stairway would have provided the only known access to the TB Terrace from the east. It is tempting to link the construction of the Stepped and Megaron 2-3 terraces, but there is no way of knowing the exact chronological relationship of these two architectural elements.

Farther north, Megaron 4 had been built on

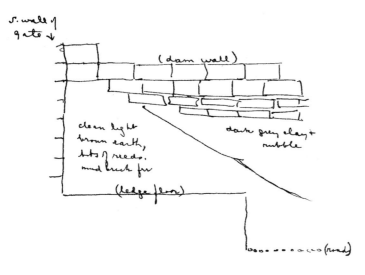

Fig. 6.25a-b. The Dam Wall after the rubble fill in the Gate Passage (above, foreground) has been removed. The layers of fill below the Dam Wall in this area are clearly visible in the photo as well as in the sketch section (left) made by G. Roger Edwards. In the background of the photo, the Drain Basin has been partially exposed. Source: Gordion Project, Penn Museum.

a platform that lay at a height comparable to both the Stepped and the Megaron 2-3 terraces (Young 1964:286–88, figs. 20–21) (Fig. 6.6). Megaron 4 is the only Destruction Level building to have been disturbed after the fire, and what remains of its contents suggested that it had once held considerable wealth. Before his death, Keith DeVries had considered the possibility that Megaron 4 was actually the residence of the king at the time of the fire, and that Megaron 3 (on the fringes of the construction zone) was then being used for storage (pers. comm. 2005). This interpretation can only be evaluated when complete inventories of these buildings and the arrangement of their contents are available.

Fig. 6.26. Removal of the Dam Wall within the YHSS 6A Gate Passage. The proximity of the Drain Basin (foreground) to the Dam Wall is clear. The relatively regular stone packing against the interior walls of the Drain Basin contrasts with its appearance today (Fig. 6.2). Source: Gordion Project, Penn Museum.

The Construction of the Dam Wall and Filling of the Early Phrygian/YHSS 6A Gateway

A tall thin wall runs from the southwest corner of the Early Phrygian/YHSS 6A Gateway diagonally across the North Court of the Gate Building (Fig. 6.5), establishing the line of the new Middle Phrygian/YHSS 5 Gate Building (compare Figs. 6.5 and 1.3). Young called this the Dam Wall because he saw its function as a barrier separating the fill of rubble and stone blocks against its ragged back (southeast) face, and the fill of clay resting against its smooth (northwest) face (Young 1955:12, figs. 29–30; 1956:252ff). The Dam Wall was built of stone blocks that are identical in color and form to those of the Early Phrygian/YHSS 6A Gate Complex, and it was not difficult to find their source: when excavated, part of the Early Phrygian/YHSS 6A Gate

Building had been demolished, including most of the north wall of the North Court, and the inner end of the south wall of the court (Figs. 6.24, 6.25; see also Young 1956:257).[6]

The first thing to consider in an attempt to determine when the Dam Wall was built is its relationship to the floor of the Early Phrygian/YHSS Gateway. Overlying the cobbled roadway within the Gateway and underlying the Dam Wall were two distinct deposits described by G. Roger Edwards when he removed part of the wall and excavated beneath it:

the dam wall was underlaid by a single stratum of very clean earth, light brown in color with a little admixture of mud brick and patches of powdery white vegetable matter probably decayed reeds. This layer is very thick adjacent to the s[outh] wall [of the gateway] …and extends from the lowest course of the dam wall here to the floor of the ledge [which runs along the wall of the Gate Passage]. The layer slopes down as it goes north and at the edge of the ledge is ca 30 cm thick. In the scarp it seems to go down and overlie the road floor…At a point 1.50 [m] from [the] s[outh]. wall this…layer is overlaid with a mixture of tough dark gray clay mixed with soft white stone rubble such as is used for wall stuffing—the beginning of the overall "clay blanket" [north] of the dam wall? (GRE NBK 45, 1953:17–18)

Several photos and a sketch section made by Edwards clearly show this stratification and indicate that the brown layer could be cut to a smooth face—a characteristic of the Middle Phrygian/YHSS 5 clay fills (Fig. 6.25a, b). Why this brown layer was put in place is not clear, but what it accomplished is readily apparent: it produced an even slope between the edge of the Early Phrygian/YHSS 6A Gateway wall and the middle of the Gateway Passage. The fill above the brown clay is less dense and may simply be intended to provide a more level surface for construction of the Dam Wall and for the Drain Basin as well. Edwards's description of the upper fill level is compatible (though not identical) with the stratum that Young describes at the bottom of the Drain Basin's interior (RSY NBK 49, 1955:102).

The base of the Dam Wall to some extent reflects the difference in the two fill deposits beneath it. The foundation course is stepped into the clean clay fill where the latter is high, along the Gateway wall (3 courses), and then has an added course near the low center of the Gateway Passage. The top of this segment of the Dam Wall is, however, relatively level. Although uncertainties remain, it is clear that an episode of filling occurred before the Dam Wall was built, and it is reasonable to accept Edwards's suggestion that the clay fill in the Gateway marks the start of laying fill inside the Gateway as well.

What the clay fills suggest is confirmed by solid rock. Young states that the masonry of the Dam Wall within the Early Phrygian/YHSS 6A Gate Passage could not have been laid once the Drain Basin was in place, since the southeast end of the Basin nearly abuts the Dam Wall (RSY NBK 49, 1955:68–70) (Figs. 6.5, 6.19, 6.25, 6.26). The assumption that

he presumably made is that the mason stood next to the smooth or northwestern face of the Dam Wall (rather than its very irregular southeastern or back face) when laying its blocks. We have already established that the Drain Basin was built before the fire, and Young's inference based on construction process places the Dam Wall before the fire as well.

Pushing the data a little further, it seems highly likely that the rubble behind the Dam Wall was raised at the same time as the wall for two related reasons. First, for the Dam Wall to fulfill its function as a barrier between stone and clay fills, it would need stability, which would be best achieved by packing the rubble fill carefully against its ragged back face, eliminating large voids in the rubble and block fill. Second, if the heavy stone fill were simply dumped in behind the Dam Wall, it is quite possible that its weight could collapse the lightly built (and not securely founded) Dam. There would be no problem in moving rubble into the Gate Passage, since the masons building the Dam Wall would be working from inside the citadel and materials placed against its rough face could be moved westward into and along the Gate Passage from the plain below. If this reconstruction of process is correct, then the filling of the Gateway had also begun before the fire.

The argument for a simultaneous laying of both the Dam Wall and rubble fill based on mechanical stability is even more critical for the trapezoidal area within the Early Phrygian/YHSS 6A North Court of the Gate Building. Even if voids were not as critical here (because the Dam Wall was founded on a flat surface), it is hard to see how this thin 4-m-high wall would stand if rubble were dumped down into the restricted space behind it from the top of the Early Phrygian/YHSS 6A Fortification Wall (Fig. 6.24). That the rubble was either dumped in or carefully laid in from the southeast is again suggested by the difference in the two faces of the Dam Wall. On the other hand, moderate amounts of rubble dumped in as the Dam Wall grew in height would presumably do little damage.

A final argument for construction of the entire Dam Wall (and thus the fill behind it) before the fire comes from the great variation in the height of this structure from one end to the other. The high point of the Dam Wall lies within the North Court, where, as stated above, the wall extends more than 4 m above the court floor; it then dips down over the wall of the gateway proper and is only 4 courses high in the middle of the gateway (Figs. 6.25, 6.26).[7] The first question is: Why would the Phrygians have bothered to carefully construct a smooth wall face that would never have been visible to the inhabitants of the Palace Quarter, i.e., if there was no one living there at the time the Dam Wall was built? A rough stone retaining wall would have served just as well (RSY NBK 49, 1955:4). Second, the varied height of the Dam Wall strongly suggests that it was never completed, and if the primary purpose of the Dam Wall was to separate stone from clay fills, then why was it abandoned when only partially built? I would suggest that Dam Wall construction ceased when the Palace Quarter was emptied as a result of the fire, and when appearance and safety were no longer of concern.

These arguments based on construction techniques and processes are the only ones available to us: no evidence of burning or charcoal within the Gateway fills were recorded by Young. It does, however, make a great deal of sense if enlargement and strengthening of the new fortification system was under way at the *start* of the major construction project that is documented by the Unfinished Project. Fortifications would presumably have a high priority when beginning something as grand as the Middle Phrygian/YHSS 5 reconstruction of the citadel.

A Revised Understanding of the Gate Area before the Unfinished Project Began

If the Stone Enclosure Wall running between Megarons 1 and 9 was put up at some time well before the beginning of the Unfinished Project, as now seems certain, it would then have blocked off the formal elite buildings around the Outer Court from the Gateway and Gate Building Courts, the latter presumably storage areas. Moreover, anyone who entered the Gateway would have been able to go up the wide TB Terrace Stairway at the south of Megaron 1 onto the TB Terrace, and through a small entrance room to the Terrace and CC buildings (Figs. 1.2, 6.6). This short straight route would have facilitated the movement of bulk goods including food, pottery

containers, wool, and other fibers into the Terrace and CC buildings where all of these materials were processed.

We cannot say whether there was a passage through the Stone Enclosure Wall into the Outer Court, but one piece of evidence suggests that there may not have been such an opening. At the east end of the Stepped Terrace, its stone retaining wall is made up of two parts. Looking at plans and photographs of the masonry of the stub wall running between the western end of the Stone Enclosure Wall and Megaron 1, the way in which the blocks were laid indicates that all but about 10–20 cm of this short north leg of walling is later, set in a gap between the northern face of the western end of the Stone Enclosure Wall and the south face of Megaron 1 (Figs. 6.5, 6.6, 6.10). An L-shaped block extending north about 10–20 cm at the western end of the Stone Enclosure Wall would thus suggest the presence of a narrow doorway leading between the enclosure wall and Megaron 1 (RSY NBK 61 1959:97). If we consider that before the Unfinished Project began, the main stairway up to the buildings on top of the TB Terrace lay to the west, a doorway between the Stone Enclosure Wall and Megaron 1 would have allowed people to move back and forth between the Terrace Buildings (where cooking took place on a massive scale) and the megarons around the Outer Court.

The presence of the Stone Enclosure Wall, with or without a doorway, does resolve a question that has puzzled just about everyone who has studied the plan of Early Phrygian/YHSS 6A Gordion. The Gate Passage and Polychrome House retained an orientation established in YHSS 6B, the time of the first formal buildings in this area. When the orientation of the megarons inside the Gate changed during the initial construction phase of Early Phrygian/YHSS 6A, anyone coming through the Gateway faced west toward an area that may have been open early in 6A, but that was eventually filled by the massive TB Terrace (DeVries 1990: fig. 4). Thus, in the latter years of the Early Phrygian/YHSS 6A period, there was only a small triangular area inside the Gateway, which was further constricted by the Stone Enclosure Wall. Access to the North and South Courts of the Gate Building, large areas that were presumably used for storage, would have been maintained, and the newly discovered TB Terrace Stairway lay in a straight line from the entrance through the Polychrome House. It therefore seems likely that during the latter part of the Early Phrygian/YHSS 6A period, the great Gate Passage was used primarily for bringing in supplies and taking out finished products such as food and textiles.

The erection of the Stone Enclosure Wall may in fact have been part of a larger building program that included a new and perhaps grander entrance that led into the Palace Quarter. Young had long argued for a second gate to the formal buildings of the Inner and Outer Courts during the Early Phrygian/YHSS 6A period. In his report on the 1959 season he states:

> The area to the [north] of the Polychrome House has not been completely investigated as yet, nor is it thoroughly understood. An impression emerges, however, and is strengthened as the area is cleared, that the [southern] gate of the city became of less importance with the passage of time…The [south] gate was evidently becoming a little-used back door to the city. The orientation of all the important buildings of the Phrygian town…suggests the existence of another and more important gate which gave access to the city from the [east]." (Young 1960:236)

Young initially looked to the east by extending a narrow trench in that direction, only to find a solid defensive wall; he then looked to the north, where he again found the fortification system, this time over a significant excavated area (Fig. 1.2; see also DeVries 1990:378–79, figs. 7, 10, 28).

If there was a second gate it would solve a second and very practical problem. Once the Drainage Basin and the Dam Wall were in place, the southern gateway was blocked, whether or not the rubble filling of the Gate Building had begun. How, then, were the tons of fill that were deposited inside the citadel brought through its fortification wall? The relatively small amount of clay and rubble needed for the construction of the Proto-C Building and other parts of the Unfinished Project could have been brought in through the door in the Brick Enclosure Wall and carried from a hypothetical gate to the east or north. If there was a gate to the west,

these materials could even have been dumped off the south end of the TB Terrace. But there must have been a more efficient way to bring in the massive fills of earth and rubble used after the fire. Only more excavation or precise subsurface testing will provide an answer to the problem of the hypothetical second gate.

Conclusions

The Phrygian rulers of the 10th and 9th centuries BC seem to have been incorrigible builders, constantly changing and remodeling their settlement at Gordion, and to some extent we can document the sequence of such changes using stratigraphy. The information preserved by the fire that destroyed much of this settlement ca. 800 BC is, however, something quite rare—an endpoint that paradoxically reveals not only details of everyday life, but also a great deal of information on construction processes and planning.

What, then, have we learned about the city plan represented by the Unfinished Project? The evidence shows that in 800 BC the gateway into the Phrygian Palace Quarter was being raised, apparently to the level of the tops of the older fortification walls (based on the preserved height of the Dam Wall). We cannot know what the form of the new gate and associated fortification walls would have been, but we can say that the new gate foundations indicate a shift in alignment that was eventually used for the Middle Phrygian Gate. Within the citadel, the Stepped Terrace and Eastern Terrace show that the Phrygians were engaged in raising the level of major public buildings around the two courts to a height compatible with that of the new gateway. Architectural fragments (Building Proto-C, the Eastern Terrace) show that the methods of construction typical of the Middle Phrygian period were also being used in the Unfinished Project: deep clay fills, rubble foundations, and multicolored squared ashlar blocks. The project was not, however, intended to change the entire area within the citadel: the Phrygians clearly wanted to leave the relatively "new" service buildings on the TB Terrace in place.

Whatever the original plan, the Middle Phrygian/YHSS 5 citadel rebuilding following the fire was literally a monumental undertaking. The use of fills to raise the level of buildings and construct enormous artificial burial mounds is also material evidence of the burgeoning political power at Gordion during the 9th and 8th centuries BC. At other times and in other places in the Near East, powerful rulers chose to use stone and sculpture to demonstrate their control over people and labor. The Phrygians used stone too, but they focused just as much attention on remodeling the landscape, creating new heights where their kings could be housed in both life and death.

Acknowledgments

Excavation and survey at Gordion since 1988 have been supported by grants from the National Endowment for the Humanities (NEH, a US federal agency), the Social Science and Humanities Research Council of Canada, the National Geographic Society, the Royal Ontario Museum, the Kress Foundation, the IBM Foundation, the Tanberg Trust, and by gifts from generous private donors. All modern archaeological research at Gordion (1950–2006) has been sponsored and supported by the University of Pennsylvania Museum; the College of William and Mary has been a co-sponsor since 1991, and the Royal Ontario Museum co-sponsored work carried out between 1994 and 2002. G. Kenneth Sams gave me permission to work on the Unfinished Project in his capacity as editor for publication of the Young excavations. Gordion Archivist Gareth Darbyshire helped me to obtain notebook facsimiles and photographs. Phoebe Sheftel provided digital drawings of many plans, and engaged in lively discussions of Building C that clarified my thinking about this structure. Publication drawings were prepared by Sondra Jarvis and Carrie Alblinger. Editorial comments on the text were provided by Robert H. Dyson, Jr., Robert Henrickson, and Peter Kuniholm. To all of them I offer my thanks.

NOTES

6.1.   This is equivalent to Phase EBB VII in the Early Phrygian sequence used by Sams 1994a:13–14.

6.2.   A large multi-roomed structure shown on previous plans of the Destruction Level (the PPB) was probably not built until the Middle Phrygian period, but this remains to be confirmed by new excavation.

6.3.   References to the notebooks include: the initials of the excavator, notebook number, year in which the notebook was written, and notebook pages. The excavators cited here are Rodney S. Young (RSY), G. Roger Edwards (GRE), and Charles K. Williams II (CKW).

6.4.   For a description of the pavement and its stratigraphic position see Voigt 1994:271–72 (CS 5), and Sams 1994a:10.

6.5.   Megaron 9 was built at the same time as the drain that runs under the stone pavement of the YHSS 6A Outer Court (Young 1964:290; Sams 1994a:10, his Phase EPB V). Its foundations are deep, set into the fill that covered the YHSS 6B Early Phrygian Building, and both the Megaron 9 foundations and the 6A drain incorporate shaped stones of soft white stone ("poros") which must come from the PAP building, demolished at the end of YHSS 6B (Voigt 1994:271, Courtyard Stages 4-5; Voigt and Henrickson 2000:49–50, figs. 6–7).

6.6.   When Young took down the Dam Wall to free the Early Phrygian YHSS 6A Gate Building, he took the opportunity to reverse what he saw as destructive "Persian" behavior, and used the Dam Wall blocks to rebuild those sections of the Early Phrygian Gate Building that had been dismantled as part of the Unfinished Project (Young 1956:258, figs. 28–29).

6.7.   I have been unable to find either elevations for the Dam Wall within the gateway or a measured drawing which would give us its height at this point.

7

Pictures in Stone: Incised Drawings on Early Phrygian Architecture

Lynn E. Roller

A group of drawings from Megaron 2, one of the buildings from the Gordion Destruction Level excavated in 1956 and 1957, has long lain in the shadow of the more famous discoveries of those early Gordion years. Yet because these drawings have the potential to offer considerable information on several aspects of the culture and society of the Early Phrygian city, they merit further attention. The greatest number of drawings were located on the exterior surface of the side and back walls of the megaron, incised directly onto the stone blocks from which the megaron's walls were constructed; two others have been noted on the Early Phrygian Gate. Rodney S. Young, who was responsible for their initial excavation and publication, nicknamed them "doodlestones" because he assumed that they were random marks and pictures scratched onto the walls of the standing building by the general public waiting outside (Young 1957:323, figs. 10–12; Young 1958:142–43, fig. 3; Young 1963, 1969a).

Young's assessment of the nature of the drawings and the circumstances under which they were incised onto the walls of Megaron 2 has rarely been challenged, except by Mellink (1983:357–58). Yet a closer review of the drawings and their position on the building walls shows that Young's initial assumption is very unlikely. It is more probable that the drawings were incised onto the individual blocks of Megaron 2 before the building was constructed, and that this was done not by casual passers-by, but by those who had access to the building blocks during the building's construction. Moreover, the range of subject matter in the drawings is greater than

Young's description would suggest. Several of the drawings do fit Young's label of "doodles," since they are little more than haphazard lines or careless drawings by an untutored hand, perhaps the product of workers who were testing their tools or simply amusing themselves. Others, however, depict complex compositions done with considerable sophistication. Some scenes reveal close familiarity with the style and subject matter of the formal sculptural programs of southeastern Anatolia, while others keenly record contemporary life around Gordion.

Since I have discussed the placement of the drawings and their relationship with Neo-Hittite sculptural style elsewhere (Roller 1999a, 2005, and 2009), this chapter addresses one potential source for the drawings, the observation of contemporary life in the early Phrygian community, with special focus on drawings of architecture. Several drawings record architectural types used within the city, as well as scenes of daily life involving animals.

The drawings depicting architectural structures form an intriguing group. They reproduce the elevation of a building, and the likeliest source for such a building is the architecture found in the city of Gordion itself. Three clear examples of architectural elevations appear on one stone block, which in its current state consists of two non-joining fragments (Gordion inventory no. ST 263a and b; Roller 2009: no. 9a and b) (Fig. 7.1a, b). The stone was recovered from the east wall of Megaron 2, where it had fallen to the ground together with a number of other incised stones, evidently as a result of the wall's collapse due to the fire that destroyed the building. Its

Fig. 7.1a. Drawing on ST 263a, actual state. Source: Gordion Archives., Penn Museum

Fig. 7.1b. Drawing on ST 263b, actual state. Source: Gordion Archives, Penn Museum.

Fig. 7.2. Drawing on ST 263a. Illustration: author.

original position on the wall of Megaron 2 is unknown. The relationship of the two fragments to each other was recorded in a drawing made at the time of excavation (Young 1957: pl. 90, fig. 12; Young 1969a:272 top). In each case one sees the rectangular face of a building surmounted by a triangular pediment, indicating that the view is that of the short end of a building with a pitched roof. One of the drawings shows a door in the building's end wall. In two cases the building is taller than it is wide, while the building's façade is nearly square in the third drawing. These factors strongly suggest that the drawings depict the elevation of one end of a Phrygian megaron, such as those constituting the most common building type in the Citadel Mound with a pitched roof and a doorway in the short end of the building (Sams 1994a:212).

This discussion of the three architectural elevations is based on the photographs of the incised stones and on my drawings of the two surviving parts of the stone, made from autopsy in 1992 and 1993 and further refined in 2001 and 2004 (Figs. 7.2, 7.3). A drawing based on tracings of the two parts of the incised block was made in 1956 and has since been published elsewhere (Young 1957: pl. 90, fig. 12; Young 1969a:272; Mellink 1983:357, fig. 1; Berndt-Ersöz 2006:396, fig. 119). But an examination of the actual stone shows that the 1956 draw-

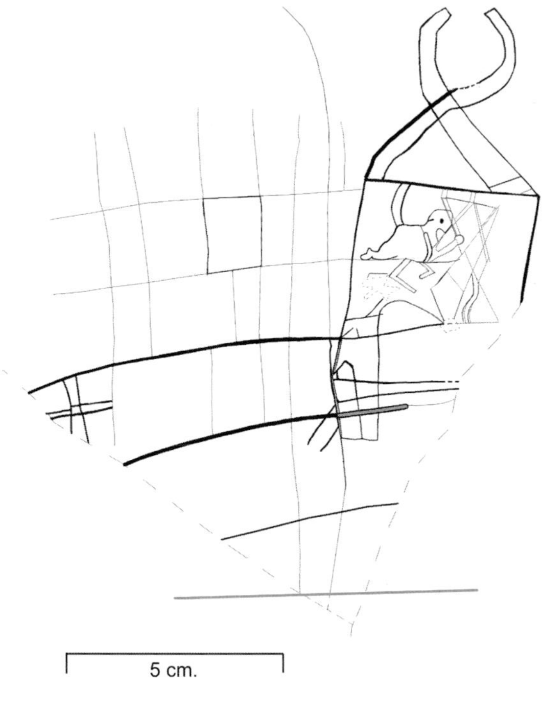

Fig. 7.3. Drawing on ST 263b. Illustration: author.

ing contains several significant errors, so the new and more accurate drawings should provide a more reliable basis for analysis. The three architectural elevations depicted on the block have usually been discussed together as a unit, but close examination reveals that they differ from each other in several ways and probably show three separate structures. The center of the three elevations, which I will examine first, seems to be the simplest and most straightforward drawing. I will then analyze the one at the left, and finally the one at the right, the most complex of the three.

The center elevation (here called Building A) depicts the wall of a building surmounted by the triangular end of a steeply pitched roof supported by a central vertical beam. Lines forming the side walls of the building continue beyond the top of the wall into the roof area, although whether this reproduces an intentional construction feature or is just sloppy drawing is not certain. Similar lines can also be seen in the elevation at the left, Building B, though these seem more clearly to be the result of careless drawing. The diagonal lines outlining the roof extend above the central ridgepole to form a V pattern; this is likely to be intentional, illustrating the extension of the sloping rafters above the ridgepole to create a decorative pattern of horns on the roof. In the center of the building's façade is a double door composed of two leaves, each made from a row of vertical beams bound together with two horizontal cross beams. To the right of the double door is a small rectangle, probably a window, while over the door is a circle with small lines inside it, presumably a form of decoration placed on the building wall. The building's wide double doors and exterior decoration above the door suggest that it was an imposing structure of some importance.

The second building (Building B), incised to the left of Building A, also depicts the end of a rectangular building, in this case a tall, narrow structure with a steeply pitched roof forming a high gable supported by a central vertical beam. Above the central point of the gable are lines in the shape of a crescent, although it is difficult to be certain whether this depicts a separate decorative element such as an akroterion placed on the building's roof, or a horn pattern formed by rafters that continued above the gable point, similar to that depicted in Building A.

Set into the center of the building's wall is a rectangle; this is likely to indicate a window, since it is too high above ground level to be a door. Lines in the pediment form small rectangles, one to the left of the central beam and two to the right; these appear to illustrate a set of windows in the pediment. The lower left portion of the building wall overlaps a drawing of a bird of prey, shown in right profile. The incised lines of the building are heavier than those of the bird; thus it seems likely that the bird was drawn first and the building was incised later over the bird.

This drawing has attracted much attention, since it has been thought to illustrate a Phrygian temple (Mellink 1983:357–58; Sams 1995:1156–57). Several reasons for this explanation have been advanced. The principal one is the overall similarity between the megaron elevation drawn on the stone and the architectural façades that appear in several cult reliefs of the Phrygian Mother Goddess Matar, both orthostates from central Phrygia and reliefs carved directly into the live rock of the Phrygian Highlands (Haspels 1971:73–111; Naumann 1983:38–62; Berndt-Ersöz 2006:21–40, 51–53; see also Roller 1999b:71–105). These cult reliefs also illustrate the short end of a building with a gabled roof and a door in the center of the wall, and in several examples an image of the goddess standing in the doorway makes their use as cult objects uncontestable.

In addition to the general similarities of appearance, a number of specific details in this drawing have been interpreted as indicators of cult. One is the presence of the rectangle in the center of the wall; I have called it a window, but others see it as a cult niche such as those found in several carved façades of the Phrygian Highlands. The windows in the pediment of the building are another feature found in several Highland cult façades. Also similar to the cult façades is the curved ornament at the peak of the gable: such curved akroterion horns are regularly found on Phrygian cult reliefs, both orthostates from central Phrygia and cult façades in the Phrygian Highlands. Finally, the position of the building over the bird of prey invites the suggestion that this building was a temple of the Phrygian goddess Matar, since a bird of prey was a frequent attribute of the goddess. I would like to examine each of these features in turn.

The general similarity between the building

type in the Megaron 2 drawing and that found in Phrygian cult reliefs is clear. Both illustrate the short end of a megaron. In Early Phrygian Gordion, however, the megaron plan was used for many buildings with a variety of functions, ranging from the Terrace Building, used for food and textile preparation, to Megaron 3, probably a residence for the elite. Thus, the presence of the megaron type in itself is not indicative of cult function. Each feature noted above in the drawing is similarly equivocal. The rectangle in the center of the building wall has some visual similarity to the cult niches in the rock monuments of Phrygia, but it makes little sense to assume that this rectangle depicted a niche. The drawing presumably was intended to represent an actual building, and a three-dimensional building would be unlikely to have a niche set in its front wall. The cult façades in the Phrygian Highlands are dummy façades that represent the exterior surface of a building with no interior space. The devotee of the cult approaches the façade knowing that it is a flat two-dimensional surface, and expects, for example, to place an offering in the façade niche or to pray to an image of a deity set in the niche. The function of an actual cult building is quite different: a worshipper knows that the building encloses space, and expects to enter the building to perform a ritual act or stand at the door and look at a sacred object such as a cult statue within the building. Assuming that the Megaron 2 drawing represents an actual building, what purpose would be served in illustrating a cult niche on the exterior wall? I therefore assume that the central rectangle on the drawing depicts a window.

The connection of the windows shown in the pediment with a Phrygian cult is also tenuous. Such windows appear in three of the carved façades in the Phrygian Highlands that replicate architectural structures, the Areyastis Monument and the Unfinished and Hyacinth Monuments at Midas City, in each case with closed shutters (Berndt-Ersöz 2006:33). The reason for their presence in the Highlands cult façades is probably because such a window was found on the actual building imitated by the façade. Thus, the purpose of the window is to be sought, not in its relationship to cult ritual, but in the role that it played in a three-dimensional building. Windows on an upper level can be a common feature of utilitarian buildings such as a barn, where they provide light and access to an upper story; gable windows also serve the practical purpose of allowing smoke to escape from a building that has an interior hearth but no chimney. Since several of the megarons in the Gordion Destruction Level had hearths set in the center of an interior room, they would have needed some means of air intake and smoke ventilation, and a gable window could well have served that purpose. The representation of pediment windows in both the Gordion incised drawing and the carved cult façades may consequently have had nothing to do with cultic function; rather, in both cases the picture or cult relief could illustrate a window used for ventilation that was actually present on a real building.

The curved ornament on the building's roof recalls similar ornaments found on building façades and on many of the cult façades (Berndt-Ersöz 2006:29–30). As noted above, the curved ornament could represent horns, i.e., sloping rafters extending beyond the roof gable, or a separate stone akroterion, of which several examples are known from Gordion (Sams 1994a:212–13; Voigt 1994:271; Voigt 2005:29). Whether made of timber or stone, the curved akroterion was a decorative feature intended to make a building appear more conspicuous and therefore more noteworthy; its presence in these drawings presumably indicates that the buildings illustrated fulfilled some special function in the community. The roof decoration in itself, however, is not a symbol of cult practice.

For many scholars the main feature of this drawing connecting it to Phrygian cult practice is the building's position overlapping the bird of prey. A bird of prey was a common attribute of the Phrygian Mother Goddess and appears in conjunction with her images from several Phrygian sites, including Gordion.[1] Drawing the building over the sacred symbol of the deity would therefore seem to link the two. Such an interpretation remains very speculative, however, since a great many of the Megaron 2 drawings show one figure incised on top of another, often without regard to subject matter.

A drawing of two human figures fighting (Gordion inventory no. ST 256, Young 1969a:270 top; Roller 2009: no. 14) illustrates this point: the right figure overlaps a lion facing right, and both figures are overlaid by two large birds, one facing left and one facing right. In another drawing (Gordion inventory no. ST 262, Roller 1999a:146, fig. 3; Roller 2009: no. 8), one sees one large quadruped which overlaps with part of another, as well as two birds standing upright and the outspread wings of a third. The same stone on which the building elevations appear provides further evidence of this circumstance, since the rear part of a quadruped can be seen below Building B with a series of random lines at the animal's right. Thus, the conjunction of the bird with the building elevation may imply a relationship between the two subjects, but it may also mean nothing. Given the frequency of drawings that combine two or more unrelated subjects, it seems best to assume that the two elements of this drawing, bird and building, are also unrelated.

None of the features that have been adduced to interpret this drawing as an illustration of a Phrygian temple is convincing. Indeed, the depiction of the window in the building's center may suggest that we are looking at the back of the building, since we would expect to see a door in the front wall. In that case the curved decoration atop the roof gable would be horns formed by the roof timbers of the building.

Turning to the third drawing, Building C (Roller 2005:127, fig. 3; Roller 2009: no. 9b), one also sees the short end of a rectangular building with a gabled roof, but with several unique features. The outline of this building's roof is drawn with parallel double lines, suggesting that more than a simple wooden beam is being depicted, and the double outline extends well above the roof gable in a curved-V with inverted arms. Here one can assume that the drawing illustrates a stone akroterion with horns that curve inward (Sams 1994a: pl. 20.3.2). Fragments of such akroteria have been found at Gordion in an Early Phrygian level, and a nearly intact akroterion, with horns that curve outward, was found in the fill above Megaron 2 (Sams 1994a: pls. 20.2, 20.3.4).

In this drawing, no door signals that we are looking at the front of a building, but an animal with a raised tail, drawn in right profile, is visible within the outlines of the building's front wall. This feature

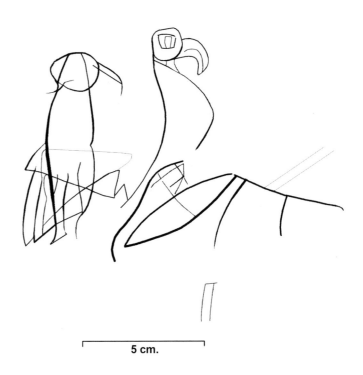

5 cm.

Fig 7.4. Drawing on ST 273. Illustration: author.

was omitted from the previously published drawing of this stone, but it can be seen in the photograph and is clearly visible on the actual stone. This is probably a lion, and here it surely represents a type of decoration on the building's façade, either a relief sculpture or a painted drawing. Next to the lion one can see crossed diagonal lines forming a lozenge pattern; these are very faint, but seem intended to illustrate some form of geometric ornament that would also have decorated the building's front façade. The combination of lion and geometric pattern implies that this drawing represents the decorated façade of an imposing public building.

The lion is one of the most frequent subjects in the group of Megaron 2 drawings, regularly shown in right profile and with a raised tail. Details such as an open mouth and sharp claws emphasize the animal's ferocity.[2] While the lion drawn on the architectural façade is too small to offer a minute level of detail, the striding pose and raised tail suggest that this animal was intended as a symbol of power, further reinforcing the imposing nature of the building's appearance. Below the building is a series of horizontal parallel lines which may represent stairs

Fig. 7.5. Drawing on ST 317, actual state. Source: Gordion Archives, Penn Museum.

Fig. 7.6. Drawing on ST 317. Illustration: author.

that led up to the building's entrance.

Thus, one can see that the drawings illustrate three rather different buildings, probably with different functions. Two—A and C—seem to show the front of impressive public buildings, while the third—B—may be the rear view of a building that is not marked as particularly special. The drawings also suggest that the concept of stone akroteria with

inward-curving horns on a Phrygian building may have originated as curved wooden rafters that were translated into stone to create a more impressive effect as an architectural decoration.

Regarding the bird that overlaps with Building B, I have argued against the assumption that the bird must connect the building with the cult of the Phrygian Mother Goddess. But if the bird was not a

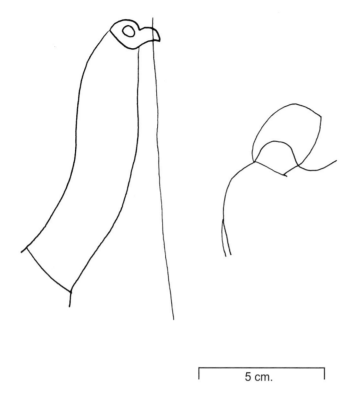

5 cm.

Fig. 7.7. Drawing on ST 281. Illustration: author.

to illustrate birds that were actually present in the daily life of the Phrygian settlement. Because a hawk or falcon was a frequent attribute of the Phrygian Mother Goddess, several scholars have used the drawings of raptors to postulate a prominent position for the goddess's cult in the Early Phrygian city, but this remains very uncertain. No image of the Phrygian Mother is known from the Early Phrygian city, nor are there any artifacts that can be definitively connected with her cult, so one cannot be sure whether the hawk was a cult symbol at this early date.

A few drawings, moreover, encourage an alternative explanation for the appearance of the raptor. Rodney Young drew attention to one (Gordion inventory no. ST 273; Roller 2009: no. 19) in which two birds appear, one resting on what seems to be an outstretched human arm (Young 1969a:275; Mellink 1983:357–58, fig. 2) (Fig. 7.4). Young suggested that this drawing may be an illustration of falconry, with the birds shown as if perched on a leather arm guard. Another drawing in the Megaron 2 group (Gordion inventory no. ST 317; Roller 2009: no. 46) supports Young's suggestion (Figs. 7.5, 7.6). One can see a man wearing a short kilt with a dagger at his waist. He is standing with his left arm outstretched and his right drawn back and up; two birds in flight are shown to each side of him. Although the drawing is somewhat crudely executed, it appears to show a man who stands as if swinging a lure over his head, perhaps to attract a falcon to return to him and perch on his outstretched arm. In this, one sees another example of falconry in action. Another drawing (Gordion inventory no. ST 281; Roller 2009: no. 21) of a bird with the sharp beak of a raptor, whose body appears to be wrapped in some type of cloak, could be intended to depict a hooded falcon (Fig. 7.7). These drawings could reflect contemporary interest in falconry.

Finally, a drawing (Gordion inventory no. ST 298; Roller 2009: no. 38) found on another stone illustrates a completely different type of architectural structure (Figs. 7.8, 7.9). The stone is cracked in several places, and its surface is partially damaged,

cult symbol, what is the reason for its presence? To answer this we need to consider the images of birds in the broader context of these drawings.

Birds form the single most common subject matter in the Gordion drawings, appearing on nearly half of all the incised stones (Roller 2009:26–27). A variety of avian species can be noted, including a duck (Gordion inventory no. ST 841; Roller 2009: no. 94), storks (Roller 2009: nos. 2, 50, 71), a chicken (Gordion inventory no. ST 839; Roller 2009: no. 50), and birds with impressive crests (Gordion inventory no. ST 394; Roller 2009: nos. 67, 104). Far and away the most common species is the bird of prey or raptor. These are frequently shown in profile, where their pronounced beak and sharp talons are displayed conspicuously (Young 1969a:274, top right; 275, top left; Roller 2005:126, fig. 1; Roller 2009: nos. 11, 69). Most of the birds appear alone or in the company of other raptors, but are not actively engaged in any activity. It is unclear whether the raptor was chosen mainly for its symbolic value, alluding to hunting or predation, or for the desire

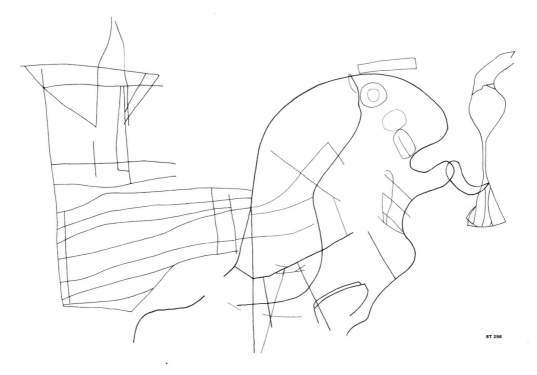

ST 298

Fig. 7.8 (top). Drawing on ST 298, actual state. Source: Gordion Archives, Penn Museum.

Fig. 7.9. Drawing on ST 298. Illustration: author.

but a drawing with several interesting features is still discernible. At the left of the drawing an irregular rectangle is formed by single vertical line on each side and a pair of horizontal parallel lines at the top and bottom. In the center of the rectangle, two parallel vertical lines are topped by an irregularly drawn triangle. Additional lines extend diagonally from the upper corners of the rectangle down toward the center. Below is a series of parallel horizontal lines, irregularly drawn. To the right of the rectangle, the head of a large lion faces right with its mouth open and its tongue hanging out; at the far right a bird with an elongated tail is shown in profile.

The drawing at the left is likely to depict the wall of a wooden structure with horizontal bracing at the top and bottom and diagonal bracing across the center, perhaps a wooden gate. This seems unlikely to be a separate building, but could be part of a wooden fortification wall, such as a stockade, or it could be a gate with two leaves. The tall pointed structure in the center may be a tower, although it would be surprising to see a tower placed in the middle of a gate, which is one reason for preferring the interpretation of a stockade wall. Alternatively, if the drawing represents a gate, the actual tower would have been placed at the side of the gate, and the drawing distorts the perspective to make the tower appear more conspicuous. The series of parallel horizontal lines below the structure could represent a flight of stairs leading up to the wall/gate. The lion and bird at the right are probably unrelated to the main subject of the drawing, another instance of drawings with unrelated subject matter shown together, as noted above. This drawing is more carelessly done and lacks the level of precision and detail found in the three drawings of megarons, so this interpretation must remain provisional. If correct, it would give us one view of a wooden wall or gate found in the Early Phrygian city.

These are but a few of the examples of the Early Phrygian drawings than can offer valuable information on both the physical and social aspects of contemporary life at Gordion. Analysis of them is not only informative, but should also induce caution in our study of the early levels of the city. We cannot simply rely on interpretations that are supported by material from later Phrygian culture and assume that these same interpretations are valid for the earliest phases of the Phrygian settlement. In this, as in other ways, the study of these Early Phrygian drawings presents both a challenge and an opportunity to expand our knowledge.

NOTES

7.1.   The examples from Gordion include four cult reliefs—Mellink 1983: pl. 72, fig. 1-3, pl. 73, fig. 2; Roller 1999b: figs. 7 and 12; a cult relief from Ankara—Roller 1999b: fig. 8; and a statue found near Ayaş—Naumann 1983:67, no. 21.

7.2.   For examples of lions, see Roller 2009: nos. 1, 4, 6, 7, 10, 29, 38, 48, 53, 56, 58, 80, 83, 98, 99, 102. See the discussion in Roller 2009:23–25.

8

Early Bronze Fibulae and Belts from the Gordion Citadel Mound

Maya Vassileva

Gordion has yielded one of the largest collections of bronze objects in the Near East from the early 1st millennium BC, rivaled only by the finds from Hasanlu and Luristan in northwestern Iran. This extensive bronze assemblage clearly demonstrates the role of Gordion, and Phrygia in general, as a major bronze-producing center in Anatolia. Nearly a thousand bronze objects of Phrygian date were excavated on the Citadel Mound between 1950 and 1974, and although all of them form part of my research, I present here my preliminary conclusions concerning only two categories of objects: fibulae and belts.[1]

Fibulae

The fibulae are the most abundant group of bronze objects found at the Citadel Mound. In view of the current re-examination of artifacts and stratigraphy prompted by the new Gordion chronology, the fibulae from this stratum are of special interest.[2] The Destruction Level on the Citadel Mound (hereafter, DL) yielded 41 fibulae: 38 are bronze, and the remaining 3 are gold, silver, and electrum (Table 8.1). It is not a coincidence that the only fibulae of precious metals were discovered in Terrace Building 2, which has often been considered a treasury because of the other elite goods found in the same room (Young 1962a:165–67, pls. 46–47; DeVries 1980a:38; Sams 1993:552).

There are several conclusions that emerge from a statistical and stylistic analysis of the fibulae. The earliest type in the city is XII.7A (Caner 1983:51–60,

type A I, 1-2; Muscarella 2003:229), and they are the most frequently discovered: 23 out of 41.[3] These fibulae have a large flat, D- or horseshoe-shaped arc, and the ends, with the characteristic "horned" catch, are usually narrower than the middle of the arc. Two rather crudely manufactured pieces have very wide arcs (B1977a and B564b), and the cone-shaped catch-ends are cast together with the pin. One interesting example shows a detachable spring and pin that fit to the catch-end by a hollow cone. The tension of the spring keeps the pin in place (B1971) (Fig. 8.1a, b).[4]

These fibulae seem earlier than the main XII.7 type, and indeed, it has already been observed that the XII.7 types derived from XII.7A, although they had a chronological overlap (Young 1981:244; Muscarella 1967:43; 2003:231). Fibulae of the XII.7A type were discovered in Tumuli W, G, KIII and IV, and S (Table 8.2), which are the earliest in the tumuli sequence (Young 1981:209–11, TumW 29–33, 35–55; Kohler 1995:39, TumG 5, pl. 21E; 97, TumS 2, pl. 52E; Körte and Körte 1904:78, No. 26; 102, Nos. 11-12). It is worth noting that in Tumulus W, which is the earliest, 26 examples of the XII.7A fibula type were discovered, but none of XII.7 type.

There are three more unpublished fibulae of this type from tumuli (two from cremation burials), but none of them originates from the burial chamber; they come either from earlier, pre-burial contexts or from secondary deposits.[5] These fibulae are mostly found in Phrygia proper, primarily at Gordion and Ankara, and so far no examples are known from the western Anatolian coast (Caner 1983:53, 68).[6] Their spread and use seem to be short-lived: they did not

Table 8.1. Types of fibulae found in the Destruction Level at the Gordion Citadel Mound.

Type of Fibulae	XII.5	XII.7A	XII.9	XII.14	'Leech'	Arched	Near Eastern	Other
Building								
CC2		3			1			
CC3		10			2	2		
Megaron 4			1					
TB2	2 (gold and silver)	1 + 1 electrum						
TB3		1			4			
TB7		2			1			1 wire-wrapped
TB8		2		1			3	
Uncatalogued		3˙						

˙ These uninventoried fibulae were found in the Gordion Museum depot, without any reference to their context. They might have originated from the DL as they are XII.7A type, badly burned, and cracked from bronze disease.

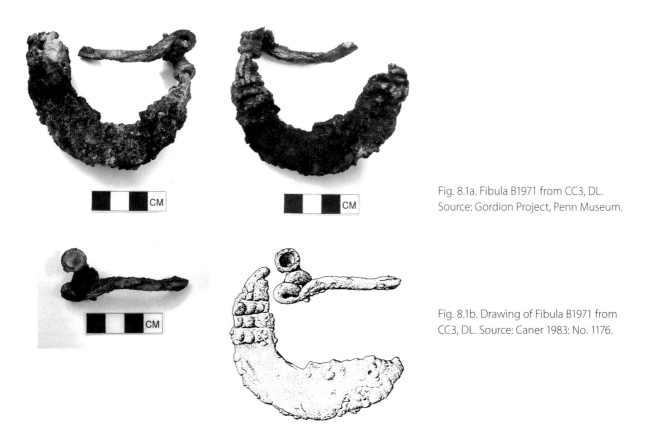

Fig. 8.1a. Fibula B1971 from CC3, DL. Source: Gordion Project, Penn Museum.

Fig. 8.1b. Drawing of Fibula B1971 from CC3, DL. Source: Caner 1983: No. 1176.

outlive by much the rebuilding of the Middle Phrygian Citadel (such as B1217, which was found in the clay deposit), and therefore help us identify the earliest contexts at Gordion.

Almost the entire variety of Phrygian (and Anatolian) fibulae types known from later contexts and other locations are missing from the DL city repertoire (already noted by Mellink 1981:269). The only

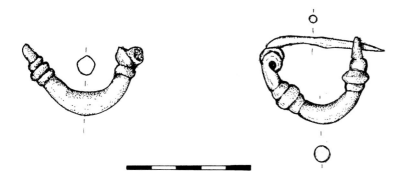

Fig. 8.2. The two arched fibulae B1988c and d from CC3, DL. Illustrations: author. Source: Gordion Project, Penn Museum.

Table 8.2. Types of fibulae found in the Gordion tumuli.

Type of fibulae	XII.2	XII.2A	XII.3	XII.4	XII.5	XII.7	XII.7A	XII.9	XII.9β	XII.11	XII.13	XII.14	Leach	NE	Other
TUMULI															
W				2					26				6		
G							1						2		
Y											1		1(?)*		1**
Q							2(?)***				1				
S							1								
KIII	1			8(?)****	1	5	24(?)	1			2				
P			14												
KIV						6	11(?)	5			3	6			
MM						40		51		33	1	19			
S1	2	3						1	7	4	19	28			
N											3	5			
J							1				3				
B														1	

* This miniature fibula lacks both ends and it is difficult to properly classify. E. Kohler considered it an imported leech fibula.

** The ends of this fibula come closer to the XII.7A type, but the arc is round in section and transversally ridged. E. Kohler described it as XII.2. Caner (1983:NI.1) regarded it as a unique type.

*** These two fibulae are badly corroded and difficult to classify. E. Kohler listed them as XII.4. My examination of the objects suggests that they are probably of XII.7A type.

**** The statistics of the fibulae found by the Körte brothers is based on their descriptions, as not all fibulae are illustrated.

exceptions are three fibulae (B1764, B1596, B1454) of type XII.14 and a XII.9, which are abundant in later contexts.[7] DeVries devoted considerable attention to an examination of their provenance.[8] If their DL context is to be accepted, then it looks as if they were already in circulation at the time of the destruction, although they became far more popular during the Middle Phrygian period. While the exact sequence of the Gordion tombs is still debated, it is significant that fibulae of types XII.9 and XII.14 appear in tumuli KIII, KIV, MM, and S1, all of which are now dated after the destruction.

It is worth noting that there are 12 imported fibulae in the DL context, which is a relatively high number, and they help in pinpointing the date of the Destruction Level. Two arched (Bogenfibeln) fibulae

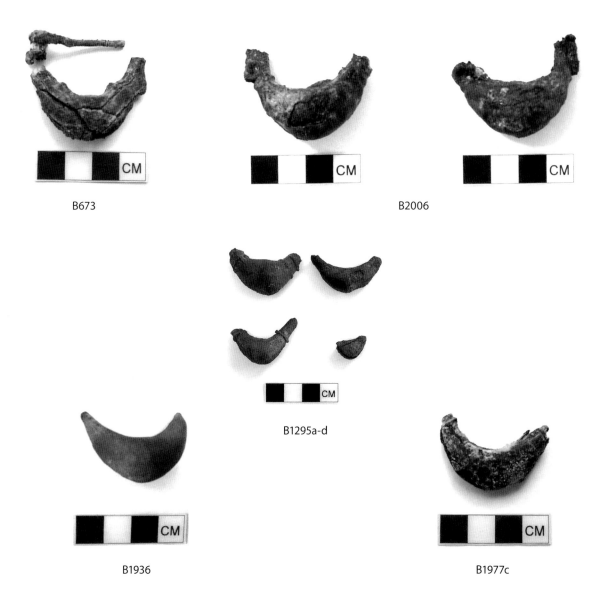

B673   B2006

B1295a-d

B1936   B1977c

Fig. 8.3a. Leech fibulae from the Gordion City Mound, DL. Source: Gordion Project, Penn Museum.

(B1988c and d), one symmetrical and one asymmetrical, were found in a clump with two XII.7A fibulae in CC3 (Fig. 8.2). They feature arcs with round sections and moldings at each end, and display Aegean affinities, although no exact parallel can be identified. Their prototypes can be found among the arched fibulae of Ertuğrul Caner's type IId, with a slightly swollen bow in the middle and two moldings at the ends, often asymmetrically set (Blinkenberg 1926, type II:7–19; Caner 1983:29–31, Nos. 7–13). They are dated ca. 1125–950 BC and all of the Anatolian examples come from the Carian coast. The asym-

metrical types in the Aegean and in the Near East, however, have long arm-shaped catch-ends, while the Phrygian examples display catches that lead directly to the molding. The exact shape of the two catch-end finials is unknown. Parallels can be cited from Cyprus (Idalion: Gjerstad 1948:348, fig. 25, 3a, No. 40), from Crete (Vrokastro: Sapouna-Sakellarakis 1978: Taf. 11, 611), as well as from Alişar, Zincirli, and Megiddo (Pedde 2000: Taf. 5, 46–47; Taf. 11, 129–130; Taf. 25, 351–353, 358, C1.2 type).

Recently, two examples of the arched fibula type were found in stratum IIa at Kaman-Kalehöyük,

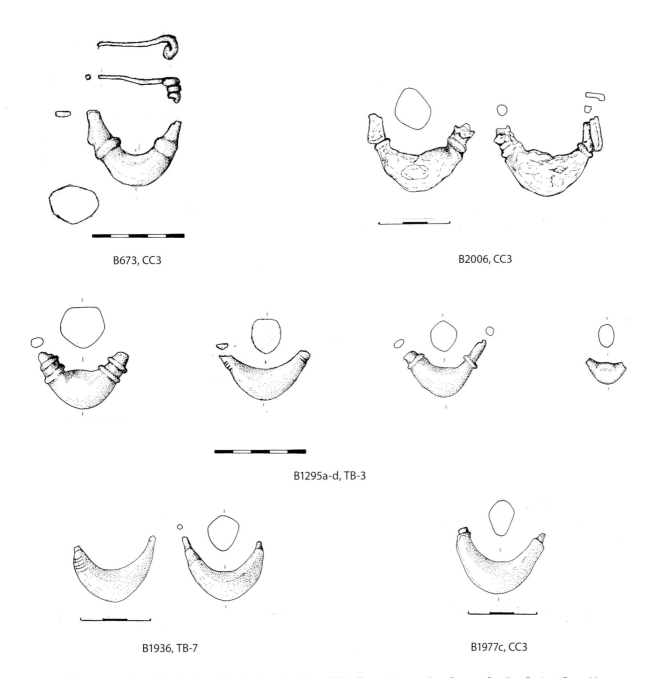

B673, CC3

B2006, CC3

B1295a-d, TB-3

B1936, TB-7

B1977c, CC3

Fig. 8.3b. Drawings of leech fibulae from the Gordion City Mound, DL. Illustrations: author. Source: Gordion Project, Penn Museum.

100 km southeast of Ankara, and they provide close parallels to the Gordion pieces (Omura 2006:6, 8, 14, figs. 8.7–8.8). Unfortunately, the strata of this site are not precisely dated and cannot offer much support to the Gordion finds in this respect (Omori and Nakamura 2006:267).

Arched fibulae began to be used in the Mediterranean during Sub-Mycenaean times and continued into the Archaic period. Some scholars believe that they originated on Greek islands (Sapouna-Sakellarakis 1978:85, type IV), and recently, a Cypriot origin for asymmetrical fibulae has been advanced with additional evidence (Giesen 2001:109, 371; *contra* Caner 1983:30). It is probably best to assume that the type developed as a result of varied contacts in the Aegean and eastern Mediterranean (as accept-

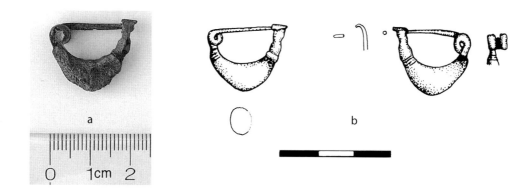

Fig. 8.4a, b. (a) Leech fibula B13a from Tumulus C. Photo: Museum of Anatolian Civilizations, Ankara. (b) Drawing of the leech fibula B13a from Tumulus C. Illustrations: author. Source: Gordion Project, Penn Museum.

ed by Giesen 2001:63), rather than to attempt to identify a precise point of origin.

The earlier Sub-Mycenaean arched fibulae, both asymmetrical and symmetrical, may have contributed to the appearance of the wide arc fibulae in the Near East ca. 900 BC (Stronach 1959:191, figs. 6.4–6.6). Our problem is that few are securely datable. The examples from Tarsus (Goldman 1956: pls. 247–249) cannot be of LBA date (Pedde 2000:175), and the Alişar parallels come from layers with a wide range of dates (von der Osten 1937:110). Most of the cited parallels that can be dated, however, fall in the late 9th/8th century BC (see Pedde's C1.2 group, Pedde 2000:175–76). No other examples of these arched fibulae were found at Gordion, either in the tumuli or in the later levels of the Citadel Mound.[9]

It is not easy to pinpoint the source of the Gordion imports. They may have originated in Cyprus, Crete, or the Aegean islands, where the arched fibula had a long history.[10] Once the fibulae began to circulate in the East, they may also have been shared among different Anatolian and Near Eastern sites. In view of the problematic dating of the Tarsus, Alişar, and Kaman-Kalehöyük parallels, however, it is still difficult to determine whether Gordion provided the immediate source for these Aegean-inspired fibulae, or vice versa. What one can say is that this type of fibula does not occur in any strata later than the Destruction Level of the Citadel Mound, which suggests its disappearance after the destruction. This assumption, together with the early history of these fibulae in the Aegean, might point to a date in the

9th century BC for the Gordion arched fibulae.

The other group of foreign fibulae at Gordion, more numerous than the previous one, is the so-called leech fibulae (B1936–TB-7; B1977b, B2006–CC3; B673–CC2; B1295a-d–TB-3) (Fig. 8.3a, b). Only the swollen, "leech," bow with tapering ends and round section is preserved in most cases. Two items (B673 and B2006) show fragments of trapezoidal or triangular catch-plates, the former having the spring and pin as well. One or two molded rings at each end can also be seen (on B1295c and B1295a, respectively, and possibly on B673 and B2006 as well). Some examples display several horizontally milled lines at each end (B1295b and B1936).

The tumuli of Gordion have furnished four specimens of this fibula type, which are among the earliest examples. Probably the best-preserved item is one of two miniature fibulae that come from Tumulus C (B13a). They originate in "Stone Complex 4," a pre-tumulus inhumation burial, originally considered by the excavator to be the main burial (Kohler 1995:25, fig. 11B). This feature is earlier than the tumulus itself, and the fibulae might be of DL or pre-DL date (Kohler 1995:26n5; Muscarella 1967: pl. XVIII.94). The piece displays a slightly different catch than the rest of the leech fibulae: it has no triangular flat catch but rather a plain hook that comes out of the bow. Its damaged state makes its outline difficult to define; it could be either rectangular or triangular (Muscarella 1967: pl. XVIII.94) (Fig. 8.4a, b).

Two more leech fibulae were discovered in the tomb chamber of Tumulus G (B11, B17), which

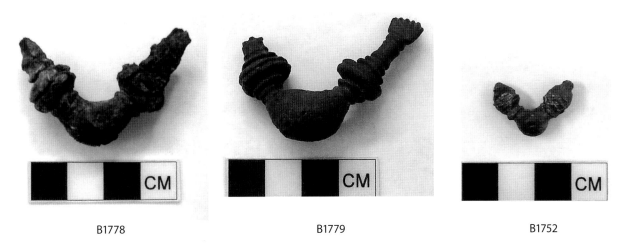

B1778   B1779   B1752

Fig.8.5a. Near Eastern fibulae from the Gordion Citadel Mound, DL. Source: Gordion Project, Penn Museum.

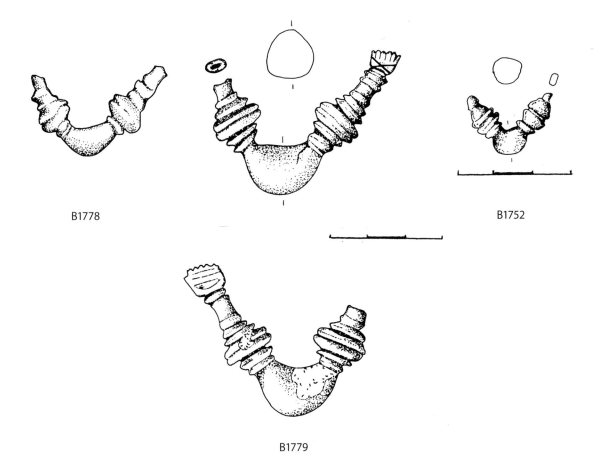

B1778   B1752

B1779

Fig. 8.5b. Drawings of the Near Eastern fibulae from the Gordion City Mound, DL. Illustrations: author. Source: Gordion Project, Penn Museum.

B1669, WSlope, 5-6, N, layer 6, Pit B

B1320, WIS, layer 5

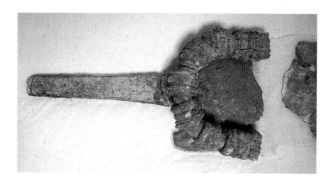

B1604, M6C, South Cellar

B1605, M6C, South Cellar, lower layer

is also considered to be among the earliest (Kohler 1995:37, 39, TumG3 and 4, pl. 21C and D). One leech fibula (B29) found in the mantle of Tumulus B may also be earlier than the tumulus itself, which is dated ca. 630 BC (Kohler 1995:1, 21, 39, 192, TumB 19).

These fibulae fall within Sapouna-Sakellarakis' type IV, especially IVd, and within Kilian's types D Ia and b (Sapouna-Sakellarakis 1978:68–69, 77–78; Kilian 1975:31–34, Taf. 6.221–237). Several SPG (ca. 850–750 BC) examples from Lefkandi can be cited as comparanda (Popham, Sackett, and Themelis 1980:S59.32, pl. 249.2; 1996:T.80.65, pl. 140, SPG II/IIIa; T.34.37, SPG IIIa, pl. 129). Kilian, however, considers them to be of Thessalian origin, because so many of them were found at Pherai, and he dates them to the 8th /7th century BC.[11] Other scholars think this type appeared under the influence of the Villanova circle in the 8th century BC, although the Italian fibulae generally have bigger swollen and hollow bows, while the Gordion examples are solid cast. Whatever their exact origin, these fibulae were certainly western imports (either Aegean or mainland Greek) to Gordion.

Unlike the case of the group of arched fibulae, we have at least two leech examples (B534 and B606) from post-DL contexts, and probably four, if the two from Tumulus B (TumB 18 and 20) are of post-DL date. Most of the parallels are again from the 8th century BC, but the Lefkandi pieces indicate that the type may date to the late 9th century BC.

The third group of imported fibulae at the Gordion Citadel Mound consists of three items with more or less triangular-shaped bows, swollen in the middle, and two bi-coni-

Fig. 8.6. Belts from the Gordion Citadel Mound: B1669, B1320, B1604, B1605. Source: Gordion Project, Penn Museum.

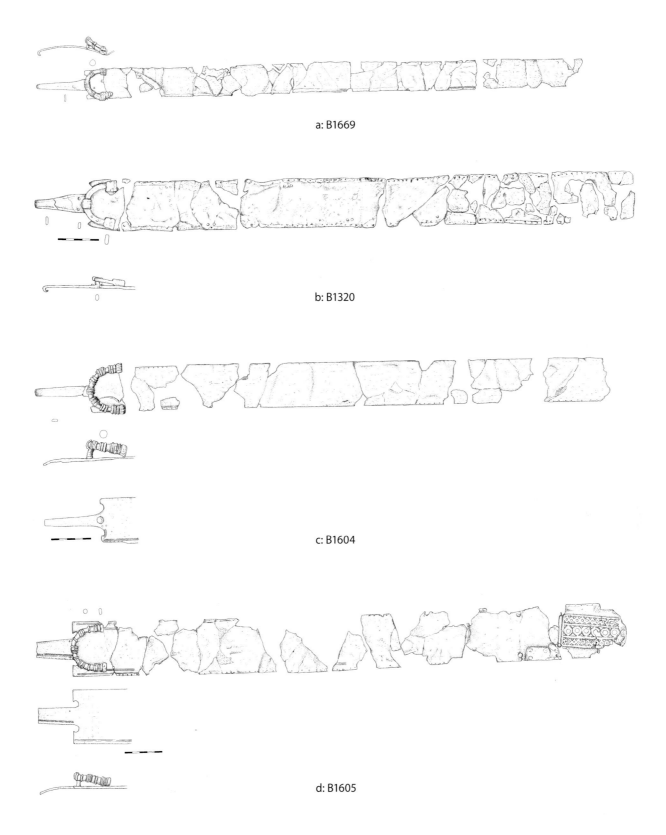

a: B1669

b: B1320

c: B1604

d: B1605

Fig. 8.7a-d. Drawings of belts from the Gordion Citadel Mound: (a) B1669, (b) B1320, (c) B1604, (d) B1605. Illustrations: author.
Source: Gordion Project, Penn Museum.

Fig. 8.8a. Bronze belt B677 from the Gordion Citadel Mound. Source: Gordion Project, Penn Museum.

cal moldings between two or more discs at each end. Most of the swellings in the middle of the bow resemble the leech fibulae, but are slightly flattened (B1779, B1778 and B1752, all from TB-8) (Fig. 8.5a, b). Caner assigned them to the group of Cypriotic and Oriental fibulae, type V (1983:180–82),

while O.W. Muscarella listed a similar piece from Tumulus B (B5) among the Aegean or western imports at Gordion (1967:82, B2, pl. XVIII.92). The preserved catch-end of B1779 is shaped in the form of a hand which bears an incised cross on the outer side. The parallel for this ornamentation on Boeo-

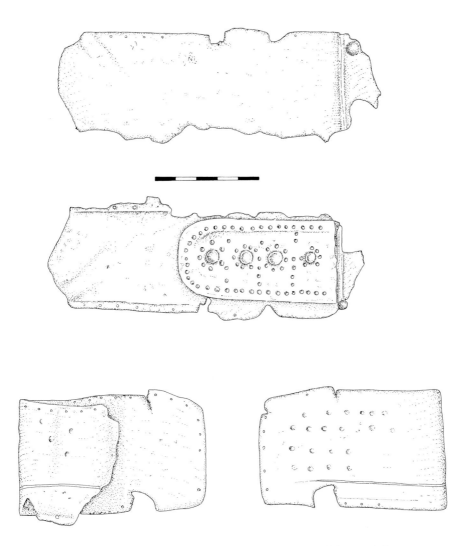

Fig. 8.8b. Drawing of parts of the belt B677 from the Gordion Citadel Mound. Illustrations: author. Source: Gordion Project, Penn Museum.

tian fibulae in Euboia, cited by Caner (1983:181), is not convincing. There is a closer example from Assur with the same ornamented hand (Pedde 2000: Taf. 23, No. 301). Two fibulae from Alişar could possibly provide parallels for the slightly swollen bow with bi-conical beads at both ends (Pedde 2000: Nos. 378–379, Taf. 26). These fall within Pedde's C1.2 group, dated to the 8th–7th century BC (Pedde 2000:175–76). Caner regards this type of fibula as an import from Alişar, which sounds plausible (1983:181, following Przeworski 1939:177).

Similar fibulae are found in other levels of the Citadel Mound and in tumuli: B5 (Tumulus B: Kohler 1995:21, TumB20, fig. 9D, pl. 11E), B1777

(WCW-2), B1595 (TrQ, clay), B1149 (KH; 6th c. BC or earlier, Muscarella 1967:83, B4). Two (B1861, B1881) were found in a 4th century BC context (PPB-7 and PPB-SE3; Caner 1983:181). Their bow swellings are smaller and more ball-like, and they bear a closer resemblance to Near Eastern triangular fibulae. Additional examples of Near Eastern triangular, or "knee-bow/elbow" fibulae have been found in Middle and Late Phrygian contexts at Gordion (B1191, B1201, B1878). These seem to have had a long period of use.

Despite initial expectations, the imported fibulae at Gordion do not offer decisive chronological guidance for the dating of the Destruction Level,

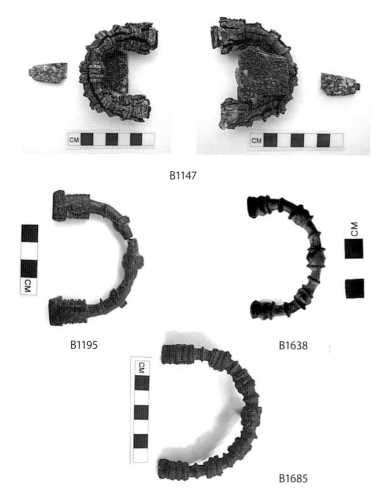

Fig. 8.9. Fibula-type belt buckles from the Gordion Citadel Mound. Source: Gordion Project, Penn Museum.

B1147

B1195   B1638

B1685

nor do the parallels of the arched and the leech types. The imported fibulae do, however, indicate early and relatively frequent contacts with the Aegean.

Belts

Bronze belts are among the most attractive objects found in Gordion and constitute a hallmark of Phrygian metalworking, which was widely imitated and exported to Greek sanctuaries. All of the examples published so far were found in tumuli. Probably the most exquisite are the three belts from Tumulus P, a child's burial at Gordion (Young 1981:17–20, TumP 34–36), which is now dated to ca. 760 BC (Sams and Voigt 2011: fig. 7.10). There are, however, more examples that were excavated on the Citadel Mound of Gordion: five complete (or almost complete) belts (Figs. 8.6, 8.7a-d, 8.8a,b), four belt buckles, and more fragments from hooks, catchplates, and bronze bands.[12] All of these examples were found in contexts that postdate the Destruction Level.

There are two pieces from the clay filling that probably represent Early Phrygian products. Both of these are belt buckles: one with a hook (B1685), which was found in the clay under the South Cellar, and another (B1147) that was discovered in a pit dug into the clay (MW2; Kohler 1995:209). It is worth noting that the former has 13 moldings on the arc and shows that pieces with numerous moldings appear relatively early in the sequence.

In his final publications, DeVries devoted considerable effort to defining the early contexts of the South Cellar. Based on the types of fibulae and belts in the deposit, he synchronized the South Cellar and

Tumulus S1 (which is later than Tumulus P: Kohler 1995:192; DeVries 2005:37–40). Two complete belts, a belt buckle, a catch-plate, and more belt fragments were discovered in this context, which DeVries dated to the late 8th–early 7th century BC (B1604, B1605, B1638, B1510, B1606, and B1607). One additional belt may also come from a similar early context (B1669). The others derive from layers and fills that can be dated between the 5th and 3rd century BC, but the bronze objects can be dated only roughly (B1320, B1195).

Phrygian belts consist of solid bronze bands with small holes running along both long sides, probably for sewing them to leather or cloth. A set of parallel incised lines also flanks both long sides, and often the lines run along the two edges of the hook. The belt buckle is of a Phrygian fibula type, covering the base of a long hook. The catch plate is a rectangular openwork piece with one rounded end, usually riveted to the band. The hook is cut from the same bronze sheet and comes out of two semi-circular cut-outs.

The bronze bands of the Tumulus P belts (as well as the silver one from the Bayındır Tumulus) show intricate patterns of incised geometric decoration. Unfortunately, x-rays of the five complete belts from Gordion revealed no decoration on the bands.[13]

One of the Tumulus P belts has a buckle resembling the XII.7 fibula type, although the front side of the bow has a ridge in the middle (TumP 36). Other examples contain more moldings on the bow, and most of them fall within the XII.14A fibula type, with 9 or 10 moldings (Muscarella 1967:25–26; Caner 1983:147–49, JIII type), although one has as many as 13 (B1685) (Fig. 8.9).[14] The Early Phrygian contexts of B1685 and B1147 are secure, which means that the number of moldings on the buckle arcs cannot be used for chronological purposes. In other words, it would be difficult to claim that earlier belts feature plainer buckles with fewer moldings.

The typological development of Phrygian belts is still unclear in many respects, but some observations on changes in shape can be made (Kohler 1995:207–10). The hook gradually becomes shorter and thicker, and is sometimes riveted to the bronze band. The bands of incised parallel lines that run along the long sides of the belt also tend to grow wider (TumS1 11–12, Ankara Tumulus I, Boğazköy Nos. 2561 and 2566; Kohler 1995:126; Özgüç and Akok 1947:63, Res. 25; Boehmer 1979:7–8). The openwork catch-plate becomes finer; relatively large arcs or circles (as on TumP 34–36) provide between two and four options for fastening, and develop into a network of smaller circles or squares with triangles, resembling weaving to some extent (Kohler 1995:126–27, TumS1 13 and 15; B1605; B1510).

The catch-plate is subsequently replaced by solid bronze plaques with a greater number of circular or square holes for the hooks (B1147, B677).[15] A border of embossed dots surrounds the holes and runs along the perimeter of the plate. The catch-plates of the earlier belts are riveted to the band and immovable, while later they are attached by a hinge (B1605, B1441, B677, and possibly B1509).[16] The hook also becomes more decorated, and a rod connecting both ends of the belt buckle is also present (Boardman 1961–62: pl. 21.c; 1967: Nos. 279, 294, 295, 298, 302). Only one of the earliest Phrygian belts has this type of buckle (Young 1981: TumP 34, fig. 9A), while it becomes frequent in the Greek examples (Jantzen 1972: Taf. 45, B116; Taf. 46, B1691, B605, B614).

The end moldings of the belt buckle become ridged rectangular blocks, while on the Greek examples they are most often hemispherical and button-like (Kohler 1995:127–28, TumS1 18, compared to the Emporio type C). Openwork D-shaped buckles consisting of two or three concentric wires are also absent from the Phrygian repertoire (Boardman 1961–62: pl. 20 d; 1967: No. 293). The use of lion heads on the ends of the fibula-type buckle seems to be an Ionian innovation and appears never to have been popular in Phrygia (Naumann and Tuchelt 1963–64:47, Taf. 31, 2–4; Barnett 1963–64: pl. 31 g; Boardman 1967:217, No. 293; Caner 1983:198, G21; Klebinder 2001:114–15; 2002:79; 2007:100–101, Kat. Nos. 711, 730, 731).[17] The belt buckles mentioned above might be compared with the exquisite gold examples from Ephesos which have a lion's head in the middle of the fibula bow (Bammer and Muss 1996: Abb. 99–100).

Recent finds at the Artemision at Ephesos and in Miletos prompt a closer examination of Phrygian-type belts (and other bronze objects) found as votives in East Greek sanctuaries (Donder 2002; Klebinder 2007). Phrygian-type belts were adopted in Ionia at the beginning of the 7th century BC and became more popular during the second half of the same century (Klebinder 2001:117; 2007:104–5). Their Phrygian prototypes can be dated to the late 8th century BC and later (i.e., those from the South Cellar, Tumuli S1 and J: Kohler 1995:64–65, TumJ 21; 126–28, TumS1 11–19). Belts like those from Tumulus P have not been found in Ionia, but the Greek items do resemble the pieces from the Gordion Citadel Mound.

Phrygian bronze belts are known primarily as grave goods in burials, either on or to the side of the skeleton. Since two of the belts and many belt fragments come from the South Cellar on the Citadel Mound, I would suggest that it was a special deposit. The elite artifacts from this deposit, such as stamp seals, an ivory figurine, and an abundance of Greek pottery also support the hypothesis that this deposit was distinct from the others (DeVries 2005:42; Dusinberre 2005: Cat. Nos. 19 and 20, 45). One of the belts was found in a pot (B1604), while the other was discovered lying partly in a pit (B1605). The latter has been repaired, and the x-rays revealed at least one additional mending. B1320 also has a repair. The fact that they were repaired suggests that at least some of them were used publicly.

I have argued elsewhere that Phrygian belts were related to the cult of the Great Goddess (Vassileva 2005b), and my belief in this link has only grown stronger. The geometric designs on some of the belts echo the patterns on Phrygian rock-cut façades and on inlaid wooden furniture from the Gordion tombs (Simpson 1988:34–35; 1998:636; Simpson 2010:91–99; Vassileva 2001:59–60). Both of these have been linked to the symbolism of Kybele's cult and to the goddess' role in Phrygian burial customs (Buluç 1988:22; Roller 1999b:102, 104, 111–12). Moreover, most of the Phrygian-type belts and fibulae found in the Greek world came from sanctuaries of goddesses: Artemis in Ephesos; a goddess in the Harbor Sanctuary on Chios (Boardman 1961–62); Hera in Samos (Boardman 1961–62:189); Athena in Erythrai (Akurgal 1993: fig. 93d); Athena Pronaia in Marmaria at Delphi (Perdrizet 1908:130, No. 702; Diod. 22.9.5; Völling 1998:250); and Aphrodite at Zeytintepe, Miletos (Donder 2002:3; Senff 2003).[18]

The use of Phrygian-type belts and fibulae as votives in Greek sanctuaries has sometimes been linked to dedications by women on the occasion of marriage or childbirth (Boardman 1961–62:189). In some cases this may have been true, but in Phrygia the belts appear to have been the attributes of men, especially rulers and aristocrats, and they seem to have been connected to the cult of the Mother (Matar). Elements of Matar's cult may have been adopted and adapted by the eastern Greeks, both men and women, who subsequently purchased or imitated the exotic belts and fibulae and used them as votives (cf. also Ebbinghaus 2006:209, 217).

If we now return to the belts from the South Cellar, a parallel with the Greek practice can be drawn if one assumes that the South Cellar belts were a special assemblage, similar to the votive deposits in sanctuaries. The belts were clearly treated with special care judging by the textile pseudomorphs found on some of their surfaces (B1605, B1510). Another interesting feature of one of the belts (B1320) is its length: one end is missing and yet the preserved length is still 1.08 m, the longest Phrygian belt for which we have evidence.[19] Beneath one of the belts (B1320) were a toggle and small chain on which a miniature silver bird was hanging (B1321, B1322, ILS322).[20] One can only guess as to the original relationship among these objects, but the bird was an attribute of Phrygian Kybele, and it is tempting to regard the entire deposit as having been related to her cult.

As I hope to have shown, fibulae and belts are among the most important bronze artifacts to have been found at Gordion. To some extent, the earliest fibulae can supplement other evidence regarding the dating of the early Phrygian city, as well as contribute to the relative chronology of the tombs. The fibulae and the belts also testify to a wider range of contacts and influences than one might have expected. In other words, the inhabitants of Gordion during the Early Phrygian period may not have been as isolated from the Aegean world as previously assumed. The belts also have the potential to lead us into the realm of Phrygian religion and its links with Aegean sanctuaries, although our grasp of these issues is still rather tenuous.

Acknowledgments

I would like to pay my respects to the memory of the late Keith DeVries, who was always so friendly and helpful and encouraged my research in countless ways. I am also happy to offer this contribution in memory of Ellen Kohler and in celebration of her long career at Gordion and in the Gordion archives of the Penn Museum.

NOTES

8.1. The chapter presents some of the results of my research as a Mellon fellow at the Metropolitan Museum of Art in New York, 2002–04, and my initial research as a 2007–08 ARIT Mellon fellow in Turkey.

8.2. Hereafter I will use the conventional abbreviations for strata and loci accepted by the Gordion team: DL = Destruction Level, TB = Terrace Building, CC = Clay Cut, KH = Küçük Höyük, NB = Gordion Notebook. I will also use the standard chronological abbreviations of Aegean archaeologists: LPG = Late Proto-Geometric, LG = Late Geometric, EO = Early Orientalizing, SPG = Sub-Proto-Geometric, and LBA = Late Bronze Age. The ramifications of the new Gordion chronology for the dating of small finds, including fibulae, are addressed in Rose and Darbyshire 2011.

8.3. I use the old fibula classification system of C. Blinkenberg, supplemented with a few subtypes described by O.W. Muscarella and R.M. Boehmer (Boehmer 1972; 1979).

8.4. Ertuğrul Caner did not believe that it fit into any of his groups (1983:175, No. 1176). All characteristics of this fibula, however, other than the attachment of the pin, fall within the XII.7A type.

8.5. One from Tumulus K (B437), one from the surface of Tumulus E (B508), and one from the habitation gravel fill under Tumulus J (B139).

8.6. An item from the Manisa Museum with unknown provenance may be an exception: Dedeoğlu 2003:29.

8.7. Judging by the published context, fibula fragment B1596 may actually be of pre-DL date. It was found in the Megaron 4 Terrace fill: NB 121:45; Sams 1994a:16. Only the catch-end is preserved, but it could pertain to a XII.13 or 14 type fibula. The possibility that it is a later intrusion cannot be completely ruled out.

8.8. Again, the possibility that it is a later intrusion cannot be excluded due to the later coarse-ware sherds reported in the notebook for the context of B1545: NB 106, 64. Muscarella (2003:233n35), however, believes that the worn appearance of B1454 (studs missing) does not support the idea that it was discarded by a later inhabitant of the city.

8.9. If the fragmentary fibula from Tumulus Y (B1513:

Kohler 1995: pl. 57A) can be considered an arched fibula, it would be the only example in a later context (see Table 8.2). The incised cross on the preserved end, however, speaks in favor of Near Eastern inspiration.

8.10. The Cretan parallels require further research. Three horse trappings from the early Greek cemetery at Knossos (Coldstream and Catling 1996a:219.f92, f102, f103a; a LG burial) provide a parallel for the iron horse bit with crescent-shaped cheekpieces from Gordion (ILS 334 and 335, TB2), discussed by Muscarella (2003:237–39). There are two more horse bit parallels from Crete, but these are not so compelling: Arkades and Prinias (Donder 1980:44; type VIe). Tomb 219 at Knossos has yielded two(?) pairs of bronze lotus-bud vessel handles (219.f85, f93, f97), very much like those of the Tumulus K-III vessel (Körte and Körte 1904:72, No. 57, Abb. 51) and similar to the Egyptian-blue lotus handles from Tumulus P (TumP 47:Young 1981:31). The few fibulae that are somewhat comparable to the Phrygian arched ones are of LPG–EO date (Coldstream and Catling 1996b:551–52).

8.11. He mentions the Gordion examples, published by O.W. Muscarella, and considers them Greek mainland imports at Gordion: Kilian 1975:32.

8.12. The total number of belts and belt fragments found on the Citadel Mound is 17. One hook (B2003) and a hinge rod (B2061), both without a context, can be added to the list in Kohler 1995:209.

8.13. Performed on August 1, 2005, in the Museum of Anatolian Civilizations in Ankara. For this I am grateful to Mr. Latif Özen, Chemical Engineer and head conservator at the Museum Laboratory.

8.14. This is unlike the NIII type in Caner 1983: Taf. 63.1141–48).

8.15. See also the examples from Samos (Jantzen 1972: Taf. 47) and Chios (Boardman 1967: pl. 90). In personal communication (June 2004), E. Kohler suggested to me that she regards B677 as Celtic rather than Phrygian. It was, in fact, found in a very late stratum on the Citadel Mound, and the x-rays show a slightly different pattern of corrosion on the belt's bronze band. Its clasp, however, is very similar to the later variants of Phrygian catch-plates: a solid bronze plate on a hinge with embossed dots surrounding the holes. See Figure 8a, b here.

8.16. See Tumulus I at Ankara (Boğazköy No. 2562), as well as the above-mentioned examples from Samos, namely B447 and B1328, and Chios; Klebinder 2001:117; 2002:79; 2007:103).

8.17. The one from Didyma was published by the excavators as an appliqué (for a furniture piece?). The lion head, which is 4 cm long, looks unusually large for the end molding of a fibula-type belt buckle. But there is an example with lion heads from Kaynarca, near Tyana in southeastern Anatolia: Akkay 1992. An example with ram heads is known from Phanai and Chios: Boardman 1967:217. Buckle ends in the shape of stylized human (?) faces can be seen on one of the Tumulus P belts: Young 1981:20, TumP 36, fig. 11.

8.18. The Samos example is the only one that comes from a burial: Völling 1998:246–47, n28; Boehlau and Habich 1996:124, Abb. 3.

8.19. Ranking second in length is TumP 35, ca. 0.95 m, but the catch-plate was shifted backwards to make it shorter (and fit the wearer). We may have a similar situation here.

8.20. The toggle is probably too heavy to have been suspended from the belt, but the silver bird might have been hanging from the bronze band.

Midas and Tumulus MM

Fig. 9.1. Panoramic view looking east from the Citadel Mound at Gordion, showing Tumulus MM at the left and other tumuli on the Northeast and South Ridges. Photo: author.

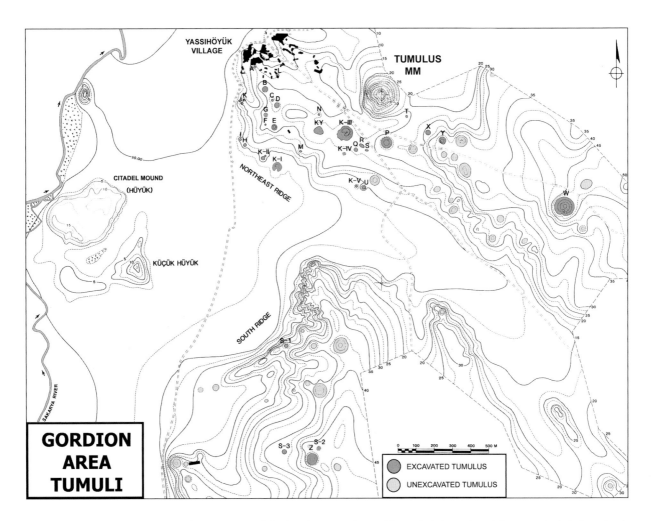

Fig. 9.2. Map of tumuli in the immediate area around Gordion (excavated tumuli have alphabetical or alpha-numerical designations). Source: Gordion Project, Penn Museum.

9

Phrygian Tomb Architecture: Some Observations on the 50th Anniversary of the Excavations of Tumulus MM

Richard F. Liebhart

The most striking and memorable feature of the Gordion landscape is the presence of over 200 tumuli, or earthen burial mounds that cover the tombs of the city's elite.[1] Ranging in date from the 9th century BC to the Hellenistic period, these tumuli vary in size from nearly imperceptible humps to the 53 m tall Tumulus MM, which is visible from nearly all parts of the Sakarya River valley (Fig. 9.1). Forty-four of the tumuli have been investigated archaeologically: 5 by the Körte brothers in 1900, 31 by the Americans, and 8 by Turkish archaeologists.[2] Rodney Young gave the tumuli that were excavated under his watch alphabetical or alpha-numerical designations (Fig. 9.2). The three greatest of these (W, P, and MM) were published in 1981, seven years after Young's death, with his descriptions augmented by other Gordion scholars under the direction of Ellen Kohler (Young 1981). Her own publication of the other excavated tumuli containing inhumations has added immensely to our understanding of Phrygian tomb construction (Kohler 1995). Her forthcoming work on the tumuli with cremation burials will complete the overall picture of the elite funerary practices of this period, even though these tumuli did not contain built wooden tomb chambers.[3]

The year 2007 marked the 50th anniversary of the excavation of Tumulus MM, and it seems fitting to take another look at this unique monument. My presentation is based on some of the observations that I have made at Gordion since 1990; these expand the original study by Young, Kohler, and Charles Williams, who made the original architectural drawings of the tomb chamber in 1961.[4] It is not possible in this brief discussion to present all the evidence for the descriptions that follow, and the reader should keep in mind that the most appropriate way to appreciate the monument is to visit in person. There, inside Tumulus MM, one will find what Rodney Young discovered fifty years ago: the oldest standing wooden building in the world. If the current radiocarbon and dendrochronological dates for the juniper logs used in the tomb are correct, and if these logs were in fact cut specifically for use in this tomb (and they almost certainly were), the construction of Tumulus MM dates to around 740 BC (Manning et al. 2001).[5] While this is too early for the occupant to have been Midas himself, the tumulus might have been the young king's first major public project, a tomb for his father. In that case, the designation MM would still be correct for this tumulus: the Midas Mound.

Figure 9.3 shows Tumulus MM and the modern entrance to the tomb, created by Young's excavation in 1957. It also shows, to the right of the museum compound, the smaller Tumulus P, slightly older than MM and covering the burial chamber of a small child. In order to accentuate the extraordinary nature of Tumulus MM, a brief discussion of the construction of a more-or-less typical Phrygian tumulus burial of the Early and Middle Phrygian periods follows, using Tumulus P as an example (Fig. 9.4).

A rectangular pit would first be dug to a depth of 1 to 2 m. The bottom of the pit might be lined with stone or simply left as an earthen floor. The tomb chamber was usually made of squared pine timbers, with rather simple joinery at the corners.

Fig. 9.3. View of Tumulus MM and Tumulus P from the top of Tumulus K-III. Photo: author.

As the tomb chamber rose, the pit outside was filled with rubble stone, thus helping to hold the wooden beams in place. The normal tomb chamber dimensions range from about 2 m square to about 3.75 m by 4.5 m (Kohler 1995: table 2). After the walls were built up to the desired height, the burial itself would take place. The body would be lowered into the chamber and the grave goods arranged; the roof beams would then be placed over the chamber. These could be in one or two layers, laid flat across the tomb chamber walls and sealing the tomb forever (in theory, at least). More rubble was added to form a mound over the chamber, then usually a sealing layer of clay, and finally the earthen mantle of the tumulus proper.

The construction of Tumulus MM shares many similarities with the other Gordion tumuli from this period, but it is exceptional in every way (Liebhart 2010). The tomb chamber proper was made from squared pine beams, with cedar and pine beams used

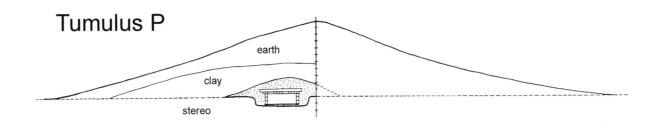

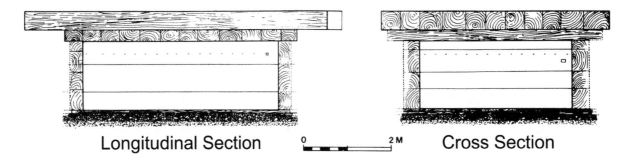

Fig. 9.4. Sections of Tumulus P and its tomb chamber. Source: Gordion Project, Penn Museum.

Fig. 9.5. Wide-angle view of the interior of the tomb chamber of Tumulus MM, taken from the northeast corner. Photo: author.

for the floor (Fig. 9.5).[6] Its interior measures 5.15 m by 6.20 m—nearly twice as large as its closest rival, the chamber of Tumulus Z.[7] The walls stand nearly 3.3 m high and are topped by a double pitched roof, similar to Phrygian megaron design, but unique among the excavated tomb chambers at Gordion. In the west wall is the entrance cut by Young in 1957, and a modern steel bridge lies in the corner where the coffin of the dead king was placed some 2,700 years ago. A modern steel frame supports the central crossbeam complex, which still shows the curving distortion caused by the tremendous weight of the tumulus above that pressed down on the chamber until equilibrium was finally reached. The bulging north wall on the right in Figure 9.5 displays another result of this pressure.

Figure 9.6 is a composite photograph of the south side of the outer casing of juniper logs that surrounds the pine and cedar tomb chamber proper. This panoramic view is made up from nine separate wide-angled photographs, and it shows the distortion common to such combined perspectives. It also illustrates one of the problems of viewing the tomb: one cannot get more than about 3 m away from the outer casing, so there is no vantage point from which one can either get a decent overall view or take a photograph that effectively illustrates the construction of the tomb chamber. The details of the tomb's construction would be easier to study and describe if the tomb had collapsed.

The following explanation of the construction of the tomb is illustrated by a series of plans, sections, and diagrams that are based both on the measurements this writer has made since 1990 and on a CAD model of the tomb restored to its original, undistorted state (Fig. 9.7).[8] This virtual tomb is still a work in progress, but it has been used to produce the plans and sections that follow, which present a sequential description of the construction of the

Fig. 9.6. Composite photograph of the south side of the outer casing of juniper logs. The concrete pilasters at the sides form part of the protective shell that was installed in 1961; the black steel support system was installed in 2002. Photo: author.

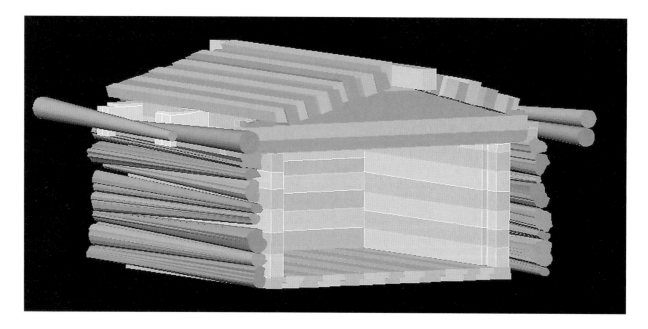

Fig. 9.7. CAD model of the tomb chamber. Drawing: author and Banu Bedel.

tomb chamber and tumulus. All of the sections are cross sections, and the point of view for all of them is looking north.

The Phrygians first dug a roughly rectangular pit some 14 m by 16 m and a little over 2 m deep (Fig. 9.8). The bottom of the pit seems to have been lined with the buff-colored limestone found so frequently in buildings on the Citadel Mound (especially during the Early Phrygian Period). Certainly the sides of the pit were lined with this stone, creating a wall

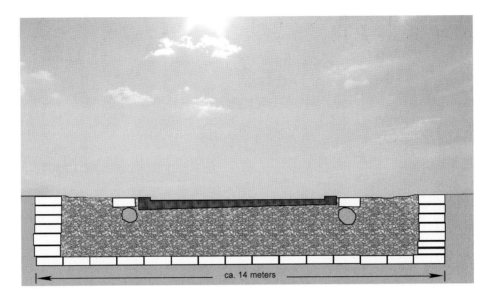

Fig. 9.8. Center cross section showing the initial stages of the tomb chamber construction (looking north). Drawing: author.

about 1 m thick, with the faces of each block roughly dressed.

Instead of building the tomb chamber in the bottom of this pit, the decision here was made to fill the pit with rubble. When the Phrygians approached the original ground level, they set large, unworked boulders more or less in the intended lines of the outer casing. On top of these boulders, and equally irregularly placed, were more of the limestone blocks. In the space between were placed juniper logs, forming what appears to have been a solid raft of logs running across what would be the width of the tomb chamber. These logs were then trimmed down flat on their tops to form a bedding surface for the cedar and pine floor beams, which formed the first layer of the tomb chamber proper.

Figure 9.9 shows how the floor was built: each floor beam had lap joints cut into one upper and one lower corner along its length (except for the first and last, which needed only one lap joint each). With this design, each floor beam would support and be supported by its neighbors. The first beam set was on the east side, and there were 13 floor beams in total, of varying widths. The floor beams seem to have been set level, but then the Phrygian builders trimmed the top surfaces to make a floor that sloped down from the middle to all four sides some 10–12 cm.[9]

Once the floor beams were in place, the first pine wall beams were set directly on top of the floor (Figs. 9.10, 9.11 [see latter in color insert]). The builders set more juniper about 35 cm outside the tomb chamber walls, and the logs became the lowest members of the outer casing seen in Figure 9.6. The spaces in-between were filled with rubble, as was the space between the juniper logs and the surrounding perimeter wall, which was also rising at the same time (there is, in fact, a rough correlation between the height of the limestone blocks and the normal height of the squared pine beams of the walls—around 30–40 cm). However, the limestone wall was not designed as a retaining wall to contain the rubble: the tumulus fill was also rising in concert with the construction of the tomb chamber complex.

Figure 9.12 shows a plan of the tomb chamber and outer casing at the level of the first wall beams. The longer east and west wall beams extend beyond the north and south walls, and their ends were fitted into shallow notched cuts in the inner faces of the juniper logs. The shorter north and south walls were set into vertical grooves cut into the inner faces of the east and west walls, creating simple but strong housed joints. Only gravity and the pressure from the rubble outside held the wall timbers in place. If these interior walls were standing alone, the joinery used to construct them would allow them to fall

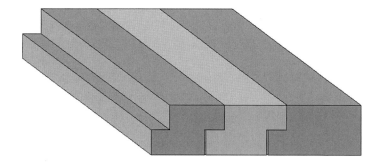

Fig. 9.9. Drawing showing the design of the tomb chamber floor system. Drawing: author.

outward, but not inward: keeping the tomb chamber intact was the prime concern for the Phrygian builders. At this level of the interior walls, there is no evidence for the use of structural dowels, pegs, or clamps of any kind. The floor beams also extended out underneath and beyond the north and south walls. The rubble filled all the spaces except the tomb chamber itself. It was only this rubble packing that held the juniper logs in place.

The entire complex, including the tumulus, rose together (Fig. 9.13). It is not known if the full diameter of the tumulus was built at this time, although there is some tantalizing evidence suggesting that it might have been. As the tomb chamber complex rose, the eighth log of the outer casing marked the location of the crossbeam systems. These were set across the side walls of the tomb chamber and extended out onto notches cut into the tops of the outer casing.

Each of the three crossbeam systems were made of two pairs of beams stacked on top of each other. Above these, two other pairs of beams formed the angle for the roof, except at the north gable support system, which actually has three pairs of beams. At the level of the crossbeams, the notching at the corners of the walls changed, and now the vertical slots were cut into the sides of the crossbeams (i.e., into the north and south walls, and into each side of the central crossbeam system; see Fig. 9.14). The effect was the same as with the lower walls: the joints were designed to withstand pressure from the outside, which, as described earlier, was the prime mechanism to keep the structure together.

The extension of the crossbeams onto the juniper logs of the outer casing would appear to tie the pine interior walls to the outer casing. However, there is again no evidence for any kind of dowels pinning the crossbeams to either the interior walls or

to the juniper logs of the outer casing. Rather than providing a lateral connection, the main role of this design was to spread the weight of the intended tumulus above onto two extra vertical lines of support.

The Phrygians understood that the juniper logs were valuable for construction projects, despite the fact that the juniper tree trunks tapered so rapidly that it was impossible to cut from a juniper log a long squared beam of useful dimensions (Fig. 9.15). Instead, the extremely slow growing junipers were not only less susceptible to rot than pine, but they were also remarkably dense and resistant to compression perpendicular to the grain.

Weight pressing down on the side of the log (as on the outer casing) would have much less effect than on a pine beam. One of the logs from the outer casing that was cut for dendrochronology has a radius of only 38.5 cm, but has 830 preserved annual rings, something on the order of ten times the number of rings one would find in a pine tree of similar dimension (Rose and Darbyshire 2011:117n5.25). This strength of the juniper is clearly in evidence in Tumulus MM, where the compression of the rubble pack and tumulus fill above the tomb chamber complex was enough to crack stones between the juniper logs, but the weight was not heavy enough to crush the fibers of the juniper logs themselves (Fig. 9.16). The Phrygians regularly used juniper logs in footings for walls and as stabilizing inserts in fortification walls and rubble fill, including in the Early Phrygian Gate Building and in the rubble fill that buried it at the beginning of the Middle Phrygian Period.

Another point is demonstrated by Figure 9.13, which shows the gable supports in place. When the tomb construction reached this level, the funeral of the dead king took place. The construction debris would have been cleared, the funeral banquet held

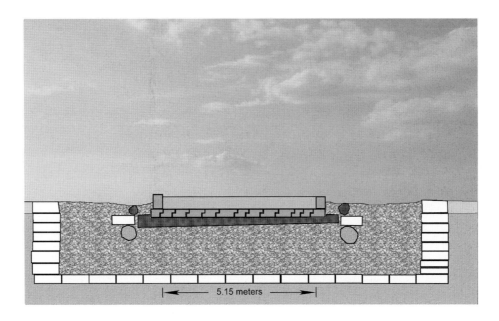

Fig. 9.10. Center cross section showing the tomb chamber built to the level of the first wall beams (looking north). Drawing: author.

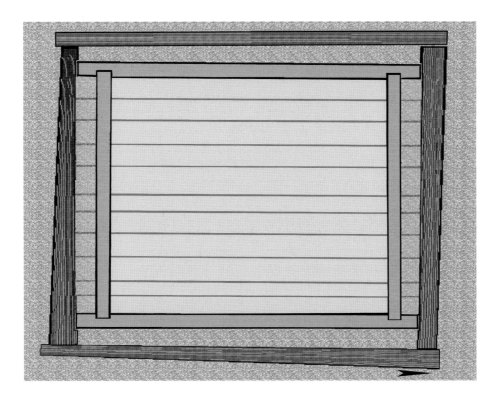

Fig. 9.12. Plan of the tomb chamber proper and the outer casing at the level of the first wall beams. Drawing: author.

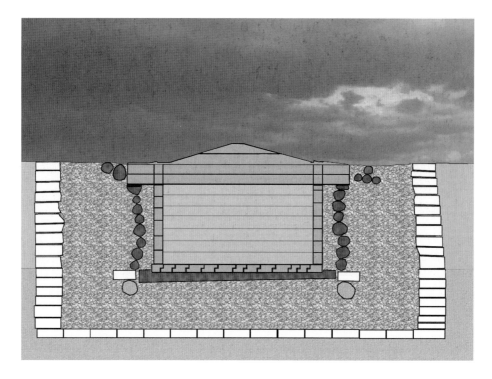

Fig. 9.13. Center cross section showing the tomb chamber built to the level of the gable supports (looking north). Drawing: author.

presumably near by, and the body and grave goods were lowered into the tomb chamber. The coffin and furniture were arranged (Simpson 2010:7–11), and any object that had a handle or other method of suspension was hung on one of 69 iron L-shaped spikes that were driven into the east, south, and west walls.[10]

Then it was simply a matter of setting the pine beams of the roof in place, and the tomb was completely closed off. A second layer of roof beams was installed, and the somewhat imperfectly understood upper roof structure was built (Fig. 9.17).[11] Certainly there were juniper logs set perpendicular to the ridge beam, but how many there were and whether the space beneath was completely filled with rubble was not recorded when the rubble over the tomb was partially cleared between the excavation in 1957 and the creation of the first set of plans and elevations in 1961.

Whatever the exact nature of this secondary roof was, we do know that rubble was piled on top and extended out past the line of the perimeter stone wall, resting in part on the tumulus fill that supported the wall on the outside (see Young 1981:85).

Presumably a clay layer was placed above the rubble, and then the tumulus proper was completed. As the tomb chamber reached its structural equilibrium, bending, groaning, and cracking under the tremendous weight it carried, the environment changed as well. The temperature and humidity levels dropped, and the fungus and microscopic agents that would normally destroy the wood were unable to complete the task, much to the amazement of everyone who has ever seen the tomb.

We should now turn to the tantalizing evidence regarding the construction of the tumulus versus that of the tomb chamber complex. In 2003, the Turkish Ministry of Culture added gutters on either side of the modern retaining wall that lines the open trench created during the 1957 excavation of the tumulus (Fig. 9.18, also Fig. 9.3). This new operation required the workers to cut back the scarp of the trench, and this, in turn, revealed a portion of tumulus stratigraphy that had for years been covered by slump and vegetation. In Figure 9.19, the darker top stratum is the dirt from the excavation. Below that is a lighter band representing the erosion debris of

Fig. 9.14. Plan of the tomb chamber proper and outer casing at the level of the cross beam systems. Drawing: author.

2700 years of exposure to the weather of the Anatolian plateau. Next one sees some of the stratigraphy of the original tumulus fill, with its characteristic diagonal pattern as the dirt was piled from the outside inward towards the center. Other layers and lenses can be made out, but the most interesting is marked by the dashed line. This relatively horizontal line is roughly 4 m above the ancient ground level, which is about the same elevation as the top of the stone perimeter wall surrounding the tomb chamber. This apparent correspondence between the tumulus construction and the tomb chamber complex suggests at least the possibility that the tumulus was indeed built up at its complete diameter from the very beginning. We are never likely to know for sure.

On a more positive note, there are certain details related to the construction techniques of the tomb chamber proper for which there is more evidence. We have already seen the lap joints of the floor beams and the housed joints used for the walls of the tomb chamber. All of these joints are simple and strong, but the construction of the tomb necessarily got more complicated at the level of the crossbeams. Figure 9.20 shows the design of the crossbeam and gable support systems. The two pairs of beams that create the crossbeam were pinned together at their ends with wooden clamps, with shapes like dumbbells or fat double T-clamps (Fig. 9.21).[12]

The use of wood for clamps of this shape is odd. It is unlikely that they were intended as structural clamps, because the grain of the wooden clamps makes their fattened ends susceptible to sheer failure (i.e., the wider parts could break off relatively easily under any significant strain, since wood has less strength against forces parallel to the direction of the grain). It is more likely that the clamps were intended to hold the beams together for some intermediate operation, during the process of fitting the crossbeams and the interior wall beams at this level. There would be no need for clamps in these positions once the upper interior wall beams were installed and the rubble was added on the outer side of the crossbeam, since the rubble would hold everything in place. Evidence from the gable supports above may lead to a better understanding of this process.

Figure 9.22 presents a section of the south end of the tomb chamber proper, showing the east and west walls below, the crossbeam system, and the gable supports. It also marks the positions of two wooden dowels, a feature of construction long anticipated but not discovered until 1999. The dowels are still *in situ*, and, like other dowels that have now been detected in the tomb, they can only be seen where the wooden beams have deformed enough

Fig. 9.15. The rapid taper of one of the few surviving large junipers in the mountains near Gordion is evident in this photograph, with the author as scale. Photo: John Marston.

to create a gap of usually a centimeter or less between two superimposed beams. The dowels come at very specific spots and seem designed for equally specific functions (almost all of the joints that can be inspected have no trace of dowels at all). The two whose locations are shown in Figure 9.22 are located between the upper member of the crossbeam and the lower member of the gable support. They are relatively small and rectangular in section, about 2.5 cm thick and about 7.5 cm wide. They are certainly not large enough to have been intended as structural elements, but like the wooden clamps in the crossbeams, these appear to have been intended as temporary support for some operation. More evidence for this operation can be seen on the face of the lower gable support beam.

Figure 9.22 also shows the locations of two lines marked by the Phrygian builders on this beam (the actual lines are black and ca. 2 mm wide). The long lower line runs parallel to the bottom of the beam about 9 cm above its lower edge. In the center is a vertical line. These are ancient layout lines marked by a Phrygian carpenter, and traces of similar lines are visible in places along the sloped edges of the upper side of this beam. The combination of dowels and layout lines suggests an explanation of the construction sequence that is illustrated in Figure 9.23. The lower gable support beam was originally set in place as a full-thickness beam with squared ends. The builders used the two dowels to hold this beam in position while they marked the layout lines and trimmed the upper surfaces to create the desired angles.[13]

Should this be the case for all the gable supports, there would be a total of 28 dowels in these beams: 8 in the south; 8 in the center; and 12 in the north, where there are three pairs of beams in the gable support system. Most of the joints between these beams are too tight to inspect

Fig. 9.16. A stone between juniper logs of the south side of the outer casing of the tomb, displaying compression fractures. Photo: author.

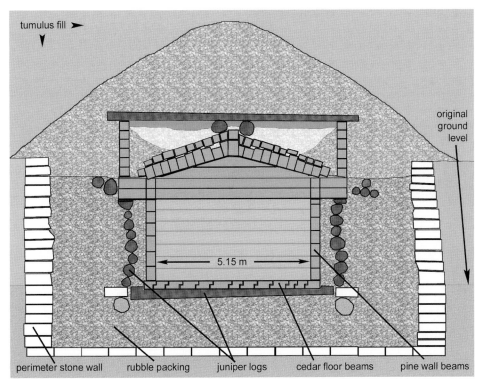

tumulus fill ➤

original ground level

5.15 m

perimeter stone wall   rubble packing   juniper logs   cedar floor beams   pine wall beams

Fig. 9.17. Center cross section of the tomb chamber complex with construction complete (looking north). Drawing: author.

for dowels, so logical extrapolation is the only recourse. These dowels and all the other ones found so far in the tomb seem to have had the same purpose: to hold the position of a beam either while it is being cut to a specific shape or length, or while a neighbor-

ing beam is being trimmed or positioned.

The actual cutting and trimming of the wooden members of the tomb chamber complex is also worthy of mention here. In the tomb today, there are thousands (if not millions) of ancient tool marks

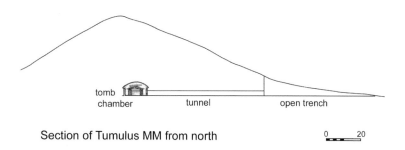

Fig. 9.18. Section of Tumulus MM from the north, showing the open trench and tunnel cut during the excavation of 1957. Source: Young 1981:83, fig. 51.

still visible, but one type this author has never seen is an ancient mark left by a saw on a structural piece of wood. Instead, what one sees in the tomb time after time are marks left by flat-bladed tools, like an axe, an adze, or a chisel. Figure 9.24 shows the end of a juniper log that displays the marks of a narrow axe blade about 4.5 cm wide, which was used to trim roughly square the end of the log (the preserved marks are not those left from felling the tree).[14] These are actually similar to the marks left

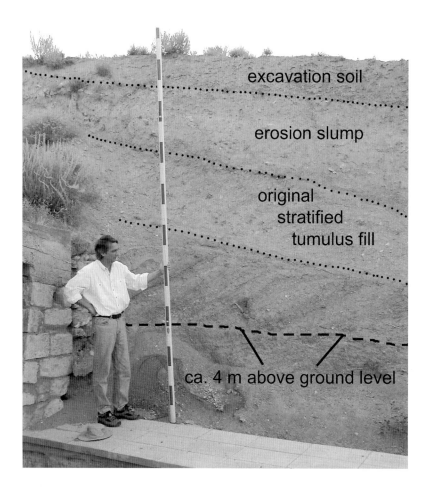

Fig. 9.19. View of the east side of the open trench in 2003, displaying part of the stratigraphy of the original tumulus construction in the recently cleaned scarp. Photo: Peter Grave.

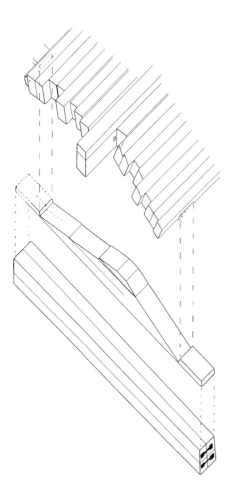

Fig. 9.21. View of the west end of the north crossbeam system, with cuttings for the clamps (portions of the original wooden clamps are still in place on some of the other beam ends). Photo: author.

Fig. 9.20. Expanded view of the crossbeam and gable support system at the north end of the tomb. Source: Young 1981:99, fig. 65.

from the trimming of the inner faces of the limestone blocks of the perimeter wall, which must have been made with a similar tool, though perhaps one with a heavier, thicker blade (Fig. 9.25). Even where one would really expect to see saw marks, like in the large notch cut in the central crossbeam to create the housed joint for the upper walls of the tomb chamber, one finds instead clear evidence for a chopping or slicing tool (Fig. 9.26). This is not to say that the Phrygians never used saws for cutting wood, and there is actually evidence for the use of a saw in the tomb chamber of Tumulus MM. A small wooden block (ca. 111 x 55 x 48 mm) used to plug a pre-construction mortise hole in the south wall of the tomb chamber was found to have clear evidence of a fine-toothed saw. However, the size of this small

piece is closer to furniture than to building material, and the use of a saw on furniture is known at Gordion (see Simpson 2010: 197-198).

There are many important questions concerning Tumulus MM, and not all of them can be addressed here. One stands out, however, and should receive some attention: "How long did it take to build the tomb?" It is hard to imagine that there could ever be a definitive answer to this question, but such a caveat does not preclude offering some thoughts based on observations made in the tomb over the course of the last 17 years. This author's short answer is: "not as long as one might think." Of all the materials used in the construction of the tomb chamber and tumulus, only the cedar used for the floor beams was likely to have been unavailable locally. However, cedar trees are still found in the mountains that line the southern coast of Turkey, so even with transportation issues of such large beams or logs, the time frame for their procurement might have been only a matter of a few weeks. There are still pine trees in the mountains northwest of Gordion that are easily big enough to supply the largest timber found in the tomb, the main ridge beam, which is 34 cm wide by 42 cm thick and 11.43 m long.

In addition, there are indications strongly suggesting that many (if not most) of the pine beams

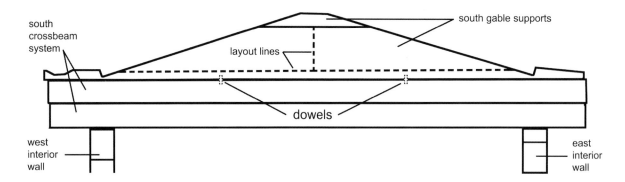

Fig. 9.22. Cross section showing the south crossbeam system and gable supports, plus the locations of the west and east walls of the tomb chamber proper (looking north). Drawing: author.

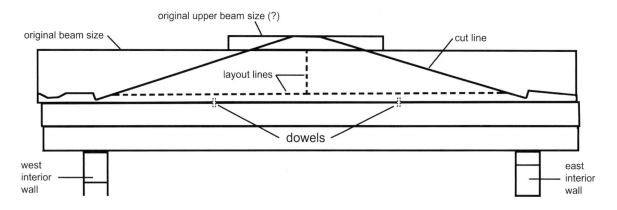

Fig. 9.23. Cross section showing the south crossbeam system with original size of gable supports, layout lines, and cut lines (looking north). Drawing: author.

used in the tomb are reused, and may therefore have been stockpiled. As described above, the joinery used in building the tomb chamber is very simple and straightforward, which a skilled or even semi-skilled worker could handle in fairly short order. The juniper logs needed only to be felled in the forest, trimmed of limbs and cut to the desired lengths, and brought to the construction site. Quarrying the soft stone used for the perimeter stone wall around the tomb chamber complex should have proved no undue burden, and these stones also could have been stockpiled. Dirt, clay, and rocks are certainly available in the immediate area, with wagons and/or pack animals used for the bulk of the transportation. Nothing here is out of the ordinary except the scale of the finished project. For the work around

the tomb chamber complex, one could envision several crews at work at the same time. Some of the curious features on the south end of the tomb chamber almost demand such a scenario.

It seems highly likely that the construction of Tumulus MM was an effort undertaken by the entire community at Gordion (and possibly much of the territory under Phrygian control, whatever that might have been). One can imagine a workforce of thousands—men, women, and children—gathering and installing the materials, particularly those materials that did not require any particular skill level, such as digging and loading dirt and clay, or picking up the millions of rocks (literally child's play?) for the rubble fill around the tomb chamber. The creation of the tumulus itself, beginning from a 1 m

Fig. 9.24. South end of a juniper log from the east side of the outer casing, showing the preserved ancient tool marks. Photo: author.

Fig. 9.25. Tool marks on the inner face of the perimeter limestone wall separating the rubble packing from the tumulus fill. Photo: author.

high outer ring (Young 1981:84) and filling inward, might seem odd at first, until one remembers that starting at the full diameter of the bottom of the conical mound would have allowed more people/ wagons/pack animals to have access to the construction site at the same time where most of the dirt would be needed. This made the building of the tumulus not only more efficient, but it also caused the

deposited soil to be compacted by foot traffic as the loading progressed inwards toward the center, level by level.

The construction of Tumulus MM was a concerted effort, with all sections built up at the same time, at least to the moment of the funeral of the dead king. A chance discovery in 2007 connects that ceremony to the actual construction of the

Fig. 9.26. View from below of the southwest notch in the central cross-beam, showing at left two of the beams from the west interior wall. Photo: author.

tomb chamber. Four names in Phrygian script were found inscribed at one end of a 9 m long roof beam, and more of them are visible at the beam's end (Fig. 9.27). One of the names, Sitsidos, is already attested in Tumulus MM—it had been written in wax that was pressed into one of the ring-handled bowls that was found in the tomb chamber during excavation. Consequently, at least one of the signatories had been a guest at the funeral banquet, and all the evidence suggested that the others were too (Liebhart and Brixhe 2009). However, investigations in 2011 showed that no other names were inscribed on this roof beam. While this alters the original hypothesis concerning the names, it still seems most likely that Sitsidos, at least, was among the funeral guests.

After the burial and closing of the tomb chamber with the roof beams, the secondary roof was built, and then the rubble was piled up on top until it cov-

Fig. 9.27. Drawing of the names inscribed on the roof beam in Tumulus MM. Drawing: Kimberly Leaman and author.

ered the entire inner complex. At that point, the rest of the tumulus was built at whatever pace the Phrygians chose—there was now no reason to hurry.

Unlike the stone pyramids of Egypt, there is almost no way that any significant portion of Tumulus MM could have been built while the king was still alive, unless he had been so gravely ill that his imminent demise was predictable. There could have been planning and stockpiling of materials, but the nature of the monument and its wooden tomb chamber precluded its partial construction and exposure to the elements. For the complete construction of Tumulus MM, one should be thinking months instead of years, and perhaps even weeks instead of months.[15]

Of course, this discussion of a timeline for the construction of Tumulus MM is the opinion of one researcher. It has nothing to do with engineering tables and charts, and it may have too much to do with working in a cool, dark, dusty place for too many years. But however much one might learn about the Phrygians, they never cease to surprise us. Perhaps in another 50 years, some future archaeologist may have the tools and techniques to answer some of these questions. With any luck and a lot of care, Tumulus MM and its tomb chamber will still be around to impress and amaze. And most likely, it will still be the oldest standing wooden building in the world.

NOTES

9.1. The total number of tumuli in the Gordion area has usually been described in print as being around 80 (e.g., in the introductory note by G.K. Sams in Kohler 1995:xxxvi, and in Liebhart and Johnson 2005:191). Recent survey work by American and Turkish researchers put the number at around 100. In 2007, Ben Marsh added to this number primarily by studying aerial photographs from the 1950s (pers. comm. 2008). The tentative count now stands at around 240 tumuli (though many of these may prove to be natural or modern features in the landscape). This larger number does seem to fit better a scenario of elite burials for a major city over a period of use from about 850–600 BC (plus what appears to have been a less frequent use down into the Hellenistic period). It would suggest that not only were members of the royal family buried in the tumuli, but many of the important non-royal inhabitants received similar honors, varying in degree according to size and location of the tumulus.

Many of the smaller tumuli visible in the early aerial photographs have been made visually undetectable today by modern plowing. The silting of the valley has no doubt covered many lower-lying small tumuli as well. Thus, the total number of identified tumuli at Gordion could rise or fall with future investigation.

9.2. The tumuli excavated by the Körte brothers are designated K-I, K-II, K-III, K-IV, and K-V (Körte and Körte 1904). The University of Pennsylvania excavations investigated Tumuli A, B, C, D, E, F, G, H, I, J, K, L, M, N, O, P, Q, R, S, T (this is still included in the list despite the fact that it was probably not a tumulus but a natural feature that produced no evidence of a burial), U, W (V was left out of the series to avoid confusion with K-V), X, Y, Z, KY, MM, S-1, S-2, and S-3, plus the salvage excavation in 1953 of an unnamed tumulus found a few kilometers west of Gordion near the modern village of Kıranharmanı (Kohler 1980, 1995; Young 1955:16–17; 1981). Turkish archaeologists from the Museum of Anatolian Civilizations in Ankara excavated Kızlarkayası A, B, and C a few kilometers north of the Citadel Mound (Saatçi and Kopar 1990); at Kıranharmanı, Tumuli A and B, and Köyönü Tümülüsü (Yağcı 1991); Mamaderisi Tumulus to the west of the Citadel Mound (Temisoy 1992); and a salvage excavation on the ridge north of Tumulus MM in 2001, which produced no finds (unpublished).

9.3. See Kohler 1980 for a preliminary discussion of the cremation burials.

9.4. The text in Young 1981:94 and footnote 13 on p. 95 make it sound as if Charles Williams made some initial drawings in 1958 and added to these in 1961, but he worked on the tomb only in 1961 while excavating at Gordion (pers. comm. 2007).

9.5. While a discussion of the dating of the tomb is beyond the scope of this chapter, there are indications that the juniper logs were indeed cut specifically for use in this tomb, and that there was no appreciable time gap between their cutting and their installation in the tomb. For an overview of Gordion's chronology, see Rose and Darbyshire 2011.

9.6. The confirmation of cedar (*Cedrus*) for at least 8 of the floor beams is a relatively recent development, and it is somewhat casually mentioned in an article describing the deterioration of some of the wood in the tomb chamber (Filley et al. 2001:13346). One sample from the floor timbers taken in 1957 had already been identified as cedar, but another was (mis-)identified as yew (*Taxus*; see Young 1981:292). The soft-rot fungus that caused the majority of the deterioration of the wood in the tomb chamber made identification of the species of wood very difficult (Blanchette and Simpson 1992). Proper identification of wood species found in the tomb often requires an electron microscope and a knowledge of the effects of soft rot on the wood cell structure (see Blanchette et al. 1991:5, 9–11. More recent analysis of the floor beams shows that pine was used for at least 3 of the floor beams (Aytuğ, Blanchette, and Held 2010:170). A complete analysis of the species of wood for every timber in the tomb still needs to be performed.

9.7.   The area of the tomb chamber is 31.93 m² in Tumulus MM versus ca. 17 m² in Tumulus Z.

9.8.   This CAD model is the product of a collaboration between this writer and my Turkish colleague Banu Bedel.

9.9.   This feature is obvious to anyone walking the tomb chamber. It had long been assumed that the curvature was due to the weight of the walls pressing down on the edges of the floor, but problems with the original floor elevations as they related to the elevations of the crossbeams in the CAD model of the tomb chamber led the author to reconsider the issue. It seems impossible for the walls to bend the floor beams across their lengths as the weight of the tumulus bore down upon the walls. It would have been even more so across the width of the tomb chamber, where the eastern wall in particular would have simply crushed the easternmost floor beam (which it actually did to a relatively small degree). What happened regularly in the tomb chamber was a localized distortion and crushing of wood fibers. In fact, the cedar floor beams appear to have held up better than many of the pine beams of the walls, although this may be due to the spreading of the weight over the length of the east and west floor beams and across all 13 floor beams at north and south. The curvature of the floor may have been an attempt by the Phrygians to divert any water entering the tomb (i.e., rainwater) out from the tomb chamber. This would at first seem to indicate that the tomb was built before the death of the king and was designed to withstand exposure to the elements. But there is no indication that the wood at any level of the tomb was exposed to the weather; in fact, the opposite seems to be true. Many surfaces are nearly as fresh as when new, with no oxidation of the wood or deterioration of any kind. Another example of the Phrygian builders' concern about keeping water out of the tomb chamber is the presence of gutters at the sides of the roof. These were created just inside the upper extensions of the lines of the east and west outer casing, with their north

and south ends cut into the upper surfaces of the ends of the gable supports. There would have been no reason at all for these gutters before the roof beams were installed. Only then would the upper members of the outer casing have created a kind of dam wall that (at least in the minds of the Phrygian builders) would have required a means of diverting any rainwater away from the tomb chamber and out into the rubble packing outside the line of the outer casing (see Fig. 9.17). These features presumably were intended for potential use after the burial took place and the rubble pile and tumulus were mounded over the tomb chamber complex (i.e., in case it rained during that period—could the tomb have been built at the end of the dry summer at a time when rains were expected?). In short, the curvature of the floor and the gutters might suggest a certain compulsive nature of the Phrygian builders, but these features do not indicate that the tomb was built in advance of the death of the king. Everything about the construction and preservation of the tomb chamber suggests that it was built relatively quickly, and that it was exposed to the elements only as long as it took to build, bury the king, and bury the tomb chamber.

9.10. There are two rows of 10 spikes in the west wall, two rows of 12 spikes in the south wall, and rows of 8, 9, and 8 in the east wall. Young (1981:100n26) seems to have miscounted the number of spikes in the south wall, giving a total of 13 for the bottom row (an easy mistake to make given the difficulty of proper lighting in the tomb chamber).

9.11. See Young (1981:94) for his discussion of this upper structure.

9.12. The south crossbeam system was treated differently than those at the center and north. At the south, the crossbeam members were of different lengths, but they still received wooden clamps. Here, the clamps fitted unusually between the ends of the lower (and shorter) southern beam and into the sides of the lower (and longer) northern beam. In addition, the wider ends of these clamps were cut in the shape of a swallow tail, unlike the squared ends of the clamps in the center and north crossbeams. Even more curiously, the actual clamps at the south end were not used in the final construction, suggesting a program of fitting these timbers away from their ultimate position, most likely in a work area just off to the side (another indication that the tumulus was built up at the same time as the tomb chamber, thus creating a surface on which to work). This upper section of the south end of the tomb chamber has a number of other odd features in its construction, and they are still under investigation.

9.13. Alternatively, the beams could have been set up in a workspace off the tomb chamber walls to be marked and cut, using the dowels as holding devices for the working of the beams and then repositioning devices for the final installation (in a similar fashion suggested in note 9 for the south crossbeams). However, the narrow and relatively delicate sections of the gable supports at either edge of the tomb roof/ceiling would have been susceptible to breakage during the transporting of the beam to its final position on the tomb. It is likely that the final cutting, at least, was done with the gable support in the position it holds today.

9.14. Young says in passing that the juniper logs at the north end (where he first encountered them during the removal of the rubble fill) each ended "in a neat, vertical face cut by sawing" (Young 1981:86). Again, without very good lighting, it is difficult to see such details as tool marks, and the ends of the juniper logs were trimmed square to their lengths. The precision is indeed remarkable, since a chopping tool was used instead of a saw. Identification of the use of an axe for trimming the ends of the juniper logs, along with analysis of many other tool marks in the tomb chamber complex, was provided by Douglas Reed in 2012 (pers. comm.).

9.15. The other tumuli at Gordion never seem to elicit suggestions of construction before the death of the occupant, presumably because their smaller sizes do not create any sense of wonder about how long it took to build them. It is only the scale of Tumulus MM that prompts such an idea. It still seems more likely that the normal Phrygian tumulus construction concepts are at work here, but writ large under the direction of Midas, who was determined to illustrate his own and Phrygia's status and power.

10

Royal Phrygian Furniture and Fine Wooden Artifacts from Gordion

Elizabeth Simpson

In 2012 the Gordion Furniture Project conducted its 32nd season of research and conservation in the Museum of Anatolian Civilizations, Ankara.[1] Many interesting advances have been made in recent years, as the team has concentrated its efforts on the furniture and other wooden artifacts from Tumulus P, Tumulus W, and the City Mound at Gordion. In order to understand these discoveries one must first review the furniture from Tumulus MM. Because these pieces were so well preserved, we studied them first; what we learned about the furniture from this tomb has been the basis for all subsequent work (Simpson 2010).

Rodney Young called the largest burial mound at the site Tumulus MM—for "Midas Mound," after the powerful Phrygian king who ruled at Gordion during the second half of the 8th century BC (Young 1981:79–80; Körte and Körte 1904:20, 23). Young eventually came to believe that the king buried beneath the mound was not Midas but his father, and the tomb's occupant has still not been identified with certainty.

The theory that the tomb was the burial of Midas' father gains support from recent C-14/dendrochronological studies, with the most recently proposed date for the cutting of the logs of the tomb's outer casing reported as 740 BC +7/-3 (see DeVries et al. 2003). This date may undergo further revision, however, and the determination reflects the date at which the outer logs were cut, giving only a *terminus post quem* for the burial.[2]

The mysterious King Midas and his dynasty feature in many of the chapters in this volume. Re-garding the furniture from Tumulus MM, the ruler becomes something of a reality. Whether the tomb was that of King Midas or his predecessor, the grave goods had, in some sense, belonged to Midas himself: if the king took the throne on the death of his father, he surely would have officiated at the final rites (Simpson 2001:33). Midas was a contemporary of the Assyrian king Sargon II (r. 721–705 BC), and has been associated by scholars with Mita of Mushki (Körte and Körte 1904:9–10, 18 [after Winckler]; Mellink 1965:318; Muscarella 1995:92). Mita appears in Sargon's annals for the years 5–13 (Luckenbill 1926:part 2, 4ff), dated to ca. 718–709 BC (Hawkins 1994:271), with Mushki, a land to the east incorporated into the Phrygian Kingdom by the late 8th century BC.

Midas was also known to the Greeks (Roller 1983, 1984). According to Herodotos, he was the first foreigner to make an offering at the sanctuary of Apollo at Delphi, dedicating his throne, which was "well worth seeing" (Herodotos 1.14; Devries and Rose, this volume). This tantalizing comment was in the minds of the excavators, from Gustav and Alfred Körte (1904:21) to Rodney Young (1974:2; 1981:260–61), so it seemed fitting that they should find Phrygian furniture at Gordion.

After Young's death in 1974, his work was continued by his colleagues and students, and in 1978 I began to study the wooden objects. My first task was to assess the early field drawings and then produce ink versions for the posthumous publication of Young's three great early tombs. Comparison between the field drawings and the excavation photo-

Fig. 10.1. The remains of the king lying on his collapsed coffin. Tumulus MM, Gordion, 1957. Source: Gordion Project, Penn Museum.

graphs, however, showed that most of the drawings were inaccurate. While many of the early renderings were published in *Three Great Early Tumuli* (1981), a new study was deemed necessary, and I was asked to republish the wooden finds.

I first went to Ankara to see the collection in 1981 and found the wood in extremely fragile condition. Working in the museum laboratory at the time was Robert Payton, conservator for the British Institute of Archaeology in Ankara. Payton took an interest in the furniture, which resulted in a collaborative effort, under my direction, to save the wood from further deterioration. This led to a major conservation project, now headed by Krysia Spirydowicz of Queen's University in Kingston, Ontario, and conducted under the auspices of the University of Pennsylvania Museum. To date, more than 40 conservators, scientists, and graduate interns have contributed to this effort. The techniques developed by the project's conservators now serve as the standard

for the conservation of dry archaeological wood (Payton 1984, Simpson and Payton 1986, Blanchette and Simpson 1992, Spirydowicz 1996, Simpson and Spirydowicz 1999, Spirydowicz et al. 2001, Simpson 2003, and Spirydowicz 2010).

The Furniture from Tumulus MM

The study and conservation of the wooden objects from Tumulus MM have revealed extensive information, not only about the king's furniture but also regarding the circumstances of the burial. None of this was obvious to Young and his team as they entered the tomb.

The first thing the excavators saw when they cut through the tomb wall was the skeleton of the king lying on a mass of textiles, covering what Young thought was a four-poster bed (Fig. 10.1). Along the west wall lay bronze jugs and what were apparently bronze and leather belts. At the south of the tomb were three large bronze cauldrons on iron stands, and inside the cauldrons were pottery vessels containing the remains of food. Leaning against the east wall were two ornate screen-like objects, which Young identified as throne backs (Fig. 10.2). To the south of these, a fancy inlaid table had collapsed, with its legs and frame preserved. Nearby were the legs and tops of eight "plain" tables, which had also fallen to the floor. Strewn over the area were bronze omphalos bowls, jugs, and dishes of various types, which had once sat on the tables or hung from nails on the walls. The tomb had contained 170 bronze vessels, 10 belts, more than 180 bronze fibulae, 18 pottery vessels, and at least 15 pieces of fine wooden furniture (Young 1981:79–190, fig. 66; Simpson 2010:viii, 7–28).

Our initial project was the inlaid table, which Young called the "Pagoda Table" because of its exotic design. The table had fallen with its square frame

intact, enabling the excavators to understand its general form. However, the early field drawings depicted an odd-looking object which Young considered ungainly (Young 1974:6–9; 1981:183–87, figs. 109–11, pls. 82–83). The table had three legs, with scroll feet, and three structural supports that rose from the feet to prop up the frame. Subsequent study has shown that the table was made of boxwood, inlaid with juniper, with a walnut top (Blanchette, Held, and Aytuğ 2010:166–67).

The excavators attempted to conserve the table by immersing it in a bath of alcohol to dry the wood and then soaking it in a solution of paraffin (Fig. 10.3). However, the wax did not enter the fine pores of the boxwood, but instead coated the surface, obscuring the contrast between the colorful woods (Simpson and Spirydowicz 1999:36; Spirydowicz 2010:137–39).

Retreatment of the table by Robert Payton began in 1982. The surface was first cleaned with sol-

Fig. 10.2. Serving stands and tables *in situ* in the Tumulus MM chamber, 1957. Source: Gordion Project, Penn Museum.

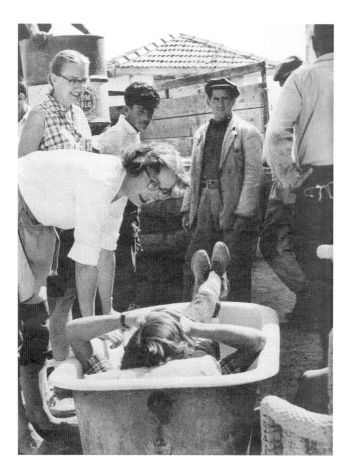

Fig. 10.3. Ellen Kohler, Grace Muscarella, Machteld Mellink (in bathtub), and other members of the staff at Gordion in 1957. The bathtub was used for the on-site consolidation of much of the wooden furniture from Tumulus MM. Source: Gordion Project, Penn Museum.

vents, and the wood was then consolidated under vacuum in a solution of Butvar-B98 (polyvinyl butyral). After consolidation, the pieces were removed from the solution, wrapped in polyethylene sheeting, and allowed to dry slowly. When the wood had dried, the surface was cleaned, and the pieces could be handled and studied. This method has been used, with some variation, for almost all the wooden objects from Gordion.

Following treatment, the wood was stronger and lighter in color. The elaborate inlay was once again visible, and detail drawings could be made of the table's 40 major components (Simpson 1983; 2010: figs. 4–20, 22–28). The sophisticated designs include mazes and other symbols, many of which were not merely "decorative" (Simpson 1988:28–29;

1996:191; 2010: figs. 9, 17). Motifs that occur on the inlaid table also appear as markings on early figurines and survive on women's dowry textiles and ritual cloths in Europe and Anatolia, down to the present (Kelly 1989, 1999; Allen 1981). Evidence suggests that these patterns were protective and empowering, with connotations of procreation and fertility (Schuster and Carpenter 1986–88, 1996). The inlaid table was covered with such apotropaic and religious symbols, suggesting a ritual function (Simpson 2010:48–56).

After completing the detail drawings, I was able to reconstruct the table on paper (Fig. 10.4). The new drawing revealed a finely crafted, complex work of art, which was far more elegant than the early drawings had suggested (Simpson 1983; 2010: fig. 21). Study revealed that the inlaid table was a portable banquet table, carried by its four handles in order to transport and serve food on its tray-shaped top. Once the table's form was clearly understood, we were able to reconstruct the actual object. This was accomplished by attaching the wood of the table to a Plexiglas frame supported on a metal stand. The initial mount was constructed in 1983, followed by an improved version in 1989 (Simpson and Payton 1986:45–46; Simpson and Spirydowicz 1999:37–39; Simpson 2010:159–62). The inlaid table could now be seen assembled for the first time in 2,700 years.

Young's "screens" were made of boxwood, inlaid with juniper, with walnut top pieces and curved "legs" set into the front faces (Fig. 10.5) (Blanchette, Held, and Aytuğ 2010:166, 168–69). As with the other wooden objects from the tomb, the initial treatment of the screens in 1957 had darkened and damaged the wood. Gordion Furniture Project conservators were able to improve the situation with the retreatment of the wood in 1983 and 1984, which revealed new information about the design and construction of the screens (Simpson and Spirydowicz 1999:41–43; Spirydowicz 2010:142–44). At the center of each face was an inlaid rosette, supported by two curved lion's legs with scroll feet. These elements were set within a grid of inlaid square designs surrounded by thousands of tiny diamonds and triangles. Each so-called

Fig. 10.4. Reconstruction drawing of the inlaid table (5212 W 80), Tumulus MM. Illustration: E. Simpson, 1985. Photo: author.

screen had a walnut top piece supported by a back leg and diagonal struts: during the course of our research, we discovered that the "screens" were actually serving stands (Fig. 10.6) (Simpson and Payton 1986:46; Simpson 2010:65–74). Their tops featured carved wooden rings which had held small bronze cauldrons, ten of which were found nearby in the tomb. With these were two bronze ladles, which had undoubtedly been used to transfer the contents of the cauldrons into other vessels (Young 1981:110–12 [MM 4–13], 123 [MM 47–48]; Simpson 2010: color pls. VIB–C).

After their conservation, the serving stands were assembled for display, mounted initially in 1984 and remounted in 1999 (Simpson and Payton 1986:47; Simpson 2010:162–63). The stands, along with the inlaid table, can now be seen assembled in the Museum of Anatolian Civilizations. In 1997, the stands were installed in new cases, designed by Erkal Saran and fabricated by MOB Mobilya-Dekorasyon A.Ş. in Ankara for the Gordion wooden objects on view in the museum (Simpson 2010:162).

With the aid of new drawings, the inlaid decoration on the faces of the stands could be analyzed and interpreted (Simpson 1988:29–37; 2010:77–83). There were 202 square designs in the field of stand A and 188 on stand B, and most were symmetrical with respect to rotations of 180°. That is, a rotation

of the original design by 180° will replicate the design exactly. However, any other operation on the design will yield one of three other options, for a total of four distinct square motifs. The Phrygian cabinetmakers played with this special feature, turning and flipping a few main designs to create a seemingly endless variety of patterns—and an overall scheme of baffling complexity.

The meaning of the rosette complex at the center of the faces of the stands has now been partially deciphered (Simpson 2010:87–110). The key to the discovery lay in the arts of the greater Near East, where symbols could be used to represent deities. One such instance occurs on the Neo-Babylonian stone tablet of King Nabû-apla-iddina (r. ca. 887–855 BC), which shows the sun god Shamash seated in his shrine at Sippar (Woods 2004). Before the god, at the center of the composition, is his symbol, a large sun disc, set up on an altar or table. This image recalls the motifs on the faces of the Tumulus MM stands. Above the seated god, the sun disc is shown again along with two other symbols. These three designs are identified by an inscription as "Sin, Shamash, and Ishtar," with Ishtar represented by a star rosette. This suggests that the rosettes on the Gordion serving stands might symbolize a Near Eastern goddess.

Fig. 10.5. Inlaid serving stands *in situ* in the Tumulus MM chamber, 1957. Source: Gordion Project, Penn Museum.

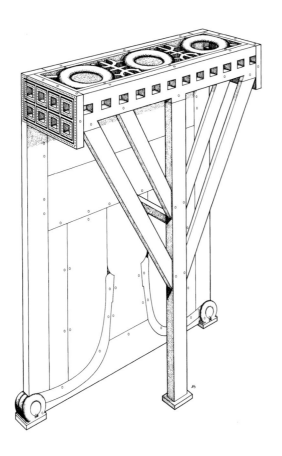

The iconography can be further decoded through a series of monuments in the Phrygian Highlands, located to the southwest of Gordion. One of the grandest is Arslan Kaya, cut from a rocky outcrop and representing a shrine of the Phrygian Mother Goddess, Matar (Haspels 1971:87–89, figs. 186–91, 523; Simpson 1998: figs. 8–9; Simpson 2010:93–96, pls. 120, 121A). The façade is decorated with geometric patterns, and a doorway in the lower part of the façade frames a niche. Inside the niche is an image of the goddess Matar, flanked by two attendant lions standing on their hind legs and touching her head with their paws. This scene can be recognized, in abstract form, on the faces of the Tumulus MM serving stands. The rosette, a symbol for the Mesopotamian goddess Ishtar, was appropriated by the Phrygians to symbolize their own great

Fig. 10.6. Reconstruction drawing of serving stand A (5229 W 81), Tumulus MM, back view. Illustration: E. Simpson, 1986. Photo: author.

goddess. Her attendant lions are represented by the curved lion legs that support the rosette from below. The Gordion stands can thus be identified as portable shrines of Matar. Like the inlaid table, the stands were important ceremonial objects utilizing powerful numinous imagery.

Tumulus MM had contained eight "plain" banquet tables, each with three curved legs and a tray-shaped top. The legs of all these tables were made of boxwood, and seven of the table tops were walnut. The eighth top (table 6) is severely decayed and cannot be identified with certainty; it may be maple or cherry (Blanchette, Held, and Aytuğ 2010:166–68). The plain tables were initially treated in 1957 (Simpson and Spirydowicz 1999:43–45; Spirydowicz 2010:144–45). Over a period of 12 years our team conserved these fragile tables, and by 1999 all had been placed in protective storage (Simpson and Spirydowicz 1999:45–48, 73–74, figs. 48, 108; Spirydowicz 2010:145–55). After retreatment the wood could be studied and drawn, allowing the form of the tables to be understood. Tenons at the tops of the legs were fit into "collars" that extended down from the lower surface of the table tops. Research has shown that this system of joinery was widespread, attested in the Middle Bronze Age tombs of Jericho and in the Pazyryk burials of the 4th century BC (Simpson 1995:1654–55, 1668–69; 2010:62–64).

Found in the northeast corner of the tomb were the remains of two stools and a chair, which were eventually identified from numerous decayed fragments of boxwood and juniper (Blanchette, Held, and Aytuğ 2010:166, 169). The chair had a carved backrest, with small animals depicted in panels, the only figural decoration from the Tumulus MM burial (Simpson 1993; 2010:111–17). Degraded chunks of reddish purple textiles showed that fine cloth had been placed on these pieces of furniture, perhaps including pillows with lofted batting (Ballard et al. 2010:211–16, 222–23).

At the north of the chamber was the king's "bed," which I had reconstructed in a drawing for Young's posthumous volume, based on his interpretation at the time of excavation (Young 1981:187–90, figs. 112–13). Subsequent research, however, showed that the "bed" was actually a coffin, carved from a huge cedar log, with ledges extending out at both ends. Four large pine blocks had braced the log

coffin, and inlaid rails were socketed into the sides (Simpson 1990; 2010:119–25). The king had lain on a bedding of textiles, including reddish purple fabric and gold-colored woven flax, which achieved its golden hue from the mineral goethite (see Ballard, this volume; Ballard et al. 2010:204–11, 220–22).

This combined research has enabled us to reconstruct the circumstances of the king's burial. The remains of the coffin, as found on the tomb floor, revealed that a ceremony had taken place before the interment: the coffin had clearly been assembled elsewhere before the burial, then disassembled, and its parts placed in the chamber in something other than their original arrangement. The contents of the tomb—which were largely banquet furnishings—were no doubt used for the ceremony. The tables, serving stands, bronze vessels, and organic residues were evidently the remains of a ritual sacrifice, followed by a gala feast, in honor of the dead king (Simpson 2001; 2010:127–35). Analysis of the food and drink residues produced the menu of the funerary banquet. The small cauldrons that sat in the tops of the serving stands contained a mixed fermented beverage made of grape wine, barley beer, and honey mead. The food consumed was a spicy stew, made with barbecued sheep or goat, honey, wine, olive oil, and apparently lentils, seasoned with anise or fennel (McGovern 2001; 2010:177–87; McGovern et al. 1999).

Furniture and Wooden Objects from Tumulus P

This rather complete picture can help with the interpretation of the Tumulus P and Tumulus W burials. These tombs produced a spectacular array of wooden objects, but they are less well preserved because the roofs of the chambers had collapsed, crushing the contents. Tumulus P covered the tomb of a small child, whose only remains consisted of teeth (Young 1981:9).

The tomb was excavated in 1956, producing at least 21 pieces of furniture and 49 additional wooden objects (Young 1981:1–77). The excavation was extremely difficult due to the condition of the chamber, and the damaged artifacts were recorded in terms of the particular roof beams or floorboards to which they had become attached. A plan was later reconstructed

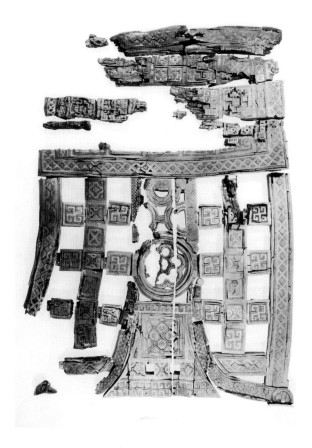

Fig. 10.7. Inlaid face of the serving stand from Tumulus P, after conservation, 1985. The serving stand incorporates fragments catalogued as 4257 W 60 and 4258 W 61. Photo: author.

Fig. 10.8. Reconstruction drawing of the face of the Tumulus P serving stand. Illustration: E. Simpson, 1987. Photo: author.

based on the excavation notes, although some of the objects were inadvertently drawn in the wrong locations (Young 1981: fig. 5; Simpson and Spirydowicz 1999: fig. 60). This affected the early interpretations, including that of a "screen," which was found in the southwest corner of the tomb along with other pieces of furniture (Young 1981:62–67); some of these pieces were partially protected by fallen roof beams that had formed a sort of lean-to over the area.

The Tumulus P "screen" was actually a serving stand made of boxwood and inlaid with juniper and yew. Its face was carved in openwork, with a large rosette at the center supported by lion legs and surrounded by elaborate inlaid patterns. Although much of the wood had deteriorated, enough survived to allow the face to be reconstructed completely (Figs. 10.7, 10.8) (Simpson and Spirydowicz 1999:52–54). This process was aided by an under-

standing of Phrygian decorative conventions, gained through our work on the Tumulus MM furniture. The stand had a curved back leg crowned with a U-shaped element, which supported a carved top piece that featured two open rings (Simpson and Spirydowicz 1999: figs. 64–65). The rings were octagonal in section, and on their inner bevels were deposits of bronze residue. This showed that bronze vessels had originally been placed in the top piece, as with the Tumulus MM stands (Simpson and Spirydowicz 1999: figs. 65–66). It was these bronze deposits that first suggested that all three "screens" were actually serving stands.

The Tumulus P stand was not well understood at the time of excavation, and the back leg was reconstructed in a peculiar manner: in early drawings a penannular wooden ring, which appeared on the plan in the southwest corner, was added at the

Fig. 10.9. Reconstruction drawing of the front face of the inlaid, studded stool, Tumulus P. The stool incorporates elements catalogued as 4256 W 59, 4337 W 72, and 4338 W 73. Illustration: E. Simpson, 1987. Photo: author.

0   10 cm

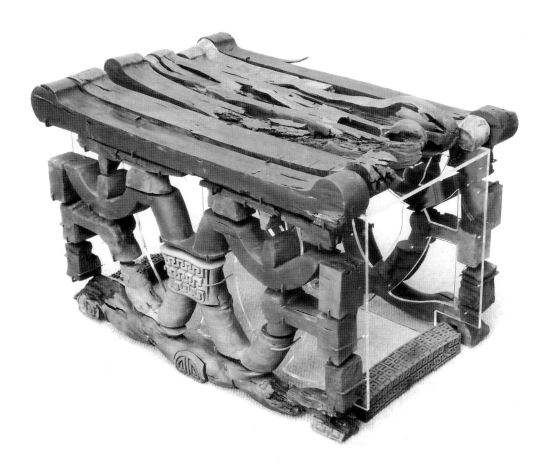

Fig. 10.10. The inlaid stool from Tumulus P, as seen from the back, reconstructed for display in the Museum of Anatolian Civilizations, 1993. Photo: author.

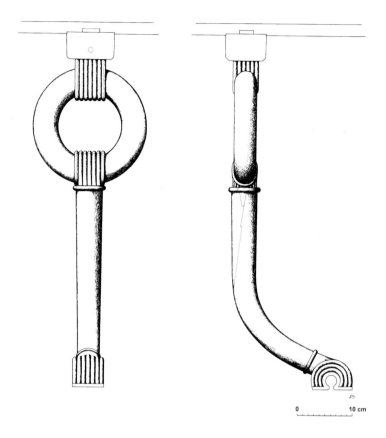

0　　　　　　10 cm

Fig. 10.11. Reconstruction drawing of one of the legs of the "Tripod Tray Table," Tumulus P. The table includes fragments catalogued as 4237 W 40, 4260 W 63, 4252 W 55, 4244 W 47, and 4253 W 56. Illustrations: E. Simpson, 1988. Photo: author.

The wood was conserved in 1984 and 1985; after treatment the pieces could be studied and the fragments positioned correctly (Fig. 10.9). The front and back faces were made from alternating strips of boxwood and yew; the boxwood strips, where inlaid, were inlaid with yew, and one yew strip was inlaid with boxwood. The two faces were joined at the top by a series of planks, and at the bottom by two stretchers that were carved on their top and outer faces (Simpson and Spirydowicz 1999: fig. 69).

The stool was reconstructed on a Plexiglas mount (1993) and is now on display in the Museum of Anatolian Civilizations (Fig. 10.10). The design of this stool is unusual and can only be understood in reference to the Tumulus MM inlaid table (Simpson 1988:35; 1996:204–6). Each face of the stool was a rendering of such a table, with the three-dimensional table "collapsed" into two dimensions for the purpose of design. As if this idea were not clever enough, the cabinetmakers then denied the implication of the third dimension by alternating the colored woods, obscuring the original intention and reducing the stool faces to a series of stripes.

The remains of several pieces of furniture were found at the north of the Tumulus P chamber, including the "Tripod Tray Table," named for its large, carved boxwood top (Simpson and Spirydowicz 1999:57–58). The table had three exceptional legs that were not initially recognized because of their fragmentary condition (Young 1981:67). At the top of each leg was a large ring, "held" above and below by moldings carved to evoke "fingers" or claws; from the bottom set extended a curved leg that terminated in a stylized animal-paw foot (Fig. 10.11). These legs had clearly belonged to the table, as proved by the mortise-and-tenon joinery.

The new reconstruction of the table's legs solved the mystery of the furniture in the tomb's southwest corner. The penannular ring that had once been attributed to the leg of the serving stand actually belonged to one of the legs of the Tripod Tray Table,

bottom of the leg (Young 1981: figs. 35–36). This reconstruction is clearly untenable, however, and when the ring is removed, the foot sits squarely on the ground (Simpson 1996:198). The pieces of the Tumulus P stand are now in storage in the Museum of Anatolian Civilizations (Simpson and Spirydowicz 1999: fig. 109).

Found near the stand in the southwest corner of the tomb were pieces of a carved wooden stool, which was inlaid in geometric patterns and studded with bronze tacks (Simpson and Spirydowicz 1999:54–56). The front face of the stool had been drawn incorrectly, due in part to the misplacement of the fragments in photographs taken at the time of excavation. In addition, the forms were drawn without reconstructing the shrunken areas, so the stool face looked odd, and the form of the stool was not understood (Young 1981:72–74, fig. 42, pl. 32A–C).

and was found at the north of the chamber, not the southwest.

Near the Tripod Tray Table were the remains of another fancy table, named the "Mosaic Table" by Young because of its boldly inlaid top (Simpson and Spirydowicz 1999:58–59). The top was made of boxwood boards, joined edge to edge and inlaid with strips of yew in a pattern of squares and crosses. It too was poorly understood and hard to envision from the early drawings (Young 1981: fig. 39). The table was treated at the time of excavation, which did not strengthen the wood but helped keep the fragments together. This facilitated our new treatment, after which the pieces could be studied and drawn. Work progressed slowly, however, because so little of the table had survived intact. Only in 2006, after 16 years of study, could the form and decoration of the Mosaic Table be reconstructed.

Many other wooden objects were found in the Tumulus P chamber; all were fragmentary, but most could be recognized in the context of the Tumulus MM furniture (Simpson and Spirydowicz 1999:56–57, 59–67). These included two plain tables, six or more stools, two footstools, a small chair or throne, and a full-size bed. The bed was reconstructed in a drawing at the time of excavation, but because of the poor condition of the fragments, the accuracy of this rendering cannot be verified (Young 1981:

Fig. 10.12. Top of the parasol from Tumulus P (4236 W 39), after conservation, 2004. Photo: author.

fig.40; Simpson and Spirydowicz 1999: fig.80). Sections survive from an inlaid "headboard" and carved footboard, along with several unplaced inlaid pieces. Although the headboard is not well understood, in 2006 the footboard and adjoining legs were successfully reconstructed in drawings. Recently studied items from Tumulus P include a parasol (Fig. 10.12), a box, 8 spoons or ladles (Fig. 10.13), and 23 plates and bowls. These ranged in size from miniature to enormous, and some were apparently made as sets (Young 1981: pls. 25–27). Most were incomplete, and a few were preserved in only one or two small remnants. One group of pieces

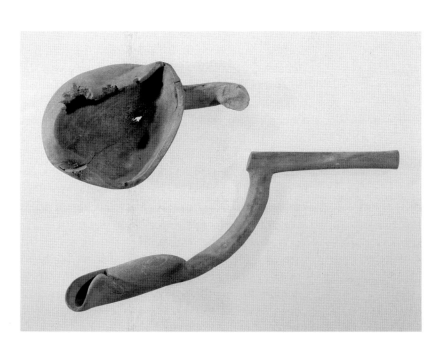

Fig. 10.13. Fragment of a ladle (4332 W 67) and spoon (4044 W 16) from Tumulus P, after conservation, 1998. Photo: author.

is presented here as a case study in order to illustrate the difficulties experienced by Young and his artists, and then by our team, in working with these extremely fragmentary objects (Figs. 10.14–10.18).

"Four fragments that do not join" were interpreted after their excavation as "fragments of a square bowl," which was catalogued as 4227 W 30. The piece was reconstructed in a drawing by J.S. Last, pictured in Young (1981: fig. 27, pl. 26I, showing the base and two rim fragments, here Fig. 10.14). The drawing showed a deep dish with a rounded contour, four small handles that extended out from the four corners at the level of the rim, and a square base. The upper surface of the rim was decorated

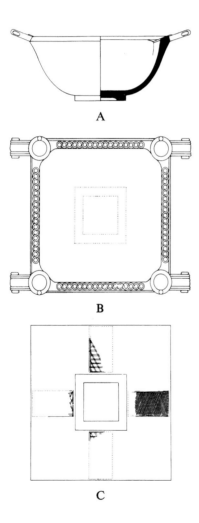

A

B

C

Fig. 10.14. Early reconstruction drawing of a "square bowl" from Tumulus P, illustrated in Young 1981: fig. 27, and originally catalogued as 4227 W 30. Source: Gordion Project, Penn Museum.

with an inscribed guilloche pattern (Fig. 10.14B), and four panels of cross-hatching were incised on the exterior of the vessel, extending from the sides of the base to the rim (Fig. 10.14C). The early drawing showed two different types of cross-hatching on the back, one type deriving from the pattern on the base fragment, and the other on the (non-joining) rim fragments. This discrepancy seemed unusual in the context of the other wooden vessels from the tomb, some of which had incised patterns on their back surfaces but never of more than one design. This suggested that we should re-examine the fragments from the "square bowl" in order to ascertain whether the early drawing was correct.

We first considered the base, without the rim fragments, and soon found other small pieces of wood that belonged to the same vessel. One of these had been catalogued as "saucer fragment with T-shaped handle" (4229 W 32) and was illustrated in Young (1981:58, pl. 26A). The "T-shaped handle" turned out to be one of three tab-like projections that were connected by a rung, forming an elaborate handle of a square, shallow dish. More pieces of this dish were extracted from the "red-trunk" group, a cache of hundreds of unlabelled fragments found inside a large red trunk, wrapped in newspaper dated 1956; these were apparently taken to Ankara shortly after the excavation of Tumulus P and placed in storage in the Museum of Anatolian Civilizations (Simpson and Spirydowicz 1999:67). This red trunk was the source of numerous "discoveries" leading to our various new interpretations of the wooden finds from Tumulus P, as it had contained fragments of many—if not most—of the wooden objects from the burial. Our "new" plate had two handles that extended out at the ends, and although the wood was in very poor condition, almost all of both handles had survived, including two pieces that joined the base fragment (Fig. 10.15). This allowed me to reconstruct the plate almost completely in drawings (Fig. 10.16). We assigned the inventory number 4229 W 32 to this object and moved on to the rim fragments that we had set aside earlier.

Two additional fragments could be associated with the rim pieces, all of which had belonged to a second plate (Fig. 10.17). It too had projecting handles, but each handle had four tab-like projections (instead of three), connected at their ends by a rung. Although very little of this plate had survived, based on the form of the other plate, this one, too, could be reconstructed almost totally in drawings (Fig. 10.18). This object retained the original catalogue number of the "square bowl" (4227 W 30), which now no longer existed. These new plates are two of the finest small artifacts from Tumulus P and are unique among the finds from Gordion.

The most endearing of the wooden objects from Tumulus P are the miniature animals—11 animals have survived in relatively complete condition, and at least one more is extant (Simpson and Spirydo-

Fig. 10.15 (at right). Plate from Tumulus P (4229 W 32), underside, including the base fragment originally attributed to the "square bowl" (see Fig. 10.14), after conservation, 2000. Photo: author.

Fig. 10.16. Reconstruction drawing of the plate from Tumulus P (4229 W 32) shown in Figure 10.15. Illustrations: E. Simpson and J. Mandrus, 2000. Photo: author.

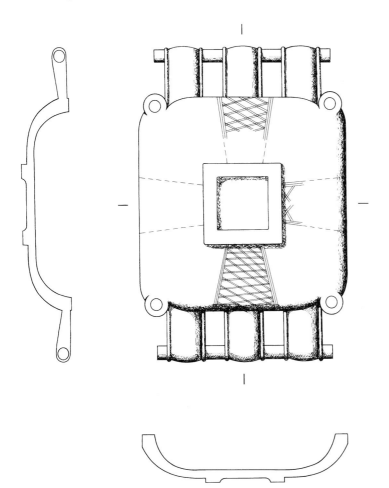

0   10 cm

wicz 1999:64–66). One of these, originally called a "horse," is less than 5 cm tall and stands on a base decorated with a zigzag pattern carved in relief (Young 1981:51, figs. 22A, 23, pl. 22A–B). The "horse" is actually a bull, as indicated by small holes in the sides of its head which had once held horns, now missing. Since 1956 this little bull had survived standing on only one complete leg. In 2004, however, we discovered that an extra animal leg from the red trunk had belonged to this bull (Fig. 10.19, left front leg). This was not obvious when we first found the leg, because it looked too large for the bull. We eventually realized that the animal had been broken before the pieces were recovered, probably when the tomb's roof collapsed; the bull's body and leg had become separated, shrinking at different rates because of the conditions associated with their respective

contexts. Also in 2004 we noticed another red-trunk fragment, a cylindrical handle, that was decorated with the same zigzag pattern as the bull (Fig. 10.19). This suggests that the two pieces had originally been attached to one another, apparently with a vertical post, and that the bull had once been mobile—in the hands of its young owner.

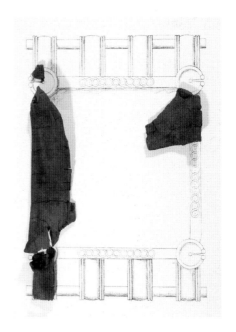

Fig. 10.17 (right). Plate from Tumulus P (4227 W 30), including fragments originally attributed to the "square bowl" (see Fig. 10.14), after conservation, 2000. The plate fragments have been positioned on a preliminary reconstruction drawing (pencil) by E. Simpson. Photo: author.

Fig. 10.18. Reconstruction drawing of the plate from Tumulus P (4227 W 30) shown in Figure 10.17. Illustrations: E. Simpson and J. Mandrus, 2000. Photo: author.

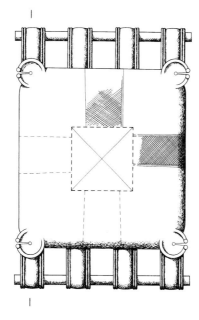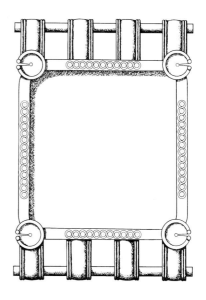

0   10 cm

Wooden Artifacts from Tumulus W

Tumulus W, the earliest of the three great royal tumuli, was excavated in 1959 (Young 1981:191–218). As with Tumulus P, the roof of the chamber had collapsed, crushing the grave goods inside. These had included the remnants of a "screen," which was apparently a serving stand like those from the Tumulus MM and P burials. Its design was quite different, however, as its front face was carved in openwork and covered with bronze studs (Simpson 1996:206–7). The Tumulus W screen had not been stored in the Museum of Anatolian Civilizations with the other wooden finds, but was found in the storeroom at Gordion in 1982. The screen was transferred to Ankara, and retreatment began in 1990. This was a difficult and time-consuming process, involving the removal of the old consolidant applied at the time of excavation, the reconsolidation of the wood,

Fig. 10.19. Small wooden bull (4033 W 5) with handle (formerly uncatalogued), after conservation, 2004. Photo: author.

and treatment of the bronze studs to inhibit further corrosion (Simpson and Spirydowicz 1999:68–70). In 1998, after eight years, the conservation of the screen was completed, and the surviving section of the carved face could be reconstructed in a drawing (Fig. 10.20). The extant fragments were attached to a Plexiglas mount, which was set onto a reproduction of the drawing, and in 2008 the drawing and mounted fragments were placed on display in the Museum of Anatolian Civilizations.

From a technical standpoint, several plates from the Tumulus W burial were among the most interesting of the wooden artifacts from Gordion (Simpson 1999:783–84; Simpson and Spirydowicz 1999:70–71, figs. 97–98). In 1995, one of the plate fragments was found to have a small pivot hole at the center of the back, suggesting that the plate had been made or finished on a lathe.[3] When we inspected the plates more closely, we noticed distinctive tool marks on the backs, indicating that the plates had indeed been made on a lathe and not merely anchored on a pivot for the finishing of the surface. These tool marks consisted of long cut marks that stopped abruptly, evidence of the back-and-forth action of the ancient rope-driven lathe. Research on the wooden objects from all three tombs has produced extensive information about the woods, tools, and techniques used by the Gordion woodworkers, situating the Phrygian craftsmen within their ancient milieu and adding greatly to our knowledge of this ancient craft tradition (Blanchette, Held, and Aytuğ 2010; Blanchette 2010; Simpson 2010:197–202).

Furniture and Wooden Objects from the City Mound

In 2007 the carbonized wooden artifacts from the City Mound at Gordion were examined and sorted, photographs were taken and preliminary drawings made, and the reorganized groups of finds were placed in archival storage. These finds included the remains of furniture and other types of objects, most of which were excavated in 1959 from Megaron 3 in the burnt debris of the Destruction Level (Young 1960:237–40; 1962a:160–63). The fragments that had survived had apparently been cov-

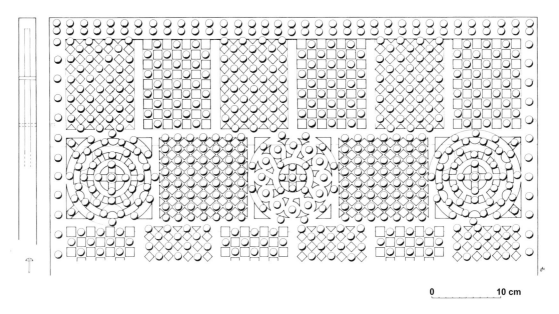

Fig. 10.20. Reconstruction drawing of the extant section of the face of the Tumulus W "screen" (6279 W 109). Illustration: E. Simpson, 1999. Photo: author.

ered by the building's fallen superstructure and then carbonized by the high heat of the fire that engulfed the city. Previous attempts to study these finds had been hampered by a mistake in the typed version of Young's Gordion Field Book 78, which replaced the word "east" as written by Young with "west" in the typed transcription (p. 29). In fact, all the furniture remains found in Megaron 3 were found along the *east* wall of the main room of the building.

These included Young's "first piece of furniture," which now consists of bronze studs and corner braces, with almost no wood remaining. Numerous ivory plaques were found in the area, but Young could not determine whether they had belonged to the "first piece of furniture" or another object that had stood nearby. The fragile plaques, preserved largely in groups of broken fragments, are carved with small, charming figures or designs of concentric squares. Young's "second piece of furniture" is represented by several inlaid chunks of carbonized wood that are now uniformly black in color, making the base wood difficult to distinguish from the inlay. The inlay technique is similar to that of the Mosaic Table from Tumulus P, suggesting that the "second piece of furniture" may have been a table with an inlaid top. In addition to the "first" and "second" pieces, numerous small fragments of inlay and bronze studs

are preserved, although it is unclear which piece (if either) these had belonged to. Finally, several finely carved wooden plaques decorated with figural or geometric designs have survived in very poor condition. Some of these were originally identified as bowls, but it now seems possible that they were flat panels, perhaps once the sides of boxes, cupboard doors, or even window shutters—although their original forms have not been determined.

These tantalizing fragments may serve to indicate the magnitude of the loss of the many fine wooden objects that once existed in the city of Midas—and to remind us of our good fortune that so many have survived intact in the tumulus burials of the necropolis.

NOTES

10.1 Figures 10.4, 10.6–13, 10.15–20 © Elizabeth Simpson; Figures 10.1–3, 10.5, and 10.14 courtesy of the Gordion Excavations, University of Pennsylvania Museum of Archaeology and Anthropology. The research and conservation of the Gordion Furniture Project is ongoing.

10.2 For an attempt to sort out the kings of the dynasty that ruled at Gordion in the 8th century BC, see Muscarella 1995:97.

10.3 The Project is grateful to Daniel Olson for suggesting we look for tool marks on the Tumulus W plates.

11

King Midas' Textiles and His Golden Touch

Mary W. Ballard

Phrygia has been famous for its garments and textiles since antiquity. A floppy, quasi-conical hat, the "Phrygian cap" has been a symbol of liberty and independence from the Roman Republic. Even today this cap is seen in the coat of arms of the United States Senate and of nations like Cuba, Colombia, and Argentina, and it is cherished by Frenchmen honoring Bastille Day, since it developed into an emblem of the French Revolution. Pliny actually credited the Phrygians with the invention of decorative weaving or embroidery in his *Natural History* (8.74.196), and the Latin word for embroiderer was "phrygio." There is, in fact, some circumstantial evidence at Gordion to support Pliny's claim: polychromatic pebble mosaics unearthed on the Citadel Mound have been viewed as textile imitations, and the variety of loomweights and spindle whorls indicate extensive weaving activity (Burke 2005). Indeed, extant fragments of tapestry weavings have been found on the Citadel Mound and additional fabrics have been found in the tumuli.

Both Louisa Bellinger (1962) and Richard Ellis (1981) studied textile fragments associated with the tombs and the citadel, and focused their examination on weave structure and pattern. They had combined and co-mingled their observations about the various fragments in order to gain a comprehensive overview of Phyrgian textile production and style, but they lacked access to analytical equipment including high magnification microscopy. This deficit can now be remedied, and technical identifications of fiber and dyestuffs should be appended to the volume on the furniture and bier in Tumulus MM (Simpson 2010).

In September 2003, textile fragments from Tumulus MM (Midas Mound) were brought to the Museum Conservation Institute, Smithsonian Institution, for analysis (Ballard et al. 2010). They can be divided into three groups, which I review below, although this chapter will focus on only one of them.

One group consisted of compact, powdery agglomerations with shadowy braid-like surface impressions, internal cords, and even a residual burr clover, fruit of the *Medicago* spp. *fabaceae* (J.W. Kress, pers. comm. 2005). While dye analysis at first seemed an impossible task, there is a curious occasion when even fugitive dyes are preserved despite fiber destruction: bacteria in the gut of keratin-eating insects cannot digest dyestuffs, so pink wool will become pink frass or purple dyed mohair, purple frass. If the fabrics had been exposed to such bacteria, then dye analysis was possible. We wondered, in particular, whether we would find evidence of the colorant Tyrian purple, the famous Royal Purple of the Phoenicians. Such a purple is technically 6,6'dibromoindigo, and can be identified by establishing the presence of bromine in the purple residue.

Using known reference standards and a special protocol against the sample, inductively coupled mass spectroscopy failed to find the presence of bromine. There is certainly no Tyrian purple present (Dussubieux and Ballard 2005). Additional possibilities remain and the research is not yet complete, even on the identity and conditions for the bacteria. Other samples are red in color, or masses of pinkish tan. Associated with these amalgamations is a second group of textiles, twined fragments that have largely lost their perpendicular element. Their consistent dark appearance suggests a utilitarian purpose, and twined textiles were often used for bags or as soft containers, such as cushion covers. The lost element might have been composed of yarns from a different fiber, one more susceptible to decay, but perhaps one to which pattern had been assigned.

The third group, the subject of this chapter, is composed of tabby (balanced plain weave) fabrics found on the king's bier and elsewhere. They may have been used as bedding or as the king's shroud, or as part of a tabby bag to hold the king's collection of fibulae. The fabrics from the bier abound with weaving errors (Fig. 11.1; see color insert). Bellinger (1962) thought the fiber might be wool, while Ellis (1981) suggested it might be cellulosic. At the Museum Conservation Institute, the identification of the fiber remained surprisingly inconclusive even with the excellent imaging of high magnification polarized light microscopy. Using scanning electron microscopy the basis of the difficulty became obvious: the yarns are not now made up of fibers; in fact, there is no extant fiber (Ballard et al. 2010). Only a hollow core remains, surrounded by a continuous golden yellow film (Fig. 11.2). Elemental analysis of this coating with energy dispersive X-ray spectroscopy showed it to be 97% iron by weight. Fourier transform infrared spectroscopy ordinarily identifies organic material, and in order to be certain, a spectrum was requested. This resulted in the tentative identification of goethite, a golden yellow inorganic mineral named after the German poet and colorist Goethe. Chemically it is known as αFeOOH, iron (III) oxide hydroxide.

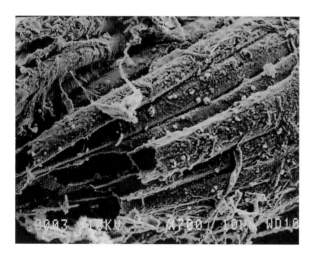

Fig. 11.2. A photomicrograph of individual fibers in a yarn of 2003-Tx-1 taken with scanning electron microscopy. Photo: author.

This was an unusually exciting discovery because it suggested that the body in Tumulus MM, which was probably that of Midas' father, may have been covered by a golden shroud. To be certain, however, we had to answer three critical questions:

1. Is this a post-burial reaction? Could it be a pseudomorph or positive formation where metal replaces natural fiber?
2. What is the explanation for a *film* of goethite rather than a powder or a mineral? Can one make goethite film on fabric?
3. An infrared spectrum identified organic matter—what definitive proof can substantiate the goethite identification?

Each can be answered in turn. First of all, the coating found is not a pseudomorph. Pseudomorphs form positive substitutions of metal inside the textile fibers; there is an affinity and reactivity between the fiber polymer and metal species, often copper. A gradual transformation takes place under certain conditions that fossilize the fibers, yarns, and fabrics (Chen, Jakes, and Foreman 1998, Jakes and Howard 1986). Iron, by contrast, tends to corrode and dissolve fiber, as a rusty tack commonly does.

Second, the formation of a goethite film on fabric can be replicated (Fig. 11.3; see color insert). Hans Kuhn, Senior Researcher at the Milliken Research Corporation, patented such a process a few years ago during the experimentation on aqueous polymeric film formation and conductive films (Kuhn 1998, 2000). Producing uniform coatings on fabrics in this manner is unusual, but it can be done. In more recent times, a polymeric binder usually adheres the pigments to a fabric, as with many images on t-shirts.

In the past, an innovative exception was the pigment coloration "khaki," carried out on fabrics using chrome and iron oxides made with mineral salts, alkali, and chromium potassium sulfate (Liles 1990, Matthews 1920). Today dyes are differentiated from pigments by their solubility in water, by their absorption into a fiber substrate, and by their reactivity with the chemical reactivity with the fiber (Table 11.1). Chemists now recognize dyes as being primarily organic molecules, having a backbone of carbon atoms, while the majority of pigments are inorganic.

Table 11.1. Properties of dyes and pigments.

Property	Dyes	Pigments
Intense color	yes	yes
Dry composition	Organic solid particles	Inorganic solid particles
Water soluble during application	yes	no
Adsorb into fiber	yes	no
React with fiber, chemically bonded	yes	no
Stability to light and air	Moderately fast to light	Can be permanent
Stability to washing, rubbing	yes	Moderately fast

In the time of King Midas, there is no record that our chemical division between organic and inorganic or between dyes and pigments was similarly defined and understood.

Dr. Kuhn laid a goethite film on polyester fabric in a method much like coloring with dyes. His process involves an aqueous solution: water, fabric, and a divalent iron source like Mohr's salt. This ammonium ferrous sulfate, a waste product from metal pickling, is the colorant source. Pyrite, also known as Fool's Gold, can be substituted. The necessary auxiliary chemicals would all have been available to the Phrygians: formic acid, ammonium formate, and urea (Kuhn 1998). All in all, the process bears a strong resemblance to the conventional dyeing of mordanted wool with natural dyes (Table 11.2) (Giles 1974, Liles 1990, Schweppe 1986). For the dyer, the procedures are quite similar. The aqueous solution is diluted for dyeing to a ratio of 100 to 50:1 (water: fabric weight) in contrast to a 20:1 ratio for goethite film formation. The temperature of the solution is gradually raised to 90° Celsius and maintained for an hour during many natural dyeings. To form goethite, the solution is also gradually raised to 90° Celsius and kept there for two hours.

Our third concern was the definitive identification of the ancient film as goethite. If one uses near infrared spectroscopy, the spectrum of a fragment from Tumulus MM matches geological mineral standards of goethite (Fig. 11.4). More precisely, with a molybdenum detection unit, the X-ray diffraction pattern from a Tumulus MM sample is a perfect match to the crystalline structure of goethite (Fig. 11.5). Raman spectroscopy also matches mod-

Table 11.2: Recipe comparison: mordant dyeing versus film-forming goethite.

Component	Mordant Dyeing	Goethite
Fabric content	Protein (wool, mohair)	Any fiber type
Liquor ratio (water: fabric weight)	100–50:1	20:1
Temperature	Raise and hold 80–90° C 1 hour	Raise and hold 80–90° C 2 hours
Colorant source	Plant or insect extract	Mohr's salt (ammonium ferrous sulfate), pyrite
Auxiliaries	Formic acid or sulfuric acid, potassium bitartrate,	
Sodium sulfate	Acetic acid, ammonium formate, urea	
pH	Monitor acidity	Monitor range 3.5-3.2-3.3

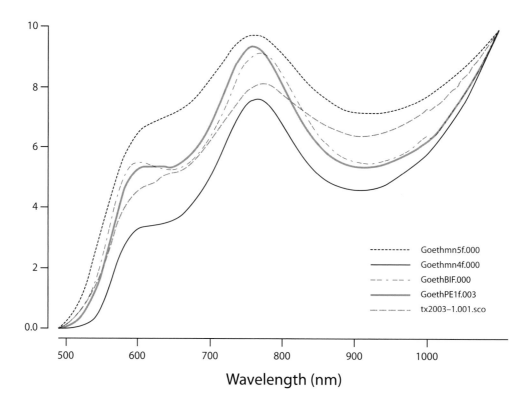

Fig. 11.4. Near infrared spectroscopy matches mining standards of goethite to 2003-Tx-1. Source: Spectral International Inc.

ern to antique goethite samples.

Yet even with such confirmation, some skepticism may remain: why would the Phrygians bother? What about the iron decorative strips on the bier (Simpson 1990)? Was the film intentional or was it just an unusual artifact of the burial conditions? The palette of natural dyes contains numerous yellows and golden hues. Yet as a group, yellow dyes are the most fugitive hue; they all tend to fade quickly, and more quickly than the reds or blues (Giles 1974; *Colour Index* 1971). Moreover, natural dyes are often fiber specific, and mordants work most easily with protein fibers (Schweppe 1986, Liles 1990).

But goethite has advantages, both in antiquity and today (Table 11.3). It is permanent; it does not fade, and the color can outlast the fabric (*Colour Index* 1971). Goethite absorbs ultraviolet light and will therefore protect the skin beneath it from sunburn and melanoma. Goethite is also a bacteriostat, supporting neither bacterial nor viral growth (Kuhn 1998). From the manufacturer's viewpoint, there

were also distinct advantages. The Phrygians making this goethite film were not dependent on a good harvest or on climate. Any fiber could be treated, regardless of its chemical composition and reactivity. Dyers using natural dyes would have needed a good harvest after proper weather conditions, and would have been limited as to the type of fiber they could dye.

There is one critical difference between mordant dyeing with natural dyes and this method of pigment coating: the goethite solution is colorless during the manufacture of the coating. That is, no colloidal suspension of goethite is floating in the aqueous solution. Under the proper conditions, the coating gradually appears on the fabric substrate (Kuhn 2000). With natural dyeing, the hue in the bath matches the color of the final fabric, with some tonal change associated with the mordant. Technically, the Phrygians were synthesizing the colorant, forming iron III hydroxide oxide. Their goethite film was synthetic.

Other evidence of their chemical acumen was

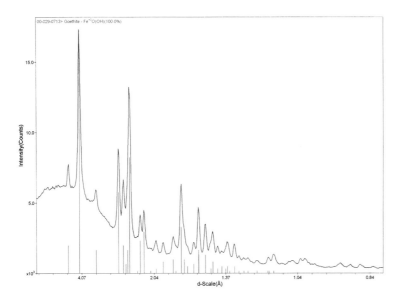

Fig. 11.5. The match between the x-ray diffraction pattern of Tumulus MM textile fragment 2003-Tx-1 and the reference pattern of goethite (the vertical bars). Illustration: author.

found in the southeast corner of the tomb (Fig. 11.6; see color insert). The dark inner gel between two strands of yarns on this tabby fabric fragment is identified as having the chemical structure of indigo (Ballard et al. 2010). This is a clever and extremely economical way to get an even, uniform dyeing from an indigo vat dye—the equivalent of a fine suit fabric instead of the fugitive coloring of blue jeans. With this method, the indigo will diffuse directly into the adjacent fiber before it is "wasted" by going into an aqueous dyeing solution. Near this fragment was another, an earthy green tabby fabric (Fig. 11.7; see color insert), which we were able to recreate: some modern handkerchief linen coated with goethite was vatted with indigo using alkali and sodium dithionite to reproduce the same long-lasting earthy green color (Fig. 11.8; see color insert).

Indigo, as a vat dye, impregnates the fiber per-

Table 11.3. Comparison of the properties of goethite film-coated fabric, Colour Index Yellow Pigment 42, versus a typical yellow natural dye, weld, *Reseda luteola L.*, Colour Index Natural Yellow 2, native to the eastern half of Anatolia (Cardon 2007; *Colour Index* 1971; Schweppe 1992).

Working Property	C.I. Natural Yellow 2	Goethite, C.I. Pigment 42
Naturally occurring collection material	Harvest leaves, inflorescences, fruits	Pyrite
Stability of collection material in storage	Damaged by heat, air drying	Stable
Stability of finished material	Stable	Stable to 100° C.
Applicability	Protein fibers premordanted with metal salt	Any fabric
Absorption	Blue light of visible wavelength	Ultraviolet, Blue light of visible wavelength
Lightfastness	ISO 3or 4, (moderately stable)	permanent
Microbial resistance	no	yes

manently only when it is reduced, when oxygen is removed from its molecule. There are various methods to achieve this reduction: slow fermentation method with urine, ferrous sulfate with lime or wood ashes, zinc-lime, or sodium dithionite with alkali (Liles 1990, Schweppe 1992). Each method has its advantages and limitations, and some methods would compromise a goethite coating already in place.

Fortunately for modern experimenters, we have the benefit of explanations from fine technical literature, references, mentors, and patient colleagues with diverse scientific training. How did King Midas and the Phrygians achieve what they did? The most reasonable explanation is that they were superb chemists, textile technologists, and chemical engineers, and that King Midas truly had a golden touch.

Acknowledgments

I am grateful for the help and support of numerous colleagues: Dr. Harry Alden, Dr. Lynn Brostoff, Roland Cunningham, Dr. Laure Dussubieux, Walter Hopwood, Joseph Koles, Odile Madden, Dr. Amadine Péquignot, the departments of Botany, Invertebrate Zoology, and Mineralogy at the Museum of Natural History; Elizabeth Simpson and Krysia Spirydowicz; Hans Kuhn and the Milliken Research Corporation; Phoebe Hauff and Spectral International, Inc.

12

In the Shadow of Tumulus MM: The Common Cemetery and Middle Phrygian Houses at Gordion

Gunlög E. Anderson

Among the most distinctive features of the now-familiar 1950 aerial photograph of Gordion are the nearly 100 tumuli that dot the landscape around the Citadel Mound (Figs. 12.1, 12.2). Better than many volumes of text, this photograph conveys the immense scale of the tumulus burials of wealthy families during the Early and Middle Phrygian period. Looking from the Citadel Mound toward the northeast today, one is overwhelmed by this extensive field of monumental burial mounds, and the view must have been even more striking in antiquity before the effects of erosion were visible (Young 1981: pl. 1A and B).

Nearly all of the studies of these tumuli have focused on their burial assemblages and the identification of their occupants. We have neglected to ask several basic questions such as who actually constructed the tumuli, where the workers lived, and what their lives were like. This chapter attempts to clarify these issues by using the evidence of houses and tombs uncovered outside Gordion's citadel during the Rodney Young excavations of the 1950s. I suggest that the residents of these houses are likely to have figured among the laborers who were engaged in Phrygian tomb construction, not unlike the situation in New Kingdom Egypt wherein the laborers' houses were situated near the Pharaonic tombs that they built (Lesko 1994).

Excavation and Research

The even ground surrounding the tumuli reveals nothing today, but as early as the 3rd millennium BC, a Hittite cemetery was situated on the western end of the Northeast Ridge (Fig. 12.3) (Mellink 1956:1); later, in the early 1st millennium BC, a Phrygian cemetery and a domestic settlement were located here. This place had the clearest view of the Citadel Mound and the surrounding plain—a view that can be experienced today by every visitor to the Expedition House (Kohler 1995: pl. 3B).

The Gordion Expedition under the direction of Rodney S. Young undertook the first season's work in this area in 1950, and he began by digging the small Tumulus A. While the first day's experience was still fresh in his mind, he described it in an April 1 letter to his colleague G. Roger Edwards: "Gold the first day, also…carved ivory, but in horrible shape. We opened a small tumulus…and only 60 cm below the present level we found a big cremation…apparently a young damsel." There was gold, silver, electrum, ivory, beads, bronze, and a terracotta perfume container. "All very satisfactory," concluded Young (Edwards 1980:159).

This experience of digging the rich grave in Tumulus A marked an encouraging beginning, but it would remain an isolated experience that contrasted with what was to follow in those first seasons on the Northeast Ridge. In the next tumulus to be excavated, B, the burial chamber had been built into the cellar of a preexisting house—an early harbinger of the complicated stratigraphy that was to mark this area (Kohler 1995: fig. 4). Searching for the burial chamber in Tumulus H, also in 1950, the excavators came upon a Phrygian cemetery of simple inhumations in plain earth graves. This cemetery turned out to be the burial ground for commoners who did not have the wealth and status of the tumulus builders. The

Fig. 12.1. Aerial view of Gordion in 1950, looking northeast. Source: Gordion Archive, Penn Museum. Image 46511/GB-50-1.

deeper levels of this Common Cemetery, on bedrock and in gravel, contained burials from a much older period, the Bronze Age. Machteld J. Mellink (1956) launched the investigation of the Bronze Age cemetery, which was continued by Ann Gunter (1991).

The discovery of the graves of the Phrygian commoners was unexpected and did not appear to be very promising when the large tumuli were still the main focus of the expedition. It was simply not practical to include the cemetery in the excavation plans. All information available to us—about the Common Cemetery and the domestic houses—is therefore based on the discoveries in pre-tumulus levels and in the mantles of the tumuli on the Northeast Ridge.

Mellink outlined the history of the "core area" of the cemetery during the Iron Age. After the end of the Bronze Age, she noted, the area "seems to have been

left in peace for a considerable time, until Phrygian settlers selected the ridge for fairly intensive habitation" (Mellink 1956:1–2). These were Phrygians of the 8th and early 7th centuries, whose houses may have been destroyed in Cimmerian raids, after which the area reverted to a cemetery during the Middle and Late Phrygian period and eventually included a Roman burial ground.

My own work on the burials and the houses in this core area includes Tumuli H and I, the extended Main Trench, the trial trenches, and the Museum Site (Figs. 12.1, 12.4–12.6) (Anderson 1980). A final publication report of the entire Common Cemetery and habitation area remains to be done. The Common Cemetery includes all burials below the ancient surface (except those identified as either Bronze Age or Roman) and all secondary burials inserted in the mantles of tumuli (Kohler 1995:4–5; A. Goldman 2000).

There have been no recent excavations on the Northeast Ridge proper, but analysis of the excavations has continued, especially due to the work of Ellen L. Kohler (1995). Kohler has pursued the demanding task of separating the artifacts found in the tumuli from the pre-tumulus material that belongs to either the domestic levels or the Common Cemetery. The mantles of the tumuli contain residual artifacts and debris from both the houses and common graves that were scooped up during the tumulus construction. Some of the artifacts resist classification, but Kohler has meticulously recreated the techniques of the tumulus builders and their funerary rituals.

The Common Cemetery

We now know that of the 14 lesser tumuli on the western end of the Northeast Ridge, a total of 12 were located on top of either houses or common graves or

Fig. 12.2. Area map of Gordion showing the Citadel Mound and Lower Town (including Küçük Höyük), and the tumuli on the Northeast Ridge and South Ridge. The Common Cemetery and Middle Phrygian settlement lie at the northwest end of the Northeast Ridge, south of the modern village. Illustration: Elizabeth Simpson, after Mahmut Akok. Source: Gordion Archive, Penn Museum. Image 102720/Plan 1978-4.

Fig. 12.3. Western part of the Northeast Ridge tumulus cemetery, from the southwest. Tumulus K-II is in a line with the top of Tumulus MM (the largest). K-III lies at the foot of MM, and Tumulus P is at the right edge of the picture. Source: Gordion Archive, Penn Museum. Image 102813/GB-81-94.

both: A, B, C, D, E, F, H, I, J, K, M, and K-II. Only G and K-I were "clean" (Kohler 1995:7). Initially it seemed as if the historical sequence described by Mellink was clear; but now, based on recent research, I would propose that the Phrygian domestic habitation and the Common Cemetery developed together as parallel phenomena, existing alongside each other for a time, although the cemetery may have outlasted the habitation. People who built their houses nearby also began burying their dead here. This assumption is supported by the great number of children and infants that were found buried in household pottery in close proximity to the habitation levels. As some of the houses were burned or abandoned, the Common Cemetery encroached upon the area, and finally the tumulus builders took advantage of the stone available in the walls of the abandoned houses.

The Common Cemetery encompassed the area between the 5 m and 20 m contour lines, from Tumulus A at the west, to Tumulus M at the east, and Tumuli H and I at the south. Burials were found scattered across an area nearly 400 m long from north to south, and about 300 m wide from east to west—close to 12 ha. Some trial trenches in this area turned up sterile soil, and it is likely that the burials were made in clusters, not evenly spread across the whole expanse (Fig. 12.1).

The classification of grave types and the dating of the Common Cemetery remain somewhat tentative because a number of graves were disturbed and a majority of them lacked grave goods. The most distinctive interments were found in the oldest levels—those of Bronze Age date, where 55 carefully organized burials were documented; most of these were in large clay vessels or pithoi, although a few were in cist graves and simple inhumations. This part of the cemetery encompassed an area of about 6,000 m^2 (Mellink 1956:3–4).

The chronology of the earliest Phrygian burials in the Common Cemetery must be inferred from the limited material we have on hand. There is scholarly agreement that Tumulus G is the earliest installation on the west end of the Northeast Ridge. Judging by the ceramic evidence, Sams now dates it to ca. 840 BC, which makes it roughly contemporary with the Terrace Building on the Citadel Mound (Sams 2005a:10–21; Voigt 2005:22–35). This would make it slightly later than Tumulus W and approximately 60 years earlier than Tumuli K-III and KY (Sams 1994a:193–94, pl. 61; Kohler 1995:38, 191–96).

Given this early date, we would need to envision the landscape of the Northeast Ridge as it was before the construction of Tumulus MM. It is conceivable that the wide expanse on both sides of the ancient road was an area set apart, bracketed, as it were, by Tumulus G on the west and Tumulus W (and others) on the east. No habitation remains were reported underneath Tumulus G or W, and the mantle fill was clean, which may indicate that the area was not yet inhabited.

Tumulus G, however, "may have been the focal point of an early Phrygian cemetery of simple graves" (Sams 1994a:194). One of these graves was a stone-lined inhumation under Tumulus D that had been supplied with a pair of low-necked jars, or dinoi, painted in the distinctive "Ladders-and-Zigzag" style, which can be dated no later than the Destruction Level on the Citadel Mound (ca. 800 BC). Children were found nearby buried in Gray Ware kraters of Early Phrygian type (Sams 1994a:84–85, 91, 95, 137, 160–61, pl. 141). In all, at least 20 burials surrounded a habitation complex of three houses in pre-tumulus levels of Tumulus D. As a rule in the Common Cemetery, household pottery was used in burials of infants and children, both inhumations and cremations: various jars, trefoil-mouthed jugs, bowls, and cooking pots.

It therefore seems likely that the smaller Tumulus G was being built high on the western end of the Northeast Ridge while the greater Tumuli W, K-III, P, MM, X, and Y were being built by ruling families on the eastern end of the ridge; and within less than a generation, the first domestic households with a common cemetery had begun to cluster around Tumulus

Fig. 12.4. Museum site on the Northeast Ridge in 1962: general view from the northeast looking to the Citadel Mound, after excavation. Source: Gordion Archive, Penn Museum. Image G-4233.

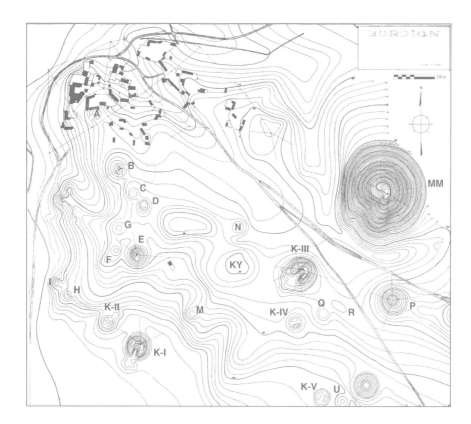

Fig. 12.5. Map showing the tumuli at the northwest end of the Northeast Ridge, several of which were excavated in 1950. The Common Cemetery and Middle Phrygian settlement lay under and around most of these burial mounds. Illustration: Mahmut Akok, 1950. Source: Gordion Archive, Penn Museum. Image 46862/Plan 1950-1.

G (Kohler 1995:38). The area around Tumuli H and I continued to be the core area, as it was intensely used throughout the Middle Phrygian period. A total of 250 graves were noted here by the excavators, and when the full extent of the Common Cemetery is finally mapped, the number of burials may exceed 300.

The most common burial type was extended, dorsal inhumation in earth and gravel, but inhumations in cists, in pits, and under sherds were also found around the houses in the excavated area (a total of 72 were recorded; 40 were noted as "uncertain"). These inhumations were not oriented in any consistent direction, but conformed to the slope of the ground (Figs. 12.2, 12.7). In the middle of the 7th century cremation was introduced into the cemetery. At least 20 cremations were arranged *in situ* and concentrated in the Main Trench, north of the houses, in Tumuli H and I (Figs. 12.3, 12.8).

As stated above, the Common Cemetery shows intensive use of the core area, expanding gradually to the northwest, north, and northeast. Around the outer periphery of the core area we can observe finds of about 20 inhumations and a couple of cremations, with 6th century grave goods of lydions and lekythoi—both imports and local imitations (Figs. 12.1, 12.6; the circle indicates graves with lydions and lekythoi). The outer perimeter of the Common Cemetery would therefore have been contemporary with the tumuli raised during the 6th century—A, C, D, E, I, M, K-I, and K-II (Kohler 1980; 1995:7).

On the whole, grave gifts were sparse. Of the 120 catalogued graves assumed to be Phrygian, less than a third (34) had modest offerings such as bracelets, earrings, rings, beads, pendants, the occasional fibula, and pottery. Infants and children, who made up about a third of all burials, were more likely than adults to have been accompanied by a small offering of beads, bracelets, or pottery such as feeding bottles.

Chronologically, two groups of burials were distinguished: a larger group of graves from the 8th to the 7th century characterized by Phrygian monochrome wares, and the much smaller 6th century group, mentioned above, associated with imports from western Anatolia, eastern Greece, and in particular, Lydia (Anderson 1980:278–81; Greenewalt 1966:35–40; Schaus 1992:151–78; Kohler 1995:50–53, pls. 28H and 29C). Burial in the Common Cemetery seems to have ended toward the close of the 6th century, which is about the same time in which the last tumulus, A (530–520 BC), was installed on the Northeast Ridge.

On the basis of this material, a general question remains: What are we to make of the many graves totally lacking grave gifts? If close to two-thirds of the graves had no material gifts, were the burials poor because the people were paupers or because of prevailing funerary customs? Our observations of grave goods may be skewed because of the ground's disturbance when the tumuli were raised. A certain number of stray finds, such as fibulae, may originally have been deposited as gifts in burials that were disturbed, whereas other chance finds, such as knives and sickles, probably came from houses. We find that the perceived, perplexing poverty of the graves is not reflected in the houses, which suggests at least a basic subsistence level of material culture.

Domestic Habitation

Early in the excavation of Tumulus H in 1950, it became clear that the mantle of the tumulus was built over the remains of a medium-sized house (Kohler 1995:43–53, figs. 18, 19). In due course, many more house walls with floors were uncovered in the H-I Main Trench, in 5 of the 13 trial trenches, and at the Museum Site (Figs. 12.1, 12.6, 12.9–12.12). At least 11 separate houses could be reconstructed. Many other indications of intensive habitation were observed—wall fragments, pits of all sizes, and terraces carved out of the bedrock and covered with habitation debris, especially large quantities of ashes and broken pottery. Apparently the builders of the

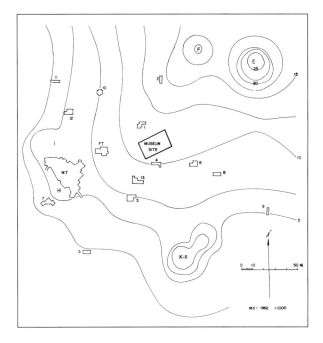

Fig. 12.6. Trench plan of the excavations of the Common Cemetery and Middle Phrygian settlement, showing the Main Trench (MT) under and between Tumuli H and I, the Field Trench (FT), trial trenches 1–13, and the Museum Site trench. Illustration: Joseph S. Last, 1962. Source: Gordion Archive, Penn Museum. Image 76583/Plan 1962-33.

tumuli had taken advantage of the ruined houses, reusing the debris and mud brick and robbing the house walls for the stones needed for the guide walls in mantle construction.

Despite the simplicity of the houses on the ridge, the builders' practical use of materials, techniques, and layouts was clear. These structures were all clustered above the floodplain between the 5 m and 17.5 m contour lines, which kept them safe from the spring flooding that is known to have occurred there (Kohler 1995:7). The geological conditions on the ridge—with hardpan, gravel up to 1 m in depth, and sand layers—made it convenient for foundations and offered good drainage; the gentle slopes were also well suited for the type of dwelling built there. Whenever possible, the builders took advantage of the incline to recess the houses into the slopes, with the outside of single-faced back walls left rough where they abutted the scarp of the earth. This building method economized on materials. For the rest, double-faced stone walls were built using

Fig. 12.7. Examples of inhumation burials from the Main Trench: (a) Extended burials (Burials A-63 and A-64 = Anderson 1980: No. 63). Source: Gordion Archive, Penn Museum. Image R-135-9/GO-1055. (b) Extended burial (Burial A-26 = Anderson 1980: No. 56). Source: Gordion Archive, Penn Museum. Image R-131-18/GO-930. (c) Cist burial (Burial A-58 = Anderson 1980: No. 5). Source: Gordion Archive, Penn Museum. Image R-135-3/GO-1050. (d) Pit burial (Burial A-49 = Anderson 1980: No. 9). Source: Gordion Archive, Penn Museum. Image R-137-7/GO-1022. (e) Pit burial (Burial A-53 = Anderson 1980: No.10). Source: Gordion Archive, Penn Museum. Image R-135-33/GO-1036. (f) Sherd burial (Burial A-45 = Anderson1980: No. 17). Source: Gordion Archive, Penn Museum. Image R-138-19/GO-1015.

either drywall technique or mud mortar. Wooden posts were typically placed at regular intervals in the walls or in corners, while mud brick was used for upper walls and internal dividers. No fixed pattern dominated in either house plans or the settlement layout, though generally a southern exposure was favored. Patches of gravel and stone pavements indicated that living spaces were planned around open courtyards.

One house found deep in the ancient ground under Tumulus H had a small megaron plan, and had been rebuilt to a final size of 5 m by 6 m (Figs. 12.9 and 12.13). Close by, a small cellar had been built to hold storage jars. Walls typically showed traces of plaster and whitewash.

Preserved walls in Tumulus H reached a height of 1.15 m. In Tumulus B, the stone cellar with its earthen wall was 1.8 m high—clearance enough for a standing adult (see Kohler 1995: fig. 4). Burned remains showed that roofs had been built of logs, reeds, and clay and were probably slightly pitched. Floors were of hard-stamped earth and gravel, typi-

d

e

f

Fig. 12.8a (top), b. Cremation burial from the Main Trench (Burial A-17 = Anderson 1980: No. 92): (a) closed and (b) uncovered. Source: Gordion Archive, Penn Museum. Images R-132-38/GO-954 and R-132-44/GO-957.

cally with inset pebbles and stone slabs. Built-in features included hearths, ovens, bins, small cupboards of mud brick, and benches of stone for millstones and grinders.

Some floors showed that the inhabitants had been forced to leave in a hurry, abandoning their household pottery of cooking pots, bowls, storage amphoras for dry goods, trefoil-mouthed jugs and round-mouthed cups for liquids, plus some finer wares—round-mouthed cups of painted ware and some of lustrous black fine ware. A large polished ring stand of a rare shape was also left on the floor (Figs. 12.14, 12.15) (Hendrickson, Vandiver, and Blackman 2002:391–400). Other household items were tripod mortars of clay or stone. Diverse stray finds from mantle fills add to the inventory that might be expected in a household, such as knives, sickles, small spatulas, axes of iron, awls and needles of bone, spindle whorls and loomweights of clay, fibulae of bronze, beads of glass and stone, and hewn stones and pieces of trimmed flint (Kohler 1995: fig. 22, pls. 28–30, 38G, 40).

In addition to these artifacts of material culture, the excavations yielded some intriguing finds of a symbolic nature, of literacy and cult. For example, someone in the house under Tumulus H—perhaps the head of the household—had scratched his name, LAGINEIOS, in old Phrygian characters on the side of a large jug, while a second (incomplete) name, OMEKAS, was found on another vessel (Young 1969b:267, figs. 4, 5).

The floor of one house held a small cultic image: a shaped, round-headed, aniconic stone. This belongs to a group of 15 similar stone idols, some plain, some showing facial features, that were found on house floors and in debris in mantle fills (Fig. 12.15). These images may possibly be grouped with the small, cut-stone relief of Kybele and a bull from a household shrine (see Kohler 1995: pls. 11, 12, 17). It is also conceivable that these small idols were considered protective household spirits, expected to keep the houses and their people safe, but discarded when the houses were destroyed. Lynn E. Roller and Machteld J. Mellink have placed these idols and the small relief within the context of the cult of the Phrygian Mother Goddess (Mellink 1983; Roller 1999b:75–82).

We have a good general understanding of the chronology of the habitation on the Northeast Ridge,

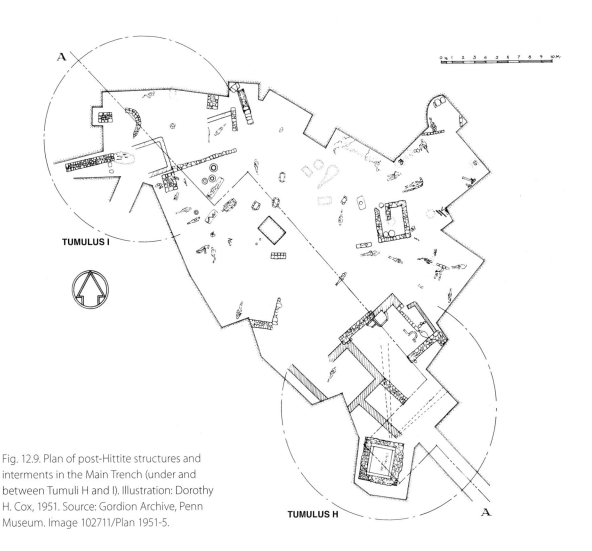

Fig. 12.9. Plan of post-Hittite structures and interments in the Main Trench (under and between Tumuli H and I). Illustration: Dorothy H. Cox, 1951. Source: Gordion Archive, Penn Museum. Image 102711/Plan 1951-5.

Fig. 12.10a (top), b. Phrygian House IV, Cut VII: (a) from the north; (b) detail of interior from the north, with cist burial A-58 visible in the foreground (cf. Fig. 12.7c). Source: Gordion Archive, Penn Museum. Images R-135-40/GO-1043 and R-135-4/GO-1051.

but many specific questions remain. The abandonment and burning of the uppermost house under Tumulus H must have occurred before the tumulus was constructed. Thanks to the gifts deposited in the burial chamber of H, including an imported East Greek bird bowl dated to ca. 640–620 BC, we have a *terminus ante quem* for the preexisting habitation here. In fact, three other tumuli on the west end of the Northeast Ridge are dated by Greek imports, and all of them were constructed on top of ruined houses: Tumulus F (640–620), Tumulus J (ca. 600), and Tumulus K (620–600). Keith DeVries concluded that "the finds from these tumuli, and sporadic finds from the Citadel Mound, document a steady flow of Greek imports soon after mid-7th century BC" (DeVries 2005:43–44). As for a more specific link, we have a pottery connection between house VII and the burial in Tumulus H that shows that the interval between the abandonment of the houses and the return of tumulus builders to the west end of the Northeast Ridge cannot have been long (Kohler 1995:194).

The onset of habitation activities is more difficult to determine. As discussed above in connection with the cemetery, however, the earliest common burials probably clustered around Tumulus G (the oldest installation here), and the pre-tumulus levels of nearby C and D were associated with several houses. Although these oldest house levels are not yet fully understood, those located high on the ridge under Tumuli C, D, and E are very likely some of the earliest house foundations.

As circumstantial evidence, we may recall how Kohler noted that after the completion of Tumulus N there was a hiatus of tumulus construction on the western end of the Northeast Ridge (Fig. 12.2) (Kohler 1995:194). Tumuli Z and S-1, the next, were built on the South Ridge. There is a possibility that Z and S-1 were diverted to the South Ridge because the western end of the ridge was still occupied by houses of commoners. A ceramic connection has been established between a painted dinos, found in Tumulus Z, and a painted round-mouthed jug from the floor of house VII (Fig. 12.16) (Anderson 1980:33; Sams 1994a:138n110; Kohler 1995:160, fig. 68D, pls. 82C, 83G). The building of the very large Tumulus Z would therefore have been contem-

Fig. 12.11. Trial trench 3, 1953: Burnt Phrygian House. Source: Gordion Archive, Penn Museum. Image R-228-7/GO-3515.

Fig. 12.12. Tumulus E, "Bakery," from the south, 1951. Source: Gordion Archive, Penn Museum. Image R-62-32/GO-762.

porary with the habitation in the Tumulus H area.

The analysis of ceramics and bronzes suggests that the houses in the area of Tumuli H and I existed from the second half of the 8th century through the first half of the 7th century (DeVries 2005:42–46). After the house under Tumulus H was burned, the area was used for common burials and, before long, for tumuli. There were still other houses higher on the ridge that may have been occupied longer and certainly were rebuilt several times. The best example is the house under Tumulus E, where there are rooms with special functions, including a "bakery" in the oldest levels, and a well-constructed "Lydian" house from the late 6th century (Fig. 12.6) (Ramage 1969; Anderson 1980:56–57).

When we look for analogies, we find that the Middle Phrygian houses on the Northeast Ridge were more developed than the simple wattle-and-daub houses of the Early Phrygian period discovered on the Citadel Mound by Mary Voigt and her team (Voigt and Hendrickson 2000:49–50, fig. 7). The builders on the ridge were certainly familiar with the

megaron plan; their techniques included substantial stone walls, mud brick, and wooden posts set in the walls. Nevertheless, they held on to their recessed floors and built-in features of ovens, plastered bins, and milling benches. Conservative, and with limited resources, the house builders on the Northeast Ridge never reached the point of using cut stone or ashlar walls. Good stone and colored pebbles, as found in the public architecture on the Citadel Mound, were simply not available to them.

Looking beyond Gordion, the best parallels for these houses are to be found on Büyükkale II, the Phrygian level at Boğazköy (Schirmer 1969: taf. 6a; Mellink 1993:294–95), and other Hittite sites in central Anatolia that were occupied by the Phrygians, such as Demirci Höyük and Kaman-Kalehöyük (Gates 1996:297). Even as late as the 1st century AD, Vitruvius gave an evocative description of a "Phrygian" house in his history of architecture (Vitruvius II.I.5), which is not so different from those on the ridge.

It is noteworthy that several construction details in the houses are duplicated in the neighbor-

Fig. 12.13a (top), b. House I, 1951: (a) level b (second level), from the northwest; (b) level c (upper level), from the south. Source: Gordion Archive, Penn Museum. Images R-67-23/GO-849 and R-63-20/GO-834.

ing tumuli. As Ellen Kohler pointed out in 1995, both the houses and the burial pits were generally cut into sloping areas, and the use of stone-weighted roofs in both cases are probably also a case in point

(1995:165, 178). Such similarities in construction are not really surprising: the construction of a tumulus like MM must have required a workforce of thousands, and even the smallest tumuli must have

Fig. 12.14. Gray ceramic ring stand from floor of House 1c under Tumulus H (Gordion inventory no. 872-P-265). Height. 11.4 cm, diameter 19.2 cm. Source: Gordion Archive, Penn Museum. Image R-122-22.

Fig. 12.15a, b. Stone idol from building underneath Tumulus B, excavated in 1950: (a) frontal view; (b) profile. From trench 4, fill over burned floor (Gordion inventory no. 58-S-1). Source: Gordion Archive, Penn Museum. Images R-849-29 and 30.

involved several hundred (Liebhart, this volume). Linking the residents of these houses to tumulus construction in the area therefore seems virtually certain. The proximity of residence and work site would have allowed for greater speed and efficiency in building, and the existence of a settlement in the vicinity of the tumuli would have provided additional security for them as well.

This is not to say that the community on Gordion's Northeast Ridge would ever have constituted the entire workforce for a tumulus, nor that such construction would have been the only means of livelihood for the residents—the tumuli were built too infrequently for that. But the inhabitants probably served as a core group of workers whenever a new tumulus needed to be constructed. It is somewhat

Fig. 12.16. Round-mouthed jug from trial trench 1, House VII (Gordion inventory no. 2380-P-745). Ht. 13.1 cm, max. diam. 13.3 cm. (a): after conservation; (b): drawing. Source: Gordion Archive, Penn Museum. Images R-525-14 and 101452.

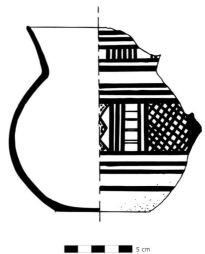

5 cm

ironic that the houses in this area were ultimately enveloped by tumuli after the destruction in the early 7th century BC, with the house stones reused as guide walls in the new mantle construction.

Conclusions

The following general scenario emerges: during the late 9th and 8th centuries, while the great tumuli were being built on the eastern end of Gordion's Northeast Ridge, the western end became occupied by a group of people who established a kind of village with its own cemetery. The people who built their houses here knew they were living upon an even older burial ground, as they found large chunks of Hittite pottery useful for constructing hearths and preparing child burials. Apparently they settled here quite purposefully, choosing the area with the best view of the Citadel Mound. They preferred again and again to rebuild their houses here, even though they were living outside the protective walls of the citadel. This left them unprotected against aggressors—even though they were able to keep watch in all directions—and some houses were burned down in the early 7th century, possibly by foreign aggressors.

People found various resources on the ridge: easy access to fresh water, different types of land, excellent gravel for houses, but only limited amounts of fine-quality stone and wood. What remains of their material culture—the accumulated finds from both the Common Cemetery and the habitation levels—show that they had tools of bronze, iron, stone, and flint; ornaments of bronze—bracelets, pins, beads, and fibulae; beads of glass and amber; great quantities of household pottery, mostly of coarse ware but also lustrous black fine and painted wares; certain pottery imports; and large storage vessels for foodstuffs and liquids.

Although there seem to have been no specialized workshops, certain large households had rooms for cooking and baking, while spindle whorls and loomweights attest to spinning and weaving activities. The residents probably depended on a mixed economy of agriculture, sheepherding, fishing, and hunting, complemented by exchanges of goods and labor with the people and markets of Gordion, to which traders came from all over Anatolia and beyond. During the time in question—possibly the entire Middle Phrygian period (800–540 BC)—the settlers were without doubt part of the considerable workforce needed for the great public works of their time, the construction and guarding of the tumuli. The similarities between the construction methods of the tumuli and those used in the houses are therefore to be expected.

What sociopolitical relations might have existed between the common folk and their ruling families? Signs of incipient literacy in the House of Lagineios suggest persons with managerial skills. The presence of cult idols and house shrines points to continuity and tradition. In other words, the materials we have studied attest to a cultural unity between the residents of the houses and the deceased in both the Common Cemetery and the lesser tumuli.

Whatever we might think of the meager grave goods in the common graves, the artifacts suggest that we are not dealing with the graves of paupers, but with a funerary custom in which gifts were uncommon. Nevertheless, common folk were honored by being offered their final resting place within respected boundaries and in a venerable context, in some sense rendered hallowed as the burial ground of elite and royal families, the leaders of the nation.

Acknowledgments

I am grateful to Ellen Kohler and Machteld Mellink for having provided such constant inspiration to me throughout my career. I also thank Gareth Darbyshire for assembling the illustrations.

13

The Throne of Midas? Delphi and the Power Politics of Phrygia, Lydia, and Greece[1]

Keith DeVries and C. Brian Rose

Excavations conducted near the Treasury of the Corinthians at Delphi in 1939 uncovered two votive pits that contained material ranging in date from the late 8th century BC to the late 5th (Figs. 13.1, 13.2) (Amandry 1939; Luce and Blegen 1939:342–43; Amandry 1977:293; Amandry 1991:191–95). Frequently referred to as the "Halos Deposit," the pits contained an extensive assortment of elite offerings that were carefully buried ca. 420 BC, including several chryselephantine figures of Archaic date (Amandry 1991:191–94; Lapatin 2001:57–67). Within one of the pits was the now celebrated ivory figurine of a man with a lion (Figs. 13.3a-d), which is nearly complete (Amandry 1939:107–9; Amandry 1944-45; Barnett 1948:16–17; Schefold 1968; Rhoads 1970; Schiering 1976; Carter 1985:216–25; Amandry 1991:199–202; Schiering 2003). The figurine is fairly large, with a height of 22 cm, and like many of the other objects in the dump, it was burned.[2]

The figure is that of a standing male holding a spear vertically in his right hand and resting his left on the head of a standing lion with profile body and frontal head. He wears a long mantle over a short tunic, with an open-ended arm ring on his right arm above the elbow. His hair is parted in the center and pulled over his ears, ending just above his shoulders. Two locks fall on his chest and end in circular knobs decorated with eight-pointed incised stars, which in turn echo an incised St. Andrew's cross on the lion's shoulder. Round holes have been drilled in the center of the man's enlarged eyes, probably for the insertion of a different material, and both eyes and eyebrows

have been incised. The lion's outstretched arms form a 90-degree angle and touch both the man's thigh and the shaft of the spear. The base is decorated with an elaborate battle^^ment meander above a course of pendant pointed leaves, and incisions have been used to delineate the hair, spear blade, and the borders of the lion's arms (Fig. 13.3d). The frontal shot is deceptive, for it makes the figures look more fully modeled than they really are (Fig. 13.3a). In profile the piece is rather plank-like, with only the heads of the lion and the lion tamer in high relief (Fig. 13.3b). The back is not modeled at all, aside from the tamer's head (Fig. 13.3c), and the large mortise in the center of the back shows that the piece was attached to something.

In Pierre Amandry's publication of the piece in 1945, he judged it to be East Greek with strong Syro-Hittite influence, and dated it to the 7th century (Amandry 1944-1945). His proposed date has been generally accepted (e.g., Hurwit 1985:126; Carter 1985:216–25), although scholars have increasingly vacillated with regard to its geographical origin, citing various regions of Anatolia as possibilities.[3] Already in 1964, Demargne could not decide whether it was East Greek or Lydian, and Boardman subsequently implied that he could not either (Demargne 1964:398, fig. 521; Boardman 1978:16, fig. 52). In 1991 Amandry himself argued that the ivory was made in Asia Minor by someone adhering to Anatolian traditions, but whether that individual was a Greek or a non-Greek was uncertain (1991:202). Other archaeologists connected to the Delphi excavations have followed his lead, although as early as

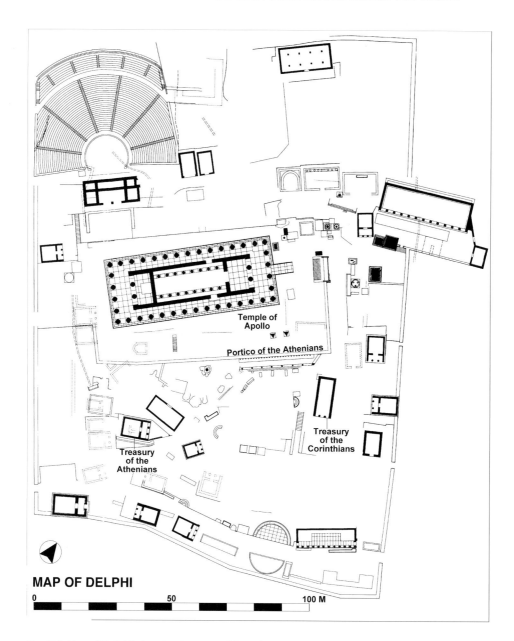

Fig. 13.1. Map of Delphi, showing location of Corinthian Treasury (308) relative to the find spot of the ivory figurine. Source: Bommelaer 1991: pl. 5.

1976, Wolfgang Schiering had already discarded the Greek possibility and judged it to be either Lydian or Phrygian (Schiering 1976).[4]

The question of provenance has now been clarified: recent discoveries near Lycian Elmalı and further research on excavated material at other sites, especially Gordion, enable us to identify the figurine as Anatolian, and specifically Phrygian. Several features of the figurine are attested throughout the Sy-ro-Hittite realm: the combination of short tunic and long mantle appear in late 8th century Neo-Hittite sculpture (Akurgal 1962: figs. 134, 142; Schiering 2003:61), as does the open arm ring worn just above the lion tamer's elbow. The latter appears to have been a relatively common attribute of Neo-Hittite kings in the 8th century, and is found on royal statues and reliefs from Zincirli, Malatya, and Carchemish, among others.[5]

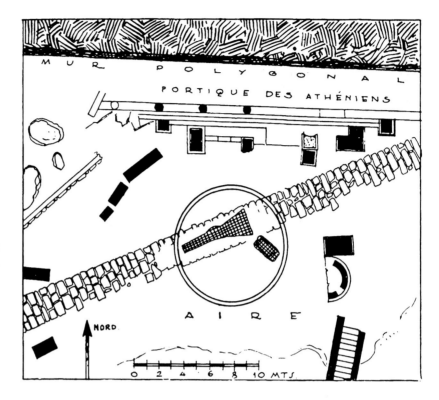

Fig. 13.2. Plan of the two votive pits at Delphi. Source: Amandry 1939:87.

In Amandry's original study, he pointed out other traits that are characteristic of Syro-Hittite sculpture, notably the "X" on the lion's shoulder and the ivy-leaf ear of the lion, but these features are also found high on the Anatolian plateau, in Phrygia. One can cite, for example, the "X" on the lion on an orthostate relief from Ankara dating to the second half of the 8th or the early 7th century, and a wooden lion with an ivy ear from Gordion, probably of the early 8th century (Fig. 13.4).[6] The fringed borders of the lion also appear consistently in Phrygian minor arts, especially in depictions of animals (Sams 1995:1153).

Particularly important is the decoration on the base, as Schiering recognized 25 years ago; it now emerges as all the more significant in the wake of Kenneth Sams's study of Phrygian ornamental motifs on Gordion pottery (Schiering 1976:48–49; Sams 1994a:140–55). A battlement meander runs across the front and two sides of the base; on the front one also finds sets of four squares with dots at their centers between the meander's rises and dips. A close parallel appears on a sherd from Phrygian Boğazköy, with a checkerboard tucked into the gaps created by the meander (Figs. 13.5, 13.6) (Bittel and Güterbock 1933:32, fig. 15, upper right; Bossert 2000: pl. 113, no. 358a, and pl. 158, no. B350; Akurgal 1955: pl. 30a). Beyond Phrygia, in the region of Tabal (south-central Anatolia), a somewhat similar motif can be identified on pottery, but in modified form, as on a sherd from Porsuk where the checkerboard is in place but the unity of the battlement meander is obscured. The border is of varying

width, and is variously rendered as solid, outline, and hatched (Fig. 13.7) (Dupré 1983:119, no. 165, pl. 82).[7] Aside from the ivory, the combination of squares and the battlement is attested on nothing outside the plateau territory of Tabal and Phrygia.

Other details of the base also evoke inner Anatolian parallels. Dotted squares appear on the garment of King Warpalawas in the rock-cut relief at İvriz dating to the second half of the 8th century (Fig. 13.8), but they are at home in Phrygia too, as on a vase from Gordion of the late 9th century (Fig. 13.9).[8] A variant of squares (rather than dots) within squares can be found on a furniture fragment from Gordion probably dating to the first half of the 8th century; the same piece features the popular Phrygian arrangement of four squares in windowpane format, which is also seen on the base of the ivory (Fig. 13.10).[9] Another instance of the four squares, with different filling ornament, appears on a silver appliqué from a tumulus of the late 8th or early 7th century at Bayındır near Elmalı, which included Phrygian inscriptions (Fig. 13.11) (Özgen and Öztürk 1996:27, fig. 33; Özgen and Özgen 1988:33, 46, fig. 53; Akurgal 1962:72, IM 42). Moreover, the same basic pendant triangle motif is duplicated in a relief of Sargon

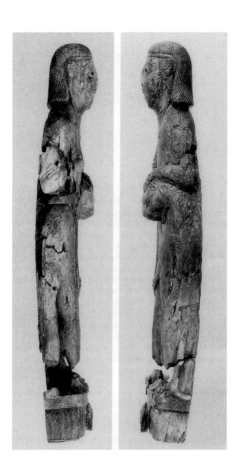

Fig. 13.3a. Ivory figurine from Delphi, front. Source: Schiering 2003: Abb. 1. Permission: Athanasia Psalti, Director, 10th Ephorate of Prehistoric and Classical Antiquities.

Fig. 13.3b. Side views of ivory figurine. Source: Schiering 2003: Abb 2. Permission: Athanasia Psalti, Director, 10th Ephorate of Prehistoric and Classical Antiquities.

Fig. 13.3c. Back view of ivory figurine. Source: Amandry 1944-45: pl. XI. Permission: Athanasia Psalti, Director, 10th Ephorate of Prehistoric and Classical Antiquities.

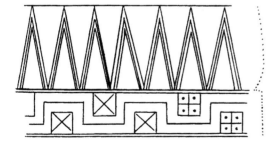

Fig. 13.3d. Drawing of base of ivory figurine. Source: Schiering 2003: Abb. 6. Permission: Athanasia Psalti, Director, 10th Ephorate of Prehistoric and Classical Antiquities.

II from Khorsabad, on the hem of a dress worn by a Phrygian tributary (Barnett 1948:9, fig. 7).[10]

Furthermore, the overall style of the ivory figurine is comparable to sculpture from Phrygian sites. A stone head from Gordion (Fig. 13.12a) has enlarged eyes reminiscent of those of the lion tamer, and when viewed from the side (Fig. 13.12b), the head features a similar cap-like rendition of the upper hair.[11] Another stone figure from Gordion has a small pursed mouth like that of the lion tamer, as well as a similar treatment of the body: the upper arms are not articulated at all, while the articulated forearms are short and cramped (Fig. 13.13) (Körte 1897:25–27, pl. II; Mellink 1983:352, pl. 72, no. 1-3). The low forehead is also a standard feature of

Fig. 13.5. Post-Hittite sherd from Boğazköy. Source: Bittel and Güterbock 1933:32, fig. 15, upper right.

5 cm

Fig. 13.4. Wooden lion with an ivy ear from Gordion. Source: Gordion Archive, Penn Museum. Image 102882.

siren attachments on the bronze cauldrons of Gordion and Van (Schiering 2003:61). Similar too is the treatment of the arms and upper body on an ivory figurine of a "priest" from the Bayındır tumulus (Fig. 13.14) (Varinlioğlu 1992; Özgen and Öztürk 1996:27, fig. 32; Işık 2001:88, fig. 4; Sare 2010). A further parallel is provided by an ivory figurine from a habitation deposit at Gordion of the late 8th or early 7th century (Fig. 13.15), the very date of the Bayındır tomb and, for that matter, one that is consistent with the date of the Ankara orthostate with the "X" on the lion's shoulder.[12] This cluster of dates furnishes a general guide to the chronology of the Delphi figurine.

The function of the Delphic ivory is especially noteworthy. It was clearly attached to something, as the mortise shows, and it must have projected horizontally since there is no cutting on the base. Moreover, the object to which it connected must have been large, judging by the size of the cutting. It therefore seems likely that the ivory formed part of a piece of furniture. In that connection, an interesting possible parallel comes from the Urartian

Fig. 13.6. Boğazköy sherds with checkerboards inserted into the meander. Source: Bossert 2000: pl. 113, no. 358a. Permission: Eva-Maria Bossert.

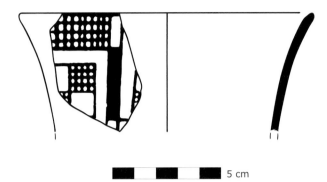

5 cm

Fig. 13.7. Non-uniform battlement meander with a checkerboard motif in-between. Iron Age sherd from level III at Porsuk. Source: Dupré 1983: pl. 82, no. 165. Permission: Institute Français d'Études Anatoliennes.

site of Toprakkale, on the eastern edge of Anatolia, where excavations produced a throne with bronze fittings (Fig. 13.16) (Barnett 1950: fig. 22; Barnett 1954). The key part is the upright member, which Barnett identified as the support for an arm on the

Fig. 13.8. Dotting in squares is apparent on the garment of Warpalawas (right) at İvriz. Source: Caner 1983: Tafel C.

basis of a cutting on the back of the lion on the top, into which the arm's tenon would presumably fit. The head of the lion rises above the arm on the Urartian piece; the same situation is apparent on the Delphic ivory as well, as demonstrated by the fully worked back of the head. Interesting too are the quite comparable heights of the two pieces: the Toprakkale support is 28 cm, and the Delphi ivory, 22.5. We can guess, then, that the Delphic ivory may have formed part of a support for the arm of a throne, probably as a kind of appliqué on the front of an upright piece of wood. The tradition of decorating wooden furniture with ivory plaques and appliqués is, of course, well attested at Gordion, as indeed throughout the Syro-Hittite realm (Simpson 2010; 1995:1653).

The presence of a meticulously carved piece of furniture in Phrygian style at Delphi prompts one to turn to the *Histories* of Herodotos, who saw a throne in the Delphic Treasury of the Corinthians that he cited as a gift of the Phrygian king Midas. He also mentioned that it was Delphi's first gift by a foreign king, and that it was well worth seeing (Herodotos 1.14). For the dates of Midas' reign we receive assistance from Assyrian records, which show that he was in power at least during the period between 717 and 709 BC, and that would fit the style of the figurine (Roller 1983; Mellink 1992:622; Berndt-Ersöz 2008). Moreover, the votive pit from which this figurine comes lies about 10 m west of the Corinthian Treasury (no. 308 on the plan) (Bommelaer 1991: pl. 5). Although little now remains of the building, its position is consistent with Pausanias'

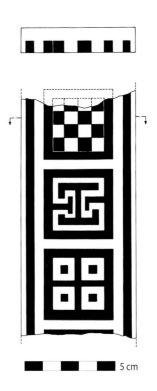

Fig. 13.9. Open-mouthed amphora from the Gordion Destruction Level, with panels on the shoulder containing the checkerboard motif, type 1B. Source: Sams 1994a: pl. 123, no. 927.

Fig. 13.10. An inlaid strip from Tumulus P. Source: Gordion Archive, Penn Museum. Image 102748.

mention of the structure in his itinerary, and a wall block that matches the form of the blocks still *in situ* bears a fragmentary inscription mentioning the Corinthians (Pausanias 10.13.5).[13]

Is the ivory lion tamer part of the throne of Midas mentioned by Herodotos? There is no absolutely conclusive proof, but the convergence of evidence is remarkable. The piece is Anatolian, and very likely Phrygian; the known dates for Midas in the late 8th century are compatible with its style; it is very likely from a piece of furniture, quite possibly a throne; and it was found close to the Corinthian Treasury, where Herodotos claims to have seen it. The conclusion that the Delphic ivory formed part of Midas' throne seems irresistible. Moreover, this may not have been Midas' only dedication: included in the

Fig. 13.11. Silver appliqué decorated with four-square pattern, from a tumulus of the late 8th or early 7th century at Bayındır near Elmalı. Source: Özgen and Özgen 1988:46, no. 53. Permission: İlknur Özgen.

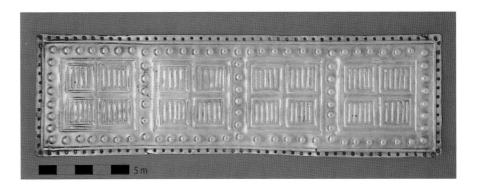

votive pit that contained the ivory figurine were two bronze cauldron attachments in the form of sirens, similar in style and date to those from Gordion Tumulus MM. (Amandry 1939:115, no. 64). The find spot alone does not prove their original presence in the Corinthian Treasury, but they are likely to have been Phrygian dedications of the time of Midas.

What of the throne's fate after Herodotos had admired it? Since the latest material in the votive pit that contained the lion tamer dates to ca. 420 BC, it looks as if the Corinthian Treasury or its storeroom burned shortly after Herodotos saw it.[14] The large quantity of carbonized wood found in the votive pits may have been remnants of the rest of the throne, although other wooden objects would almost certainly have been deposited in the pits as well (Amandry 1991:193). The proposed destruction of the throne in the late 5th century also fits with the literary evidence: we never hear of the throne again after the time of Herodotos, and it clearly was not in the Corinthian Treasury in the late 1st or early 2nd century AD when Plutarch mentions what survived of its once celebrated offerings, which was not much (Plutarch, *Moralia*, 399F).

Midas' model was subsequently followed by several members of the Lydian royal family, whose dazzling gifts were also deposited in the Corinthian Treasury: Gyges provided six gold mixing bowls—each of which weighed over 400 lbs., while Croesus supplied four silver chests and a gold statue of a lion weighing approximately 570 lbs. (Herodotos I.14; 1.50–51). Alyattes also sent a gift—an enormous silver bowl in a welded iron stand (Herodotos I.25), although its site of dedication is not recorded.

At least by the 5th century, then, it looks as if the Corinthian Treasury served as a showplace for prestige gifts by Anatolian kings, with ivory, gold, and silver prominently displayed. Why the Corinthian Treasury in particular received this assemblage is not readily apparent. The only literary attestation of a link between Corinth and Lydia involved Periander, who reportedly sent young boys

Fig. 13.12a, b. Fragmentary statuette from Gordion, possibly Matar or her male attendant, 7th–6th c. BC. Ht.: 14 cm. (a) frontal view; (b) side view. Source: Gordion Archive, Penn Museum. Images R-783-13 [Fig. 12a], R-783-14 [Fig. 12b].

5 m

Fig. 13.13. Fragmentary statuette from Gordion, now in Istanbul, possibly Matar or her male attendant. Ht.: 22cm. Source: Mellink 1983:352, pl. 72, no. 1-3.

from Corcyra to Lydia to be castrated (Herodotos 5.91–93). While this may indicate a political connection between the two areas, it does not explain the unique configuration of Corinth's Treasury. It seems more likely that the Corinthians acquired the objects after the Persian conquest of Lydia, either by purchase, loan, or gift.

When precisely the assemblage entered the Treasury is unclear, but its political reception during the 5th century may be retrievable. The Athenian Treasury at Delphi, constructed shortly after 490 BC, almost certainly featured spoils taken from the Persians, and the same may have been true for the Stoa of the Athenians at Delphi, which was situated next to the Corinthian Treasury.[15] The political and economic rivalry between Corinth and Athens after the Persian Wars was strong, and the two cities fought on opposite sides during the Peloponnesian Wars (M. Miller 1997:33). If viewed in this light, Corinth's decision to acquire the royal offerings of Phrygia and Lydia is not at all surprising in that it would have allowed Corinth, like Athens, to showcase the trappings of eastern luxury.

Not all of the items named above were initially dedicated in the Corinthian Treasury: Croesus's golden lion was first situated next to the Temple of Apollo, and was added to the Treasury only after the temple burned in 548 (Herodotos I.51). The throne of Midas must also have been displayed in a different location when it was first dedicated, since it would have reached Delphi nearly 100 years before the Corinthian Treasury was constructed.[16] The throne may have been positioned in the Temple of Apollo at first, but if so, it must have been moved prior to the fire of 548 BC, since Herodotos' comments imply that it was still intact when he saw it.

Despite the preponderance of evidence pointing to a Phrygian provenance, there will always be some degree of doubt as to whether the Delphic ivory formed part of a gift offered by Midas or by another Anatolian monarch. What is not in doubt, however, is the desirability of Delphi as a dedication site for the rulers of Anatolia, and for Midas and the Lydians in particular. In Midas' case the dedication was perhaps to be expected: his wife was Greek, from Aeolian Kyme (Aristotle, fr. 611.37; Pollux *Onom.* 9.83),

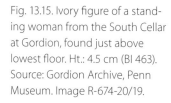

Fig. 13.14. Ivory figurine of a "priest" from the Bayındır tumulus D, near Elmalı. Source: Özgen and Öztürk 1996:27, fig. 32.

Fig. 13.15. Ivory figure of a standing woman from the South Cellar at Gordion, found just above lowest floor. Ht.: 4.5 cm (BI 463). Source: Gordion Archive, Penn Museum. Image R-674-20/19.

2 cm

and he clearly wanted to be viewed as a power broker in and around Anatolia. The fact that his name and career were still deemed worthy of mention at Delphi over 200 years after his death highlights the prescience of his decision, although he could not have imagined the role that his throne would subsequently play in the power politics of Lydia and Greece.

NOTES

13.1. This text is an updated version of a paper given by Keith DeVries on January 5, 2002, at the 103rd Annual Meeting of the Archaeological Institute of America in Philadelphia: *AJA* 106, p. 275; Deshmukh 2002. The paper was revised by Dr. DeVries in a draft dated February 7, 2005, but he passed away before he could complete his work on it: Sams 2007. The paper has been modified for article format by Brian Rose, who added several sections throughout the manuscript, including the discussion of Delphi, Corinth, and the Lydians. For assistance with the bibliography, footnotes, and illustrations, we thank Peter Cobb and Gareth Darbyshire.

13.2. The height of the figures without the base is 18.5 cm: Amandry 1944–45:149; Akurgal (1961:188–

90, fig. 144) published the complete group; Amandry (1991:202) records a total height of 22.5 cm.

13.3. In an unpublished Master's thesis from 1970, Bonnie Rhoads states: "My contention is that this ivory is as characteristically Oriental as it is Ionian Greek, and that by stylistic analysis it is possible to classify it as the work of an artist whose cultural ties are more strongly linked to Near Eastern tradition. An Anatolian provenance is very likely" (p. 5).

13.4. In 2003 Schiering published an updated study of the ivory group and suggested that it might be the work of a Phrygian artist. He also posed the question of whether it might have been part of the throne of Midas. Dr. DeVries and Dr. Schiering maintained a correspondence about the ivory for several years, beginning in January of 2002.

13.5. Akurgal 1962: pls. 106, 107 (Malatya); 121 (Carchemish); 126, 127, 129 (Zincirli); Parrot 1961: figs. 36, 38 (Gilgamesh in the palace of Sargon II, Khorsabad); fig. 41 (Assurnasirpal II, Kalakh); fig. 43 (Khorsabad relief of Sargon II). Nearly all of these examples date to the second half of the 8th century BC. The exact pose of the

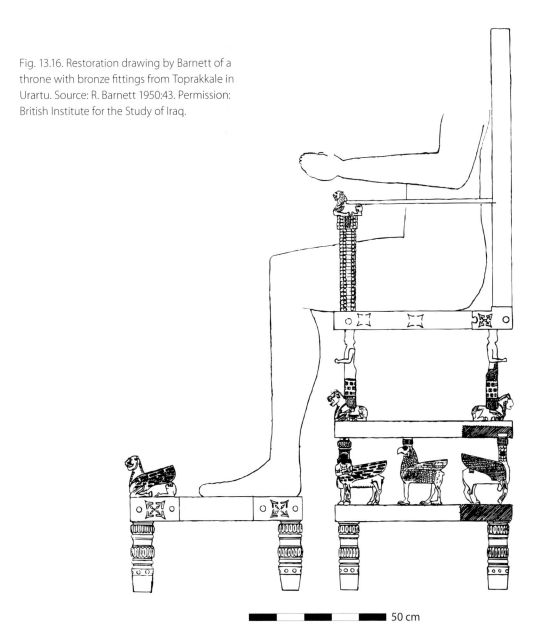

Fig. 13.16. Restoration drawing by Barnett of a throne with bronze fittings from Toprakkale in Urartu. Source: R. Barnett 1950:43. Permission: British Institute for the Study of Iraq.

50 cm

lion and his tamer are duplicated on no other known work of art, although a similar scheme appears in one of the reliefs from the Khorsabad palace of Sargon II, Midas' contemporary (Parrot 1961: figs. 36, 38).

13.6. Amandry 1944–45:161–62. For the date of the Ankara orthostates: Buluç 1988:21n2. For images: Güterbock and Özgüç 1946:74–75, figs. 22–24. The wooden lion is from Tumulus P: Young 1981:51, TumP 107, pl. 22C-F.

13.7. Dupré (1983:99–100) does not describe this as a meander, but rather as a checkerboard motif; it is identified as a meander by Sams (1994a:146–47, n164).

13.8. For the relief at İvriz in Tabal: Akurgal 1962:139–41, pl. 140; the vase's decoration is Sams' checkerboard motif, type 1B (1994a:149, fig. 64). Examples from the destruction level: Sams 1994a:283, no. 879, pl. 110; 289, no. 927, pl. 123.

13.9. An inlaid strip from Tumulus P: Young 1981:76, fig. 47, pl. 33A, Tumulus P 163.

13.10. Carter (1985:222) suggests that the motif is dependant on Near Eastern leaf capitals, although those leaves are usually overlapping.

13.11. From an earth fill with pottery extending in date

from at least the 7th century to at least the 6th. Mellink 1983:352, pl. 72, nos. 4-5; DeVries 1990:398, fig. 37; Roller 1999b:77, S93, fig. 14.

13.12. The ivory figure was found in the "south cellar" deposit: Young 1966:269, pl. 74, fig. 5. This context was recently analyzed by DeVries (2005). For the date of the Ankara orthostates: Buluç 1988:21n2.

13.13. For the inscribed block: Daux and Salač 1932:128, no. 153, fig. 16; La Coste-Messelière 1957:28, figs. 18, 312.

13.14. The latest object is a lamp dating to about 420 BC: Amandry 1991:193.

13.15. For the date and function of the Athenian Trea-sury, see Neer 2004:67. The construction date of the Stoa of the Athenians and the nature of its spoils are contro-versial. Walsh (1986) has argued that the Stoa's spoils had been taken by Athens during the Peloponnesian Wars, but most scholars would date the Stoa's construction to the immediate aftermath of the Persian Wars, and believe that at least some of its spoils were those of the Persians: Han-sen 1989; Mercanti 2006.

13.16. Midas must have sent the throne at some point during the last quarter of the 8th century, and the Corin-thian Treasury was not constructed until the last quarter of the 7th, allegedly by Cypselus: Herodotos I.14.

The Middle and Late Phrygian Citadel

YASSIHÖYÜK/GORDION
Middle Phrygian Period
YHSS Phase 5

0   50   100 M

Fig. 14.1. Plan of the rebuilt or New Citadel at Gordion, Middle Phrygian period, ca. 800 BC. The excavations in Operation 46 are indicated in gray. Source: Gordion Project, Penn Museum.

14

The Rebuilt Citadel at Gordion: Building A and the Mosaic Building Complex

Brendan Burke

The new Middle Phrygian Citadel at Gordion dates to the period after the great fire destruction of the Early Phrygian level/YHSS 6A (Fig. 14.1). The fire is now dated to around 800 BC and the initial rebuilding occurred shortly after that (Voigt 2005:31). As Sams (2005a:18) and Voigt (2005:32–35) have recently highlighted, throughout Phrygian times (Early, Middle, and Late) Gordion was composed of two mounds, an eastern one extensively excavated by Young and the less-explored western mound. The two mounds were divided by a large street that was filled in toward the end of the 4th century, creating the single flat-topped mound of today. Excavations along the southeastern edge of the mound have revealed the remains of two of the most impressive new citadel structures excavated by Rodney Young: Middle Phrygian Building A and the Late Phrygian Mosaic Building (Young 1951:6–10; 1953b:9, 14–17; 1955:1–2; 1965:6–7; Mellink 1988:228–29). These two buildings, which are the focus of this chapter, framed the southwestern edge of the eastern citadel.

Although excavations have revealed no indications of Early Phrygian structures lying below Building A, it is possible that the Early Phrygian Citadel extended this far as well. One major feature recognized fairly early on at Gordion is that the structures of the new Middle Phrygian Citadel often reflect older, Early Phrygian buildings below (Young 1962b:10; Edwards 1959:264). In the 1952 campaign, in Early Phrygian strata, Young's team excavated a wall 8 m thick, located to the northwest of Building A and below the Persian Gate building, which they inter-preted as part of an earlier fortification wall of the city (Young 1955:11, pl. 6, fig. 23; 1962a:167–68). The full extent of this part of the earlier citadel fortifications has not yet been determined, although it continues in the direction of Building A and the Mosaic Building (Fig. 14.2). A probable date for this large wall is early 9th century/YHSS 6B.

The part of the eastern citadel where Building A and the Mosaic Building are located is a significant one. The material excavated there by Young dates to the Hellenistic, Late Phrygian, and Middle Phrygian periods and provides important information for the history and organization of the new citadel after the Early Phrygian destruction level (DeVries 1990). In the course of several centuries, Phrygian culture at Gordion adopted certain Lydian, Achaemenid, and Hellenistic features, showing that it was fertile ground for other cultural influences to take root (Voigt and Young 1999).

Building A is one of the largest structures at Gordion, rivaling the Early Phrygian Terrace and Clay Cut Buildings in scale, and it was in use for quite a long time (Fig. 14.3). Built sometime in the 8th century BC, it remained in use without major modifications until the construction of the Late Phrygian/Achaemenid Mosaic Building. At that point Building A was dramatically altered, losing the southern two of its original six units with the construction of the Mosaic Building (Fig. 14.4). A heavily modified Building A and the Mosaic Building continue in use at least until the late 4th century BC.

The Mosaic Building is a large complex of highly decorated rooms and courts most likely used for administration and political receptions, perhaps cult activity. The historical context in which the Mosaic Building was constructed is quite different from the preceding Middle Phrygian period, when the Gordion citadel reached its most elaborate form and largest extent. After the mid-6th century Gordion was part of the Achaemenid Empire and no longer a center of political power in central Anatolia, although it maintained strategic importance and was well equipped with supplies (Briant 2002:705–6).

Architecturally, however, the citadel was in decline, with many Middle Phrygian buildings gradually falling out of use (Edwards 1959:266; Voigt and Young 1999). The Mosaic Building is one of the few impressive public structures that we know of on the eastern mound, and recent fieldwork in the area has given us a new perspective on this unusual building.

Chronology

Building A and the Mosaic Building should first be situated in their historical and archaeological contexts relative to other well-known monuments at the site. Gordion's chronology had initially been established by relative sequencing of strata and monuments, historical texts (Classical and Near Eastern), and comparanda with finds elsewhere.

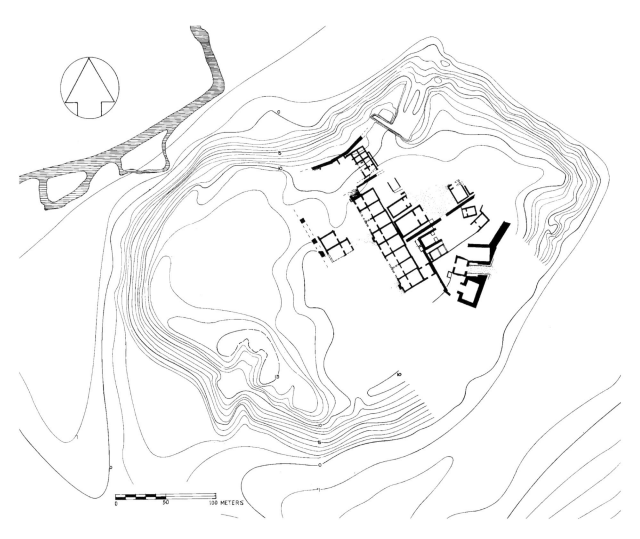

Fig. 14.2. Plan from 1969 of Early Phrygian Gordion showing citadel fortifications continuing in the direction of Operation 46. Source: Gordion Project, Penn Museum.

Three long-held chronological markers at Gordion, as established by Rodney Young, were the dates for Tumulus MM (formerly thought to be early 7th century), the Early Phrygian destruction level (formerly thought to be 696 or 676 BC), and the rebuilding of the citadel (formerly thought to be late 7th century BC). Stratigraphic analysis combined with radiocarbon and dendrochronology samples from the Destruction Level and Tumulus MM have up-ended the traditional chronology. The Destruction Level is now placed near 800 BC; the rebuilding followed immediately after, and the construction of Tumulus MM was completed around 740 BC (Rose and Darbyshire 2011). Stylistic developments in metal (especially metal bowls and fibulae) and Greek imported ceramics also fit into the revised chronology much more satisfactorily (Sams, this volume; DeVries 2005).

These chronological revisions impact the study of Building A and the Mosaic Building in several ways. Not only should we now view Early Phrygian architecture within an historical context over one hundred years earlier than previously believed, but the construction date of the Middle Phrygian eastern citadel built over the destroyed Early Phrygian one also falls back in time. If the rebuilding now begins just after the Destruction, or as Voigt and DeVries have maintained, immediately before it, then the initial construction date of Building A was probably soon after 800 BC (Voigt and DeVries, this volume).

Building A

Building A is located near the entry to Gordion's main citadel, which seems to have been the primary entrance point during both Early and Middle Phrygian times (Fig. 14.5). Blocks of limestone cut for the Early Phrygian Gate were covered with a rubble fill by the Middle Phrygian rebuilders, thereby creating a platform for a new fortification wall and gate. The Middle Phrygian entrance complex sits atop the leveling retaining wall, which has a rubble core and a stepped, multicolor ashlar Glacis, rising perhaps 20 m or more above the plain below (see Young 1956:260–61 and pl. 83, figs. 11 and 13). Today all that remains of the Middle Phrygian entrance are the Glacis, parts of the exposed rubble core, and

a few gypsum blocks of the gate itself toward the southwest, close to Building A (Fig. 14.6).

Constructed during the Middle Phrygian rebuilding, Building A's footprint measures approximately 76 x 22 m, and it was probably planned in relation to the gate complex. Although only two units of Building A were preserved completely when Young excavated the complex in the 1950s, it was possible for him to reconstruct in plan this massive structure with a total of six units, each with an anteroom and a main room behind. The reconstruction of all six units is based on fragmentary cross-walls and foundations located to the south that were used as the foundations of the Achaemenid Mosaic Building. The individual units are separated by side walls that are 2.5 m wide, which is rather massive for interior walls. Each unit is just over 10 m wide, and no back wall was found in the earlier excavations to determine the exact depth of the Building A units.

The few finds discovered in and around Building A do not point to a specific function. Unlike the Early Phrygian Citadel, Middle Phrygian buildings and later structures were not suddenly destroyed by a fire and sealed in a clay layer; they were used and re-used for centuries and then heavily robbed, thereby making it difficult to reconstruct their primary function. In the case of Building A, the early excavators report finding pithoi and burnt grain on the floor, indicating that at least part of this building was used for food storage. There are also some indications of elite goods, including an ivory plaque described below from Unit 4, and a fragment of a white group cup by the Penthesilea Painter, ca. 470–450 BC, from the floor of Unit 1 (DeVries 1997:449–50, fig. 5). Since the walls of Building A are quite massive, measuring approximately 2.5 m for each interior wall, a defensive use should not be ruled out, nor should a second story.

One comparison for the plan and construction techniques of Building A is the fortification system reported at the large citadel near the village of Hacıtuğrul, excavated by Burhan Tezcan beginning in 1973 and sometimes referred to as Yenidoğan (Mellink 1973:179–80; 1974:117; 1975:210; 1976: 272; 1977:300; 1980a:508–9; 1982:566; Tezcan 1981:43–45; Sams and Temizsoy 2000:56). This large Phrygian site is located about 20 km NW of Gordion, on the north side of the Polatlı-Ankara

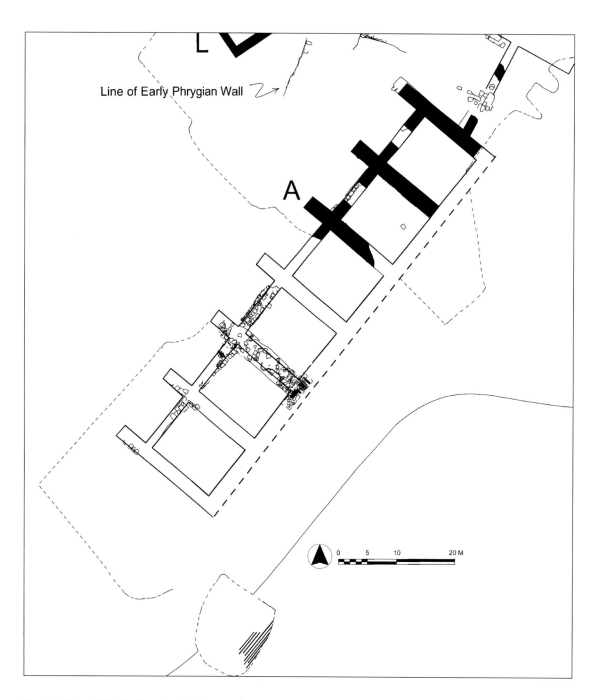

Fig. 14.3. Plan of Middle Phrygian Building A, 8th century BC. The line of the Early Phrygian wall is indicated. Drawing: Brendan Burke after David Scahill.

road, and features a fortification system made up of ashlar masonry over a rubble fill (Fig. 14.7). Cross walls run into the citadel, perpendicular to a massive main wall, thereby creating a series of bastions comparable to the units of Building A. Hacıtuğrul shares many similarities with Gordion's fortifications, as Mellink noted in her annual reports. The Middle Phrygian occupation at Hacıtuğrul continued in the 7th and 6th centuries, as at Gordion, and Phrygian inscriptions and decorative terracotta re-

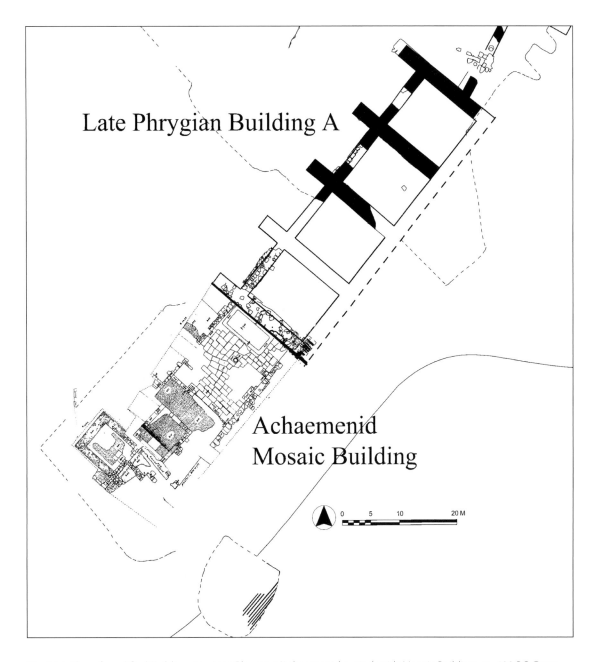

Fig. 14.4. Plan of modified Building A in Late Phrygian/Achaemenid period, with Mosaic Building, ca. 400 BC. Drawing: Brendan Burke after David Scahill.

vetments were found with reused Middle Phrygian blocks (Mellink 1980a:509). There are also at least three tumuli located near the citadel.

On the Gordion mound, a team under my direction has been investigating the area to the southwest of Building A since 2001, when work sponsored by the 1984 Foundation and the University of Victo-

ria began in what is known as Operation 46. In this area we found Hellenistic houses and other structures that made use of stones robbed from earlier Phrygian buildings. Domestic structures with walls made of plundered cut blocks and rough fieldstones of Hellenistic date show continuous modifications and reuse.

In 2006 we extended Operation 46 to the east so that Building A could be further investigated, and opened a new trench, Operation 56. Fieldwork focused on Unit 4 of Building A, where cleaning allowed us to determine old excavation lines and cuts from the previous work in the 1950s (Fig. 14.8). Not surprisingly, given the presence of reused Middle Phrygian blocks in the Hellenistic levels, the walls of this unit were heavily robbed of stone blocks. Prominent robber trenches located 10.10 m apart had taken out much of the dividing side walls of the anteroom. Several surfaces built up against these walls showed that Building A stood for centuries and was continually modified over time.

The plans drawn in the 1950s focused on the overall form and dimensions of Building A, based heavily on robbed trenches and foundation levels only. This has left us with some vexing questions to answer. The state plans show only Unit 1 with a central passageway between the anteroom and main room (Young 1955: fig. 3) (Figs. 14.9, 14.10). The walls of Unit 2 are drawn as solids, and as it stands today, there is little to indicate a passage into the main room. But the design of Building A seems to have been heavily influenced by that of the Terrace and Clay Cut Buildings, which consistently have a passageway between anteroom and main room. Our cleaning in 2006 revealed the top of the crosswall between the anteroom and main room of Unit 4 but produced no evidence of a threshold. Some burning was noted in the earlier excavation, however, and traces of ash were still present when we cleaned the top of the wall. It is possible that in a later use a passageway was constructed with wooden elements that subsequently burned. It does not look as if the building was originally constructed with passageways through each of the six units.

Another major issue concerns the back wall of Building A. No wall was reportedly found during the 1950s excavations, and the 1956 restored plan of

Fig. 14.5. Photo of Building A remains in 2006. The Early and Middle Phrygian Gates are visible to the east. Photo: author.

Fig. 14.6. Photo of Middle Phrygian Glacis, with parts of the exposed rubble core and gypsum blocks, in 2006. Photo: author.

wooden timbers that are typical of Middle Phrygian construction (Fig. 14.11). Samples were taken from nine of the juniper logs that we discovered for radiocarbon and dendrochronology testing. Initial reports from Sturt Manning of the Caroline and Malcolm Wiener Laboratory of Dendrochronology at Cornell indicate that only two samples provide secure dendrochronology dates. The last ring of one sample (GOR-204) dated to 1513 in the relative Gordion dendrochronological sequence, giving the sample's final ring an absolute date of ca. 993 BC. This is far too early for the construction of Building A, and since there was no bark preserved, this must be viewed as a *terminus post quem*. One possibility is that the timbers were from an Early Phrygian structure that was damaged in the great fire and subsequently reused as a foundation course for the Middle Phrygian back wall.

the Persian level shows a back wall extending to the top of the Glacis, making the main rooms improbably deep (Young 1956: pl. 84, fig. 15). In 2006, I extended the trench that cleared the robbed side wall to see if we could find evidence for a back wall. Fortunately, another heavily robbed wall was found running perpendicular to the side wall; this proved to be the elusive back wall, which allows us to estimate the full depth of one of Building A's rooms at about 12 m.

The robbed-out back wall had a rubble foundation like the side walls, coupled with the laid

A primary-use surface was uncovered inside the main room of Unit 4, which yielded a beautiful carved ivory plaque approximately 5 x 7 cm (Fig. 14.12). The carving shows two rounded volutes with a fruited palmette growing in the middle. Bunches of small fruits on three stems extend from both ends of the volutes. The palm tree itself has six branches evenly divided by a small chevron design in the up-

Fig. 14.7. Ashlar fortification walls at Hacıtuğrul (Yenidoğan), 20 km NW of Gordion, in 2006. Photo: author.

per center, allowing three curved palm branches with fruited ends to curve over on each side. The design, which evokes a sense of fertility and abundance, was probably used as a decorative furniture inlay. Although splintered, the full plaque can be restored and has good parallels with other ivory finds from Tumulus D at Bayındır, near Elmalı, at the Urartian site of Altıntepe (Özgüç 1969), and at Gordion itself (6670 BI 391 fd. June 14, 1961, City Mound–CW1, NB86, pp. 195–96; see Sheftel 1974 and Young 1960:240). This ivory and others examples from Gordion are North Syrian in style and date to the mid-8th century, but some features, such as the raised edges on the branches and clustered bunches of fruit, also suggest connections with Anatolian traditions, in particular Urartian. Its context, on the earliest floor of Unit 4, provides a good date for the

primary use of Building A in the 8th century.

Building A was heavily modified when the Mosaic Building was constructed, presumably in the 5th century (see below). Units 5 and 6 were dismantled during the construction of the paved exterior court along the north side of the Mosaic Building complex. When both Building A and the Mosaic Building went out of use, presumably near the beginning of the Hellenistic period, stone robbers made use of the large cut blocks employed in their construction. The side walls of Units 1 and 2 extended toward the edge of the mound, where access was relatively easy, and the robbing seems to have continued until the Young campaign began. The excavation of Building A in 1951 exposed walls that showed a great deal of subsidence along the eastern side of Building A since antiquity. The side walls, in particular, curved down the slope of the mound and were rather unstable. As Young noted in 1955, the subsidence has implications for the geomorphology of this part of the mound: the fact that the anteroom cross-wall, running perpendicular, is fairly well preserved and seems not to have subsided suggests that there may have been an Early Phrygian wall below it that provided support (Young 1955:11).

Probably dated to a later phase of Building A, perhaps the 4th century, is an unusual deposit of vessels uncovered by the Young team above the main room of Unit 4 (NB 32, Trench D, pp. 46–47; trench N, pp. 134–35) (Figs. 14.13, 14.14). The pots are uniformly large and were wheel-made but finished by hand at the top. These were nicknamed "flower pots" by the excavators because they were found upside down with holes in the bottom. One is incised with an A, probably a potter's mark, and some have streaks of dripped paint from the rim down. Since the necks of the vessels were often damaged, it is conceivable that the pots were used for the production of cheese. In this scenario, the neck would have been weakened when cheese acids had concentrated

in the upside-down pot, while the holes at the vessel's top would have let gases escape. These pots are anomalous at Gordion, and more research needs to be done on them in the future.

Found near the "flower pots" and shown in early excavation photos and plans was a mud-lined pit that may be contemporary with the vessels (Fig. 14.15). From excavation photographs one can see that the pit was embedded in rubble, with orthostate blocks along the base of the walls. It is possible that this is a later, Hellenistic cellar constructed after the Mosaic Building went out of use.

The Mosaic Building Complex

By the 5th century, in the southeastern sector of the Eastern Citadel Mound, there had been a major renovation that included construction of the Late Phrygian/Achaemenid Mosaic Building (Young 1953b:18–19). From Xenophon we know that Pharnabazos was at Gordion in 407 BC, in the company of Lacedaemonian ambassadors who had been

Fig. 14.8. Building A, main room of unit 4, showing cross wall and robber trench cleared in 2006. Photo: author.

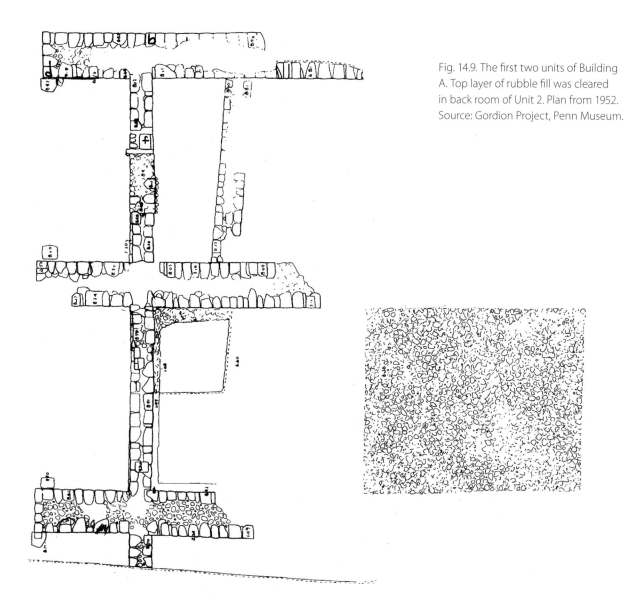

Fig. 14.9. The first two units of Building A. Top layer of rubble fill was cleared in back room of Unit 2. Plan from 1952. Source: Gordion Project, Penn Museum.

sent to meet with Persian authorities (*Hell.* I.4.2). As Briant describes it, although Gordion was no longer the capital city of Phrygia, it probably took on major importance during the Achaemenid period as a supplier of agricultural goods (2002:644). The Spartan general Agesilaos attacked Gordion in 396 BC, when it was under the command of a Persian named Rathines/Ratanes, and the city was still described as a "fortress built on a hill and well supplied" (*Hell. Oxy.* 21.6). It is within this historical context that one should reconstruct Gordion's Mosaic Building.

At this time the two southernmost units of Building A were replaced by the elaborately deco-

rated Mosaic Building complex (Fig. 14.16). Much of this striking building was uncovered in the early 1950s, and today it is difficult to grasp how truly splendid it once was (Fig. 14.17). The multi-room structure was at least 35 m in length and 11 m wide. It was entered through a court paved with large cut andesite blocks. Within this pavement a stone ring was placed, presumably intended as a planter in the courtyard. This area led the visitor on axis to a stepped entrance with columns on either side. Only one column base was found *in situ*, with red paint still preserved on it. Inside, the large, wide anteroom was decorated with a mosaic of small, colorful river stones laid in meander patterns. This room could have been a waiting area for visitors seeking entrance to the main chamber, which was roughly square and also decorated with a meander mosaic. Along the back wall, centrally placed, was a rectangular base set off by dark glassy pebbles. If this was the platform for a throne, as Mellink suggested, it would follow the general iconographic pattern for an enthroned Great King, such as that shown on the eastern bas-relief in the Treasury of Persepolis (Mellink 1988:228; Paspalas 2005: fig. 1).

The excavation of a robber trench to the south and west of the rectangular base yielded an impressive agate Achaemenid cylinder seal showing a kingly worship scene (Dusinberre 2005:51–54). The seal

shows two bearded figures with crowns and robes standing on sphinxes; these, in turn, flank a central figure who also wears a crown and emerges from a winged disc. This group surrounds a fire altar which is directly above an encircled crowned figure. Accompanying this complex iconography is an Aramaic inscription, dateable to the mid-5th century BC, that identifies it as the "Seal of Bn, son of Ztw, (hyashana)" (Dusinberre 2005:52; 2008).

As the seal is not from a primary context, it is by no means certain that it is related to events that took place in the Mosaic Building, but the heavy-handed Persian imagery suggested early on that this area may have been the location for the Great King's representative (Young 1955:2; Mellink 1988:228). It is

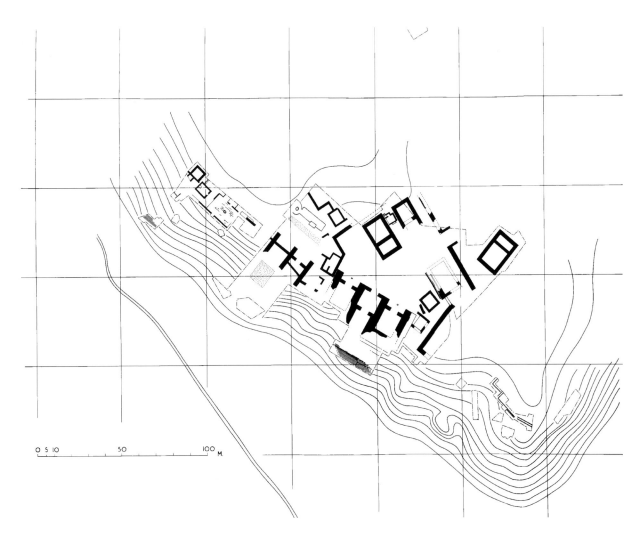

Fig. 14.10. Middle Phrygian Gate, the Glacis, first two units of Building A. Plan from 1952. Source: Gordion Project, Penn Museum.

Fig. 14.11. Robbed-out back wall of Building A, unit 4, with juniper timbers used as foundational support, 2006. Photo: author.

also possible that if there was indeed a formal audience hall in the Mosaic Building, it could date to a period *after* the conquest of the Persian Empire by Alexander the Great. As Paspalas (2005) has recently shown, an enthroned central figure would fit into many of the new courtly rituals of the Macedonians in the east.

The fill above and around the Mosaic Building revealed several examples of painted architectural terracottas from elaborately roofed buildings, most of them likely used on the Mosaic Building itself (Glendinning 1996). During the cleaning of 2006 some newly recovered roof tiles came to light, including fragments of a Theseus and Minotaur scene, rampant lions, and floral-star patterns (Fig. 14.18). Young's initial report makes it clear that these deposits should be associated with a period after the Mosaic Building went out of use: "The mosaic floor is covered by a mass of large squared blocks which lie stacked

Fig. 14.12. Ivory plaque with volutes and fruited palmettes, ca. mid-8th century BC. Photo: author.

Fig. 14.13. "Flower pots" in situ, found in unit 4 Building A. Photo from 1955. Source: Gordion Project, Penn Museum.

and partly overlapping, where they assume the position of a shapeless tumble. They are all intermingled with broken roof tiles and I am inclined to think that as they lie they were assembled by stone robbers, rather than fallen" (NB 31, Friday, May 9, 1952).

Fortress Gordion

Middle Phrygian Building A was built on a large rubble Glacis fronted with colored ashlar blocks that, together with the gate complex itself, created an impressive façade for any visitor to the site. Beyond this façade to the south, an outer circuit wall and fortification system protected the Lower Town at Gordion. This system, centered on a fortress known as the Küçük Höyük, was excavated by Young's team in the 1950s and 60s (Young 1957:324–25; 1958:140–41; Edwards 1959:264). The relationship between modified Building A, the later Mosaic Building, and the larger fortification walls of the Küçük Höyük will

Fig. 14.14. "Flower pot." Photo: author.

Fig. 14.15. Mud-lined pit between unit 4 Building A and Achaemenid Mosaic Building. Photo from 1952. Source: Gordion Project, Penn Museum.

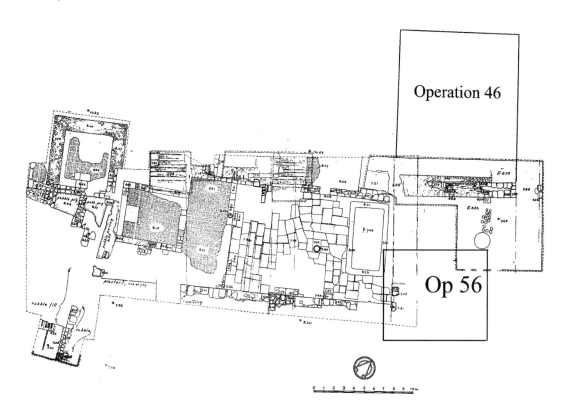

Fig. 14.16. Plan of Achaemenid Mosaic Building and modified Building A. Recent excavation units, Operations 46 and 56, are indicated. Source: Gordion Project, Penn Museum.

be the subject of future inquiries as research continues on the Middle and Late Phrygian defenses. The chronology of the Küçük Höyük is difficult to determine, yet it was a massive complex—12 m in height, at least 50 m long, and over 10 m wide. We know that there was a major military siege of this structure: two skeletons were found in the collapse, as were large numbers of arrowheads, some of which were still embedded deeply in the mud-brick walls. Lydian pottery and Attic imports indicate a destruction date of about 540 BC, perhaps coinciding with a known battle between Cyrus the Great of Persia and Croesus of Lydia (Briant 2002).

When trying to place the initial construction of Middle Phrygian Building A in historical context, one's thoughts turn to Midas, familiar as both as an historical ruler of the late 8th century, and as a figure of Greek legend epitomizing eastern kingship. Assyrian references to the Mushki ruler "Mita" are

probably the Semitic variant of the Phrygian name "Midas." From these texts Midas emerges as an ambitious king who, early in his reign, tried to oppose Assyrian influence in Asia Minor with the aid of diplomatic alliances, espionage, and minor skirmishes (Luckenbill 1926:8; Postgate 1973). Mita provided moral and economic support to disloyal Assyrian allies, including Pisiri of Carchemish in 717 BC and the King of Tabal (Grayson 1991:91–92). A visual record of one of these alliances may be preserved on the İvriz relief, showing Warpalawas of Tyana wearing a Phrygian garment, fastened with a Phrygian fibula (Mellink 1979). Herodotos credits Midas as the first foreign king to make a dedication at Delphi, and part of King Midas' throne may actually have been found near the Treasury of the Corinthians, if the suggestion by Keith DeVries regarding the ivory lion tamer figurine is accepted (DeVries and Rose, this volume).

Fig. 14.17. Photo from 1951 excavation of Achaemenid Mosaic Building. Source: Gordion Project, Penn Museum.

Midas may well have been the sponsor of the monumental Building A, although there is admittedly no concrete evidence to link him with the new structure. Either way, Building A was clearly intended to increase even further the visitor's sense of the citadel's impregnability and, by extension, the power of the Phrygian state.

The focus of recent excavations in Gordion's southeastern sector was to map diachronic changes in material culture, with particular reference to ancient technologies in domestic areas, and to understand how these changes relate to the larger historical events in central Anatolia during the post-Early Phrygian era. What we have found is that public architecture in the area, Building A and the Mosaic Building, document remarkable changes at Gordion over time, from the reign of King Midas up to the conquest of Alexander the Great, as few other sectors of Gordion have done.

Fig. 14.18. Photo of architectural terracotta with floral-star pattern, from robber fill of Building A, 2006. Photo: author.

15

Pontic Inhabitants at Gordion? Pots, People, and Plans of Houses at Middle Phrygian through Early Hellenistic Gordion

Mark L. Lawall

A striking feature of the imported Greek amphoras found at Gordion is the frequent presence of jars from Pontic producers, especially from the south coast of the Black Sea, during the 4th and very early 3rd century BC. In this period, and even earlier, the Aegean types present at Gordion tend to echo those found at sites along the northern coast of the Black Sea. From such indications in Gordion's amphora record, I concluded in an earlier paper that late Classical/earliest Hellenistic Gordion was heavily dependent on an overland route roughly due north to modern Ereğli (ancient Herakleia) for much of its amphora supply (Lawall 2010). In this chapter I propose to push that conclusion even further.

My argument is as follows. First, a survey of Gordion's amphora record from the Middle Phrygian through Early Hellenistic phases demonstrates striking similarities with the broader Pontic amphora record. At this point, normally, I would go no further than concluding (1) that Gordion shared some suppliers with Pontic sites, and (2) that the northerly overland route between Gordion and Ereğli was important to this amphora trade, especially during the latter part of the Late Phrygian period and into the early Hellenistic period. A detail of early Hellenistic house construction brought to light in the most recent excavations, however, raises the possibility of Pontic inhabitants at Gordion. That detail is the stone-built bin in the corner of a room excavated by Brendan Burke in Operation 46, just west of Building A (Figs. 15.1 and 15.2).[1] Such bins, despite

their obvious simplicity, are not common—at least they are not commonly known or reported. They are easier to find, however, in early Hellenistic houses at sites along the north coast of the Black Sea.

Middle Phrygian through Early Hellenistic Amphoras at Gordion

The prosperous Middle Phrygian period at Gordion included the earliest arrival of Greek fineware imports and very few amphoras.[2] Two major classes of amphoras belong to this phase. Most common are fragments of amphoras from the region of Lesbos and the adjacent mainland, primarily of a very dark red fabric (Abramov 1993:26, 29, 32; Clinkenbeard 1982; Dupont 1998:156–62; Monakhov 2003:47–49). Unfortunately most of the stratigraphically earliest examples involve poorly diagnostic handle fragments. Even so, the presence of amphoras of this class at the Phrygian capital fits neatly with Nigel Spencer's discussion of the grey ware tradition (of which these amphoras, despite their red fabric, are a part) that linked Lesbos with Phrygia (Spencer 1995; Lawall 2002[2003]:200 and 215–16).

The second class originated in the region of Klazomenai as early as the second half of the 7th century BC (Abramov 2001:7–16; Ersoy 1993:396–403; Monakhov 2003:50–55; Sezgin 2004). The earliest examples, with heavy triangular rims, belong to Sezgin's group 1, in use from the mid to late 7th

Fig. 15.1 Overview, looking south, of excavations in Operation 46. Photo: Brendan Burke.

ing Lydian) pottery at Gordion encourages attention to an east-west trade route (DeVries 2005). Even so, there may have been a concurrent trade route north from Gordion at an early period since the same mix of Lesbian and Klazomenian amphora types alongside East Greek finewares appears at numerous Archaic Pontic sites.[3] The situation brings to mind the old, and now seemingly out of favor, suggestion of a trade route through Anatolia linking Sinope with the Near East (Boardman 1980:240).

The Late Phrygian/Achaemenid period at Gordion, from ca. 540 to the arrival of Alexander in 334/3, witnessed a striking increase in Greek imports both in finewares and amphoras (DeVries 1990, 1996, and 2005).[4] The first of three major periods of Late Phrygian/Achaemenid imports falls at the very end of the 6th and the early years of the 5th century. The second period covers especially the third quarter of the 5th century; Greek imports then reappear through the 4th century.

Amphoras from the region of Lesbos continue to appear in the Late Phrygian period, though many date to the mid–late 6th century. The toes found so far can all date before ca. 500; they do not yet show the very tall narrow bases found in deposits associated with the Persian sack of Athens (cf. Roberts 1986: nos. 408–411). The examples from Gordion are generally similar to the many such late Archaic forms published from Pontic sites (Monakhov 2003:48–49) and from Hellespontine Phrygia (at Daskyleion, see Atila 2003: nos. 50–59, and in the Troad, see Lawall 2002[2003]: 200 and nos. 1–13). The few fragments of Lesbian grey amphoras are likewise largely limited to the 6th century, but one of them may date within the 5th century due to the sharp ridge under the rim and the handle slightly overlapping the rim (Clinkenbeard 1982; Monakhov 2003:43–47 and pls. 27–29; Abramov 1993). An outward leaning wedge rim on a bulging neck may belong to a red-clay amphora type generally as-

century (Sezgin 2004:170–72). A few other Klazomenian fragments at Gordion continue well into the 6th century. A decorated neck fragment belongs to the Attic SOS type of the 7th century, and a single wall fragment with streaky brown slip is identifiable as from either an Attic SOS or *à la brosse* amphora type of the Middle or Late Phrygian period (Johnston and Jones 1978).

The few fragments from this period have little to offer as far as identifying pots with people. The amount of Greek, East Greek, and western Anatolian (includ-

Fig. 15.2. Detail of the corner bin with loomweights in the Operation 46 house. Photo: Brendan Burke.

sociated with the northwestern Aegean (Monakhov 2003:77–78, pls. 52, 53). The Chian amphoras in this phase are nearly all datable between the late 6th century and ca. 480. There are a few fragments that can be dated later in the 5th century, but no certain examples of the late 5th century straight neck jars (Knigge 1976:23–24; De Marinis 1999; Abramov 2002; Monakhov 2003:11–24).

Amphoras of the southeastern Aegean fall into two chronological groups. The late 6th century is well represented by fully rounded rims, but airfoil and echinoid rims of southern Ionia and Caria are not found (Dupont 1998:164–86; Monakhov 2003:25–42). A few fragments with taller neck and bobbin-shaped body and knob toe date later in the 5th century (Grace 1971: fig. 3.3; Dupont 1998: fig. 23.9d-g; Monakhov 2003: fig. 15.7 and figs. 19, 20).[5] From the middle of the 5th century on, the southeastern Aegean region also takes up a broadly flaring mushroom-shaped rim (Zeest 1960:91–92; Lawall 2004a:451–53; Nørskov 2004:285–91;

Monakhov 2003:102–4). One early representative of this type may come from Erythrai, to judge from the appearance of its fabric as compared with that of roughly contemporary amphoras stamped with the abbreviation EPY (Carlson and Lawall 2005-2006[2007]; Carlson 2004; Buzoianu 1999: pls. 5, 6, no. 16.670). A larger group of rims is better dated within the 4th century, probably in its second half. These rims show a surprisingly consistent fabric that resembles later amphoras of Kos (Kantzia 1994, Georgopoulou 2001).

Amphoras from the northeastern and north-central Aegean are most readily identifiable from the third quarter of the 5th century and again nearer the middle of the 4th century. Most securely identified are the stem toes attributable to Mende, but other rims and toes likely belong to the same general class (Lawall 2004a:445–54; 1997; 1995:116–73). Foremost among these is a series of extremely micaceous jars with a cadeucus or other simple stamp on the handles; production at Mende or elsewhere around the Chalkidike seems likely (Bon and Bon 1957: nos. 2183–2184, 2202, 2219, 2226; Vaag, Nørskov, and Lund 2002: nos. A84 and G72; Grace 1956: nos. 216–220 and 245–248; Garlan 1989:477–80; Akamatis 2000: nos. PAR82–91; Peirce 2001: nos. 13.21–13.23; Robinson 1950: no. 1101; and Monakhov 1999:212, fig. 87.1). Thasian stamped amphoras include only one example from before ca. 325 BC (Gordion SS217 = Garlan 1999: no. 648).

Gordion also began to receive amphoras from Herakleia Pontike during the 4th century. Most of the fragments are quite small bits of rims or toes, but one of the few stamped fragments is a rim and neck sherd with the stamp of the fabricant Archelas in an inverted heart-shape with eponym Ia- (Fig. 15.3). This combination has been assigned by V.I. Kac to the Early Magistrate Group (390s–380s BC) (Kac 2003:275). A second stamped neck fragment may carry the eponym Kallias I of the 360s–350s BC (Kac 2003:276) with a fabricant starting with Δ..., perhaps Dionysios (Teleaga 2003:83) (Fig. 15.4). The third Herakleian stamp shows simply a strung bow. The better-preserved fragments (Monakhov 2003: pls. 86–88) and the few stamps indicate that these imports began to arrive early in the 4th century.

The rarity of Herakleian amphoras in the Aegean compared with their presence at Gordion provides

Fig. 15.3. Herakleian amphora stamp with the fabricant Archelas and the eponym abbreviation IA (SS110); not to scale. Photo: author.

Fig. 15.4. Herakleian amphora stamp with the eponym Kallias I (I627); not to scale. Photo: author.

route between the area of Gordion and the area of Herakleia; he followed the route by taxi and reported it quite easy going (Gürsan-Salzmann 2001:24–25). If a route linking Gordion and the northern coast existed in antiquity, it seems likely that it may have been used for both commerce and herding. At the same time, the increasingly organized Persian infrastructure for tribute collection and maintenance of their empire could have made Gordion a likely marketing point. For the present purposes, the main point of importance here is the higher presence of Herakleian stamps at Gordion than at sites in the Aegean or along the west coast of Turkey. This fact alone indicates a greater degree of connection between Gordion and the Pontic coast.

Alexander's famous knot-splitting visit to Gordion (Arrian, Anab. I.29 and II.3), heralding the Early Hellenistic period, did not lead to immediate changes in the record of the amphora imports. The event that does seem to have had a major impact is the arrival of the Galatians into Anatolia in the 270s and their settlement in the Gordion region, perhaps in the 260s (DeVries 1990; Voigt 2003; Darbyshire, Mitchell, and Vardar 2000; Mitchell 2005:280–93; Arslan 2002:41–55). Before the arrival of the Galatians, the early Hellenistic amphora imports to Gordion were dominated by those from the southeastern Aegean and the Pontic region, with northern Greece represented primarily by stamped amphoras from Thasos.

The often steeply sloping mushroom rims of the southern Aegean amphoras show a very similar fabric to that seen in earlier examples (Monakhov 2003: pl. 79.4, 5, and 7). There are, however, fragments attributable to Rhodes or the vicinity that span the last quarter of the 4th and the first decades of the 3rd century (Grace 1963; Philimonos-Tsopotou

positive evidence for a northerly trade route from Gordion to the Black Sea coast. The possibility that Herakleia at a prodigiously early date began to use relatively complex amphora markings could indicate rapid economic growth in that city; however, both the chronology of these stamps and their association with Herakleia have been the topics of debate (Kac 2003, Teleaga 2003; cf. Pavlichenko 1999, Balabanov 2006). Even those arguing for a later chronology would still place the material found at Gordion within the 4th century; and even those arguing for points of origin other than Herakleia would still put the production within the Pontic region.

Whichever region was producing these jars, now at such a scale of production and/or trade that control by stamping was necessary, that area was surely thriving. The associated merchants might seek out new markets, even if they required overland transport. Keith DeVries advised me that there was, until the last decade or so, a very active transhumant

Fig. 15.5. Sinopean amphora stamp of Pasichares and Hekataios (SS225); not to scale. Photo: author.

and early 3rd century, including a fragmentary stamp of the late fabricant Etymos from the end of the 4th and early part of the 3rd century (Kac 2003:277). A Chersonesan toe (Monakhov 1989: pl. 24) and two Sinopean fragments (including a stamp of Pasichares and Hekataios) (Fig. 15.5) may also date within this early Hellenistic period.[6]

It might be appropriate to include the Thasian amphoras with this Pontic group. While it is generally accepted that Thasian exports to the Black Sea began to decline during the last quarter of the 4th century (Debidour 1999, Lazarov 1999), the absolute Thasian presence in the Pontic region continued to be significant into the early 3rd century. The rarity of earlier Thasian material at Gordion coupled with Gordion's ongoing connection to the Pontic coast raises the possibility that these Thasian imports arrived via the Black Sea rather than the Hellespontine region.

The arrival of Galatian settlers in the 260s BC marks the end of any direct imports from the Pontic region; a few Thasian stamped handles may date to the 230s, as might a few Erythraian fragments. These could have come from either the Aegean or the Black Sea, but there is nothing of the expected later Sinopean or Chersonesan amphoras. I have argued elsewhere that a sudden influx of Rhodian amphoras at the very end of the 3rd and the beginning of the 2nd century is better attributable to military maneuvers around Gordion than to other forms of commerce (Lawall 2008).

From the late 6th through the first half of the 3rd century, the record of amphora imports at Gordion recalls various aspects of amphora circulation in the Black Sea. In the 6th and 5th centuries, Gordion shares many of the types that are present at Pontic sites; and what is rare at Pontic sites is also rare at Gordion. In the 4th and early 3rd century, the combination of a strong Thasian presence with substantial imports from the Pontic producers continues this link to Pontic trade patterns.

2004: pls. 24 and 60). A piriform, hollowed knob toe is a form well paralleled along the central coast of Ionia in the early 3rd century (Lawall 2004b: figs. 4, 5; Bylkova 2004: fig. 7; Kac et al. 2002:Ad80). Chian amphora rims may belong to this phase or to the end of the Late Phrygian period, but the extant toes are better dated within the later 4th or early 3rd century (Monakhov 2003:21–23, types V-B and V-C; Vaag, Nørskov, and Lund 2002: figs. 27, 28, and pls. 30, 31; and Lawall 2002[2003]: figs. 2–4).

There are rare imports from central Greece in this period, including one Corinthian rim (Koehler 1978: nos. 77 and 80; Monakhov 1999: fig. 222.3), and a group of poorly identified jars with a narrow rounded rim, short neck, and thick handles. Such jars are found in late 4th and early 3rd century contexts in Greece (e.g., Schmid 2000: fig. 188, nos. 60, 61; Doulgéri-Intzessiloglou and Garlan 1991: figs. 21, 22; Callaghan 1992: pl. 86, no. 60; Vanderpool, McCredie, and Steinberg. 1962: pl. 20, no. 4).

The material securely identified with the north Aegean in this period is largely limited to the Thasian amphora stamps of the period from ca. 310 to the 280s. Of the 47 Thasian stamps recorded at Gordion from this period, the most common eponyms include Aristeides, Archenax, Deinopas, Pythion, and Skymnos (Avram 1996, Debidour 1986, Garlan 1999 and 2004–05).

Pontic imports continue in this period. Some of the Herakleian fragments may date to the late 4th

House Bins

The house in Operation 46 (Fig. 15.1) appears to establish another connection to the Black Sea. In the southernmost corner of the room (Fig. 15.2), Brendan Burke and the workmen uncovered a low, curving stone wall. The bin formed by this wall and the walls of the room contained fine clay and numerous donut-shaped loomweights. Pottery from the room dates the construction and use of this building to the 3rd century BC. Such corner bins are not commonly found at sites around the Aegean basin. Only a few examples can be cited, and these lie along the north coast of the Aegean: the 5th or 4th century houses at Messembria-Zone (Tsatsopoulou-Kaloudi 2001: fig. 11) and Argilos (Bonias and Perrault 1996[1997]: figs. 2, 3).[7]

Third-century corner bins and other stone-built bins are more common in houses in the Pontic region. At Olbia Pontica, in houses seeming to date to the 3rd century, corner bins are very common (Leipunskaya 1995: fig. 1 and pl. 3; and others that are unpublished). The phasing of the buildings involved is still uncertain, but many of those with bins seem to have been in use in the 3rd century. Five different houses at Kerkinitis, all in use in the 3rd century, include corner bins (Kutaysov 1990: unnumbered plan after fig. 37, unnumbered plan after fig. 54, fig. 56.1, fig. 57 and fig. 62). Four similar bins also appear at Baclanya Skala in a complex of rooms thought to have been built in the first quarter of the 3rd century BC (Maslennikov and Buzhilova 1999: fig. 1; Fedoseev 2004:370). There are two corner bins in the rural house at Pustyany Bereg I, whose occupation is dated to the 4th and 3rd centuries BC (Maslennikov 2003: fig. 4.1). Likewise, at Zolotaya Balka in the Dneiper basin there are bins in two rooms in one complex, and a third in a large megaron-form building (Wasowicz 1975: figs. 19, 20).

From the Chersonesan chora, in a farmhouse with 4th and 3rd century activity, there is a bin in the corner of one room (Saprykin 1994: fig. 24). Another corner bin appears in a house at Kyta in its 4th to 3rd century phase (Molev 2003: fig. 5). While there is no information available as to the contents of these various bins, an undated stone-built bin at Tiritake near modern Kerch has been illustrated with its loomweights piled *in situ* (Munk Højte 2005: fig. 8c); the bin from Gordion Operation 46 also contained loomweights. While not overwhelming in number, even these eight sites, often with multiple bins, provide a better prototype for the behavior at Gordion than do the late 5th or early 4th century houses in northern Greece, noted earlier. Obviously a more thorough survey of Aegean and Pontic house plans (stone-by-stone plans and not the often-published reconstruction plans) would assist in clarifying this apparent pattern.

When considered alongside the Pontic character of the amphora assemblage at Gordion, these bins may indicate that we are dealing not simply with a strong north-south trade route linking Gordion to the Black Sea, but with a visible presence of Pontic immigrants. Imported goods always leave open the question of whether they simply attest to trade or whether people from the supplying region were actually using the foreign goods on site. When those imports are accompanied by a change in how one arranges one's house (perhaps even where one piles loomweights when not in use), then people accompanying the imported ceramics become a much more likely possibility.

NOTES

15.1. I thank Brendan Burke for information about this feature.

15.2. For the current overall phasing of the site, see Voigt 2005:22–35; and DeVries 2005.

15.3. For examples of this mix of East Greek finewares and amphoras at Histria, especially from Lesbos and Klazomenai, see Condurachi 1966 and Alexandrescu 2005; at Torikos, see Onaiko 1980; at Berezan, see Solovyov 1999, Posamentir 2006, and Dupont 2005.

15.4. For activity around Gordion in this period, especially the unsuccessful siege by Agesilaos in 396 BC, see *Hell. Oxyrh.* 21(16).6. Xen. *Hell.* I.4 has Pharnabazos at Gordion in 408/7.

15.5. The typology presented by Dupont 1998:164–86 covers the necessary Pontic and Aegean/Mediterranean evidence and discusses the continuing difficulties with sorting out the products of different cities and regions. For the perspective on these typologies from Pontic sites, see Monakhov 2003:25–42.

15.6. See Garlan 2004:145, no. 163 suggesting a date in the late 280s BC. Cf. also Fedoseev 1999.

15.7. I thank Nick Cahill and Barbara Tsakirgis for comments on the general rarity of such bins in Greek houses.

Conservation Management at Gordion

16

Resurrecting Gordion: Conservation as Interpretation and Display of a Phrygian Capital

Frank Matero

"Whatever withdraws us from the power of our senses; whatever makes the past, the distant, or the future predominate over the present, advances us in the dignity of human beings."—Samuel Johnson, *A Journey to the Western Isles of Scotland* (1775)

Archaeological Heritage and Conservation

Archaeological heritage and its conservation have become important issues in contemporary discourse on the use, management, and display of the past. Archaeological sites have long been a part of heritage, well before the use of the term "heritage." Current concerns can be attributed to the perception among the public and professionals alike that archaeological sites, like the natural environment, are nonrenewable resources that are disappearing at an alarming rate. This situation is attributable to a wide array of causes ranging from neglect and poor management to increased visitation and vandalism, from inappropriate past treatments to over-development for tourism (Matero et al 1998). Despite the global increase in the scale of these problems, counter-efforts of recovery, documentation, stabilization, interpretation, and display have been at the heart of archaeological preservation since the late 19th century (Demas 2000).

Like all disciplines, archaeology and conservation have been shaped by historical habit and contemporary concerns. Both disciplines address the past and its value to inform the present. Both have

also begun to expand the notion of "site" to include a more comprehensive understanding and vision of the cultural landscape. This in turn has demanded a more open, values-based approach that attempts to place artifacts and sites into a larger regional scale and contemporary social context, which recognizes the input of all stakeholders and especially culturally and locally affiliated groups.

The practices of traditional archaeology and conservation are by their very nature oppositional. Excavation, as the primary physical method by which archaeologists study a site, is an invasive process that is both destructive and irreversible. In the revealing of a site, structure, or object, excavation is not a benign reversal of site formational processes but rather a traumatic invasion of a site's physico-chemical equilibrium, resulting in immediate or gradual deterioration if preventive measures are not taken.

Conservation, on the other hand, seeks to safeguard cultural resources from loss and damage, based on the belief that material culture possesses important scientific and aesthetic evidence as well as the power to evoke memory and emotional responses. The informational value embodied in the materiality of objects and sites can be expressed as *integrity*, which is a common requirement for heritage designation in many conservation charters and codes of ethics. Integrity can manifest itself in various states as purity or completeness of form, physico-chemical composition, or context. Its definition will be a function of the values and significance to the viewer, and will vary for the archaeologist, art historian, conservator, and cultural affiliate. Integrity has come to be seen as an expression of authenticity, a quality that conveys some truthfulness of the original in time and space.

But archaeological sites are also places. If we are to identify and understand the nature and implications of certain physical relationships with locales established through past human thought and experience, we must do it through the study of *place*. Places are contexts for human experience, constructed in movement, memory, encounter, and association (Tilley 1994:15). They are more than the physical realities of a site. While the act of remembering is acutely human, the associations and meaning specific places can have at any given time will change. In this respect, conservation itself can become a way of reifying cultural identities and historical narratives over time.

Archaeological sites are what they are by virtue of the disciplines that study them. They are made, not found, constructed through time, often by neglect or destruction, amnesia, and then re-discovery. As heritage they are a mode of cultural production constructed in the present but having recourse to the past (Kirshenblatt-Gimblett 1998:7). Display as an interface mediates sites and transforms what is shown into heritage. The popular notion of archaeological sites as ruins is based on a long-standing tradition of cultivating a taste for the Picturesque (Thompson 1981). But contemporary modes of interpretation as well as an interest in displaying non-traditional sites such as Neolithic mounds or rusting industrial landscapes have begun to challenge such accepted definitions and approaches.

With advances in the scientific investigation of sites and artifacts beginning in the early 20th century, many sites were exploited for their finds and then often left unprotected and uninterpreted for public viewing. Today there is a new appreciation for a site's potential for interpretation and display, perhaps even an overzealous interest in the potential of many sites to be places for experience, education, and recreation.

Beginning with the Fourth International Congress of Architects in Madrid in 1904 and later with the Charter of Athens following the International Congress of Restoration of Monuments in 1931, architects, engineers, conservators, and archaeologists have been concerned with the identification and codification of a set of universal principles to guide the intervention of structures and sites of historic and cultural significance.

For archaeological sites, display and interpretation encompass a variety of options: reconstruction or anastylosis, building a protective enclosure or shelter, reburial, or the selected removal of components to the safety of a museum. Each choice has a significant impact on the context and the component. As we are now becoming acutely aware, interventions addressing only the material condition of objects, structures, and places of cultural significance without considering associated cultural beliefs and practices (i.e., intangible values) can sometimes compromise a site. Thus, establishing cultural and community context and engaging in dialogue with professionals and affiliates are critical.

The complexity of and professional responsibility for the archaeological investigation of sites now requires provisions for conservation whether it is a plan for visitation and display or closure and reburial. This is certainly the case in Turkey where most excavations now require a conservation plan for the treatment of its finds and the development of the site and its vicinity. Such is the philosophical and pragmatic context that the current Gordion project must address in its efforts to respond to a 60-year history of excavation, weathering, and limited conservation.

Gordion the Site

What are we to make of the site of Gordion? What narratives should be told utilizing the remains of the Phrygian's ancient citadel and its landscape? As a place in history, Gordion is known more for its real and fanciful associations with King Midas and Alexander the Great than its visited realities. What is Gordion's place in the larger perception of Turkey's past and the display of its archaeological legacy?

Archaeological research at Gordion has revealed a complex settlement history extending over 3,800 years from ca. 2500 BC to the 14th century AD (Fig. 2.1). A major conflagration around 800 BC destroyed much of the complex, already under renovation, thereby necessitating a complete rebuilding of the citadel that encapsulated the earlier buildings and fortifications under a carefully laid clay and rubble fill up to 5 m thick. This destruction and the Phrygians' response to fill and rebuild has had the fortunate effect of preserving much of the Early Phrygian citadel plan, including buildings and pavements, fortification walls, and associated finds. The rapid destruction and subsequent filling also preserved the more subtle processes of building alterations in progress just before the fire (see Voigt, this volume).

Continuous occupation of the site and reuse (robbing) of building materials from each succeeding period, combined with Rodney Young's excavation strategy, essentially left a largely Early Phrygian plan exposed, albeit partially. Like Thera and Pompeii, Gordion now displays a moment in time preserved by catastrophe and by the ancient Phrygians' rebuilding program, revealed and edited through modern excavation. This aspect of the site is a significant factor in determining how Gordion's citadel should be conserved and, more importantly, presented and displayed. Given the fact that excavation has ceased for the moment, a conservation plan for both the citadel and the surrounding landscape has now taken priority, its phasing a result of past efforts and new concerns.

Site Conservation 1950–1974

During Young's long tenure at Gordion (1950–1974), little site preservation occurred other than some remedial cement capping of the gate complex in 1956 and partial reburial of the rear wall of Megaron 2 in 1961, prompted by the removal of selected stones covered by incised "doodles" (see Roller, this volume). Young did make efforts to preserve the extraordinary burial in Tumulus MM by engaging the Turkish Archaeological Service to structurally reinforce the inner chamber.

Only the gate appears to have been subjected to minor reconstruction when, during its excavation in 1955, the northwest ramp wall of the North Court and the top of the southwest ramp wall of the South Court were rebuilt with stone blocks that had been recycled during the Middle Phrygian period in the construction of the later "dam wall" (see Voigt, this volume). In 1961 an important pebble mosaic—the earliest of its type—from Megaron 2 was cut and lifted in panels and transported to the Gordion Museum, where it was later re-installed under an outdoor shelter. Despite the popularity of lifting ancient mosaics at that time, the result is usually damaging, and in this case, the piecemeal transfer of a clay-based pebble mosaic seriously compromised the overall integrity of this remarkable pavement (Figs. 16.1 and 16.2).

Site Conservation 1978–1987

After Rodney Young's death in 1974, excavation at Gordion ceased until 1988. During that period, several site conservation initiatives were begun to limit the cumulative damage resulting from exposed walls, abandoned trenches, and unsupported baulks, and to monitor perceived structural problems at the gate complex and Tumulus MM.

Site Conservation 1988–Present

Soon after excavations resumed, Director G. Kenneth Sams began a new conservation program. In 1989 Tumulus MM and the gate became the initial focus of attention, and in 1993, consideration was given as to how best to stabilize and display the Terrace Building.

In 1999 conservator Mark Goodman introduced a well-developed set of formal guidelines for site conservation and a priority program based on condition and significance. Plumbline measurement monitoring began at the gate, a French drain was installed, and a temporary scaffolding system was built. In 2002 low-pressure gravity grouting was begun on the dry-laid masonry gate on the recommendation of Sir Bernard Feilden (Fig. 16.3). For the Terrace Building, TB4 masonry was rebuilt and an elaborate system of temporary protection employing sandbag buttressing and soil capping of the splayed walls was begun at TB1, 2, and 8, and later extended to the entire building and other masonry features (Fig. 16.4).

The tragic death of Goodman in 2004 brought the Architectural Conservation Laboratory of the University of Pennsylvania (ACL-UPenn) to the site, and, together with Middle East Technical University (METU), a comprehensive conservation and management program was developed for the citadel and its vicinity.

Fig. 16.1. Megaron 2 during excavation and discovery of pebble mosaic pavement, 1956.Source: Gordion Archive, Penn Museum.

Site Conservation Program

In recent years, heritage professionals have become more aware of values-based planning, especially for archaeological sites (Lipe 1974, Demas 2000). It is the goal of the current conservation program to develop a detailed site and regional management plan by 2012 after gaining greater familiarity with the physical and social dimensions of Gordion, the nearby town of Yassıhöyük, and the surrounding vicinity.

As a physical place, Gordion is conspicuously defined by the citadel's constructed earthen mound, which rises above a flat plain surrounded by satellite constructions (e.g., fortifications, lower town, and roads) and an extensive royal cemetery of tumuli and natural features (Fig. 2.1). The excavation or subtractive revealing of the early citadel, once situated upon and now within the excavated mound, con-

tributes to today's inherited physical reality, as do the subsequent spoil heaps and the now partially exposed Phrygian, Hellenistic, Roman, and Byzantine structures.

The Mound and Its Excavation

From the earliest years of archaeological research at Gordion, the site has been understood as a complex landscape. New appreciation of the site as part of a regional cultural landscape is now underway by the Graduate Program in Restoration at Middle East Technical University. Until that study is complete, a focus on the citadel and its immediate built features will continue to dominate the conservation discussions. Critical to this dialogue and subsequent ac-

Fig. 16.2. Current display of lifted Megaron 2 mosaic at the Gordion Museum, 2005. Photo: author.

tions is the consideration of both the constructed (and deconstructed) mound itself and, by extension, the scarps that define the current extent of the excavation and the exposed citadel core (Fig. 16.5).

The first-order priority of the conservation plan is the ancient constructed form of the mound in terms of its mass and contour, as well as its dynamic reshaping by subsequent occupation and its disfigurement by excavation and weathering. Large-scale interventions, already underway, include the selective removal of excavation spoil dumps that have significantly altered the external form of the ancient mound, and the infill of dangerously eroded scarps that now rim the excavation and undermine the visitor circuit above. Also critical to the stabilization of the mound, the scarps, and the surrounding tumuli is the development of a re-vegetation plan to curtail erosion, already begun by the site's archaeobotanist, Naomi Miller (see Miller, this volume).

Internally, the extent of the citadel, and especially the Early Phrygian period revealed by excavation deep within the mound, has created a unique situation for viewing. From the flat top of the mound, visitors have an extraordinary 360-degree view into the extensively excavated citadel. Unlike many such stratified sites, the citadel's diachronic urban plan can be understood relatively easily if the legibility of the building fabric is maintained and reinforced. This remains one of the site's most significant aspects and is currently threatened by the instability of both the eroding scarps and baulks and the poorly presented and eroded architectural fabric (Fig. 16.4). A new visitors' circuit utilizing the different vantage points above has been designed with 12 canopied wayside pavilions, each addressing a different set of themes depending on the views inward and outward toward the surrounding ancient and modern landscape (Fig. 16.6). Here the expansive views allow a

Fig. 16.3. Grouting the Early Phrygian Gate, 2003. Photo: Mark Goodman.

Fig. 16.4. General view of the Terrace Building with its temporary stabilization, 2001. Photo: Mark Goodman.

Fig. 16.5. Site plan of phased conservation activities over the next five years. Source: Penn Architectural Conservation Laboratory.

simultaneous narrative that can easily shift in theme or time, such as the military landscapes of ancient and modern (Battle of Sakarya) Anatolia.

Architecture

The perception of any urban plan depends on the relationship of its parts. Gordion's surviving architectural features allow us to discern and understand the citadel's plan (albeit partial) with its buildings, fortification walls, entrance gate, paved areas, and enclosed and open spaces. The overall relationship of this plan is currently illegible due to structural deterioration and a variety of earlier conflicting preservation/presentation techniques. In order to re-establish the architectural form and structural stability of the buildings, a range of techniques including selective reburial, stabilization, restoration, and partial reconstruction have been implemented simultaneously. Architectural form and building fabric are currently being interpreted according to a set of guidelines that carefully mediate between the re-establishment of overall plan and the preservation of architectural fabric. Authenticity here is a relative term that must find its balance in protecting future archaeological value while exposing and displaying ancient structures for viewing.

The excavation photographs from the 1950s and 60s reveal a site very different from the current landscape. At the time of excavation many buildings and enclosure walls were readily discernible, constructed of stone and mud brick with evidence of heavy timber framing (wall slots), and standing in some cases over 1 m in height. Pavements of stone, cobble, mosaic, and plaster clearly differentiated interior and exterior spaces. Although years of prolonged exposure degraded these materials (mud brick) and construction techniques (splayed rubble core masonry walls), some features such as the stone pavements and megaron walls were subsequently

reburied for protection. Currently, various presentation techniques are under development to reveal and display walls and pavements by excavation, capping, encapsulation, replication, and reburial.

Differentiation of buildings dating to the various phases of occupation (such as Early and Middle Phrygian) is difficult, especially where buildings and features continued in use but were modified. Fortunately or not, Young excavated down to the Destruction or Early Phrygian level, leaving very few of the later Middle Phrygian buildings in place. Where excavation has revealed these, or even earlier Bronze Age structures, a method of physical differentiation is being explored to build a sense of time into the urban plan. This is possible, as many of the earlier buildings are barely discernible by walls or pavements and can be imprinted on the ground as shallow perimeter plans. Final decisions will depend on the details and legibility of such theoretical schemes

Fig. 16.6. Visitor circuit with new stone steps, railings, and wayside pavilion design. Source: Penn Architectural Conservation Laboratory.

on site when viewed from the visitor circuit above. In this regard, recent examples of interpretation at similar sites in Turkey offer comparable solutions for consideration, such as at Hattusa (Seeher 2007).

Any physical intervention at Gordion must be preceded by the obligation to continue to study, document, and analyze the construction of Early and Middle Phrygian architecture. The intentional burial of the early citadel after the fire has provided a unique opportunity to record in detail the preserved materials and methods of Phrygian builders. Stones of many varieties, clay mortars and plasters, mud brick, painted terracotta tiles, pebble and cobble pavements, and (indirectly) wooden timber framing are all preserved for material and architectural analyses that could contribute much to an understanding of Phrygian building technology.

At the Terrace Building—a large linear building of successive rooms where goods were produced, processed, and stored—the architectural evidence (as well as associated finds) is well preserved, thus demanding an intervention approach that preserves the construction integrity as well as the visual legibility of this building's unique plan and the individual associated interior features (walls, floors, openings, hearths, and storage bins). Here recent conservation methods have included a range of techniques including selective stone block replacement, mechanical repair of original stones (grouting, adhesive repair, and pinning), and *in situ* wall stabilization (cable stitching) (Fig. 16.7). The end result is the preservation of the ancient walls as found without disassembly or reconstruction (as attempted earlier), thus preserving their structural integrity as well as overall form.

The entrance to the Citadel Mound affords a slightly different example of how one might reconcile the conservation, stabilization, and interpretation of built form at the urban scale. From all evidence Gordion was a raised fortified settlement with a series of ashlar walls and one or more gate structures. Today, as in antiquity, one approaches the citadel up a ramp through the massive gate (Fig. 16.8). The current Early Phrygian Gate survives nearly complete due to intentional burial during the Middle Phrygian period for a superimposed gate above it. Although the later gate was largely destroyed by subsequent reoccupation and stone reuse, Young's excavations removed much of the Middle Phrygian fill, which formed an

imposing stepped polychrome platform Glacis from which the later gate rose. While the stepped Glacis is still partially visible, Young's spoil heaps have significantly changed the immediate topography around the gate entrance and the overall outer contour of the Phrygian mound. The result is a confusing and less impressive entrance compromised by the looming spoil mounds, and it is dangerously unstable due to the exposed unsupported Middle Phrygian fill.

Current solutions to this complex problem address the three-fold requirements of (1) restoring the experiential sense of arrival and entry clearly intended by the Phrygians in their architecture and setting, (2) the display of time revealed and understood through the physical superimposition of building and stratigraphy, including the later rubble fill for the construction of the Middle Phrygian Gate, and (3) the necessity for stabilization and public safety. This will be achieved by re-establishing public entry to the citadel through the existing Early Phrygian Gate while at the same time exhibiting and interpreting the later Middle Phrygian Glacis and rubble fill. Such a plan will require the removal of the current excavation ramp and Young's spoil heaps, which disfigure the entrance and the distinctive mound profile. The cut rubble fill will be stabilized with limestone-filled gabions, which provide essential buttressing of this critical feature while visually referencing its rubble stone construction.

Although the actual Middle Phrygian Gate is long gone, the presence and height of the rubble fill and the few remaining ashlar blocks of the later gate attest to the massive rebuilding project the Phrygians undertook after the Destruction. Here, within a compressed space surrounded by the later fill, one can experience time as stratified space (Fig. 16.8). Entry into the early citadel through the gate on the cobble ramp brings the visitor into full view of the citadel and provides a unique opportunity to comprehend Phrygian architecture and its spatial intent. Few buildings from this period in Turkey exist to this degree. In this context, the goal of site conservation is to *resurrect* ancient Gordion, not in a literal physical sense, but rather in an experiential way that would re-establish both its impressive monuments and its *longue durée* for the viewer.

Despite the completeness of its form, the Early Phrygian Gate is not without structural problems.

a

Fig. 16.7a-f. Terrace Building (TB2),
demonstration of various wall masonry
conservation techniques: (a) before treatment; (b) stone replacement; (c) drilling
for adhesive repair; (d) structural retrofit-
ting; (e) wall capping; (f) after treatment.
Source: Penn Architectural Conservation
Laboratory.

b

c

d

e

Fig. 16.7 cont'd.

f

Fig. 16.8a (top), b. Gate entrance showing Early and Middle Phrygian masonry and trenched later Phrygian fill, view looking northwest (a) and east (b). Source: Penn Architectural Conservation Laboratory.

The use of dry-laid rubble stone fill behind the battered ashlar walls of the gate has rendered the structure potentially unstable, especially in a seismically active region. This became evident in the 1990s when a bulge and cracking were observed on the northwest corner of the South Court, which only worsened after the 1999 earthquake. Because of the incredible rarity and integrity of the gate, any further remedial effort to stabilize the masonry must be minimal (i.e., not disassembly). Therefore, in advance of any structural solutions, mid-range laser imaging (scanning) and a stone-by-stone conditions survey of the gate have been recently completed, and structural and environmental monitoring is currently underway (Fig. 16.9).

In addition, an innovative program of protecting the gate and wall tops using "soft" vegetative capping holds great promise in ultimately providing a maintainable, sustainable solution that is both aesthetically acceptable and cost effective for so large a site (Fig. 16.10) (see Miller, this volume). These are some of the larger projects currently underway at the citadel that respond to the need for immediate stabilization, and interpret the site to the public during on-going conservation and excavation. While the process is open-ended and will benefit from professional and public input during this phase, its goals and objectives are based on a long-term plan that recognizes the site's potential as an important visitor destination.

Like all places of human activity—including heritage—archaeological sites are constructed. Despite their fragmentation, they are complex creations that depend on the legibility and authenticity of their components for meaning and appreciation. How legibility and authenticity of such structures and places are realized and ensured must be thoughtfully considered and understood for effective site conservation. From the broadest perspective, archaeology and conservation should be seen as a conjoined enterprise; for both, physical evidence has to be studied and interpreted. Such interpretations are based on a profound and exact knowledge of the various histories of the thing or place and its context, on the materiality of its physical fabric, and on its cultural meanings and values to the public over time. This requires the application of a variety of specialized technical knowledge, but ideally the process must be brought back into a cultural context so that the archaeology and conservation projects become synonymous.

Fig. 16.9. Laser-image of the gate and surrounding area. Source: Penn Architectural Conservation Laboratory.

a

b

c

d

e

Fig. 16.10a–e. Installation of vegetative "soft" caps on north gate complex: (a) existing concrete cap prior to intervention; (b) capillary break layer; (c) filter layer; (d) completed "soft" caps; (e) view looking east of completed north gate "soft" wall caps. Source: Penn Architectural Conservation Laboratory.

17

Working with Nature to Preserve Site and Landscape at Gordion

Naomi F. Miller

There are two main categories of built remains at Gordion: the settlement occupied intermittently from the Early Bronze Age to the War of Independence, and over 100 burial tumuli erected primarily during the Middle Phrygian period. Both categories are, in principle, protected by Turkish law, but part of the ancient settlement as well as most of the tumuli lie in deeply plowed and irrigated fields, and the damage has been considerable. Additional deterioration has been caused by natural forces: wind and water erosion, freezing and thawing, and root disturbance.

Plants grow almost anywhere, and they can impede or enhance the preservation of archaeological ruins. By managing the open-air archaeological site of Gordion as a very specialized kind of garden within the broader historical landscape, we solve several problems and create a variety of opportunities. I cannot say that all of our strategies are of proven value, but I present here some of the approaches I have used in collaboration with the Gordion conservation team led by Frank Matero.

Problems in Preservation

To dig is to destroy, so ordinarily the best way to preserve a site is to leave it unexcavated. Even so, deep-rooted plants frequently disturb subsurface remains. Post-excavation preservation of exposed building levels needs to consider the deep- and shallow-rooted plants that can destroy or obscure architectural remains, although such consideration

is often absent in site management plans. The tumuli present a somewhat different problem: the roots generally are not deep enough to disturb the tomb chambers below, although erosion channels and overall surface erosion remain significant issues that need to be resolved.

At Gordion, we are working with nature rather than against it, using our knowledge of the habits and growth cycles of the native vegetation to determine which plants should be encouraged or discouraged to grow in particular parts of the site. There are three key goals that underlie this project: to understand the basic characteristics of plants that grow in the region; to maximize the diversity of the desirable species in the plant cover, thereby making it harder for the undesirables to grow; and to apply that knowledge to managing vegetation at the site. The surfaces of tumuli and unexcavated settlement mounds, where minimal intervention can have dramatic results with remarkably little effort, might be thought of as parkland. Excavated areas with exposed architecture can also benefit from effective use of vegetation cover, but require more active intervention and maintenance.

Even if a roof is erected over an excavated area, seeds will blow in and trash will accumulate, causing standing structures to suffer from fluctuating environmental conditions. Zero-maintenance, therefore, is a goal that can never be reached for open-air archaeological sites. The most effective management plan is one that utilizes local human and physical resources, and can be maintained and adapted by local authorities after the experts have left. I admit that this part of our plan at Gordion remains un-proven, but many of the villagers at Gordion already are experienced farmers and gardeners who understand the regional climate and soils. With orientation and some training, a local labor force could be developed.

Opportunities

Actively managing plantings and vegetation has a direct benefit for site preservation, but also creates opportunities that go well beyond that narrow mission. The native steppe vegetation of central Anatolia has supported wildlife and domestic flocks for millennia. Biodiversity is high for an arid region, and the healthy steppe has a solid cover of plants that prevents erosion, absorbs light and heat from the sun, and helps maintain the water table. Overgrazing is one problem, but both agricultural and urban development consume land that would otherwise support dense vegetation. The archaeological precinct provides a protected expanse of terrain that can serve as a refuge for rare and interesting plants. Admittedly, the beauty of the native steppe vegetation is subtle, and most people prefer to look at trees, but visitors can be guided into an appreciation of the central Anatolian steppe. With the native steppe established, environmental education can teach both schoolchildren and adults to value the biodiversity in their own backyard—for its ecosystem "services," its potential economic and aesthetic values, and as a way to begin to understand the daily lives and surroundings of the ancient inhabitants of Gordion.

In addition to the indirect touristic benefits of mound and site stabilization, the area that can be protected and managed with minimal labor input could serve as an engine for economic development: ecotourism (not just archaeological tourism, but also bird-watching, botanizing, etc.); a dairy industry based on the improved rangeland combined with the reintroduction and development of Anatolian stock varieties; and developing seed sources for native-plant gardening in the surrounding region.

In contrast to agricultural fields, which are brown for most of the year and a rather uniform green the rest of the time, the steppe vegetation is beautiful and varied year-round. In the archaeologi-cal site as garden, certain areas can be "coded" to different levels of "wildness" that will create a visually varied plantscape that draws the viewer's gaze to the visible archaeological remains.

We are quite intentionally *not* trying to restore the landscape to its "original" state, although archaeobotanical studies at the site have provided valuable information about the vegetation from the Late Bronze Age to the Medieval period (Miller 2010). In ancient times, for example, tasty pasture plants like *Trigonella* were more numerous, while today's overgrazed pasture is filled with plants that have spines/prickles or chemical defenses that render them unpalatable. Even if we could use this information to re-create the types and proportions of plants, the vegetation cover has changed over time. Furthermore, Tumulus MM may have been bare in antiquity, either from grazing or intentional clearance: without vegetation, the surface reflects light so that the mound stands out in the viewshed for miles around, and this could well have been the desired effect.

No one type of plant can be said to be the best for the purpose of preservation (Table 17.1). Archaeological sites experience a variety of wind and weather conditions and are characterized by many different zones, while slopes face all directions with different moisture conditions on the upper and lower slope. But economic, scientific, and aesthetic concerns make the native steppe plants of central Anatolia particularly desirable. They have evolved in this environment and, once established, should not require watering or expensive care. The native vegetation also includes many perennial plants that stay green well into the summer or even year round.

The Vegetation Improvement Program on Tumulus MM

When erosion became a major issue in Turkey in the early 1990s, the authorities became concerned about conditions on Tumulus MM, which is across the street from the Gordion Museum in the village of Yassıhöyük. The tumulus dates to the Middle Phrygian period and is about 53 m high and 300 m in diameter (Young 1981). I suggested then that an uninterrupted cover of plants would slow wind and water erosion by reducing exposed bare ground; the

Table 17.1. Plants mentioned in the text.

Latin binomial	English common name	Attributes	Usefulness
Trigonella sp.	fenugreek	small annual; excellent pasture plant	tumuli, excavated
Bromus tomentellus, B. cappadocicus	bromegrass	tall tufted perennial grass	tumuli, scarps
Stipa arabica, S. holosericea, S. lessingiana	feathergrass	tall tufted perennial grass	tumuli, south, west-facing scarps
Melica ciliata	silky spike melic	medium tufted perennial grass	tumuli, north-facing scarps
Hordeum murinum	wall barley	short annual grass; avoided by grazers	tumuli, excavated, wall stubs
Taeniatherum caput-medusae	Medusa-head grass	medium annual grass	tumuli, excavated
Androsace maxima	greater rock jasmine	inconspicuous annual	tumuli, excavated, wall stubs
Atriplex cf. *lasiantha*	orache	invasive annual, deep spreading root	bad for excavated and surrounding area
Peganum harmala	Syrian (wild) rue	deep rooted woody perennial, prolific seed production; avoided by grazers	bad for excavated and surrounding area
Scabiosa sp.	scabious	many species, some small annuals	tumuli, excavated, wall stubs
Nigella arvensis	love-in-a-mist	medium annual	tumuli, excavated
Festuca ovina	sheep fescue	medium tufted perennial grass	tumuli, excavated, north-facing scarps
Poa bulbosa	bulbous bluegrass	short tufted perennial grass	tumuli, excavated, wall stubs
Alyssum sp.	alyssum	inconspicuous annual	tumuli, excavated, wall stubs
Carduus nutans	musk thistle	tall biannual, deep taproot, prolific seed production; avoided by grazers	bad for excavated and surrounding area
Amblyopyrum cf. *muticum*	none	tall annual grass	tumuli
Krascheninnikovia ceratoides	Pamirian winterfat	large woody perennial	may need to be controlled on tumuli
Onopordum anatolicum	thistle	tall biannual, deep taproot, prolific seed production; avoided by grazers	tumuli
Descurainia sophia	herb sophia	tall annual, prolific seed production	tumuli, roots not very deep, but too tall
Asperugo procumbens	German-madwort	sprawling annual	bad for excavated and surrounding area
Bromus tectorum	cheatgrass	medium annual grass, prolific seed production	tumuli, scarps; fast-growing, but should decline under stable conditions

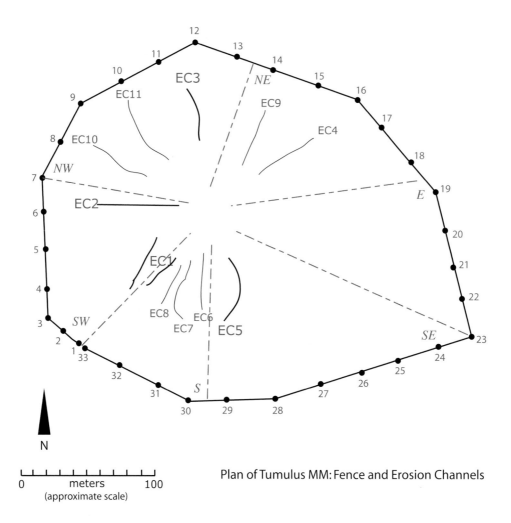

Fig. 17.1. Tumulus MM schematic plan, showing sectors and location of erosion channels. Source: author.

total amount of water flowing downhill would also decrease, as the roots absorb water and keep most of it in the aboveground biomass. When asked how to accomplish this, I suggested that a fence around the mound would keep keep flocks, tourists, and children off the mound (Miller 1994). In the spring of 1996, İlhan Temizsoy, director of the Museum of Anatolian Civilizations, arranged for the mound to be fenced (Fig. 17.1).

The vegetation management program on the great tumulus is intended to improve the overall plant cover, reduce the depth and number of erosion channels, and control the mud over the largest channel, which is above the tourist entrance to the tomb chamber. An annual vegetation survey allows us to monitor our progress and anticipate problems.

Even though Tumulus MM had very little plant cover to begin with, many rare species survived out of the reach of animals. The fence has allowed these plants to repopulate the mound. Although there had been no obvious improvement in the vegetation cover by the summer of 1996, it was clear by the summer of 1997 that the fence had begun to work: the vegetation cover inside the fence was denser than what lay outside (Miller 1998, 2000). Within a few years, the shallowest erosion channels nearly disappeared under new growth. There were clear differences in plant taxa depending on slope and aspect. After a few more years, plants began to recolonize the harsher south side, although the vegetation remains sparser than on the well-watered north. Since 2005, slender tufts of feathergrass have established

Fig. 17.2a-c. Looking down Erosion Channel 3: (a, above left) 1997, mud brick; (b, above right) 1999, with post 12 in background, seeded annuals visible; (c, right) 2002, bare surface largely gone. Photos: author.

themselves even on the steepest part of the south slope. There are also differences from one year to the next: after the particularly harsh winter and spring of 2004, for example, the prolific annual wall barley (*Hordeum murinum*) was greatly reduced for several growing seasons.

Sometime between the summers of 1998 and 1999, a carelessly discarded cigarette burned a large swath of the vegetation of the northeast sector of the mound. The area was immediately recolonized by an annual grass, probably *Amblyopyrum muticum*, which I had introduced into Erosion Channels 3 and 5 (EC-3, 5), but the burn did raise the issue of fire hazards. Unlike sections of the American prairie, which has adapted to periodic fires and which was maintained in its open state by the management practices of indigenous populations (see, e.g., Weiser and Lepofsky 2009), the absence of grazing had led

Fig. 17.3a–d. Erosion Channel 1: (a, top) 2000: brick "platform" and diversion channel visible; (b, bottom) 2006: regrowth; (c) 2007: new rows of mud-brick; (d) 2008: growth after one (drought) year. Photos: author.

to an accumulation of dry plant matter. Both Remzi Yılmaz, our foreman, and a grass specialist with whom I spoke, Musa Doğan, felt that fire would damage the roots of the perennial grasses and retard vegetation recovery. The Gordion project director, G.K. Sams, therefore purchased a weed-whacker to cut a swath several meters wide along the inside and the outside of the fence in the fall of 2000. The initiative was eliminated during the wet winter of 2001, but fire preventation remains a concern for site management here and elsewhere in Turkey.

With the successful recovery of the vegetation on Tumulus MM, it seemed appropriate to consider the introduction of controlled grazing. Hüseyin Fırıncıoğlu, a range management specialist now retired from the Field Crop Research Center (Tarla Bitkileri Merkez Araştırma Enstitüsü), has been advising us since 2004. Although heavy grazing reduces biodiversity (Fırıncıoğlu, Seefeldt, and Şahin 2007), Dr. Fırıncıoğlu pointed out that moderate grazing would improve the plant cover (Fırıncıoğlu et al. 2009), and advised us to use a mixed flock

Fig. 17.3c (above), d (below)

of about 45 sheep and 5 goats (for the woody vegetation) for about a week. If done at the end of September, all the seeds of the spring and summer-flowering plants will have dispersed, especially the perennial grasses we are trying to encourage. This controlled grazing actually enhances seed set, as the hooves of the sheep and goats bury the seeds, and the dung provides fertilizer. In addition, grazing limits some of the excess vegetative matter, and so reduces the fire hazard. Our success with this program has been spotty, in part because the shepherds were reluctant to promote grazing in an area that they thought harbored snakes. But in 2009 Ayşe Gürsan-Salzmann introduced us to a shepherd who was willing to cooperate. For the record, I always encounter tortoises on Tumulus MM, yet in more than ten years of monitoring, I have seen only one shed snake skin (and no snakes).

In 1997, the three deepest erosion channels constituted one of our most pressing problems: EC-1, EC-3, and EC-5 (Fig. 17.2). The force of water flowing in the channels is great enough to move stones. In collaboration with Kurt Bluemel, an expert in ornamental grasses and landscaping, we decided to line two of the channels with mud brick. The first year's experiment focused on EC-3 and EC-5, which were very successfully treated by using mud brick to slow and absorb the torrents that flow down the mound during heavy rains (Miller and Bluemel 1999). The mud brick in question came from a village structure that had been disassembled; the owner was happy to provide the bricks for free as long as we hauled them away. After the initial positioning in 1997, we sowed seeds of annual plants in spaces between horizontal rows of bricks, which set the stage, a few years later, for the growth of vegetation around the channels. That first year we used seeds of fast-growing annual grasses: wall barley, which already grew at the site, and cf. *Amblyopyrum muticum*, which did not.

In 1998, both the fence and the bricks proved so successful that the Museum of Anatolian Civilizations asked us to develop a plan for the more problematic area above the entrance, EC-1. That channel covers a much larger area, which meant that it was unrealistic to line the channel as we had done on EC-3. Moreover, machinery or even hand-carrying so many bricks would displace the soft soils and struggling plants of the mound surface. Ideally, bricks would be set in horizontal bands, with the lower ones acting as steps for the work higher up. Leaving a meter or more between rows would keep labor costs down and leave open ground for plants to colonize.

Such plans must, of course, involve all key area stakeholders, and the museum authorities thought it better to create continuous sluices in the side channels with a brick platform in the center. This approach effectively prevented seedlings from establishing themselves. In June of 1999, Miller documented the work that had been carried out in EC-1, and since almost no plants were growing in the heavily bricked channel, permission was granted to rearrange some of the bricks in EC-1 to allow plants to become established. In 2006 bricks were laid in the erosion channel above the tomb entrance (EC-1) in horizontal rows; after two years had passed, the bricks were no longer visible, and vegetation is slowly establishing itself over much of the channel (Fig. 17.3).

Another ongoing problem has been erosion on either side of the entrance to the tomb. Sometime in the 1990s, several channels which have since filled in were dug to divert water from the entrance. In 2003 the authorities decided to cut back the earth along the entrance to the tomb, and subsequently added impermeable cement gutters next to the walls lining the entry. After two years, both gutters silted up near the tomb antechamber, so the problem clearly has not been solved. Despite our interventions, the south side (at the right, as one faces the entrance) is particularly problematic since it is bare of vegetation.

An important part of the vegetation improvement program involves monitoring any changes that occur, thereby allowing us to assess our various interventions (mainly the fence, but also the bricks and minimal addition of seeds). The vegetation survey was begun in 1998, and has been conducted nearly every year since then.

In order to assess our progress, it is important to know what is growing on the mound at any given time. To that end, I developed a system for making vegetation transects that was inspired by Masters (1997). Superficial inspection showed that the vegetation cover changes depending on slope and aspect, so I numbered the fence posts and divided the mound roughly into six sectors (SW, NW, NE, E, SE, and S) based on dominant vegetation just inside the fence. I then assembled a ring of garden

hose that encircles an area of about one square meter (3.54 m circumference). Starting from one post
in each sector, I set the hoop down every 15 paces
(approximately 10 m) and listed the plant taxa visible within them. I also estimated slope and percent
of area covered by plants, noting whether they were
just vegetative, in flower, fruit, or dry. On a separate
chart, I noted types in the vicinity of the hoop but
not actually within it.

The north side is clearly more favorable to plant
growth than the south, and run-off makes the lower
slopes substantially wetter than the upper ones. Some
of the present distribution of plants has probably
been affected by the history of grazing. For example,
the prevalence on the lower slopes of spiny or unpalatable plants, such as thistles (*Onopordum anatolicum* and *Carduus nutans*), wall barley, and Syrian rue
(*Peganum harmala*) reflects the fact that grazing was
most intense towards the base of the mound, favoring
the survival of these anti-pastoral types (Fırıncıoğlu
et al. 2009). In nearly all years, over 100 species of
plants have been recorded within the hoops (over
100 m²), with rainfall serving as a key variable in observed biodiversity from one year to the next.

Tumulus MM: Problems and Opportunities

From the perspective of both preservation and
finance, minimal intervention using locally available
labor and materials proved extraordinarily effective
in creating a dense plant cover on the tumulus. The
native perennial grasses produce less biomass because
they grow slowly, thereby reducing maintenance
costs and fire hazards. The improved vegetation is
tremendously valuable for ecological restoration in
that it provides a seed bank for the immediate vicinity and for potential expansion of improved rangeland, gardens, and other projects, such as the Citadel
Mound.

Up to now, the vegetation project has provided no direct economic benefit to the village of
Yassıhöyük. We hoped that our methods would
demonstrate the value and relative ease of restoring
grazing lands by letting over-grazed pasture rest for
a few years. The native steppe vegetation is naturally
rich in edible pasture grasses and legumes, yet over-

grazing reduces the fodder plants and encourages the
spiny and inedible plants. We also hoped that the
mound could serve as a seed bank for the development of a local nursery business if native plant gardening becomes as popular in Turkey as it is in the
United States,

Because we are trying to preserve a historical
landscape for posterity, the other tumuli require just
as much attention. The smaller tumuli do not appear
to have the same erosion problems as those on Tumulus MM, but they are still threatened by plowing
and irrigation. Much of what we have learned about
restoring the native vegetation on Tumulus MM can
be applied to them as well, if the authorities allow
the intervention. Should that happen, there could
be positive ramifications for ecological restoration,
education, tourism, and economic development.

To Plant or Not to Plant

When we began the project, my own fantasy was
to use masses of bright red poppies to line the bare
spot on Tumulus MM where children used to slide
down the mound. More seriously, visitors and team
members frequently ask what we planted on Tumulus
MM to make it so green, and the answer is: very little.
Before we learned that the fence was sufficient treatment for most of the protected enclosure, we assumed
that we would have to plant seeds or transplant seedlings in the bare areas. To that end, we carried out
several experiments in various places: sowing seeds
directly, growing seedlings from seeds, transplanting
clumps of grasses, and putting seeds in mudballs that
were subsequently set in the ground. In order to reduce the impact on the already stressed native vegetation, we did not want to collect seeds or dig up whole
plants on a massive scale from the wild. Harvesting
seeds of common plants does not hurt the local populations, because the ripest seeds get dispersed in place
in the course of harvesting. For transplants, we also
chose common types. For the most part, we harvested
the fenced tumulus and Citadel Mound.

In some bare areas there is a pressing need for
new vegetation that will keep undesirable plants
from moving in, and in such situations, a variety
of common annuals with easily collected seeds have
proven useful (Fig. 17.4). Some annual wall barley,

a

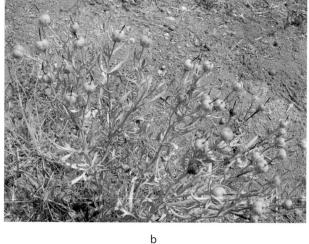

b

c

Fig. 17.4a-c. Some plants mentioned in the text:
(a) *Nigella arvensis*, (b) *Peganum harmala*, (c) *Stipa arabica*. Photos: author.

cf. *Amblyopyrum muticum*, and a few other types sprinkled between the rows of bricks to stabilize the soil surface in EC-3 and EC-5 did their job. In various places we have been able to spread *Androsace maxima* (rock jasmine), *Taeniatherum caput-medusae*

(Medusa-head grass), and *Nigella arvensis* (love-in-a-mist), among others. Most perennials are much harder to grow from seed, as we discovered when we planted some *Stipa arabica* (feathergrass) on Tumulus MM over EC-1: none sprouted. We have had some luck with the seeds of the perennial grass *Poa bulbosa* (bulbous bluegrass) (see Citadel Mound, below). This grass is particularly useful because its leaves and inflorescences are short, it has shallow roots, is very common, and grows prolifically on flat areas (see Citadel Mound, below).

Digging up plants in the wild or at the site will open the area to colonizers of bare ground (i.e., plants that thrive in disturbed areas, which tend to be invasive annuals that we do not want). Part of a large grass clump can be pulled from the ground, broken into smaller clumps (say, 2–3 cm), leaving a healthy, if somewhat smaller, plant in place. We have had our greatest successes with transplanting clumps of perennial grasses. After an initial failure in 1997, when we transplanted three *Stipa arabica* plants from the Citadel Mound to the area above the entrance to MM, we successfully transplanted *Stipa arabica*, *Festuca ovina* (sheep fescue), *Melica ciliata* (melic), and *Poa bulbosa* to appropriate spots on the Citadel Mound. We have had less luck with *Stipa holosericea*, and the perennial bromegrasses, *Bromus tomentellus* and *B. cappadocicus*. Although the transplants are sturdy, the clumps do better with supplemental watering if the winter is dry.

When we began the erosion control program on Tumulus MM, I considered incorporating seeds into the mud-brick that lined the erosion channels to give the plants a headstart. Some years later, Frank Matero told me that elders of the Santa Clara and San Ildefonso pueblos put seeds in mudballs against insect predation, and this seemed like a possible solution to our plant propagation problem. For us, the mudball technique allows us to set out the seed in the dry season, when we are at the site (see Miller 2006 for mudball production demonstration). The mudballs seem to work best for the large perennial grasses, especially *Stipa arabica* and *Festuca ovina*. For annuals such as Medusa-head grass and rock jasmine, simply planting seeds works just as well or better.

The Citadel Mound

Plants can and do grow almost anywhere on open-air archaeological sites, obscuring the ruins completely or emerging from cracks in the masonry. In either case, root damage will work against the long-term preservation of the structures. The character of the vegetation itself, and how its components interact with each other, will determine the positive or negative effect of plants on the ruins. Tourists visiting Gordion see the remains of the royal precinct, destroyed by a catastropic fire in about 800 BC (DeVries et al. 2003). The clean stratigraphic break marks the beginning of the Middle Phrygian period, the heyday of tumulus construction.

In 1992 I suggested that one way to reduce below-ground water damage to the ruins was to encourage perennial tufted grasses to grow in the excavated rooms, in the hope that they would crowd out the deep-rooted plants. This meant a change in what had become standard procedure: vegetation management in the fenced area of the Citadel Mound had consistently been limited to weeding in the central excavated area in early June. Yet the seeds of grasses that we would like to encourage (*Stipa arabica*, melic, sheep fescue) ripen in June and July, so the unintended result of this schedule was that just when the potentially valuable plants have focused their energies on reproduction, we prevented them from spreading by seed. At the same time, one of our deep-rooted pests, Syrian rue, was not affected at all, because it flowers, fruits, and seeds prolifically during the summer; in fact, its growth was actually

encouraged, since any competition was effectively removed. Starting in the mid-2000s, G. Kenneth Sams directed the weeders to spare the large perennial grasses. The result is that melic has established itself on several north-facing scarps, and *Stipa arabica* is also beginning to spread (Fig. 17.5).

In 2004 I recommended that we schedule two cuttings per year: one for tourists, and one in midsummer to remove the most numerous undesirable summer-seeding plants. In particular, the Syrian rue and orache (*Atriplex* cf. *lasiantha*) should be cut when the seed pods are forming. Since fruiting is the most energy-demanding part of a plant's life cycle, cutting at that point will weaken the plant, and greatly reduces the spread of new plants from seed.

Preservation through Vegetation Management: The Terrace Building Soft Cap Project

In 2006 we began a more active intervention program on the Citadel Mound. Frank Matero wanted to try using a soft cap to protect the wall stubs based on historic preservation practice in Great Britain (see Lee, Viles, and Wood 2009). The goal was to see if the Turkish equivalent of a sod layer on top of the wall stubs would insulate them by reducing intra-annual fluctuation of moisture and temperature. My task was to identify both appropriate and inappropriate species in the native vegetation, collect seeds, and give the conservation team some basic understanding of the botanical issues. I also wanted to demonstrate that an archaeological site is and should be regarded as a living thing, in a very real sense.

The conservation team laid geotextile on top of the wall stub dividing Terrace Building units 1 and 2 and covered it with a 5–10 cm layer of clean earth (Keller and Matero 2011). The wall top was divided into four sections: one-third was covered with transplanted *Poa* clumps, one-sixth with a *Poa* seed mix, one-sixth with *Poa* mudballs, and one-third was left as a "no treatment" control area, and covered with stone. Over the next few years, maintenance involved removing undesirable plants from the wall (especially orache), and leaving those that are not harmful (Fig. 17.6).

A variety of plants appropriate for this experiment already flourish in the Citadel Mound. *Poa*

Fig. 17.5a–c. Citadel Mound: (a, top) 2005, view east across Terrace Building to Citadel Gate (modern scaffolding), Tumulus MM, and other tumuli; (b) 2006, view west across Terrace Building; (c, opposite page) 2006, John Marston investigating melic growing on a north-facing slope near the Citadel Gate. Photos: author.

Fig. 17.5c.

bulbosa, an inconspicuous perennial grass that forms small, short clumps and already grows profusely on-site was the obvious candidate for the "sod." There are also short, shallow-rooted plants that grow easily on wall stubs, such as *Scabiosa* sp., *Alyssum* sp., rock jasmine, and wall barley. We collected seeds of rock jasmine, in particular, for the wall tops because it is inconspicuous and grows well on shallow exposed soil. For the sediment banked against the stub, we added seeds of the somewhat taller Medusa-head grass, an attractive annual that could help stabilize the soil quickly without causing root damage below. For the flat area within the room, a variety of medium-tall perennial grasses that thrive under different conditions were put in mudballs (sheep fescue, feathergrasses, and perennial bromegrasses). Only some of the sheep fescue sprouted, but it did not survive the drought of 2007 and the trampling by workers in the area. Despite two years of drought in 2008 and into 2009, the Medusa-head grass re-

seeded itself, but has not thrived due to competition from many other plants. After three years, the *Poa* clumps are well established and successfully prevent undesirable plants from moving in. The seeded area has produced a number of widely spaced tufts. The *Poa* mudballs did not work well at all, and other plants have taken root in the control area.

The Soft Cap Project has demonstrated the value or worthlessness of various approaches in the relatively arid central Anatolian plateau. Even if *Poa* did nothing to insulate against moisture and temperature fluctuation, it kept undesirable (i.e., deep-rooted) plants at bay. Over the next few years, the conservation team will extend the Terrace Building soft cap experiment to the other wall stubs, and they have begun a similar project on top of the Early Phrygian Gate, which had a cracked cement capping. *Poa* seeds are easy to collect, and the plain surrounding the Citadel Mound is covered with *Poa* clumps that can be responsibly harvested. The *Poa bulbosa* clumps transplanted to the wall stubs could also be interspersed with seeds from a variety of short annuals with shallow roots to colonize the inevitable cracks between the clumps.

Citadel Mound: Problems and Opportunities

In many places, *Poa* is already doing a good job of keeping larger plants out of the excavated structures. As with Tumulus MM, a cover of slow-growing perennial grasses whose delicate roots descend less than about 20 cm from the surface would go a long way toward protecting the ruins below. Some plants, notably Syrian rue, have deep roots (encountered during excavation as deep as about 3 m). Others, especially the musk thistle (*Carduus nutans*) and orache, are undesirable because they produce so many seeds. Inhibiting the growth of these three types could be accomplished by cutting and removing them at appropriate times. An early June cutting could be followed by a second one when the plants (Syrian rue and orache especially) are flowering or going to seed, which would prevent new plants from establishing themselves.

The collapsing baulks at the edges of the excavated area are still a problem, and more active in-

Fig. 17.6. Terrace Building 2 experiment, 2007. Poa clumps in foreground, seeded and mudballed in middle ground, "no treatment" in background. Photo: author.

on south-facing slopes. Two other perennial feathergrass species grow in the region, as do two perennial species of bromegrass.

All of my suggestions are based on the presumption that managing the vegetation within the confines of the site can, in the long term, reduce labor costs, improve the aesthetic and intellectual experience for visitors, and protect the unexcavated areas. An uninterrupted cover of shallow-rooted species is the best way to achieve these goals. The general principle is that the roots of densely growing plants will take in water from precipitation and return it to the aboveground biomass. Shallow rooted perennials with sod-like form have the additional advantage of keeping undesirable (i.e., deep-rooted) plants from taking root.

Open-air Archaeological Site as Garden

Because the site is open-air, any long-term management plan must have a major botanical component. It would help if we started thinking of the open-air archaeological site as a specialized kind of garden with several management zones, each with its own problems and solutions. At sites in naturally wooded regions, like the Athenian Agora, preservationists must contend with trees (see Mauzy 2006); at Gordion, we are fortunate that the region's natural vegetation is steppe. Our goal is to establish a non-natural collection of relatively shallow-rooted native plants, mainly grasses, whose slender roots do not go very deep; typically, the taller the grass, the deeper the root mass, from about 2 cm to a maximum of about 50 cm. Other perennials and some annuals have deep spreading roots or deep tap roots. A good reason to reduce the populations of those plants, even in areas where they are not harming the underlying ruins, is that they produce seeds that spread into areas where one does not want them. By

tervention would improve the aesthetics of the site. Tall perennial grasses could be planted in small clumps on the collapsed profiles, and even watered, until they establish themselves. These plants are non-invasive, unlike annuals such as *Descurainia sophia*, orache, *Asperugo procumbens*, *Bromus tectorum*; and in the unlikely event that they did spread to the wall stubs, it would be easy to control their growth. If these plants were massed, they would also effectively direct the visitor's gaze toward key areas of the site. Several types of plants are ideal for this purpose: melic and sheep fescue grow well on north-facing slopes, and feathergrass (*Stipa arabica*) has been spreading gradually shifting the standing biomass (i.e., living plants) to slow-growing perennials and non-invasive annuals, the undesirable plants will decline in proportion.

One implication of the site as garden is that the requirements of the living plants must be taken into account. Perennial plants take many years to establish themselves. Any management plan should involve minimal disruption to the soil surface once the plantings are set in order to get the full benefits of their low maintenance cost. With site as garden, long-term management will clearly need the practical experience of gardeners and botanists, although villagers can be trained to take care of the grounds, thereby providing additional income for them.

Native Steppe Plant Demonstration Area on the Yassıhöyük Museum Grounds

As an archaeobotanist, my hope is that visitors to the site will develop an appreciation for the beauty of the landscape and the diversity of its flora, not just the artifacts and ruins of Gordion. Yet the sad truth is that most of our tourists come in groups and have neither the time nor inclination to inspect plants as they walk around. I therefore considered the idea of developing a garden on the grounds of the Gordion Museum in Yassıhöyük, and in 2006, when Mecit Vural, a botanist from Gazi University, visited the site, we were able to make this idea a reality. A plot measuring about 5 x 10 m was set aside, and at the urging of Dr. Vural, we arranged for gypseous soils to cover an equivalent area adjacent to the original one the following year. For this ongoing project, maintenance is minimal: I selectively weed the plot for a few hours over the course of a few days in June, and during the summer I collect seeds and make some mudballs to be set out later in the year. Our foreman, Zekeriya Utgu, and Dr. Vural distribute the seeds and mudballs, and transplant some larger specimens as well. Dr. Vural has provided explanatory signage, and I have prepared a one-page flyer that could be distributed to museum visitors. The out-of-pocket cost has been minimal—primarily trucking in the gypsum, and buying some animal dung fertilizer.

Conclusions

Although I have used the metaphor of archaeological site as garden, it is not my intention to restore the vegetation to some hypothetical earlier state. Rather, as a garden evolves and changes over the year and from year to year, the program at Gordion aims to use the resilience of the native vegetation to highlight and protect specific archaeological remains, such as wall stubs, as well as the traces of ancient landscape that have formed part of the viewshed since the tumuli were constructed over 2500 years ago.

Beyond the immediate benefits for erosion control, biodiversity preservation, rangeland improvement, and ecotourism development at the site, much of what we have learned has potential applications for other parts of Turkey. Several archaeological sites in Turkey already have programs in place that share some features with our goals for Gordion. The Kerkenes project, for example, has a strong program promoting ecologically sustainable development within the context of the archaeological project (Kerkenes and Ehrhardt n.d.). The Çatalhöyük project is a leader in integrating the preservation of an open-air archaeological site with its cultural landscape and local development issues (Orbaşlı 2004). Finally, the Bin Tepe cemetery at Sardis, with dozens of tumuli threatened by the expansion of olive production, has historic landscape preservation issues most similar to ours; their education program is a model well worth duplicating (CLAS n.d.) None of these projects, however, is actively incorporating the native vegetation into their overall management strategy.

One of the most exciting aspects of the conservation work on the Tumulus MM and the Citadel Mound is its wide-ranging significance even beyond the successful conservation of one of the major archaeological sites of Turkey. Developing Gordion as a tourist destination can only be enhanced by treating the archaeological resources—the settlement and surrounding tumuli—as part of a working cultural landscape (Miller 2011). Farming and herding are part of that landscape, as are the natural flora and fauna. Increasingly, Turkish as well as foreign tourists will look for both cultural and natural attractions, and archaeologists will need to work collaboratively with villagers, museum officials, and specialists in historic preservation if a successful site management plan is to be formulated. What we have undertaken at Gordion represents the beginning of that process.

Acknowledgments

In addition to all the people mentioned by name in the body of this text, I have had the pleasure of working with many collaborators over the years. Included among them are: Keith DeVries, who first showed me the grassy steppe between Yassıhöyük and Şabanözü—the inspiration for this project; Mac Marston, who has helped with the vegetation survey and seed collecting during four field seasons; Richard Liebhart and Ayşe Gürsan-Salzmann, who have provided tremendous moral and practical support in the field; Remzi Yılmaz and Zekeriya Utgu, who supervised or personally carried out much of the physical work on Tumulus MM and the museum botanical garden. The TB2 wall stub experiment was devised by Sarah Stokely and Kelly Wong, who commented after a plant tour that she could see how the site is a living thing. I am grateful that my former supervisor Stuart Fleming and excavation director Mary Voigt agree that archaeobotany is about more than just charred seeds and wood. Yener Yılmaz and the University of Pennsylvania Museum provided funding for my travel during non-excavation years.

18

Gordion Through Lydian Eyes

Crawford H. Greenewalt, Jr.

"Gordion Through Lydian Eyes," the title proposed by Brian Rose for this chapter,[1] recalls the brilliant conceit of Walter Andrae, in his book *Das Wiedererstandene Assur* (1977), to introduce the Assyrian city through an imagined visit in the early 7th century BC by a traveler from Greek Ionia, who has guidance from Assyrian friends.[2]

A Lydian from Sardis arriving at Gordion towards the middle of the 6th century BC (after ten days of upland travel) would have found a landscape broadly similar to that of his homeland, with river valley and mountains. Today, the Sakarya (ancient Sangarios) River valley is less cultivated and the surrounding mountains at Gordion more barren, respectively, than the Hermos River Valley and Tmolos mountain range at Sardis; but in antiquity, the two landscapes may have been more comparable in those respects. Mountains at Gordion, however, are farther away from the city than Mt. Tmolos, which looms over Sardis; in addition, the Gordion landscape with its elevation some 600 m higher than that of Sardis would have had much colder winters, and its plant community would have been distinctly different, lacking that great staple of lower Mediterranean lands, the olive.[3]

The remoteness of the surrounding mountains at Gordion might have reassured less-advantaged Lydians of Sardis, where the proximity of Mt. Tmolos (Fig. 18.1) included the threat of its predatory and destructive animals—leopard, hyena (Fig. 18.2a, b), and pig. For the Lydian visitor who belonged to a privileged class, however, nearby mountains were welcome. With his horse and retainers, he could enjoy the challenges of hunting dangerous animals, as well as fleet-footed deer and elusive wild goat in their

habitat (Fig. 18.3); and with gracious permission of his majesty, he was occasionally allowed to cut timber in the mountain forest preserves of Taranza. Furthermore, his three strong sons all belonged to his majesty's cavalry, and their horses had been superbly trained (even in "above the ground" exercises like the *levade, courbette, capriole,* etc., of modern times), largely because they had been raised in the exclusive highland pastures of nearby Mt. Tmolos.[4]

"Come back another time and hunt with us," said his Phrygian host. "Deer we also have in plenty, likewise wild goat, who control our forest growth too well; and, beneath our glorious canopy of heaven even the timorous hare makes joyous hunting—with the help of our trained falcons (Fig. 18.4). As for mountain predators, they live far from the city, to be sure; but nearby river swamps are a haven of troublesome pig, and our vast surrounding plains bring us wolves, which in winter are a constant menace.[5]

Outside Gordion, as at Sardis, final resting places of local greats and their families were marked by artificial hills; they were distributed, however, in several parts of the surrounding land, not displayed together in a distant but prominent ridge opposite the city, like the burial hills of Lydian greats near Sardis. Gordion hills lacked the stone curb walls (*crepides*) at their bases and the "phallic" markers on their summits, which were characteristic of burial hills at Sardis, as in parts of the East Greek world. "The small burial hills show that Phrygian lesser gentry have begun to ape their betters, as Lydian upstarts at Sardis continually agitate for permission to do," said the Lydian (Fig. 18.5). "Ours have done that here for countless generations," replied his Phrygian host.[6]

Fig. 18.1. Sardis: distant view from the north (Bin Tepe), showing Acropolis and Mt. Tmolus. Photo: Archaeological Exploration of Sardis, Harvard Art Museums.

The biggest burial hill at Gordion, which commemorated the most illustrious of past greats at Gordion, was much higher than any of the others. At Sardis, two burial hills were even larger, including one recently built to commemorate his late majesty, Alyattes, father of the reigning monarch (Fig. 18.6). On the other hand, some of the Phrygian hills were far more venerable, older by eight-to-nine generations than the earliest at Sardis.[7]

Nearing the city, our Lydian visitor admired its outer defenses: with high walls (standing 14 m or about 46 feet high), regularly spaced bastions, and, at strategic locations along the fortification line, several 'podium forts' that rose even higher (one with a building that rose four stories above the *chemin de ronde*). At Sardis, the city wall had few towers, but was at least as high, and much thicker (20 m or nearly 65 feet thick at its base). One of the gates was strengthened by an outer glacis (30 m or nearly 100 feet thick) and a ditch as well (Fig. 18.7a, b).[8]

Like Sardis, Gordion also had a fortified citadel; it, however, was relatively low—and (as ancient viewers would have understood) artificially created through continuous occupation.[9] The citadel of Sardis, on the other hand, was a natural hill at the foot of the Tmolos range, and resembled a small mountain (Fig. 18.8a, b): its heights were made impregnable by nature and reportedly a royal lion; its rough, jagged slopes were partly tamed by orderly white terraces, rising tier on tier and proclaiming the power of Lydian monarchy to subdue all that is wild and uncouth (Figs. 18.9–18.12).[10]

Our Lydian visitor began his first morning at Gordion with commercial activity: purchasing several bales of fine sheep wool and goat hair, hazelnuts brought from the Black Sea, and a few slaves trained in Phrygian music—forever appealing to Ionian neighbors of Lydia.[11]

For some of these items he could only barter, using materials and manufactured goods brought from

Fig. 18.2a. Leopards on an architectural terracotta at Gordion (inventoried 4880 A179). Photo: Archaeological Exploration of Sardis, Harvard Art Museums.

Sardis, like rock crystal and finished products of jewelry, and glass, including the opaque red kind, the technical production of which had been mastered in Lydia. Some Phrygian merchants, however, accepted coin money, including both the "white gold" issues of his Lydian majesty's forebears, and the issues of pure gold and silver recently struck at Sardis.[12]

Having finished his transactions, the Lydian was invited to refresh himself before visiting the inner city. After washing face and hands with water, he rubbed them with scented salve. "Not *bakkaris* from your Aegean plant," said his Phrygian host, "but a highland version of our own, which we package in containers that resemble yours" (Fig. 18.13).[13]

"Unfortunately, our Phrygian producers want to hoax local clientele with containers of seemingly normal size but reduced capacity" (Fig. 18.14). "Ours want to do the same," said the Lydian. "Indeed, your people doubtless learned business skullduggery from us."[14]

Handed a libation dish that might have come from Sardis itself (Fig. 18.15), the Lydian poured out a thanks offering to the great goddess—"Mother," as she was simply called in Phrygia—and to Kandaules (Hermes to the Greeks) for safeguarding his goods as well as for fending off highwaymen and footpads during his upland journey.[15]

Liquid refreshment for our Lydian visitor was offered in a Phrygian side-spouted sieve cup, familiar to

Fig. 18.2b. Hyena shot at Sardis in 1922 by L.C. Holden, Jr. Photo: L.H. Holden, Jr.

Fig. 18.3. Wild goat, deer, and boar in painted pottery of East Greek (left) and Sardis (right) styles and conventions. Reconstructions: author.

Fig. 18.4. Bridle ornaments of bone, in the form of raptors seizing hares; from the Citadel Mound at Gordion (inventoried 7172-7176 BI410-414). Source: Gordion Project, Penn Museum.

him from replicas and variants at Sardis. The drink was beer, and sieve devices in cups of this kind effectively held back the chaff that invariably floated in beer, likewise the lees that too often also accumulated in wine. Spouts were a time-honored sipping device in the highlands, as well as further east; nevertheless—perhaps only because of the ribald jokes made by Ionian neighbors—our Lydian visitor disliked them, and preferred to drink from simple rims, like those of the deep cups (skyphoi) ubiquitous at Sardis and used more and more frequently also at Gordion.[16]

"For your drink, here is a tasty Spring-time relish," said his Phrygian host, passing our Lydian visitor two quail eggs and a dish of white "truffles." Pointing to the latter, he said, "Those you can never find in your lowland country."[17]

To enter the inner city, our Lydian visitor first ascended a steep glacis, faced with light and dark stone in stepped construction; and, after passing through a strong gate, beheld a complex of important buildings, arranged in rows and organized in an inner and outer series. Their orderly arrangement, he was told, had always existed: long before the great lord of Phrygia had been laid to rest under his mighty hill, even before a conflagration, nearly ten generations earlier, which had destroyed much of the inner citadel (Voigt, this volume).

Inner citadel buildings had a familiar look, with their double-pitched roofs and their gables with double windows, both of which were also present in Lydian architecture,[18] and with their roof and revetment tiles that resembled those of Sardis in specific decorative motifs. Gordion forms were not always so crisply defined as those at Sardis; some Gordion images could be downright primitive, and some motifs were totally different.[19]

Timber played a major role in terrace and wall construction, as well as in freestanding supports and roofs. Inner citadel buildings at Gordion were less open in front and lacked the freestanding columns that, with their slender fluted shafts, added grace to buildings at Sardis.[20]

Fig. 18.5. Bin Tepe, seen from Sardis. Photo: Archaeological Exploration of Sardis, Harvard Art Museums.

Fig. 18.6. Tomb of Alyattes, Sardis. Photo: Archaeological Exploration of Sardis, Harvard Art Museums.

Our Lydian visitor was pleased to see, however, that in decoration the physical ambience and paraphernalia of life in the inner city was tolerably modern and civilized, even if *farouche* survivals of a cruder past still circulated (Fig. 18.16). This was to be expected, of course, in backwoods regions like central Anatolia.[21]

Since a close and well-to-do relative of his host had died a few days before, our Lydian was invited to attend the funeral ceremonies. At Gordion, all elite graves were marked by earthen hills; there was no alternative form, like the rock-cut chamber tombs of Phrygian highlands, and of city cemeteries at Sardis. Tomb chambers of tumuli at Gordion were made of wood rather than the stone of tumulus tomb chambers at Sardis, and unlike the latter, they had no doors. All burial items were lowered in from above.

The corpse was laid out on a fancy couch, made of wood veneered in ivory and in form resembled those standard at Sardis; many corpses at Gordion, however, were buried in dug-out wooden sarcophagi (sometimes hewn from sweet-smelling Phoenician cedar), or were cremated. The latter treatment was rare at Sardis, but widely practiced in Greek cities of the coast. Our Lydian visitor noted approvingly that although the deceased had been a soldier, serving with distinction in his late majesty's war against the Medes, weaponry was omitted in his grave offerings.

Before the grave was closed, the Lydian visitor shared with assembled mourners a potent cocktail that combined wine, beer, and mead, and reportedly had been a traditional drink at Gordion for countless generations. As they began their return to the town, our Lydian visitor said, by way of comforting his host, "He has passed over the threshold and through the door"; his host murmured affirmatively, but only half comprehendingly.[22]

* * * * *

However suggestive the above narrative might be—and was meant to be—as an essay in reconstructing daily life realities from a combination of archaeological and other evidence, there should

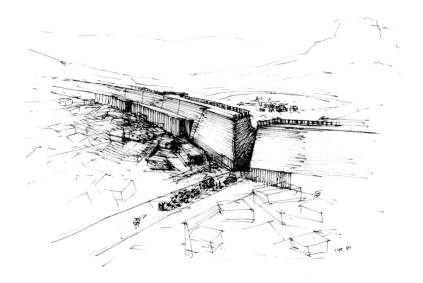

Fig. 18.7a, b. Sardis, Lydian city defenses. (a) inside looking west; (b, below) outside, looking east. Reconstruction sketches: P. T. Stinson.

be no doubt that, in addition to sailing perilously close to the wind with respect to some evidence, it is fundamentally simplistic: largely based on a pastiche of chance survivals and discoveries from the archaeological record that are cited as if they constitute adequate documentation. Greek literary and epigraphical texts of Classical and Hellenistic eras attest highly complex regulations and procedures concerning travel, city visitation, business transactions, rites of the dead, etc. The absence of such evidence from text-destitute Iron-Age and Archaic eras of western Anatolia hardly signifies that similar complexities did not exist then, and that the first half of the 1st millennium BC in Phrygia and Lydia was somehow a less complicated era.[23]

Furthermore, the narrative ultimately has to be abandoned, because of inadequate archaeological evidence from both Gordion and Sardis. Walter Andrae's Ionian visitor to Assur stayed in a private house, saw palaces and temples, received basic information about Assyrian religion and ritual, and witnessed a religious festival; he also marveled at Assyrian written records: long texts of official chronicle on stone and fired clay, and private business accounts, recorded in minute detail.

Phrygian houses, where a visitor might have stayed, are only broadly understood, and nearly the same could be said for comparable Lydian houses at Sardis.[24] The palace and administrative center at Gordion presumably is represented by some or all Middle

Fig. 18.8a, b. Sardis Acropolis. (a, top) view looking north; (b) view looking east. Photo: Archaeological Exploration of Sardis, Harvard Art Museums.

Phrygian citadel buildings. At Sardis, however, no Archaic administrative buildings have been located.[25]

Does the multi-megaron complex of Burnt and Archaic levels at Gordion belong to a traditional Anatolian palace type, with forerunners in Early Bronze Age Troy (perhaps also Demirci Höyük)? Did the Lydian Palace complex at Sardis belong to that type, or was it something entirely different— perhaps a model for the palaces of Cyrus at Pasargadae and his successors at Persepolis, as some have

Fig. 18.9. Sardis, terrace walls on lower Acropolis slopes (sectors ByzFort and F49). Reconstruction sketch, view looking south: P. T. Stinson.

thought?[26] Temples are a mystery for both Gordion and Sardis. At Gordion, some—conceivably many—of Archaic-level Buildings A-Z might have been "temples" (rather than administrative buildings); but their plans suggest little about use and ritual, unless the small semi-subterranean chamber between Buildings C and G reflects rites of purification or initiation, or was an heroon (as suggested by M.J. Mellink). Sardis so far has produced no candidates for temples.[27]

Although writing existed at Gordion already in the second half of the 8th century BC (on wax smears and wood of Tumulus MM), early Phrygian texts are short, only partly intelligible, and uninformative about history, government, diplomacy, commerce, and religious ritual. The situation elsewhere in Phrygia and western Anatolia

Fig. 18.10. Sardis, terrace wall on lower Acropolis slope (sector ByzFort; with excavator Christopher Ratté), view looking south. Photo: Archaeological Exploration of Sardis, Harvard Art Museums.

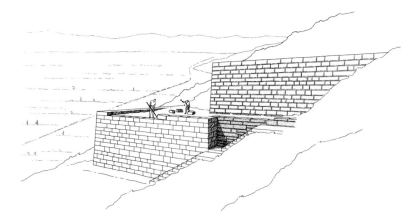

Fig. 18.11. Sardis, terrace walls on upper Acropolis slope near the summit. Reconstruction sketch, view looking east: P.T. Stinson.

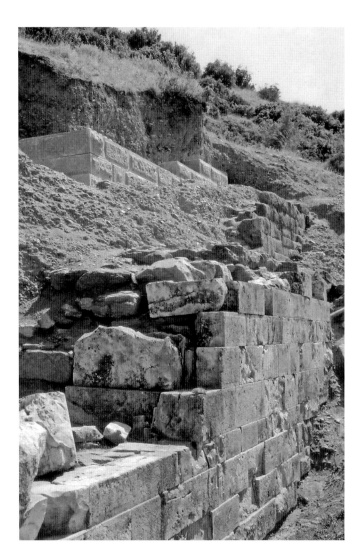

Fig. 18.12. Sardis, terrace walls on upper Acropolis slope near the summit, view looking south. Photo: Archaeological Exploration of Sardis, Harvard Art Museums.

is similar: less than 120 texts in Lydian are known, and those consist of formulaic grave epitaphs and dedications, as well as one or two words on pottery, coins, and seals. The absence of substantial and substantive contemporaneous texts is a fundamentally important lacuna, not least because, as mentioned above, it tends to dull and blunt our sensitivity to potential complexities that only texts can document.[28]

＊ ＊ ＊ ＊ ＊

The mounds and tumuli of Gordion might seem a prosaic assemblage, broadly similar in kind to hundreds of others throughout Anatolia and the Near East, enlivened by no romantic columns of marble, toppled architraves, or rock-cut façades. But in their august landscape setting of highland Anatolia, with its coronal surround of distant mountains and vast canopy of sky, they are landmarks that deeply impress—quite apart from their yield of fabulous riches: the Burnt Stratum and its extraordinary contents; intact burial assemblages of the elite; intricately carved and inlaid wooden furniture; early pebble mosaics; Archaic murals; quantities of architectural terracottas, many in context assemblages; seven hoards of gold and silver coins; exotic glasses; and rich ceramic assemblages.[29]

For that remarkable material, credit belongs, first and foremost, to the pioneers of Gordion excavation—Gustav and Alfred Körte, and Rodney S. Young: the Körte brothers, who made rich discoveries in a single season of excavation, and published an exemplary

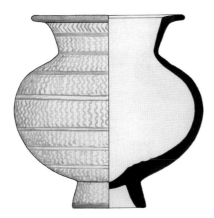

Fig. 18.13. Lydion from Gordion, Tumulus A. Individual wiggly lines evidently were inspired by Lydian marbling, created with a multiple brush that applied glaze matter in overlapping bands and irregular concentrations (inventoried 9 P9). Illustration: author, 1965.

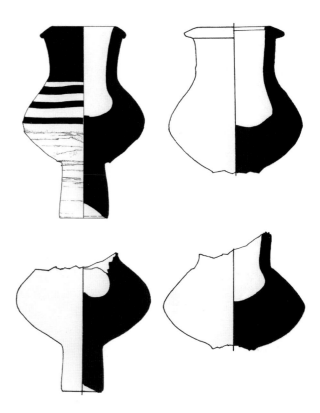

Fig. 18.14. "Late" lydions from Gordion, Citadel Mound (inventoried 2855 P935, upper left; 2528 P819, upper right; 6951 P2696, lower left; 1482 P452, lower right). Illustration: author, 1965.

report four years later[30]; Rodney Young, discoverer of the Burnt Layer and of defenses in the Küçük Höyük, excavator of Tumulus MM and of much else discussed at this conference.

Rodney Young was a born leader: strong, charismatic, "bigger than life" (Fig. 18.17). Several of his great qualities, however, elude those who knew him slightly or not at all, partly because he played down his achievements and disguised his strengths. He enjoyed posing as the ultimate "bull in a china shop": the slightest flex of his broad shoulders toppling shelf upon shelf of priceless Sèvres and Meissen porcelain—heirloom tureens, *veduta* and *paté-sur-paté* vases, dinner services commissioned by Catherine the Great—all crashing noisily to the floor, and shattering to smithereens, hopelessly irreparable. On the contrary, the silent partner of Rodney Young's decisiveness and courage was tact: he planted his ideas so subtly that recipients innocently imagined them to be their own, and, proudly espousing them, added their promotion of them to his. Most important of all was his virile optimism, a basic tenet in his way of life, which he radiated, invigorating those around him.

As has been abundantly clear in this conference, field seasons directed by Kenneth Sams and Mary Voigt have yielded a broader, deeper understanding

of Gordion in place and time. They have contributed major discoveries and meticulous publications, and addressed major, difficult, and time-consuming problems, most of which had been viewed as insignificant or non-existent in earlier seasons, notably problems of architectural conservation and site management.

This conference honors two Gordion stars, whose careers spanned both pioneering and mature field seasons: Keith De Vries,[31] successor of Rodney Young as Gordion Project director; and Ellen Kohler, expedition registrar and conservator. Keith and Ellen both were champions in hiding their lights under bushels, but Ellen was the super champion. As registrar and conservator, Ellen did by herself what eight people at Sardis do, and much besides: teaching staff assistants, maintaining order, tranquility, and security in the expedition compound; making important discoveries that had been missed by others; not to mention typing and mailing all Rodney Young's correspondence during five-month field seasons.

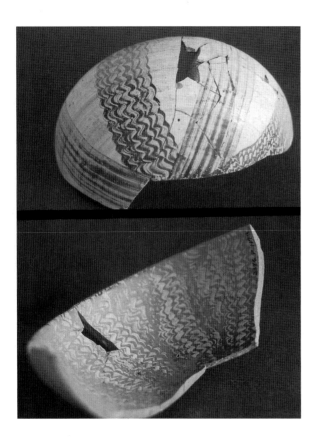

Fig. 18.15. Marbled omphalos phiale from Gordion, Citadel Mound (inventoried 3376 P1173). Source: Gordion Project, Penn Museum.

Who sorted out and reassembled the North Syrian ivory frontlet and blinker fragments from their seemingly hopeless jumble of powdery fragments, consulted Richard Barnett about reconstruction, and single-handedly consolidated and restored them? Who recognized the tiny countermarks on Lydian electrum coins and precisely recorded them? Who saw in less than two minutes that 42 silver tetradrachms of Alexander the Great—laid out for checking in the CAT room at Gordion—had been reduced to 41; stopped a busload of 35 American Embassy families, who had just inspected the coins and were returning to Ankara, carefully explained to them the importance of every single coin in the hoard, and subsequently was sent the missing coin— all neatly accomplished without accusation, humiliation, or official bureaucratic tedium? Ellen Kohler, of course, is the party responsible, and for much, much more. That will become increasingly clear as field documents continue to be consulted and two and two are put together.

In the same game spirit with which Ellen Kohler happily plunged into icy waters of the Black Sea one chill Spring day (Fig. 18.18), she gladly undertook and brought to glorious fruition formidable tasks that are basic to understanding the riches of Gordion. Those riches are shared by others because of her.[32]

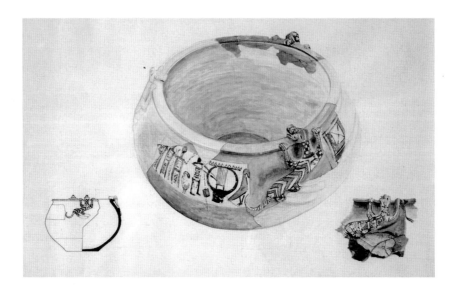

Fig. 18.16. Dinos from Tumulus J (inventoried 1997 P634). Reconstruction watercolor: author, 1965.

Acknowledgments

During the preparation of this chapter, many people helped with information and ideas: J.K. Anderson, M. Ballard, N.D. Cahill, J.V. Canby, G. Darbyshire, M.-H. Gates, K.W. Harl, A. Holliman, A. Mat-Öztekin, M.M. Miles, L.E. Roller, and G.K. Sams.

NOTES

18.1. This text substantially remains that of the oral presentation (May 22, 2007). Apart from a few attempts to avoid terms loaded with meaning from other cultures (and therefore substituting, e.g., hills, or burial hills for tumuli; greats for royalty-aristocracy), the conversational speech in this exercise is not intended to evoke ancient terminology. The model is the direct, clear, unpretentious prose, acceptable in spite of anachronisms, used by Robert Van Gulick for his Judge Dee stories. The subjects of some conversational exchanges in this text are highly improbable, with their archaeologically focused perspective (e.g., lydion capacities) and are simply vehicles for information. Some ideas are largely whimsical (e.g., wolves, quail eggs, white truffles). For the difficulties of creating casual conversational speech in historical fiction, Yourcenar 1992,

Fig. 18.17. Rodney Young at Gordion. Source: Gordion Project, Penn Museum.

Fig. 18.18. Ellen Kohler, in impromptu swimming suit, enjoys a swim in icy waters of the Black Sea, May 1961. Source: Gordion Project, Penn Museum.

reference to which was kindly supplied by M.M. Miles.

18.2. Andrae 1977; for Andrae's life and career, see also Andrae 1961 and Andrae and Boehmer 1992.

18.3. Travel time, by horseback, is a very rough guess. Steady, relaxed travel by a small party on horseback in 1831 for the 145 km distance from Smyrna to Alaşehir took three days (unpublished letter of S.F. Du Pont, reporting a trip made in late March and early April; Hagley Museum, Wilmington DE; letter no. 9-251). A hypothetical overland route from Sardis to Gordion that would have included Bagis (modern Güre), Midas City, and followed the Sangarios River from modern Mahmudiye (southwest of Eskişehir) is roughly estimated at about 460 km (without allowance for grade). For the Gordion landscape, Kealhofer 2005:144–48; Marsh 2005; Gürsan-Salzmann 2005. For olive trees in Anatolia, see Hoffner 1974:116–17.

18.4. Royal control of forests at Taranza (the location of which has not been identified and is presumed to have been on Mt. Tmolos) is attested, not for Lydian times, but for the Hellenistic era, under Antiochos III, as indicated in his letter to the Sardians of 213 BC; Gauthier 1989:13–33, especially14, 27; Ma 1999:61–63. For control of the forests of Lebanon by Antiochos III, see Josephus, *Jewish Antiquities* 12.138–44; Brown 1969:208–10. For control of the forests by Assyrian King Sargon II and the emperor Hadrian, see Meiggs 1982:75, 85–86; Kuniholm, Griggs, and Newton 2007. For Lydian cavalry, Herodotos 1.80; cf. Mimnermos fr. 14 (ed. Gerber; ap. Stobaeus, 3.7.11); Nicolas of Damascus, *FGrHist* 90 F 62; see also Greenewalt 2010a. Lydian "above the ground" exercises are pure speculation. Such exercises are proposed for the Greek world in Anderson 1961:124, 127. According to J.K. Anderson (pers. comm. 2007), Captain V.S. Littauer, who was a graduate of the Spanish Riding School, doubted their existence in Greek antiquity, perhaps because ancient literature makes no reference to the many years of highly specialized training and the exceptional aptitude of individual horses on which success in those exercises depended. But Henry Wynmalen, another authority on modern equitation, thought them entirely possible. Mounted horses shown on architectural terracottas reportedly from Düver and winged horses on horizontal simas from Sardis are rearing, but not performing the *levade*, in which the forefeet are "drawn up under the body" (Podhajsky 1958:33). Mounted horses on architectural terracottas from Buruncuk/Larisa, however, have their forefeet somewhat drawn up; Åkerström 1966:55 and pls. 26, 27. The bearded male head on a fragmentary terracotta from Sar-

dis might belong to a rider; Ramage 1978:15–16, no. 2. For the rearing horse, see Xenophon, *de Equitandi ratione* 11. Highland valleys suitable for summer pasturage and horse raising exist in Mt. Tmolos, above Sardis; but horse raising there by the Lydians also is pure speculation, unless they are the "accustomed pastures" of Herodotos 1.78 (a reference kindly supplied by A. Hollmann). For depictions of Greek horse training, Moore 2004:52–53.

18.5. For deer in Phrygian art, Akurgal 1955:1–6, pls. 1–6; Sams 1994a: pl. 126 (painted amphoras of Alişar open-mouthed type); Young 1960a:240, pl. 60, fig. 25 (ivory plaque from burnt level, M3); Young 1981:35–36, pls. 16, 17 (painted pottery jugs from Tumulus P, nos. 55, 56); for deer hunting on architectural terracottas at Gordion, Åkerström 1966:144–45, 152–53, pls. 73–75; for deer horn at Gordion, Young 1960b:3. Wild goats nibble trees on architectural terracottas at Gordion, Åkerström 1966:142–43, 148–49, 151, 159–60. The theme was familiar in antiquity: domesticated goats mounting trees are shown in the Sumerian "ram in the thicket" sculpture from Ur: D.P. Hansen in Zettler and Horne, *Treasures from the Royal Tombs of Ur* 1998:42, 61–63. In a Greek comedy by Eupolis (fr. 13, eds. Koch, Edmonds; Storey 2003:67–74), a goat chorus boasts of the many trees it crops. Archaic plastic oil flasks in the shape of hares, suspended after having been caught in hunting, from Gordion and Sardis have respective inventory numbers 5990 P2234 and P67.78: 7464. For bone bridle ornaments showing raptors seizing hares, Young 1964:283, pl. 84, fig. 14. Might Gordion "doodles" of the 9th century showing raptors near a possible human arm attest falconry in Phrygian culture? See Young 1969a:275; Mellink 1983:351–54, 357 (the latter reference kindly supplied by J.V. Canby), Roller, this volume, and Roller 2009. Much representational evidence for falconry in Hittite culture is presented and discussed in Canby 2002 (reference kindly provided by M.-H. Gates, substance kindly provided by J.V. Canby). If falconry was practiced in Phrygia, it might have been a continuation of Hittite tradition, and/or of traditions of Thrace, the reported homeland of the Phrygians, where what might have been falconry is reported by later Greek and Latin sources: Epstein 1943:501–3; Lindner 1973:111–15. Falconry evidently was not practiced in the Mediterranean world of Greece and Rome before Late Antiquity, although its practice in India was evidently reported by Ktesias in the 4th century BC: ap. Aelian, *de natura animalium* 4.26; Epstein 1943:503; Lindner 1973:111–19. For falconry in Achaemenid Iran, Epstein 1943:500–501. For wild creatures in western Anatolia, Kumerloeve 1967:364–66 (hyena), 375–77 (leopard), 180–381 (wild pig), 381–89 (deer), 394–98 (wild goat); Kumerloeve 1956 and 1976 (leopard); Banoğlu 1958:10–18 (wild goat), 18–23 (boar), 24–29 (leopard), 37–39 (wolf); Turan 1984:57–59 (wild goat), 66–69 (boar), 81–82 (leopard), 84–85 (wolf); Üstay 1990:54–65 (wild goat), 98–121 (boar), 147 (leopard), 134–43 (wolf). Figure 18.2b shows a hyena that disturbed Sardis villagers in 1922 and was killed by a member of the Butler Expedition, L.C. Holden, Jr. Hyenas reportedly posed a nighttime danger at Sardis as late as 1960; and jackals could be heard at night in the mid 1960s. For wild pig at Gordion, Gürsan-Salzmann 2005:173. Wolves at Gordion during winter months in the early 1960s were reportedly commonplace.

18.6.   For the tumuli at Gordion, see Körte and Körte 1904:36–145; Young 1981; Kohler 1980 and 1995. The great tumulus cemetery at Sardis is located 7–8 km north of the city site, and has long had the Turkish name Bin Tepe (thousand mounds); 120 tumuli have been counted there (C.H. Roosevelt, pers. comm. 2007). For tumulus *crepides* and "phallic" markers in Lydia, Roosevelt 2003: respectively, 154–55 and 176–78; Roosevelt 2009:142, 153; for examples at Larisa/Buruncuk in Aeolis, Meyer-Plath in Boehlau and Schefold 1940–42:109–11. For symbolic doors, Roosevelt 2006; for an alternative identification, Polat 2005. Several small tumuli in the cemetery at Bin Tepe belong to the second half of the 6th century BC; for small tumuli at Sardis as a phenomenon of the early Persian era, perhaps reflecting circumstances of Persian rule that encouraged Lydians to express their cultural identity: Dusinberre 2003:141–44; Roosevelt 2003:344–51; Roosevelt 2009:140–50. At Gordion, small tumuli had been constructed since the 9th century. Tumulus G has been dated to the 9th century; Tumuli X and Y are contemporaneous with the Burnt Level (G.K. Sams, pers. comm. 2007). For small tumuli at Gordion of 6th century date, Körte and Körte 1904:104–45 (Tumuli II, I, V), Kohler 1995.

18.7.   The great tumulus at Gordion, "MM," has a diameter "a little short of" 300 m and a height of "about" 53 m; Young 1981:79. The tumulus in the Bin Tepe Cemetery called Koca Mutaf Tepe, which has become commonly identified as the burial mound of Alyattes (since the account of Anton von Prokesch, later Prokesch von Osten, in 1825; earlier by Robert Wood, in 1750) has an estimated diameter of 355.2 m and a height of 61.46 m (from the bottom of a reported crepis wall; von Olfers 1859:545). Civil engineer T. Yalçınkaya has calculated that the Tumulus of Alyattes contains nearly 787,000 m³

of earth and slightly more than 40,500 m³ of cut stone (for the crepis), and chipped stone, and clay (around and over the burial chamber), and has estimated that construction would have taken two years and seven-to-eight months with a labor force of somewhat over 2,400 men and 600 horses; Yalçınkaya 2000. A tumulus at Bin Tepe nearly as large as Koca Mutaf Tepe is located further to the west and is called Kır Mutaf Tepe; Roosevelt 2009:142–44. None of the tumuli excavated at Bin Tepe, Sardis, or elsewhere in Lydia are demonstrably earlier than the 6th century BC; McLauchlin 1986:159–61, 174–206, 212; Dusinberre 2003 and Roosevelt 2003, supra, n. 6. To be sure, unidentified earlier tumuli may exist. At Gordion, however, Tumulus W is now dated to the late 9th century; Tumulus MM is dated to ca. 740.

18.8.   For towers/bastions of the outer defenses at Gordion, Edwards 1959:264 and pl. 64, fig. 4. "Podium forts" were located at the Küçük Höyük and at Kuş Tepe, and probably other places along the circuit, G. Darbyshire has surmised. A fortification ditch also appears to have existed at Gordion (Rose, this volume). For outer defenses of Sardis, Greenewalt et al. 2003:92–93, fig. 29A, B. The ditch at Sardis has not been located, but its existence is implied by a level discrepancy between the lowest exposed part of the Glacis and the cobbled road surface that passes through a gate immediately to the north. The reconstruction drawing in fig. 29A, cited above, was made before continuing excavation had exposed deeper levels of the Glacis. A single tower has been tentatively identified at the east end of the circuit. Excavation nearby was conducted in 2000.

18.9.   I.e., the "city mound," from Gustav and Alfred Körte's *Stadthügel*, which was a man-made *tell*, or *höyük*.

18.10. The Acropolis of Sardis rises 300 m above the river plain. For the sheer side facing Mt. Tmolos and the lion (carried around the Acropolis by King Meles), Herodotos 1.84. For the terraces, Greenewalt 1986:301; 1987:385; 1988:41–42; Özgen and Öztürk 1996:22, figs. 17, 18; Cahill 2008.

18.11. For Phrygian wool, Herodotos 5.49.5. For hazelnuts, DeVries 1980a:36; for slaves and music, Roebuck 1959:49, with references. Angora goats, from which mohair comes, flourish in the highlands; Tamur 2003:4–5, 47–48. There is no evidence for their existence in antiquity; Leiser 1993–94. For fine goat hair threads recovered at Sardis in a Lydian house that was destroyed in the mid 6th century BC, see Cahill in Greenewalt et al. 1990:154–55. Fine goat hair is obtained from goats of many kinds, however, not exclusively from the Angora goat.

18.12. For rock crystal at Sardis, see McLauchlin 1989. Alabanda was reported as a source for rock crystal of poor quality by Pliny the Elder (*NH* 37.9.23) and is reported as a source also of good quality rock crystal by geologist Yılmaz Savasçin (pers. comm. 2006). Rock crystal wasters (hunks, chips) have been recovered in large quantities in Archaic deposits at three excavation sectors of Sardis (HoB, PN, MMS), and in one (MMS) in contexts that clearly antedate the Persian capture of the 540s. For worked rock crystal at Sardis in the form of a lion, lenses, and jewelry, including a pyramidal stamp seal, see Hanfmann 1965:7, 9, fig. 7; Greenewalt, Ratté, and Rautman 1995:18; Curtis 1925:25 no. 49, 26 no. 50, 43 no. 114. Cullet and parts of beads of opaque red glass recovered at Sardis in a workshop of the first half of the 6th century BC show that opaque red glass was worked at Sardis, if not made there: Brill and Cahill 1988; Moorey 1994:212–14. There is no evidence for opaque red glass at Gordion. Ivory is omitted as an acquisition or sale commodity since high-quality carved ivories of the 6th century BC have been recovered at both Gordion and Sardis. Whether electrum and bimetallic currency in gold and silver would have been used at the same time is questionable. Sealed deposits that contain both are so far unknown. For an assemblage of 45 Lydian electrum coins at Gordion, Young 1964:283; Bellinger 1968. Croeseid coins of gold and silver are not reported from excavations at Gordion (K.W. Harl, pers. comm. 2007); for gold and silver croeseids in contexts at Sardis that demonstrably antedate the Persian conquest, see Cahill and Kroll 2005; for a hoard of gold croeseids at Sardis, see Shear 1922. For a recent general account of Lydian coins, see Kroll 2010.

18.13. "I anointed the nostrils with bakkaris, such as Croesus…" Hipponax fr. 104 (ed. Gerber; ap. Athenaeus 15.690a and Ox. Pap. XVIII, p. 184). According to Hesychios, s.v., *bakkaris* was "a kind of unguent from the plant of the same name; some (say it is) from myrtle, and some that it is a Lydian unguent." Pliny, *NH* 21.16.29–30, reports unguents made from the plant *baccar*, called *baccaris* by some. Dioscurides, *De Materia Medica*, s.v. bakkaris (pp. 55–56 no. 44, ed. Wellmann) gave a description; and the Morgan Library manuscript includes an image. For the Lydian salve containers now called lydion (an ancient vessel name that was applied in antiquity to a different shape), see Greenewalt 1972: 132–34. Apart from slight shape and decoration differences between lydions at Sardis and Gordion, there is no evidence that their contents differed. The association with *bakkaris, brenthium,* and

other Lydian salves and ungents was first proposed by Rumpf 1920. For Lydian cosmetics and their containers, see Greenewalt 2010b.

18.14. Containers with reduced capacity were produced at Gordion and Sardis. There is little evidence for their date, apart from late 6th century context material of one in a grave at Kameiros in Rhodes; Jacopi 1931:263–64, fig. 290 on p. 266; Greenewalt 2010b:206. There is no evidence that they were being produced as early as the middle of the 6th century. Herodotos, 1.94, called the Lydians the first *kapeloi*, but without pejorative implications; Roebuck 1959:58–60.

18.15. The model for the libation dish illustrated in Figure 18.15 is an omphalos phiale with marbled decoration from Gordion, inventoried 3376 P1173; Cahill 2010:489, no. 108. Remains of similar ones have been recovered at Sardis. For similar omphalos phialai from Miletos and Didyma, see Kerschner and Ehrhardt n.d.; Cahill 2010:492–93, nos. 113–14. For Phrygian "Mother," Brixhe 1979:41–43; for Kubaba/Kybebe/Kybele in Lydia, Hawkins 2004:218–22 and Munn 2006:120–25. For "Hermes *Kunanches*, to the Maeonians Kandaules," Hipponax fr. 3a (ed. Gerber) and the learned comments of Hawkins 2004:290–318.

18.16. For side-spouted sieve cups at Gordion, see Sams 1977; 1994a:67–70. The shape is not common at Sardis, but several examples are attested. The best preserved has Lydian marbled decoration and comes from a Lydian tomb (Greenewalt 1978:38 and pl. 13, fig. 2; now in New York, Metropolitan Museum of Art). There are fragments of others (e.g., Sardis Expedition P97.117: 10689; probably Metropolitan Museum of Art no. 26.199.18). The cups are not difficult to drink from (*pace* Moorey 1980:195–96); an Archaic wall painting fragment from Gordion seems to show a person drinking from the spout of a small pitcher (Mellink 1980b:92–93 and fig. 4). See also Greenewalt 2010c:131, fig. 6 (where the drinker is J.K. Anderson). For Greek literary references to side-spouted cups, see Archilochos fr. 42 (ed. Gerber; ap. Athenaeus 10.447b); cf. Hipponax fr. (cf. fr. 56, ed. Gerber; ap. Pollux 6.19). For a Lydian or Lydian-type skyphos with streaky-glaze decoration at Gordion, see Young 1953a:164, fig. 8.

18.17. A present of quail eggs was given to Gordion Expedition staff in 1961 (by a workman whose wife the Expedition had helped). *Phasianidae* family members appear on Archaic architectural terracottas from Midas City in Phrygia and elsewhere in western Anatolia: Åkerström 1966:107, 115, 134, 208–9, pls. 53, 59; Hostetter 1994:10–11; Ateşlier 2006:68–69. White "truffles," called *domalan* and *keme* in Turkish (Latin *Terfezia*), appear in the countryside around Gordion during spring months. They are detected from cracks that they make in the ground surface, and are levered out with long sticks. (The writer once participated in an unsuccessful domalan-hunting excursion.) A. Mat-Öztekin, who kindly provided the Latin name, also wrote that a celebrated springtime dish in the region of Gaziantep is "keme kebabı."

18.18. For a plan of inner citadel buildings A–Z, see Sams 2005a:26, figs. 3, 4. For similarities in plan between inner citadel buildings of the Burnt Level and of the Middle Phrygian level, see Young 1964:282. The gable with double windows is attested for Phrygia in a "doodle" on masonry of Burnt Level Megaron II at Gordion, as well as in rock-cut façades of the Phrygian highlands. The only evidence for a gable with double windows in Lydia is the interior painted decoration of a tomb of the 6th century BC, located a few kilometers west of Sardis, at Ahmetli. On the other hand, there is little evidence otherwise for Lydian gable design; that gables were common in Lydian architecture is indicated by Lydian raking sima roof tiles. For the doodles, see Roller, this volume, Fig. 7.2; Young 1957:323, pl. 90, fig. 12, and 1960a:227, fig. 6 (the drawing in Young, however, omits the top horizontal window border). For Phrygian highland gables with double windows, see Haspels 1971: pls. 513–515, 601–602 (Unfinished, Areyastis, and Hyacinth Monuments). For the tomb at Ahmetli, see Stinson in Greenewalt et al. 2003:140–41, no. 50 (with illustrations), and Stinson 2008; for Lydian raking sima tiles, Åkerström 1966:70–71, 73–76.

18.19. For abstractly rendered "Theseus and the Minotaur" figures in Phrygian tiles, see Åkerström 1966:141, pls. 76–79; for more realistic rendering of the same in Sardis tiles, Shear 1926:9–12; Hostetter 1994:5–10 and figs. 18, 19, 21, 22 (and for an explanation for the presence of Theseus—if he was the intended hero—in those tiles: Simon 1996:14–15. For free-field composition in a hunting scene on Gordion terracottas, Åkerström 1966:141, pls. 70, 73–75.

18.20. The use of wood at Gordion strikes modern excavators as prodigal, but probably only because wall footings of the Burnt Level and artificial fill supporting the Archaic level are so well preserved. For half-timbered construction of Burnt Level buildings, see Young 1960b:3–7. Large timbers were used as tie beams in artificial fill on

exterior sides of the Citadel Mound, when the occupation surface of the Middle Phrygian stratum was raised above the burnt stratum. When R.S. Young first visited the site, villagers were extracting those timbers to re-use them in their houses (one beam was reused as the ridgepole of a small barn, belonging to one Muzaffer, who died in 1963). For timber used in Middle Phrygian wall construction, Young 1955:8; 1956:255. The front room of the Gordion megaron unit was closed in front and entered through a doorway, not an open porch like megarons of the Greek world (and Early Bronze Age Troy). The evidence for columns at Sardis is slight but significant. It consists of column representations on Archaic naiskoi (evidently votive offerings to the Mother Goddess; recovered re-used in the Late Roman Synagogue), on one of which the columns are fluted; and a stylobate on the Acropolis spur at sector ByzFort: Hanfmann and Ramage 1978:42–51, nos. 6, 7 (naiskoi); Ratté in Greenewalt, Ratté, and Rautman 1993:27–28, 31, fig. 25 (stylobate).

18.21. "Modern and civilized" refers to Greek stylistic impact, which was strong at Sardis, although its source may not have been fully identified by ancient Anatolians with Greek culture. For 6th century mural painting at Gordion in an East Greek style, Young 1956:255–56; Mellink 1980; Bingöl 1997:36–39. The "farouche" example in Fig. 18.16, a ceramic dinos (from the lower mantle of Tumulus J, perhaps used in ceremonies associated with the Tumulus J burial), has been dated by G.K. Sams "not earlier than the last quarter of the seventh century." For a discussion of the dinos, see Kohler 1995:68–69, no. TumJ 36 (inventoried 1997 P634). Whether material of such date and style would still have circulated in the mid 6th century BC may be questioned.

18.22. For city cemeteries at Sardis, located in the Paktolos valley, chamber tombs dominate the archaeological record: more than 1,100 were excavated by the Butler Expedition between 1910 and 1914; for their form, see Butler 1922:157–67. Cist graves, sarcophagus inhumations, and tumuli also existed: Greenewalt 1972 (cist graves); Greenewalt, Ratté, and Rautman 1993:35–37 (sarcophagus inhumations); Greenewalt et al. 1985:81–84 (tumulus); Baughan 2010. Inhumation burials of the 6th century at Gordion included those designated II (Körte and Körte 1904:104–29), C, S-2, S-3 (Kohler 1995); cremation burials include M, I, and A (Kohler 1980:66–70). That the ivory cymation and other ivory fragments from II (Körte and Körte 1904:110–12) belonged to a kline was supposed by K. DeVries and has been argued by E. Baughan

(2004:100–103). For the use of *Cedrus libani* for the coffin of Tumulus B, see Kohler 1995:11. For cremation and inhumation at Gordion, Kohler 1980, 1995; in Archaic graves of Rhodes (Ialysos and Kameiros), Gates 1983. The scarcity of weaponry in Iron Age and Archaic tombs at Gordion (Kohler 1995:213) and Archaic tombs at Sardis and the East Greek world (e.g., Rhodes [Ialysos, Kameiros], Kos, Samos, Pitane) contrasts with the prominence of weaponry in tombs of other cultural eras and regions; e.g., Iron Age graves of mainland Greece, Classical and Hellenistic tombs of Macedonia and Italy (e.g., Boardman and Kurtz 1971:39–40, 62–63). For the cocktail, McGovern et al. 1999; McGovern 2000:24–25. Reference to the door by the Lydian visitor endorses the theory that the symbolic door was a concept in Lydia before the earliest physical examples, which have been dated to the mid 6th century BC and later, perhaps all after the Persian conquest in the 540s BC: Roosevelt 2006; 2009:153–55; Polat 2005.

18.23. Alain Bresson, entitled "Coming In and Out of a Greek City: A View from the Inscriptions" (delivered at the University of California at Berkeley, April 18, 2007).

18.24. For houses on the northeast ridge at Gordion, see Anderson, this volume. For highly interpretive reconstructions of Phrygian houses at Pazarlı, see Koşay 1941:3–5, 14–15, and pls. XXXVII–XXXIX. Individual spaces of a few Lydian houses of the first half of the 6th century BC are well preserved, but little is known about complete house units: Cahill 2002; Cahill in Greenewalt et al. 2003:58–59.

18.25. Frustratingly for the archaeologist, however, if ancient claims (Vitruvius 2.8.9–10; Pliny, *NH* 35.172) that the Palace of Croesus still stood and functioned in Roman times as a public building (i.e., a *gerousia*) are true, that important building should be relatively accessible in the archaeological landscape (not deeply buried, like much of the Lydian city).

18.26. For the Palace of Croesus as a model for palaces in Persia, see Hanfmann 1977; Nylander 1970:117–18.

18.27. For the Painted House at Gordion, see references to mural painting in an East Greek style, above, n. 21. A Sanctuary of Kybele at Sardis is cited by Herodotos (5.102). There also are a well-preserved altar of the 6th century BC (Ramage in Ramage and Craddock 2000:72–79), sculptural dedications that were found re-used in the Late Roman Synagogue (Hanfmann and Ramage 1978:42–51, nos. 6, 7; 58–60, no. 20), and some peculiar ritual offerings (Greenewalt 1978).

18.28. For early Phrygian texts at Gordion, Young 1969b; for Lydian texts, Gusmani 1964:250–70; 1980:148–59. The situation reflects not failure to write by Phrygians and other western Anatolians, but their choice of impermanent writing materials (presumably skins or the like). As the late Ruggero Stefanini often remarked, that practice stands in stark contrast with the use of clay as a writing material by the Hittites of the 2nd millennium and by other Near Eastern peoples in the 1st millennium. The texts of the latter groups constitute an *embarras des richesses* in the archaeological record. The situation was often noted at Gordion: one morning Rodney Young said he had dreamt the previous night that the kinds of semi-baked clay loomweights that are ubiquitous at Gordion (Burke 2005:75–78, and fig. 6-5 on p. 75) really were a form of official document. "You just peeled off an outer clay layer, and—lo and behold—long texts in Phrygian became exposed," he said. "And just to think: all these years we'd been throwing them at each other."

18.29. For wooden furniture, early mosaics, glass, and architectural terracottas, see Simpson 1988, and Simpson and Spirydowicz 1999 (furniture); Young 1965 (mosaics); von Saldern 1959 (glass); Åkerström 1966:136–61, and Glendinning 2005 (terracottas); for Archaic murals, supra n. 21. Of the seven coin hoards, four contained Hellenistic tetradrams, with 114, 42, 50, and 100 coins per hoard; one of 110 Persian sigloi; one of 45 Lydian electrum coins; and one of 5 Hellenistic gold coins (2 of which were octadrahms). For these, see Cox 1953, 1966 (tetradrachms and gold coins); Bellinger 1968 (Lydian coins). The hoard of gold coins reportedly contained another octadrachm of Seleucus III: Houghton and Lorbeer 2002:333.

18.30. For excavation by the Körte brothers, Gustav (1852–1917) and Alfred (1866–1946) at Gordion in 1900, Körte and Körte 1904; Sams 2005a:10. For biographical accounts of A. Körte, Schadewalt 1936, Thierfelder 1980; of G. Körte, Schwingenstein 1980, 1988; of R.S. Young, Pritchard 1975, Thompson 1975, DeVries 1980b.

18.31. Sams 2007; Darbyshire 2007.

18.32. Ellen L. Kohler attended the conference in which the text above was read, but died (November 3, 2008) before this volume went to press. Her nickname "El-bayan"—the writer recollects her saying in 1961—was given her by Raci Temizer, one-time Gordion Expedition commissioner, later Director of the Museum of Anatolian Civilizations in Ankara.

Bibliography

Abramov, Alexandr P. 1993. Antichnye amfory. Periodizatsiya i khronologiya (Ancient amphoras. Periodization and chronology). *Bosporskiy Sbornik* 3:4–135.

———. 2001. Tipologiya i khronologiya klazomenskikh amfor (Typology and chronology of Klazomenian amphoras). *Drevnosti Bospora* 4:7–16.

———. 2002. Tipologiya i khronologiya amfor o Khios (Typology and chronology of amphoras of Chios). *Drevnosti Bospora* 5:7–26.

Akamatis, Ioannis. 2000. *Ενσφάγιστες λαβές αμφορέων απο την αγορά της Πέλλα. Ανασκαφή 1980–1987. Οι ομάδες Παρμενίσκου και Ρόδου.* Athens: Athens Archaeological Society.

Åkerström, Åke. 1966. *Die Architektonischen Terrakotten Kleinasiens.* Skrifter Utgivna Svenska Institutet I Athen 4 XI. Lund: Gleerup.

Akkay, M. 1992. Objets phrygiens en bronze du tumulus de Kaynarca. In *La Cappadoce méridionale jusqu'à la fin de l'époque romaine: état des recherches. Actes du Colloque d'Istanbul 1987*, pp. 25–27. Paris: Institut français d'Études Anatoliennes.

Akurgal, Ekrem. 1955. *Phrygische Kunst*, Ankara: Archaeologisches Institut der Universität Ankara.

———. 1961. *Die Kunst Anatoliens: von Homer bis Alexander*, Berlin: W. de Gruyter.

———. 1962. *The Art of the Hittites*, trans. C. McNab, London: Thames & Hudson Ltd.

———. 1993. *Eski Çağda Ege ve İzmir.* İzmir: Yaşar Eğitim Kültür Vakfı.

Alexandrescu, Petre. 2005. *Histria VII. La zone sacrée d'époque grecque (fouilles 1915–1989).* Bucarest: Editura Enciclopedică.

Allen, Max. 1981. *The Birth Symbol in Traditional Women's Art from Eurasia and the Western Pacific.* Toronto, ON: Museum for Textiles.

Amandry, P. 1939. Rapport préliminaire sur les statues chryséléphantines de Delphes. *Bulletin de Correspondance Hellénique* 63:86–119.

———. 1944–45. Statuette d'ivoire d'un dompteur de lion, découverte à Delphes. *Syria* 24(3-4): 149–74.

———. 1977. Statue de taureau en argent. *Bulletin de Correspondance Hellénique. Supplément IV*:273–93.

———. 1991. Les fosses de l'Aire. In *Guide de Delphes: le Musée*, pp.191–226.

Anderson, Gunlög E. 1980. The Common Cemetery at Gordion. Ph.D. diss., Bryn Mawr College, Philadelphia.

Anderson, John K. 1961. *Ancient Greek Horsemanship.* Berkeley, CA: University of California Press.

———. 1985. *Hunting in the Ancient World.* Berkeley CA: University of California Press.

Andrae, Walter. 1961. *Lebenserrinerungen eines Ausgräbers.* Berlin: Walter de Gruyter.

———. 1977. *Das Wiedererstandene Assur.* 2nd ed. Munich: Beck.

Andrae, E.W., and Rainer M. Boehmer. 1992. *Bilder eines Ausgräbers / Sketches by an Excavator. Die Orientbilder von Walter Andrae 1898–1919.* Deutsches Archäologisches Institut, Abteilung Baghdad. Berlin: Gebr. Mann.

Arslan, Melih. 1989. Mama Deresi Frig Tümülüsü Kurtarma Kazısı/Rescue Excavation at the Phrygian Tumulus in Mama Creek. *Müze* 1:62–66.

Arslan, Murat. 2002. The Impact of Galatians in Asia Minor. *Olba* 6:41–55.

Asouti, Eleni. 2003a. Wood Charcoal from Santorini

(Thera): New Evidence for Climate, Vegetation and Timber Imports in the Aegean Bronze Age. *Antiquity* 77(297): 471–84.

———. 2003b. Woodland Vegetation and Fuel Exploitation at the Prehistoric Campsite of Pınarbaşı, South-Central Anatolia, Turkey: The Evidence from the Wood Charcoal Macro-Remains. *Journal of Archaeological Science* 30(9): 1185–201.

———. 2005. Woodland Vegetation and the Exploitation of Fuel and Timber at Neolithic Çatalhöyük: Report on the Wood Charcoal Macro-Remains. In *Inhabiting Çatalhöyük: Reports from the 1995–9 Seasons*, ed. I. Hodder, pp. 213–58. Cambridge: McDonald Institute for Archaeological Research and British Institute at Ankara.

Asouti, Eleni, and Jon Hather. 2001. Charcoal Analysis and the Reconstruction of Ancient Woodland Vegetation in the Konya Basin, South-Central Anatolia, Turkey: Results from the Neolithic Site of Catalhöyük East. *Vegetation History and Archaeobotany* 10(1): 23–32.

Asouti, Eleni, and Phil Austin. 2005. Reconstructing Woodland Vegetation and Its Exploitation by Past Societies, Based on the Analysis and Interpretation of Archaeological Wood Charcoal Macro-Fossils. *Environmental Archaeology* 10:1–18.

Ateşlier, Suat. 2006. Euromos Arkaik Mimari Terrakottaları Üzerine İlk Gözlemler (First Preliminary Report on the Archaic Architectural Terracottas from Euromos). *Arkeoloji Dergisi* 8:59–78.

Atila, Cenker. 2003. Daskyleion'da ele geçen arkaik ve klasik dönem amphoralar. Yüksek lisans thesis, Ege University, İzmir.

Avram, Alexandru. 1996. *Histria VIII, Les timbres amphoriques 1. Thasos*. Bucarest: Editura Enciclopedică.

Balabanov, Petar. 2006. "About the Origins of Englyphic Stamps." Paper presented at the First International Round Table. Production and Trade of Amphorae in the Black Sea, April 27–29, Batumi and Trabzon.

Ballard, Mary W., Harry Alden, Roland H. Cunningham, Walter Hopwood, Joseph Koles, and Laure Dussubieux. 2010. Appendix 8: Preliminary Analyses of Textiles Associated with the Wooden Furniture from Tumulus MM. In E. Simpson, *The Gordion Wooden Objects. Volume I: The Furniture from Tumulus MM,* pp. 203–223. Culture and

History of the Ancient Near East 32. Leiden: Brill.

Bammer, Anton, and Ulrike Muss. 1996. *Das Artemision von Ephesos. Das Weltwunder Ioniens in archaischer und klassischer Zeit*. Mainz: Philipp von Zabern.

Banoğlu, Niyazi A. 1958. *Turkey. A Sportsman's Paradise*. Ankara: Turkish Press, Broadcasting, and Tourism Department.

Barnett, Richard D. 1948. Early Greek and Oriental Ivories. *JHS* 68:1–25.

———. 1950. The Excavations of the British Museum at Toprak Kale near Van. *Iraq* 12.1:1–43.

———. 1954. The Excavations of the British Museum at Toprak Kale, near Van: Addenda. *Iraq* 16.1:3–22.

———. 1963–64. Review of Acquisitions 1955–1962 of Western Asiatic Antiquities (II). *British Museum Quarterly* 27 (3–4):79–88.

Baughan, Elizabeth P. 2004 Anatolian Funerary *Klinai*: Tradition and Identity. Ph.D. diss., University of California at Berkeley.

———. 2010. Lidya Gömü Gelenekleri/Lydian Burial Customs. In *Lidyalılar ve Dünyaları / The Lydians and Their World*, ed. N.D. Cahill, pp. 273–304. İstanbul: Yapı Kredi Yayınları.

Bellinger, Alfred R. 1968. Electrum Coins from Gordion. In *Essays in Greek Coinage Presented to Stanley Robinson*, eds. C. M. Kraay and G. K. Jenkins, pp. 10–15. Oxford: Clarendon Press.

Bellinger, Louisa. 1962. Textiles from Gordion. *Bulletin of the Needle and Bobbin Club* 46(1–2): 5–33.

Bennett, Julian, and Andrew L. Goldman. 2009. A Preliminary Report on the Roman Military Presence at Gordion, Galatia. *Limes XX. XXth Congreso Internacional de Estudios Sobre la Frontera Romana—XXth International Congress of Roman Frontier Studies, León (España), Septiembre, 2006,* ed. Á. Morillo, N. Hanel and E. Martín, 1:1605–16. Madrid: Ediciones Polifemo.

Berducou, Marie. 1996. Introduction to Archaeological Conservation. In *Historical and Philosophical Issues in the Conservation of Cultural Heritage*, ed. N.P. Stanley Price, M.K. Talley, Jr., and A.M. Vaccaro, pp. 248–59. Los Angeles, CA: Getty Conservation Institute.

Berndt, Dietrich. 2002. *Midasstadt in Phrygien: eine sagenumwobene Stätte im anatolischen Hochland*. Mainz: Philipp von Zabern.

Berndt-Ersöz, Susanne. 2006. *Phrygian Rock-Cut Shrines. Structure, Function, and Cult Practice.* Leiden: Brill.

———. 2008. The Chronology and Historical Context of Midas. *Historia* 57:1–37.

Bingöl, Orhan. 1997. *Malerei und Mosaik der Antike in der Türkei.* Kulturgeschichte der Antiken Welt 67. Mainz: Philipp von Zabern.

Bird, Douglas W., and James F. O'Connell. 2006. Behavioral Ecology and Archaeology. *Journal of Archaeological Research* 14(2): 143–88.

Bittel, Kurt, and Hans Gustav Güterbock. 1933. Vorläufiger Bericht über die dritte Grabung in Boğazköy. *Mitteilungen der deutschen Orient-Gesellschaft* 72:1–53.

Blanchette, Robert A. 2010. Appendix 4: Assessment of Wood Deterioration in the Furniture and Coffin from Tumulus MM. In E. Simpson, *The Gordion Wooden Objects. Volume 1: The Furniture from Tumulus MM,* pp. 171–76. Culture and History of the Ancient Near East 32. Leiden: Brill.

Blanchette, Robert A., Benjamin Held, and Burhan Aytuğ. 2010. Appendix 3: Wood Species Analysis. In E. Simpson, *The Gordion Wooden Objects. Volume 1: The Furniture from Tumulus MM,* pp. 165–70. Culture and History of the Ancient Near East 32. Leiden: Brill.

Blanchette, Robert A., and Elizabeth Simpson. 1992. Soft Rot and Wood Pseudomorphs in an Ancient Coffin (700 B.C.) from Tumulus MM at Gordion, Turkey. *Journal of International Association of Wood Anatomists* 13(2): 201–13.

Blanchette, Robert A., Kory R. Cease, André R. Abad, Robert J. Koestler, Elizabeth Simpson, and G. Kenneth Sams. 1991 An Evaluation of Different Forms of Deterioration Found in Archaeological Wood. *International Biodeterioration* 28:3–22.

Blinkenberg, Christian. 1926. *Fibules Grecques et Orientales.* Copenhagen: Andr. Fred. Høst.

Boardman, John. 1961–62. Ionian Bronze Belts. *Anatolia* 6:179–89.

———. 1967. *Excavations in Chios 1952–1955. Greek Emporio. BSA* Suppl. 6. Oxford: Thames & Hudson.

———. 1978. *Greek Sculpture: The Archaic Period, a Handbook.* New York: Thames & Hudson.

———. 1980. *The Greeks Overseas. Their Early Colonies and Trade.* London: Thames & Hudson.

Boardman, John, and Donna C. Kurtz. 1971. *Greek Burial Customs.* London: Thames & Hudson.

Boehlau, Johannes, and K. Schefold, eds. 1940–42. *Die Bauten. Larisa am Hermos. Die Ergebnisse der Ausgrabungen 1902–1934.* 3 vols. Berlin: Walter De Gruyter.

Boehlau, Johannes, and Edward Habich. 1996. *Samos—die Kasseler Grabungen 1894 in der Nekropole der archaischen Stadt.* Kassel: Staatliche Museen Kassel.

Boehmer, Rainer M. 1972. *Die Kleinfunde von Boğazköy.* Wissenschaftliche Veröffentlichungen der Deutschen Orient-Gesellschaft 87. Berlin: Gebr. Mann.

———. 1979. *Die Kleinfunde aus der Unterstadt von Boğazköy.* Boğazköy–Hattusa. Ergebnisse der Ausgrabungen 10. Berlin: Gebr. Mann.

Bommelaer, Jean-François. 1991. *Guide de Delphes: le site.* Paris: École française d'Athènes.

Bon, Anna-Maria, and Antoine Bon. 1957. Les timbres amphoriques de Thasos. *Études thasiennes 4.* Paris: École française d'Athènes.

Bonias, Zisis, and Jacques Y. Perrault. 1996[1997]. Ἄργιλος, πέντε χρόνια ανασκαφής. *ΑΕΜΘ* 10B:663–80.

Bossert, Eva-Maria. 2000. *Die Keramik phrygischer Zeit von Boğazköy.* Boğazköy-Hattuša. Ergebnisse der Ausgrabungen 18: Mainz: Philipp von Zabern.

Bottema, Sytze, and Henk Woldring. 1990. Anthropogenic Indicators in the Pollen Record of the Eastern Mediterranean. In *Man's Role in Shaping of the Eastern Mediterranean Landscape*, ed. S. Bottema, G. Entjes-Nieborg, and W. van Zeist, pp. 231–64. Rotterdam: Balkema.

Boyer, Peter, Neil Roberts, and Douglas Baird. 2006. Holocene Environment and Settlement on the Çarşamba Alluvial Fan, South-Central Turkey: Integrating Geoarchaeology and Archaeological Field Survey. *Geoarchaeology* 21:7.

Brantingham, P. Jeffrey. 2003. A Neutral Model of Stone Raw Material Procurement. *American Antiquity* 68(3): 487–509.

Briant, Pierre. 2002. *From Cyrus to Alexander: A History of the Persian Empire,* trans. P. Daniels. Winona Lake, IN: Eisenbrauns.

Brill, Robert H., and Nicholas D. Cahill. 1988. A Red Opaque Glass from Sardis and Some Thoughts on Red Opaques in General. *Journal of Glass Studies* 30:16–27.

Brixhe, Claude. 1979. Le Nom de Cybèle. *Die Sprache* 25:40–45.

Brixhe, Claude, and Michel Lejeune. 1984. *Corpus des inscriptions paléo-phrygiennes.* Mémoire 45. Paris: Editions Recherche sur les Civilisations.

Brown, John P. 1969. *The Lebanon and Phoenicia. Ancient Texts Illustrating Their Physical Geography and Native Industries.* Vol. I, *The Physical Setting and the Forest.* Beirut: American University of Beirut Press.

Bruce, I.A.F. 1967. *An Historical Commentary on the Hellenica Oxyrhynchia.* Cambridge: Cambridge University Press.

Bryce, Trevor. 2005. *The Kingdom of the Hittites.* Oxford: Oxford University Press.

Buluç, Sevim. 1988. The Architectural Use of the Animal and Kybele Reliefs Found in Ankara and Its Vicinity. *Source: Notes in the History of Art* 7(3-4): 16–23.

Bunimovitz, S. 1992. The Middle Bronze Age Fortifications in Palestine as a Social Phenomenon. *Tel Aviv* 19:221–34.

Burke, Brendan. 2005. Textile Production at Gordion and the Phrygian Economy. In *The Archaeology of Midas and the Phrygians: Recent Work at Gordion*, ed. L. Kealhofer, pp. 69–81. Philadelphia, PA: University of Pennsylvania Museum of Archaeology and Anthropology.

de Busbecq, Ogier G. 1927. *The Turkish Letters of Ogier Ghiselin de Busbecq, Imperial Ambassador at Constantinopole*, trans. E.S. Foster. Oxford: Clarendon Press.

Butler, Howard C. 1922. *Sardis I. The Excavations, Part I, 1910–1914.* Leiden: Brill.

Buzoianu, Livia. 1999. Types d'amphores hellénistiques découvertes à Callatis. In *Production et commerce des amphores anciennes en Mer Noire*, ed. Y. Garlan, pp. 201–14. Aix-en-Provence: Publications de l'Université de Provence.

Bylkova, Valeria P. 2004. The Chronology of Settlements in the Lower Dniepr Region (400–100 BC). In *Chronologies of the Black Sea Area in the Period c. 400–100 BC*, ed. V.F. Stolba and L. Hannestad, pp. 27–247. Aarhus: Aarhus University Press.

Cahill, Nicholas D. 2002. Lydian Houses, Domestic Assemblages, and Household Size. In *Across the Anatolian Plateau. Readings in the Archaeology of Ancient Turkey*, ed. D.C. Hopkins, pp. 173–79. Boston, MA: American Schools of Oriental Research.

———. 2008. Mapping Sardis. In *Love for Lydia. A Sardis Anniversary Volume Presented to Crawford H. Greenwalt, Jr.*, ed. N.D. Cahill. pp. 111–24. Sardis Report 4. Cambridge, MA: Archaeological Exploration of Sardis.

———, ed. 2010. *Lidyalılar ve Dünyaları / The Lydians and Their World.* İstanbul: Yapı Kredi Yayınları.

Cahill, Nicholas D., and John H. Kroll. 2005. New Archaic Coin Finds at Sardis. *American Journal of Archaeology* 109:589–617.

Callaghan, Peter. 1992. Archaic to Hellenistic Pottery. In *Knossos: From Greek City to Roman Colony*, ed. L.H. Sackett, pp. 89–136. *BSA* Supplement 21. Athens: British School of Archaeology at Athens.

Canby, Jeanny V. 2002. Falconry (Hawking) in Hittite Lands. *Journal of Ancient Near Eastern Studies* 61:161–80.

Caner, Ertuğrul. 1983. *Fibeln in Anatolien* I. Prähistorische Bronzefunde Bd. 14.8. Munich: Beck.

Cardon, Dominique. 2007. *Natural Dyes: Sources, Tradition, Technology and Science.* London: Archetype.

Carlson, Deborah N. 2004. Cargo in Context: The Morphology, Stamping, and Origins of the Amphoras from a Fifth-century BC Ionian Shipwreck. Ph.D. diss., University of Texas, Austin.

Carlson, Deborah N., and Mark L. Lawall. 2005–2006[2007]. Towards a Typology of Erythraian Amphoras. *Skyllis* 7:32–39.

Carter, Jane B. 1985. *Greek Ivory-Carving in the Orientalizing and Archaic Periods.* New York: Garland.

Chabal, L. 1992. La Représentativité Paléo-Écologique des Charbons de Bois Archéologiques Issus du Bois de Feu. *Bulletin de la Société Botanique de France* 139:213–36.

Chen, Hsiou-lien, Kathryn A. Jakes, and Dennis W. Foreman. 1998. Preservation of Archaeological Textiles Through Fibre Mineralization. *Journal of Archaeological Science* 25:1015–21.

Çilingiroğlu, Altan, and Mirjo Salvini, eds. 2001. *Ayanis I. Ten Years' Excavations at Rusahinili Eidurukai 1989–1998.* Documenta Asiana VI. Rome:

Istituto per gli Studi Micenei ed Egeo-Anatolici.

CLAS. *Central Lydia Archaeological Survey*, directed by Christopher H. Roosevelt and Christina Luke. Online at: http://www.bu.edu/clas/welcome/ (verified December 24, 2009).

Clinkenbeard, Barbara G. 1982. Lesbian Wine and Storage Amphoras: A Progress Report on Identification. *Hesperia* 51:248–67.

Coldstream, John N., and Hector W. Catling. 1996a. *Knossos North Cemetery Early Greek Tombs.* Vol. I, *Tombs and Catalogue of Finds. BSA* Suppl. 28. London: British School of Archaeology at Athens.

———. 1996b. *Knossos North Cemetery Early Greek Tombs.* Vol. II, *Discussion. BSA* Suppl. 28. London: British School of Archaeology at Athens.

Colour Index, 3rd edition, 1971. Bradford: The Society of Dyers and Colourists.

Condurachi, Emil, ed. 1966. *Histria II.* Bucarest: Editura Academiei Republicii Socialiste România.

Cox, Dorothy H. 1953. *A Third Century Hoard of Tetradrachms from Gordion.* Philadelphia, PA: The University Museum, University of Pennsylvania of Archaeology and Anthropology.

———. 1966. Gordion Hoards III, IV, V, and VII. *American Numismatic Society Museum Notes* 7:19–55.

Crowfoot, John W., and Grace M. Crowfoot. 1938. *Early Ivories from Samaria.* Samaria-Sebaste 2. London: Palestine Exploration Fund.

Cummer, Wilson W. 1969. "Gordion Architect's Notes for 1969." Unpublished document in Gordion Archive, University of Pennsylvania Museum of Archaeology and Anthropology, Philadelphia.

———. 1973. "Gordion: Architect's Report—1973." Unpublished document in Gordion Archive, University of Pennsylvania Museum of Archaeology and Anthropology, Philadelphia.

Curtis, C. Densmore. 1925. *Jewelry and Gold Work, Part I: 1910–1914.* Sardis XIII. Rome: Sindacato Italiano Arti Grafiche.

Dandoy, Jeremiah R., Paige Selinsky, and Mary M. Voigt. 2002. Celtic Sacrifice. *Archaeology* 55(1): 44–49.

Darbyshire, Gareth. 2007. Keith DeVries. *Expedition* 49(2):6.

Darbyshire, Gareth, and Gabriel H. Pizzorno. 2009a.

Gordion in History. *Expedition* 51(2): 11–22.

———. 2009b. Building Digital Gordion. *Expedition* 51(2): 23–30.

Darbyshire, Gareth, Steven Mitchell, and Levent Vardar. 2000. The Galatian Settlement in Asia Minor. *Anatolian Studies* 50:75–97.

Daux, Georges, and Antoine Salač. 1932. *Inscriptions depuis le Trésor des Athéniens jusqu'aux bases de Gélon.* Fouilles de Delphes 3.3. Paris: École française d'Athènes.

Debidour, Michel. 1986. En classant les timbres thasiens. In *Recherches sur les amphores grecques*, ed. J.-Y. Empereur and Y. Garlan, pp. 311–34. *BCH* Suppl.8, Athens: École française d'Athènes.

———. 1999. *Kleitos*, un magistrat thasien attesté sur les rives de la mer Noire. In *Production et commerce des amphores anciennes en Mer Noire*, ed. Y. Garlan, pp. 81–89. Aix-en-Provence: Publications de l'Université de Provence.

Dedeoğlu, Hasan. 2003. *The Lydians and Sardis.* Istanbul: A Turizm Yayınları.

Demargne, Pierre 1964. *The Birth of Greek Art*, trans. S. Gilbert and J. Emmons. New York: Golden Press.

De Marinis, Raffaele C. 1999 Anfore chiote dal Forcello di Bagnolo S. Vito (Mantova). In *KOINA. Miscellanea di studi archeologici in onore di Piero Orlandini,* ed. M. Castoldi, pp. 255–78. Milan: Edizioni ET.

Demas, Martha. 2000. Planning for Conservation and Management of Archaeological Sites: A Values-Based Approach. In *Management Planning for Archaeological Sites,* ed. Jeanne Marie Teutonico and Gaetano Palumbo, pp. 27–52. Los Angeles, CA: Getty Conservation Institute.

Deshmukh, Prema. 2002. Museum Mosaic: People, Places, Projects. *Expedition* 44(1): 46.

DeVries, Keith. 1980a. Greeks and Phrygians in the Early Iron Age. In *From Athens to Gordion: The Papers of a Memorial Symposium for Rodney S. Young,* ed. K. DeVries, pp. 33–50. Philadelphia, PA: The University Museum, University of Pennsylvania.

———. 1980b. Rodney Stuart Young, 1907–1974. In *From Athens to Gordion. The Papers of a Memorial Symposium for Rodney S. Young,* ed. K. DeVries, pp. xv–xvii. Philadelphia, PA: The University Museum, University of Pennsylvania.

———. 1986. Gordion 1984. *Araştırma Sonuçları Toplantısı* 3(1985): 261–66.

———. 1987a. Gordion Work 1985. *Araştırma Sonuçları Toplantısı* 4(1986): 203–6.

———. 1987b. Phrygian Gordion before Midas. In *Anatolian Iron Ages: The Proceedings of the Second Anatolian Iron Ages Colloquium Held at İzmir, 4–8 May 1987*, ed. A. Çilingiroğlu and D.H. French, pp. 6–12. Oxford: Oxbow.

———. 1988a. Gordion 1986. *Araştırma Sonuçları Toplantısı* 5(1) (1987):4 23–26.

———. 1988b. Gordion and Phrygia in the Sixth Century B.C. In *Phrygian Art and Archaeology*, ed. O. Muscarella. Special issue of *Source: Notes in the History of Art* 7(3/4): 51–59.

———. 1990. The Gordion Excavation Seasons of 1969–1973 and Subsequent Research. *AJA* 94:371–406.

———. 1996. The Attic Pottery from Gordion. In *Athenian Potters and Painters*, ed. J.H. Oakley, W. D. E. Coulson, and O. Palagia, pp. 447–55. Oxford: Oxbow.

———. 1997. The Attic Pottery from Gordion. In *Athenian Potters and Painters, the Conference Proceedings*, ed. John H. Oakley, William D.E. Coulson, and Olga Palagia, pp. 447–55. Oxford: Oxbrow Books.

———. 2002. The Throne of Midas? Paper presented at the Annual Meeting of the Archaeological Institute of America, 3–6 January, Philadelphia.

———. 2005. Greek Pottery and Gordion Chronology. In *The Archaeology of Midas and the Phrygians: Recent Work at Gordion*, ed. L. Kealhofer, pp. 36–55. Philadelphia, PA: University of Pennsylvania Museum of Archaeology and Anthropology.

———. 2007. The Date of the Destruction Level at Gordion: Imports and the Local Sequence. In *Anatolian Iron Ages 6: Proceedings of the Sixth Anatolian Iron Ages Colloquium Held at Eskişehir, 16–20 August 2004*, ed. A. Çilingiroğlu and A. Sagona, pp. 79–102. Ancient Near Eastern Studies Supplement Series 20. Leuven: Peeters.

———. 2008. The Age of Midas at Gordion and Beyond. *Ancient Near Eastern Studies* 45:30–64.

———. 2011. The Creation of the Old Chronology. In *The New Chronology of Iron Age Gordion,* ed. C. Brian Rose and Gareth Darbyshire, pp. 13–22.

Philadelphia: University of Pennsylvania Museum of Archaeology and Anthropology.

DeVries, Keith, Peter I. Kuniholm, G. Kenneth Sams, and Mary M. Voigt. 2003. New Dates for Iron Age Gordion. *Antiquity* 77 (29) (http://antiquity.ac.uk/ProjGall/devries/devries.html).

Diehl, Michael W., and Jennifer A. Waters. 2006. Aspects of Optimization and Risk in the Early Agricultural Period in Southeastern Arizona. In *Behavioral Ecology and the Transition to Agriculture*, ed. D.J. Kennett and B. Winterhalder, pp. 63–86. Berkeley, CA: University of California Press.

Donder, Helga. 1980. *Zaumzeug in Griechenland und Cypern*. Prähistorische Bronzefunde 16.3. Munich: Beck.

———. 2002. Funde aus Milet. XI. Die Metallfunde. *Archäologische Anzeiger* 1:1–8.

Doulgéri-Intzessiloglou, Argyroula, and Yvon Garlan. 1991. Vin et amphores de Péparéthos et d'Ikos. *Bulletin de correspondance hellénique* 114:361–89.

Draycott, Catherine, and Geoffrey Summers. 2008. *Sculpture and Inscriptions from the Monumental Entrance to the Palatial Complex at Kerkenes Dağ, Turkey*. Chicago: The Oriental Institute at the University of Chicago.

Dupont, Pierre. 1998. Archaic East Greek Trade Amphoras. In *East Greek Pottery*, ed. Robert M. Cook and Pierre Dupont, pp. 142–92. London: Routledge.

———. 2005. Archaic Greek Amphoras from Berezan in the Hermitage Collection. In *Borisfen—Berezan': Arkheologicheskaia kollektsiia Ermitazha*, ed. S.L. Solovyov, pp. 41–69. St. Petersburg: Hermitage State Museum.

Dupré, Sylvestre 1983. *Porsuk I: la céramique de l'âge du bronze et de l'âge du fer*. Paris: Institut français d'Études Anatoliennes.

Dusinberre, Elspeth R.M. 2003. *Aspects of Empire in Achaemenid Sardis*. Cambridge: Cambridge University Press.

———. 2005. *Gordion Seals and Sealings: Individuals and Society*. Gordion Special Studies III. Philadelphia, PA: University of Pennsylvania Museum of Archaeology and Anthropology.

———. 2008. Circles of Light and Achaemenid Hegemonic Style in Gordion's Seal 100. In *Love for*

Lydia: A Sardis Anniversary Volume Presented to Crawford H. Greenewalt, Jr., ed. N.D. Cahill, pp. 87–98. Cambridge, MA: Harvard University Press.

Dussubieux, Laure, and Mary Ballard. 2005. Using ICP-MS to Detect Inorganic Elements in Organic Materials: A New Tool to Identify Mordant or Dyes on Ancient Textiles. *Materials Issues in Art and Archaeology VII*, ed. P.B. Vandiver et al. pp. 291–96. Warrendale, PA: Materials Research Society.

Dyson, Robert H., Jr. 1989. East of Assyria: The Highland Settlement of Hasanlu. *Expedition* 31(2-3), special issue.

Ebbinghaus, Susanne. 2006. Begegnungen mit Ägypten und Vorderasien im archaischen Heraheiligtum von Samos. In *Stranieri e non cittadini nei santuari greci. Atti del convegno internationale*, ed. A. Naso, pp. 187–225. Udine: Le Monnier Università.

Edwards, G. Roger. 1958. Letter to R.S. Young, July 8, 1958. Unpublished document in Gordion Archive, University of Pennsylvania Museum of Archaeology and Anthropology, Philadelphia.

———. 1959. Gordion Campaign of 1958: Preliminary Report. *AJA* 63:263–68.

———. 1963. Gordion: 1962. *Expedition* 5(3): 42–48.

———. 1980. Postscript. In *From Athens to Gordion: The Papers of a Memorial Symposium for Rodney S. Young*, ed. K. DeVries, pp. 159–61. Philadelphia, PA: The University Museum, University of Pennsylvania.

———. 1984. Letter to R.H. Dyson, Jr., December 17, 1984. Unpublished document in Gordion Archive, University of Pennsylvania Museum of Archaeology and Anthropology, Philadelphia.

Ellis, Richard. 1981. Appendix V: Textiles: The Textile Remains. In Rodney S. Young, *Three Great Early Tumuli*, pp. 294–310, pls. 99–101. The Gordion Excavations Final Reports Volume 1. Philadelphia, PA: The University Museum, University of Pennsylvania.

Epstein, Hans J. 1943. The Origin and Earliest History of Falconry. *Isis* 34(6):497–509.

Ersoy, Yaşar E. 1993. Clazomenae: The Archaic Settlement. Ph.D. diss., Bryn Mawr College, Bryn Mawr, PA.

Fedoseev, Nikoklai F. 1999. Classification des timbres astynomiques de Sinope. In *Production et commerce des amphores anciennes en Mer Noire*, ed. Y. Garlan, pp. 27–47. Aix-en-Provence: Publications de l'Université de Provence.

———. 2004. O keramicheskikh kleymakh, "sravnitel'nikh obyemakh importa" i poselenii "Baklaniya Skala." *Drevnosti Bospora* 7:366–403.

Filley, Timothy R., Robert A. Blanchette, Elizabeth Simpson, and Marilyn L. Fogel. 2001. Nitrogen Cycling by Wood Decomposing Soft-rot Fungi in the "King Midas Tomb," Gordion, Turkey. *Proceedings of the National Academy of Sciences of the United States of America* 98 (23): 13346–50.

Finkelstein, I. 1992. Middle Bronze Age 'Fortifications': A Reflection of Social Organization and Political Formations. In *Tel Aviv* 19:201–20.

Fırıncıoğlu, Hüseyin K., Steven S. Seefeldt, and Bilal Şahin. 2007. The Effects of Long-Term Grazing Exclosures on Range Plants in the Central Anatolian Region of Turkey. *Environmental Management* 39:326–37.

Fırıncıoğlu, Hüseyin K., Steven S. Seefeldt, Bilal Şahin, and Mecit Vural. 2009. Assessment of Grazing Effect on Sheep Fescue (*Festuca valesiaca*) Dominated Steppe Rangelands, in the Semiarid Central Anatolian Region of Turkey. *Journal of Arid Environments* 73:1149–57.

Foley, K. 1995. The Role of the Objects Conservator in Field Archaeology. In *Conservation on Archaeological Excavations,* ed. N.P. Stanley-Price, pp. 11–19. Rome: ICCROM.

Foley, R.L. 1985. Optimality Theory. *Anthropology.* Man 20:222–42.

Ford, Richard I. 1979. Paleoethnobotany in American Archaeology. *Advances in Archaeological Method and Theory* 2:285–336.

Garlan, Yvon. 1989. Le comblement d'un puits public à Thasos. 2, Les timbres céramique. *Bulletin de correspondance hellenique* 113:477–80.

———. 1999. *Les timbres amphoriques de Thasos. 1, Timbres protothasiens et thasiens anciens.* Études thasiennes 18. Athènes: École française d'Athènes.

———. 2004–05. En visitant et revisitant les ateliers amphoriques de Thasos. *Bulletin de correspondance hellenique* 128-129:269–329.

Garlan, Yvon, and Hikmet Kara. 2004. *Les timbres céramiques sinopéens sur amphores et sur tuiles trouvés à Sinope: Présentation et catalogue.* Varia Anatolica 16. İstanbul: Institut français d'études Anatoliennes.

Gates, Charles. 1983. *From Cremation to Inhumation: Burial Practises at Ialysos and Kameiros during the Mid-Archaic Period, ca. 625–525 B.C.* Occasional Paper 11. Los Angeles, CA: UCLA Institute of Archaeology.

Gates, Marie-Henriette. 1996. Archaeology in Turkey. *AJA* 100:277–335.

Gaukroger, Sean. 1995. "1995 Field Note Summary." Unpublished document in Gordion Archive, University of Pennsylvania Museum of Archaeology and Anthropology, Philadelphia.

———. 1996. "Survey Note Book/Planner." Unpublished document in Gordion Archive, University of Pennsylvania Museum of Archaeology and Anthropology, Philadelphia.

———. 1997. "Survey Field Notes 1997." Unpublished document in Gordion Archive, University of Pennsylvania Museum of Archaeology and Anthropology, Philadelphia.

Gauthier, Philippe. 1989. *Archaeological Exploration of Sardis. Nouvelles Inscriptions de Sardes II.* Centre de Recherche d'Histoire et de Philologie de la IVe Section de l'École pratique des Hautes Études, III. Hautes Études du Monde Gréco-Romain 15. Geneva: Droz.

Genz, Hermann. 2003. The Early Iron Age in Anatolia. In *Identifying Changes: The Transition from Bronze to Iron Ages in Anatolia and Its Neighboring Regions*, ed. B. Fischer, H. Genz, E. Jean, and K. Köroğlu, pp. 179–91. İstanbul : Türk Eskiçağ Bilimleri Enstitüsü.

Georgopoulou, Viktoria. 2001. Κωακοί αμφορείς από την Καρδάμαινα (αρχαία Αλάσαρνα) της Κω. In *Ιστορία–Τέχνη–Αρχαιολογία της Κω. Α΄ διεθνές επιστημονικό συνέδριο*, ed. G. Kokkorou-Alevra, A. A. Laimou, and E. Simantoni-Bournia, pp. 107–14. Athens: Archaiognosia.

Giesen, Katharina. 2001. *Zyprische Fibeln. Typologie und Chronologie.* Jonsered: Paul Astroms.

Giles, Charles Hugh. 1974. *A Laboratory Course in Dyeing.* 3rd ed. Bradford: Society of Dyers and Colourists.

Gjerstad, Einar. 1948. *The Swedish Cyprus Expedition: Part 2.* Stockholm: The Swedish Cyprus Expedition.

Glendinning, Matthew. 1996. Phrygian Architectural Terracottas at Gordion. Ph.D. diss., University of North Carolina at Chapel Hill.

———. 2005. A Decorated Roof at Gordon: What Tiles are Revealing about the Phrygian Past. In *The Archaeology of Midas and the Phrygians. Recent Work at Gordion*, ed. L. Kealhofer, pp. 82–100. Philadelphia, PA: University of Pennsylvania Museum of Archaeology and Anthropology.

Godwin, H., and A.G. Tansley. 1941. Prehistoric Charcoals as Evidence of Former Vegetation, Soil and Climate. *Journal of Ecology* 29:117–26.

Goldman, Andrew L. 2000. The Roman-Period Settlement at Gordion, Turkey. Ph.D. diss., University of North Carolina, Chapel Hill.

Goldman, Hetty. 1956. *Excavations at Gözlü Kule, Tarsus.* Princeton, NJ: Princeton University Press.

Grace, Virginia R. 1956. Stamped Wine Jar Fragments. In *Small Objects from the Pnyx II*, pp. 117–89. *Hesperia* Suppl. 10. Baltimore, MD: American School of Classical Studies at Athens.

———. 1963. Notes on the Amphoras from the Koroni Peninsula. *Hesperia* 32:319–34.

———. 1971. Samian Amphoras. *Hesperia* 40:52–95.

Grayson, A.K. 1991. Assyria: Tiglath-Pileser III to Sargon II (744–705 B.C.). In *The Cambridge Ancient History, Vol. 3, Part 2: The Assyrian and Babylonian Empires and Other States of the Near East, from the Eighth to the Sixth Centuries B.C.*, ed. John Boardman, I.E.S. Edwards, N.G.L. Hammond, E. Solberger, and C.B.F. Walker, pp. 71–102. Cambridge: Cambridge University Press.

Greenewalt, Crawford H., Jr. 1966. Lydian Pottery of the Sixth Century B.C.: The Lydian and Marbled Ware. Ph.D. diss., University of Pennsylvania, Philadelphia.

———. 1972. Two Lydian Graves at Sardis. *California Studies in Classical Antiquity* 5:113–45.

———. 1978. *Ritual Dinners in Early Historic Sardis.* Berkeley, CA: University of California Classical Studies.

———. 1986. Sardis: Archaeological Research in 1984. *Kazı Sonuçları Toplantısı* 7(1985): 299–310.

———. 1987. Sardis: Archaeological Research in 1985. *Kazı Sonuçları Toplantısı* 8.1(1986): 381–99.

———. 1988. Sardis: Archaeological Research in 1986. *Kazı Sonuçları Toplantısı* 9.2(1987): 41–

58.

———. 2006. Sardis. In *Stadtgrabungen und Stadtforschung im westlichen Kleinasien: Geplantes und Erreichtes*, ed. W. Radt, pp. 359–72. Byzas 3. İstanbul: Ege Yayınları.

———. 2010a. Atçılık/Horsemanship. In *Lidyalılar ve Dünyaları/The Lydians and Their World*, ed. N.D. Cahill, pp. 217–23. İstanbul: Yapı Kredi Yayınları.

———. 2010b. Lydia Kozmetiği/Lydian Cosmetics. In *Lidyalılar ve Dünyaları/The Lydians and Their World*, ed. N.D. Cahill, pp. 201–16. İstanbul: Yapı Kredi Yayınları.

———. 2010c. Afiyet olsun!/Bon Appetit! In *Lidyalılar ve Dünyaları/The Lydians and Their World*, ed. N.D. Cahill, pp. 125–33. İstanbul: Yapı Kredi Yayınları.

Greenewalt, Crawford H., Jr., Christopher Ratté, and Marcus L. Rautman. 1993. The Sardis Campaigns of 1998 and 1999. *Annual of the American Schools of Oriental Research* 51:1-43.

———. 1995. The Sardis Campaigns of 1992 and 1993. *Annual of the American Schools of Oriental Research* 53:1–36.

Greenewalt, Crawford H., Jr., Donald G. Sullivan, Christopher Ratté, and Thomas N. Howe. 1985. The Sardis Campaigns of 1981 and 1982. *BASOR*, Suppl. 23:53–92.

Greenewalt, Crawford H., Jr., Nicholas D. Cahill, Hasan Dedeoğlu, and Peter Herrmann. 1990. The Sardis Campaign of 1986. *BASOR,* Suppl. 26:137–77.

Greenewalt, Crawford H., Jr., Nicholas D. Cahill, P.T. Stinson, and F.K. Yegül. 2003. *The City of Sardis. Approaches in Graphic Recording.* Cambridge, MA: Harvard University Art Museums.

Gremillion, Kristen J. 1996. Diffusion and Adoption of Crops in Evolutionary Perspective. *Journal of Anthropological Archaeology* 15(2): 183–204.

Gunter, Ann C. 1991. *The Bronze Age.* The Gordion Excavations Final Reports Vol. 3. Philadelphia, PA: University of Pennsylvania Museum of Archaeology and Anthropology.

Gürsan-Salzmann, Ayşe. 2001. The Women of Yassıhöyük, Turkey: Changing Roles in a New Economy. *Expedition* 43(3): 19–28.

———. 2005. Ethnographic Lessons for Past Agro-Pastoral Systems in the Sakarya-Porsuk Valleys. In *The Archaeology of Midas and the Phrygians: Recent Work at Gordion*, ed. L. Kealhofer, pp. 172–89. Philadelphia, PA: University of Pennsylvania Museum of Archaeology and Anthropology.

Gusmani, Roberto. 1964. *Lydisches Wörterbuch*. Heidelberg: Carl Winter–Universitätsverlag.

———. 1980. *Lydisches Wörterbuch*. Heidelberg: Carl Winter–Universitätsverlag.

Güterbock, Hans. 1946. *Ankara Bedesteninde Bulunan Eti Müzesi Büyük Salonunun Kılavuzu: Guide to the Hittite Museum in the Bedesten at Ankara,* trans. Nimet Özgüç. İstanbul: Milli Eğitim Basimevi.

Hanfmann, George M.A. 1961. The Third Campaign at Sardis (1960). *BASOR* 162:8–49.

———. 1965. The Seventh Campaign at Sardis (1964). *BASOR* 177:2–37.

———. 1977. On the Palace of Croesus. In *Festschrift für Frank Brommer*, ed. U. Höckmann and A. Krug, pp. 1445–54. Mainz: Philipp von Zabern.

———. 1980. On Lydian Sardis. In *From Athens to Gordion: The Papers of a Memorial Symposium for Rodney S. Young*, ed. Keith DeVries, pp. 99–131. Philadelphia: The University Museum, University of Pennsylvania.

Hanfmann, George M.A., and Nancy H. Ramage. 1978. *Sculpture from Sardis: The Finds Through 1975.* Sardis Report 2. Cambridge: Harvard University Press.

Hansen, Donald P. 1998. Art of the Royal Tombs of Ur: A Brief Interpretation. In *Treasures from the Royal Tombs of Ur*, ed. Richard Zettler and Lee Horne, pp. 43–72. Philadelphia: University of Pennsylvania Museum of Archaeology and Anthropology.

Hansen, Ove. 1989 On the Dedication of the Athenian Stoa at Delphi. *Classica et Mediaevalia* 40:133–34.

Haspels, C.H.E. 1971. *The Highlands of Phrygia*. Princeton, NJ: Princeton University Press.

Hawkins, J.D. 1994. Mita. *Reallexicon der Assyriologie* 8:271–73.

———. 2000. *Corpus of Hieroglyphic Luwian Inscriptions*. Vol. 1, *Inscriptions of the Iron Age*. Berlin: Walter de Gruyter.

Hawkins, Shane H. 2004. Studies in the Language of Hipponax. Ph.D. diss., University of North Carolina at Chapel Hill.

Henrickson, Robert C., Pamela B. Vandiver, and M. James Blackman. 2002. Lustrous Black Fine Ware at Gordion, Turkey: A Distinctive Sintered Slip Technology. *Materials Issues in Art and Archaeology* 4:391–400. Pittsburgh, PA: Materials Research Society, Pittsburgh.

Henrickson, Robert C., and Mary M. Voigt. 1998. The Early Iron Age at Gordion: The Evidence from the Yassıhöyük Stratigraphic Sequence. In *Thracians and Phrygians: Problems of Parallelism. Proceedings of an International Symposium on the Archaeology, History and Ancient Languages of Thrace and Phrygia, Ankara, 3-4 June 1995*, ed. N. Tuna, Z. Aktüre, and M. Lynch, pp. 79–106. Ankara: Middle East Technical University.

Hoffner, Harry A., Jr. 1974. *Alimenta Hethaeorum. Food Production in Hittite Asia Minor.* American Oriental Series, 55. New Haven, CT: American Oriental Society.

Hostetter, Eric. 1994. *Lydian Architectural Terracottas.* Illinois Classical Studies Suppl. 5. Atlanta, GA: Scholars Press.

Houghton, Arthur, and Catherine Lorbeer. 2002. *Seleucid Coins. A Comprehensive Catalogue. Part I, Seleucus I through Antiochus III.* New York: American Numismatic Society.

Hueber, F., and E. Riorden. 1994. Plan von Troia 1994 and Troia. Freilegende Ruinen und Besucherwege 1994. *Studia Troica* 4:115–20.

Hurwit, Jeffrey M. 1985. *The Art and Culture of Early Greece, 1100–480 B.C.* Ithaca: Cornell University Press.

Işık, F. 2001. Elfenbeinfiguren aus dem Artemision von Ephesos. In *Der Kosmos der Artemis von Ephesos*, ed. U. Muss, pp. 85–100. Vienna: Österreichisches Archäologisches Institut.

Ivantchik, A.I. 2001. The Current State of the Cimmerian Problem. *Ancient Civilizations from Scythia to Siberia* 7:307–39.

Jablonka, Peter. 2006. Leben ausserhalb der Burg—Die Unterstadt von Troia. In *Troia. Archäologie eines Siedlungshügels und seiner Landschaft*, ed. Manfred Korfmann, pp. 167–80. Mainz: Philipp von Zabern.

Jacopi, Giulio. 1931. *Esplorazione Archeologica di Camiro.* Vol. 1, *Scavi nelle Necropoli Camiresi.* Clara Rhodos 4. Rhodes: Istituto Storico Archeologico.

Jakes, Kathryn A., and John H. Howard III. 1986. Formation of Textile Fabric Pseudomorphs. *Proceedings of the 24th International Archaeometry Symposium*, ed. Jacqueline S. Olin and Marion James Blackman, pp. 165–77. Washington, DC: Smithsonian Institution Press.

Jantzen, Ulf. 1972. *Ägyptische und orientalische Bronzen aus dem Heraion von Samos.* Samos 8. Bonn: Meier-Arendt.

Johnston, Alan W., and Richard E. Jones. 1978. The "SOS" Amphora. *BSA* 73:103–41.

Jones, Janet D. 2005. Glass Vessels from Gordion. Trade and Influence along the Royal Road. In *The Archaeology of Midas and the Phrygians: Recent Work at Gordion*, ed. L. Kealhofer, pp. 101–16. Philadelphia, PA: University of Pennsylvania Museum of Archaeology and Anthropology.

Kac, Vladimir I. 2003. A New Chronology for the Ceramic Stamps of Herakleia Pontike. In *The Cauldron of Ariantas. Studies Presented to A.N. Ščeglov on the Occasion of His 70th Birthday*, ed. P. Guldager Bilde, J.M. Højte, and V.F. Stolba, pp. 261–78. Aarhus: Aarhus University Press.

Kac, Vladimir I., Sergei Yu. Monakhov, Vladimir F. Stolba, and Alexander N. Ščeglov. 2002. Tiles and Ceramic Containers. In *Panskoye I, The Monumental Building at U6*, ed. L. Hannestad, V.F. Stolba, and A. Ščeglov, pp. 101–25. Aarhus: Aarhus University Press.

Kantzia, Chaido. 1994. Ενα κεραμικό εργαστήριο αμφορέων του προτου μισού του 4ου αι. π.X. στην Κω. In *Γ΄ επιστημονική συνάντηση για την ελληνιστική κεραμική*, pp. 323–54. Athens: Archaeological Receipts Fund.

Kealhofer, Lisa. 2005. Settlement and Land Use: The Gordion Regional Survey. In *The Archaeology of Midas and the Phrygians. Recent Work at Gordion*, ed. L. Kealhofer, pp. 137–48. Philadelphia, PA: University of Pennsylvania Museum of Archaeology and Anthropology.

Keller, Meredith, and Frank G. Matero, eds. 2011. *Gordion Awakened: Conserving a Phrygian Landscape / Canlanan Gordion: Frig Peyzajının Korunması.* Philadelphia: Architectural Conservation Laboratory.

Kelly, Mary. 1989. *Goddess Embroideries of Eastern Europe.* McLean, NY: Studiobooks.

———. 1999. Living Textile Traditions of the Carpathians. In *Folk Dress in Europe and Anatolia: Beliefs about Protection and Fertility*, ed. L. Welters, pp. 155–78. Oxford: Berg.

Kennett, Douglas J., and Bruce Winterhalder, eds. 2006. *Behavioral Ecology and the Transition to Agriculture.* Berkeley, CA: University of California Press.

Kerkenes Eco-Center and Environmental Studies, directed by Françoise Summers. Online at http://www.kerkenes.metu.edu.tr/keco/index.html.

Kerschner, Michael, and Norbert Ehrhardt. n.d. Weihungen lydischer Keramik in Milet und Didyma. *Archäologischer Anzeiger.* Forthcoming.

Kilian, Klaus. 1975. *Fibeln in Thessalien von der mykenischen bis zur archaischen Zeit.* Prähistorische Bronzefunde 14.2. Munich: Beck.

Kirshenblatt-Gimblett, Barbara. 1998 *Destination Culture: Tourism, Museums, and Heritage.* Berkeley, CA: University of California Press.

Klebinder, Gudrun. 2001. Bronzegürtel aus dem Artemision von Ephesos. In *Der Kosmos der Artemis von Ephesos*, ed. U. Muss, pp. 111–22. Sonderschriften Bd. 37. Vienna: Österreichisches Archäologisches Institut.

———. 2002. Ephesos und Phrygien. Eine Untersuchung der Beziehungen anhand der Bronzen aus dem frühen Artemision von Ephesos. In *Temenos. Festgabe für Florens Felten und Stefan Hiller,* ed. B. Asamer, P. Höglinger, C. Reinhold, R. Smetana, and W. Wohlmayr, pp. 75–82. Vienna: Phoibos.

———. 2007. *Bronzefunde aus dem Artemision von Ephesos.* Vienna: Österreichischen Akademie der Wissenschaften.

Knigge, Ursula. 1976. *Der Südhügel.* Kerameikos: Ergebnisse der Ausgrabungen 9. Berlin: Walter de Gruyter.

Koehler, Carolyn G. 1978. Corinthian A and B Transport Amphoras. Ph.D. diss., Princeton University, Princeton, NJ.

Kohler, Ellen L. 1980. Cremations of the Middle Phrygian Period at Gordion. In *From Athens to Gordion. The Papers of a Memorial Symposium for Rodney S. Young,* ed. Keith DeVries, pp. 65–89. Philadelphia, PA: The University Museum, University of Pennsylvania.

———. 1995. *The Lesser Phrygian Tumuli. Part 1, The Inhumations.* The Gordion Excavations (1950–1973) Final Reports, Vol. 2. Philadelphia, PA:

The University Museum, University of Pennsylvania.

Korfmann, Manfred. 1992. Die prähistorische Besiedlung südlich der Burg VI/VII. In *Studia Troica* 2:105–22. Mainz: Philipp von Zabern.

Körte, Alfred. 1897. Kleinasiatische Studien II. Gordion und der Zug des Manlius gegen die Galater. *Mitteilungen des Deutschen Archäologischen Institut. Athenische Abteilung* 22:1–51.

Körte, Gustav, and Alfred Körte. 1904. *Gordion: Ergebnisse der ausgrabung im Jahre 1900.* Berlin: Druck und Verlag von Georg Reimer.

Koşay, Hamit. 1941. *Türk Tarih Kurumu Tarafından Yapılan Pazarlı Hafriyatı Raporu / Les Fouilles de Pazarlı enterprises par la Société d'Histoire Turque.* Türk Tarih Kurumu Yayınları V. 4. Ankara: Türk Tarih Kurumu.

Krebs, John R., and Nicholas B. Davies. 1981. *An Introduction to Behavioural Ecology.* Sunderland, MA: Sinauer Associates Inc.

Kroll, John. 2010. Sardeis Sikkeleri/The Coins of Sardis. In *Lidyalılar ve Dünyaları / The Lydians and Their World*, pp. 143–55. İstanbul: Yapı Kredi Yayınları.

Kuhn, Hans H. 1998. Adsorption at the Liquid/Solid Interface: Metal Oxide Coated Textiles. In AATCC, *Book of Papers: 1998 International Conference & Exhibition.* Research Triangle Park, NC: American Association of Textile Chemists and Colorists.

———. 2000. *Textile Composite with Iron Oxide Coating.* U.S. Patent Number 6,022,619.

Kumerloeve, Hans. 1956. Zur Verbreitung des Leoparden (Panthera pardus L.) in Anatolien. *Der Zoologische Garten* 22:154–62.

———. 1967. Zur Verbreitung kleinasiatischer Raub- und Huftiere sowie einiger Grossnager. *Säugtierkundliche Mitteilungen* 15:337–409.

———. 1976. Leoparden, Panthera pardus tulliana (Valenciennes, 1856). *Zentralanatolien, Säugetierkundliche Mitteilungen* 24:46–48.

Kuniholm, Peter I. 1977. Dendrochronology at Gordion and on the Anatolian Plateau. Ph.D. diss., University of Pennsylvania, Philadelphia.

———. 1996. Long Tree-Ring Chronologies for the Eastern Mediterranean. In *Archaeometry '94: The Proceedings of the 29th International Symposium on Archaeometry,* ed. S. Demirci, A.M. Özer, and

G.D. Summers, pp. 401–9. Ankara: TÜBITAK.

Kuniholm, Peter I., Carol. B. Griggs, and Maryanne A. Newton. 2007. Evidence for Early Timber Trade in the Mediterranean. In *Byzantina Mediterranea. Festschrift für Johannes Koder zum 65. Geburtstag,* ed. K. Belke, E. Kislinger, A. Külzer, and M.A. Stassinopolou, pp. 365–85. Vienna: Böhlau.

Kutaysov, Vadim A. 1990. *Antichniy gorod Kerkinitida.* Kiev: Naukova Dumka.

La Coste-Messelière, Pierre de. 1957. *Le trésors de Delphes: Photos de Georges de Miré.* Paris: École française d'Athènes.

Lapatin, Kenneth. 2001. *Chryselephantine Statuary in the Ancient Mediterranean World.* Oxford: Oxford University Press.

Last, Joseph S. 1955–56. "Gordion Architect's Log 1955–1956." Unpublished document in Gordion Archive, University of Pennsylvania Museum of Archaeology and Anthropology, Philadelphia.

———. 1958–59. "Gordion Architect's Log 1958–1959." Unpublished document in Gordion Archive, University of Pennsylvania Museum of Archaeology and Anthropology, Philadelphia.

Lawall, Mark L. 1995. Transport Amphoras and Trademarks: Imports to Athens and Economic Diversity in the Fifth Century B.C. Ph.D. diss., University of Michigan, Ann Arbor.

———. 1997. Shape and Symbol: Regionalism in Fifth-century Transport Amphora Production in Northeastern Greece. In *Trade and Production in Premonetary Greece, Production and the Craftsman. Proceedings of the Fourth and Fifth International Workshops, Athens 1994 and 1995,* ed. C. Gillis, C. Risberg, and B. Sjöberg, pp. 113–30. SIMA Pocket-Book 143. Jonsered: Paul Åströms förlag.

———. 2002[2003]. Ilion before Alexander: Amphoras and Economic Archaeology. *Studia Troica* 12:197–243.

———. 2004a. Amphoras Without Stamps: Chronologies and Typologies from the Athenian Agora. In *ΣΤ΄ επιστημονική συνάντηση για την ελληνιστική κεραμική,* pp. 445–54. Athens: Archaeological Receipts Fund.

———. 2004b. Archaeological Context and Aegean Amphora Chronologies: A Case Study of Hellenistic Ephesos. In *Transport Amphorae and Trade in the Eastern Mediterranean,* ed. J. Eiring and J. Lund, pp. 171–88. Monographs of the Danish Institute in Athens 5. Athens: Danish Institute in Athens.

———. 2008. Rhodian Amphora Stamps from Gordion, 189 BC. In *ΦΙΛΙΑΣ ΧΑΡΙΝ (Philias charin): Mélanges à la mémoire de Niculae Conovici,* ed. A. Avram, V. Lungu, and M. Neagu Călăşi, pp. 111–20. Bucharest: Daim.

———. 2010. Pontic, Aegean and Levantine Amphoras at Gordion. In *Production and Trade of Amphorae in the Black Sea. International Round-Table Conference, Batumi-Trabzon, 27–29 April 2006,* ed. D. Kassab Tezgör and N. Inaishvili. İstanbul: Institut français d'Études Anatoliennes.

Lazarov, Mikhail. 1999. Les importations amphoriques thasiennes à Odessos. In *Production et commerce des amphores anciennes en Mer Noire,* ed. Y. Garlan, pp. 195–200. Aix-en-Provence: Publications de l'Université de Provence.

Lee, Zoë, Heather A. Viles, and Chris H. Wood, eds. 2009. Soft Capping Historic Walls: A Better Way of Conserving Ruins? English Heritage Research Project, unpublished report. http://www.geog.ox.ac.uk/research/arid-environments/rubble/swc/swc-report.pdf.

Leipunskaya, Nina O. 1995. Excavations in the Lower City of Olbia, 1985–1992: Preliminary Results. *EMC/CV* n.s. 14:23–44.

Leiser, Gary. 1993–94. Travellers' Accounts of Mohair Production in Ankara from the Fifteenth through the Nineteenth Century. *The Textile Museum Journal* 30:5–34.

Lesko, Leonard, ed. 1994. *Pharaoh's Workers: The Villagers of Deir el Medina.* Ithaca, NY: Cornell University Press.

Liebhart, Richard F. 1988. Timber Roofing Spans in Greek and Near Eastern Monumental Architecture during the Early Iron Age. Ph.D. diss., University of North Carolina, Chapel Hill.

———. 2010. The Tomb Complex in Tumulus MM at Gordion. In *Tatarlı. Renklerin Dönüsu. The Return of Colours. Rückkehr der Farben,* ed. L. Summerer and A. von Kienlin, pp. 268–79. İstanbul: Yapı Kredi Yayınları.

Liebhart, Richard F., and Jessica S. Johnson. 2005. Support and Conserve: Conservation and Environmental Monitoring of the Tomb Chamber of

Tumulus MM. In *The Archaeology of Midas and the Phrygians: Recent Work at Gordion*, ed. L. Kealhofer, pp. 191–203. Philadelphia, PA: University of Pennsylvania Museum of Archaeology and Anthropology.

Liebhart, Richard F., and Claude Brixhe. 2009. The Recently Discovered Inscriptions from Tumulus MM at Gordion: A Preliminary Report. *Kadmos* 48:141–56.

Liebhart, Richard F., Gareth Darbyshire, Evin Erder, and Ben Marsh. n.d. A Fresh Look at the Tumuli of Gordion. In *Tumulus as Sema: Space, Politics, Culture and Religion in the First Millennium BC*, ed. Olivier Henry and Ute Kelp. İstanbul: Koç University. Forthcoming.

Liles, James N. 1990. *The Art and Craft of Natural Dyeing*. Knoxville: University of Tennessee Press.

Lindner, Kurt. 1973. *Beiträge zu Vogelfang und Falknerei im Altertum*. Quellen und Studien zur Geschichte der Jagd. Berlin: Walter de Gruyter.

Lipe, William D. 1974. A Conservation Model for American Archaeology. *Kiva* 39(1-2): 213–43.

Luce, S.B., and E.P. Blegen. 1939. Archaeological News and Discussions. *AJA* 43.1:310–45.

Luckenbill, Daniel D. 1926. *Ancient Records of Assyria and Babylonia*. Chicago, IL: University of Chicago Press.

Ma, John. 1999. *Antiochos III and the Cities of Western Asia Minor*. Oxford: Oxford University Press.

Manning, Sturt, Bernd Kromer, Peter I. Kuniholm, and Maryanne W. Newton. 2001. Anatolian Tree Rings and a New Chronology for the East Mediterranean Bronze-Iron Ages. *Science* 294:2532–35.

Marsh, Ben. 1997. Alluvial Burial of Gordion. *Anatolica* 23:23–26.

———. 1999. Alluvial Burial of Gordion, an Iron-Age City in Anatolia. *Journal of Field Archaeology* 26.2:163–75.

———. 2005. Physical Geography, Land Use, and Human Impact at Gordion. In *The Archaeology of Midas and the Phrygians: Recent Work at Gordion*, ed. L. Kealhofer, pp. 161–71. Philadelphia, PA: University of Pennsylvania Museum of Archaeology and Anthropology.

Marsh, Ben, and Lisa Kealhofer. n.d. *Millennial-scale Patterns of River and Small-Stream Sedimentation in the Gordion Region, Central Anatolia*. Forthcoming.

Marston, John M. 2007. Reconstructing the Functions of Domestic and Industrial Space through Charcoal Analysis at Gordion, Turkey. Paper presented at 72nd Annual Meeting of the Society for American Archaeology, Austin, TX.

———. 2009. Modeling Wood Acquisition Strategies from Archaeological Charcoal Remains. *Journal of Archaeological Science* 36(10): 2192–200.

Maslennikov, Alexandr A. 2003. Rural Territory of Ancient Cimmerian Bosporos. In *Ancient Greek Colonies in the Black Sea*, ed. D.V. Grammenos and E.K. Petropoulos, pp. 1155–1213. Thessaloniki: Archaeological Institute of Northern Greece.

Maslennikov, Alexandr A., and Alexandra P. Buzhilova. 1999. Ifigeniya na Meotide (Materialy k obsuzhdeniyu sushestvovaniya ritual'noy dekapitatsii v antichnom Priazoviye). *Drevnosti Bospora* 2:174–83.

Mason, Randall, and Erica Avrami. 2000. Heritage Values and Challenges of Conservation Planning. In *Management Planning for Archaeological Sites*, ed. John K. Papadopoulos and Richard M. Leventhal, pp. 13–26. Los Angeles, CA: Getty Conservation Institute.

Masters, Linda A. 1997. Monitoring Vegetation. In *The Tallgrass Restoration Handbook for Prairies, Savannas, and Woodlands*, ed. S. Packard and C.F. Mutel, pp. 279–301. Washington, DC: Island Press.

Matero, F., K.L. Fong, E. Del Bono, M. Goodman, E. Kopelson, L. McVey, J. Sloop, and C. Turton. 1998. Archaeological Site Conservation and Management: An Appraisal of Recent Trends. *Conservation and Management of Archaeological Sites* 2(3): 129–42.

Matthews, Joseph Merritt. 1920. *Application of Dyestuffs to Textiles, Paper, Leather, and Other Materials*. New York: J. Wiley.

Mauzy, Craig. 2006. *Agora Excavations 1931–2006, A Pictorial History*. Athens: American School of Classical Studies at Athens.

McGovern, Patrick E. 2000. The Funerary Banquet of "King Midas." *Expedition* 42(1): 21–29.

———. 2001. Meal for Mourners. *Archaeology* 54(4): 26–33.

———. 2010. Appendix 5: Chemical Identification of the Beverage and Food Remains in Tumulus

MM. In E. Simpson, *The Gordion Wooden Objects. Volume 1: The Furniture from Tumulus MM*, pp. 177–87. Culture and History of the Ancient Near East 32. Leiden: Brill.

McGovern, Patrick E., D.L. Glusker, R.A. Moreau, A. Nuez, C.W. Beck, E. Simpson, E.D. Butrym, L.J. Exner, and E.C. Stout. 1999. A Funerary Feast Fit for King Midas. *Nature* 402 (Dec. 23): 863–64.

McLauchlin, Barbara K. 1986. Lydian Graves and Burial Customs. Ph.D. diss., University of California, Berkeley.

———. 1989. Rock Crystal Working at Sardis: A Local Industry. *AJA* 93:250.

Meiggs, Russell. 1982. *Trees and Timber in the Ancient Mediterranean World*. Oxford: Clarendon Press.

Mellink, Machteld. 1956. *A Hittite Cemetery at Gordion*. Philadelphia, PA: The University Museum, University of Pennsylvania.

———. 1959. The City of Midas. *Scientific American* (July 1959): 100–12.

———. 1964. A Votive Bird from Anatolia. *Expedition* 6(2): 28–32.

———. 1965. Mita, Mushki and Phrygians. *Anadolu Araştırmaları* 2:317–25.

———. 1973. Archaeology in Asia Minor. *AJA* 77:169–93.

———. 1974. Archaeology in Asia Minor. *AJA* 78:105–30.

———. 1975. Archaeology in Asia Minor. *AJA* 79:201–22.

———. 1976. Archaeology in Asia Minor. *AJA* 80:261–89.

———. 1977. Archaeology in Asia Minor. *AJA* 81:289–321.

———. 1979. Midas in Tyana. In *Florilegium Anatolicum. Mélanges offerts à Emmanuel Laroche*. pp. 249–57. Paris: E. de Boccard.

———. 1980a. Archaeology in Asia Minor. *AJA* 84:501–18.

———. 1980b. Archaic Wall Paintings from Gordion. In *From Athens to Gordion. The Papers of a Memorial Symposium for Rodney S. Young*, ed. Keith DeVries, pp. 91–98. Philadelphia, PA: The University Museum, University of Pennsylvania.

———. 1981. Conclusions. In Rodney S. Young, *Three Great Early Tumuli*, pp. 263–72. The Gordion Excavations Final Reports 1. Philadelphia, PA: The University Museum, University of Penn-

sylvania.

———. 1982. Archaeology in Asia Minor. *AJA* 86:557–76.

———. 1983. Comments on a Cult Relief of Kybele from Gordion. In *Beiträge zur Altertumskunde Kleinasiens. Festschrift für Kurt Bittel*, ed. R.M. Boehmer and H. Hauptmann, pp. 349–60. Mainz am Rhein: Philipp von Zabern.

———. 1988. Anatolia. *The Cambridge Ancient History*. Vol. 4, *Persia, Greece and the Western Mediterranean c. 525 to 479 B.C.*, ed. John Boardman, N.G.L. Hammond, D.M. Lewis, and M. Ostwald, pp. 211–33. 2nd ed. Cambridge: Cambridge University Press.

———. 1992. The Native Kingdoms of Anatolia. In *The Cambridge Ancient History*. Vol. 3, Part 2, *The Assyrian and Babylonian Empires and Other States of the Near East, from the Eighth to the Sixth Centuries B.C.*, ed. John Boardman, I.E.S. Edwards, E. Sollberger, and N.G.K. Hammond, pp. 619–65. Cambridge: Cambridge University Press.

———. 1993. Phrygian Traits at Boğazköy and Questions of Phrygian Writing. *Istanbuler Mitteilungen* 43:293–98.

Mercanti, Daniela. 2006. La stoà degli Ateniesi a Delfi. *Ostraka, Rivista di antichità* 15:331–40.

Miller, John L., Bruce Lightbody, Richard Smith, Robert Bell, Wilson W. Cummer, William C.S. Remsen, Keith Dickey, Tim Matney, and Kimberly E. Leaman. 1974–2004. "Gordion Architect's Log 1974–2004." Unpublished document in the Gordion Archive, University of Pennsylvania Museum of Archaeology and Anthropology, Philadelphia.

Miller, Margaret C. 1997. *Athens and Persia in the Fifth Century BC. A Study in Cultural Receptivity*. Cambridge: Cambridge University Press.

Miller, Naomi F. 1984. The Use of Dung as Fuel: An Ethnographic Model and an Archaeological Example. In *Paléorient* 10(2): 71–79.

———. 1985. Paleoethnobotanical Evidence for Deforestation in Ancient Iran: A Case Study of Urban Malyan. *Journal of Ethnobiology* 5:1–21.

———. 1991. Forest and Wood Use at Gordion: Analysis of Wood Charcoal Recovered in 1988 and 1989. *MASCA Ethnobotanical Lab Report 10*. Philadelphia: The University Museum, University of Pennsylvania.

———. 1994. Some Botanical Considerations for the Conservation and Preservation of Tumulus MM at Gordion. *Anadolu Medeniyetleri Müzesi 1993 Yıllığı*:181–83.

———. 1997. Farming and Herding along the Euphrates: Environmental Constraint and Cultural Choice (Fourth to Second Millennia B.C.). *MASCA Research Papers in Science and Archaeology* 14:123–32.

———. 1998. Archaeobotanists Preserve Midas's Wealth. *Anthropology Newsletter* 39(4): 14–15.

———. 1999a. Erosion, Biodiversity, and Archaeology: Preserving the Midas Tumulus at Gordion / Erozyon, Bioçeşitlilik ve Arkeoloji, Gordion'daki Midas Höyüğü'nün Korunması. *Arkeoloji ve Sanat* 93:13–19 + plate.

———. 1999b. Seeds, Charcoal and Archaeological Context: Interpreting Ancient Environment and Patterns of Land Use. *TÜBA-AR* 2:15–27.

———. 2000. Plants in the Service of Archaeological Preservation. *Expedition* 42(1): 30–36.

———. 2006. Mudball: The Movie. On line: http://www.sas.upenn.edu/~nmiller0/mudball.html.

———. 2007. Roman and Medieval Charcoal from the 2004 Excavation at Gordion, Operations 52, 53, 54, and 55. *MASCA Ethnobotanical Lab Report 41*. Philadelphia, PA: The University Museum, University of Pennsylvania.

———. 2010. *Botanical Aspects of Environment and Economy at Gordion, Turkey*. Philadelphia, PA: University of Pennsylvania Museum of Archaeology and Anthropology.

Miller, Naomi F., and Kurt Bluemel. 1999. Plants and Mudbrick: Preserving the Midas Tumulus at Gordion, Turkey. *Conservation and Management of Archaeological Sites* 3:225–37.

Miller, Naomi F., Melinda A. Zeder, and Susan R. Arter. 2009. From Food and Fuel to Farms and Flocks: The Integration of Plant and Animal Remains in the Study of Ancient Agropastoral Economies at Gordion, Turkey. *Current Anthropology* 50: 915–24.

Mitchell, Stephen. 2005. The Galatians: Representation and Reality. In *A Companion to the Hellenistic World*, ed. Andrew Erskine, pp. 280–93. Oxford: Blackwell.

Molev, Yevgeniy A. 2003. Kyta. In *Ancient Greek Colonies in the Black Sea*, ed. D.V. Grammenos and E.K. Petropoulos, pp. 841–93. Thessaloniki: Archaeological Institute of Northern Greece.

Monakhov, Sergei Yu. 1989. *Amfory Khersonesa Tavricheskogo IV–II vv. do n.e.* (Amphoras of Tauric Chersonesos 4th–2nd c. BC). Saratov: Saratov University.

———. 1999. *Grecheskiye amfory v prichernomor'ye. Kompleksy keramicheskoy tary VII–II vekov do n.e.* (Greek amphoras of the northern Black Sea: Complexes of ceramic containers 7th–2nd c. BC). Saratov: Saratov University.

———. 2003. *Grecheskiye amfory v Prichernomor'ye: Tipologiya amfor vedyzhikh tsentrov-eksporterov tovarov v keramicheskoy tare* (Greek amphoras in the northern Black Sea: Amphora typology of leading commercial export centers in ceramic containers). Moscow: Kimmerida Press.

Moore, Mary B. 2004. Horse Care as Depicted in Greek Vases before 400 B.C. *Metropolitan Museum Journal* 39:35–67.

Moorey, P. Roger S. 1980. Metal Wine-Sets in the Ancient Near East. *Iranica Antiqua* 15:181–97.

———. 1994. *Ancient Mesopotamian Materials and Industries. The Archaeological Evidence*. Oxford: Clarendon Press.

Munk Højte, Jakob. 2005. Archaeological Evidence for Fish Processing in the Black Sea Region. In *Ancient Fishing and Fish Processing in the Black Sea Region*, ed. T. Bekker Nielsen, pp. 133–60. Black Sea Studies 2. Aarhus: Aarhus University Press.

Munn, Mark. 2006. *The Mother of the Gods, Athens, and the Tyranny of Asia: A Study of Sovereignty in Ancient Religion*. Berkeley, CA: University of California Press.

Muscarella, Oscar W. 1967. *Phrygian Fibulae from Gordion*. London: Quaritch.

———. 1989. King Midas of Phrygia and the Greeks. In *Anatolia and the Ancient Near East: Studies in Honor of Tahsin Özgüç*, ed. Kutlu Emre, Barthel Hrouda, Machteld J. Mellink, and Nimet Özgüç, pp. 333–44. Ankara: Türk Tarih Kurumu Basımevi.

———. 1995. The Iron Age Background to the Formation of the Phrygian State. *Bulletin of the American Schools of Oriental Research* 299/300:91–101.

———. 2003. The Date of the Destruction of the Early Phrygian Period at Gordion. *Ancient West and*

East 2(2): 225–52.

Naumann, Friederike. 1983. *Die Ikonographie der Kybele in der phrygischen und der griechischen Kunst.* Istanbuler Mitteilungen, Beiheft 28. Tübingen: Wasmuth.

Naumann, Rudolf, and Klaus Tuchelt. 1963–64. Die Ausgrabung im südwesten des Tempels von Didyma 1962. *Istanbuler Mitteilungen* 13/14:15–62.

Neer, Richard. 2004. The Athenian Treasury at Delphi and the Material of Politics. In *Classical Antiquity* 23.1:63–93.

Nørskov, Vinnie. 2004. Amphorae from Three Wells at the Maussolleion of Halikarnassos: Something to Add to the Typology of Mushroom Rims. In *Transport Amphorae and Trade in the Eastern Mediterranean*, ed. J. Eiring and J. Lund, pp. 285–91. Monographs of the Danish Institute in Athens 5. Athens: Danish Institute in Athens.

Nylander, C. 1970. *Ionians in Pasargadae: Studies in Old Persian Architecture.* Boreas 1. Uppsala: Almqvist & Wiksell.

Omori, Takayuki, and Toshio Nakamura. 2006. Radiocarbon Dating of Archaeological Material Excavated at Kaman-Kalehöyük: Initial Report. *Kaman-Kalehöyük* 15:263–68.

Omura, Sachihiro. 2006. Preliminary Report on the 20th Excavation Season at Kaman-Kalehöyük (2005). *Kaman-Kalehöyük* 15:1–61.

Onaiko, Nadezhda A. 1980. *Archaicheskii Torik, antichnyi gorod no severo-vostoke Ponta.* Moscow: Nauka.

Orbaşlı, Aylin, and Louise Doughty. 2004. *Çatalhöyük Management Plan.* English version downloaded from http://www.catalhoyuk.com/smp/index.html (verified December 24, 2009).

Orthmann, Winfried. 1971. *Untersuchungen zur Späthethitischen Kunst.* Bonn: Habelt.

Özgen, Engin, and İlknur Özgen. 1988. *Antalya Museum.* Ankara: Turkish Republic Ministry of Culture and Tourism.

Özgen, İlknur, and Jean Öztürk. 1996. *Heritage Recovered. The Lydian Treasure.* Ankara: Republic of Turkey Ministry of Culture.

Özgüç, Tahsin. 1969. *Altıntepe* 2. Ankara: Türk Tarih Kurumu Basımevi.

———. 1999. *Kültepe-Kaniš/Neša sarayları ve mabetleri* (The palaces and temples of Kültepe-Kaniš/Neša). Ankara: Türk Tarih Kurumu Basımevi.

Özgüç, Tahsin, and Mahmut Akok. 1947. Die Ausgrabungen an zwei Tumuli auf dem Mausoleumshügel bei Ankara. *Belleten* 11(41): 57–85.

Panshin, A.J., and C. de Zeeuw. 1970. *Textbook of Wood Technology.* 3rd ed. New York: McGraw Hill.

Parrot, André. 1961. *The Arts of Assyria.* New York: Golden Press.

Paspalas, Stavros. 2005. Philip Arrhidaios at Court—An Ill-advised Persianism? Macedonian Royal Display in the Wake of Alexander. *Klio* 87(1): 72–101.

Pavlichenko, Natalia. 1999. Les timbres amphoriques d'Héraklée du Pont: Bilan et perspectives de recherché. In *Production et commerce des amphores anciennes en Mer Noire*, ed. Y. Garlan, pp. 13–19. Aix-en-Provence: Publications de l'Université de Provence.

Payton, Robert. 1984. The Conservation of an Eighth Century B.C. Table from Gordion. In *Contributions to the Paris Congress on Adhesives and Consolidants*, ed. N.S. Brommelle, E. Pye, P. Smith, and G. Thomson, pp. 133–37. London: International Institute for Conservation of Historic and Artistic Works.

Pearsall, Deborah M. 1983. Evaluating the Stability of Subsistence Strategies by Use of Paleoethnobotanical Data. *Journal of Ethnobiology* 3(2): 121–37.

———. 2000. *Paleoethnobotany: A Handbook of Procedures.* 2nd ed. San Diego, CA: Academic Press.

Pedde, Friedhelm. 2000. *Vorderasiatische Fibeln. Von der Levante bis Iran.* Abhandlungen der Deutschen Orient-Geselschaft 24. Saarbrücken: SDV Saarbrücken.

Peirce, Sarah. 2001. The Greek Transport Amphorae. In *Torone I: The Excavations of 1975, 1976, and 1978*, ed. A. Cambitoglou, J.K. Papadopoulos, and O. Tudor Jones, pp. 495–513. Athens: Athens Archaeological Society.

Perdrizet, Paul. 1908. *Monuments figures, petits bronzes, terres-cuites, antiquites diverses.* Fouilles de Delphes V. Paris: École francaise d'Athènes.

Philimonos-Tsopotou, Melina. 2004. *Η ελληνιστική οχύρωση της Ρόδου.* Athens: Ministry of Culture.

Piperno, Dolores R., and Deborah M. Pearsall. 1998. *The Origins of Agriculture in the Lowland Neo-*

tropics. San Diego, CA: Academic Press.

Podhajsky, Alois. 1958. *The Spanish Riding School of Vienna*. Vienna: Brüder Rosenbaum.

Polat, Gürcan. 2005. Bir Anadolu-Akhaemenid Dönemi Ölü Kültü Geleneği: Tümülüs Önünde Steller ve Seramoni Alanları. *Olba* 11:1–23.

Popham, Mervyn R., L. Hugh Sackett, and Petros G. Themelis, eds. 1996. *Lefkandi III. The Toumba Cemetery. Plates*. London: Thames & Hudson.

———. 1980. *Lefkandi I. The Iron Age. The Settlement. The Cemeteries. BSA* Suppl. 11. London: Thames & Hudson.

Posamentir, Richard. 2006. The Greeks in Berezan and Naukratis: A Similar Story? In *Naukratis: Greek Diversity in Egypt*, ed. A. Villing and U. Schlotzhauer, pp. 159–67. London: British Museum Press.

Postgate, J.N. 1973. Assyrian Texts and Fragments. *Iraq* 35:13–36.

Prayon, Friedhelm. 1987. *Phrygische Plastik. Die früheisenzeitliche Bildkunst Zentral-Anatoliens und ihre Beziehungen zu Griechenland und zum Alten Orient*. Tübinger Studien 7. Tübingen.

Pritchard, James B. 1975. Rodney Stuart Young (1907–1974). *American Philosophical Society Year Book*, pp. 186–90. Philadelphia, PA: American Philosophical Society.

Przeworski, Stefan. 1939. *Die Metallindustrie Anatoliens in der Zeit von 1500–700 vor Chr. Rohstoffe, Technik, Produktion*. Leiden: Brill.

Ramage, Andrew. 1969. Studies in Lydian Domestic and Commercial Architecture at Sardis. Ph.D. diss., Harvard University, Cambridge, MA.

Ramage, Andrew. 1978. *Lydian Houses and Architectural Terracottas*. Sardis Monograph 5. Cambridge, MA: Harvard University Press.

Ramage, Andrew, and Paul Craddock. 2000. *King Croesus' Gold. Excavations at Sardis and the History of Gold Refining*. Sardis Monograph 11. Cambridge, MA: Archaeological Exploration of Sardis.

Rathgen, Friedrich. 1898. *Die Konservirung von Alterthumsfunden*. Berlin: W. Spemann. English ed., 1905. *The Preservation of Antiquities; A Handbook for Curators,* trans. G. Auden and Harold Auden. Cambridge: Cambridge University Press.

Remsen, William C.S. 1987. "Gordion 1987 Architect's Report." Unpublished document in Gordi-on Archive, University of Pennsylvania Museum of Archaeology and Anthropology, Philadelphia.

———. 1992. "Gordion 1992 Archaeological Excavations: Appendix A." Unpublished document, Gordion Archive, University of Pennsylvania Museum of Archaeology and Anthropology, Philadelphia.

———. 1993. "Gordion Excavation Grid System." Unpublished document, Gordion Archive, University of Pennsylvania Museum of Archaeology and Anthropology, Philadelphia.

Rhoads, Bonnie 1970. The "Lion Tamer" Ivory from Delphi. M.A. thesis, Dept. of Art History, University of Oregon.

Roberts, Sally R. 1986. The Stoa Gutter Well. A Late Archaic Deposit in the Athenian Agora. *Hesperia* 55:1–74.

Robinson, David M. 1950. *Excavations at Olynthos. Part XIII, Vases Found in 1934 and 1938*. Baltimore: Johns Hopkins University Press.

Roebuck, Carl. 1959. *Ionian Trade and Colonization*. Monographs on Archaeology and Fine Arts sponsored by the Archaeological Institute of America and the College Art Association of America 9. New York: Archaeological Institute of America.

Roller, Lynn E. 1983. The Legend of Midas. *Classical Antiquity* 2:299–313.

———. 1984. Midas and the Gordian Knot. *Classical Antiquity* 3:256–71.

———. 1999a. Early Phrygian Drawings from Gordion and the Elements of Phrygian Artistic Style. *Anatolian Studies* 49:143–52.

———. 1999b. *In Search of God the Mother: The Cult of Anatolian Kybele*. Berkeley, CA: University of California Press.

———. 2005. A Phrygian Sculptural Identity? Evidence from Early Phrygian Drawings in Iron Age Gordion. In *Anatolian Iron Ages 5. Proceedings of the Fifth Anatolian Iron Ages Colloquium Held at Van, 6–10 August 2001*, ed. A. Çilingiroğlu and G. Darbyshire, pp. 125–30. British Institute at Ankara, Monograph 31. Ankara.

———. 2009. *The Incised Drawings from Early Phrygian Gordion*. Gordion Special Studies 4. Philadelphia: University of Pennsylvania Museum of Archaeology and Anthropology.

———. 2011. Phrygian and the Phrygians. In *Oxford Handbook of Ancient Anatolia*, ed. Sharon Steadman and Greg McMahon, pp. 560–78. Oxford: Oxford University Press.

Roosevelt, Christopher H. 2003. Lydian and Persian Period Settlement in Lydia. Ph.D. diss., Cornell University, Ithaca, NY.

———. 2006. Symbolic Door Stelae and Graveside Monuments in Western Anatolia. *AJA* 110:65–91.

———. 2009. *The Archaeology of Lydia, from Gyges to Alexander*. Cambridge: Cambridge University.

Rose, Charles Brian. 2008. Separating Fact from Fiction in the Aeolian Migration. *Hesperia* 77.3:399–430.

Rose, Charles Brian, and Gareth Darbyshire, eds. 2011. *The New Chronology of Iron Age Gordion*. Gordion Special Studies 6. Philadelphia, PA: University of Pennsylvania Museum of Archaeology and Anthropology.

Rumpf, Andreas. 1920. Lydische Salbgefässe. *Mitteilungen des Deutschen Archäologischen Instituts, Athenische Abteilung* 45:163–70.

Saatçi, Tahsin, and Asım Kopar. 1990. Gordion Kızlarkayası Tümülüsü Kazısı. *Anadolu Medeniyetleri Müzesi* 1989 Yıllığı:68–78.

———. 1991. Gordion Kızlarkayası Kazısı—1989. I. *Müze Kurtarma Kazıları Semineri, 19–20 Nisan 1990*:151–62.

Salisbury, K.J., and F.W. Jane. 1940. Charcoals from Maiden Castle and Their Significance in Relation to the Vegetation and Climatic Conditions in Prehistoric Times. *Journal of Ecology* 28:310–25.

Salzmann, Dieter. 1982. *Untersuchungen zu den antiken Kieselmosaiken*. Berlin: Gebr. Mann.

Sams, G. Kenneth. 1974. Phrygian Painted Animals: Anatolian Orientalizing Art. *Anatolian Studies* 24:169–96.

———. 1977. Beer in the City of Midas. *Archaeology* 30:108–15.

———. 1978. Schools of Geometric Painting in Early Iron Age Anatolia. In *Proceedings of the Xth International Congress of Classical Archaeology*, ed. E. Akurgal, pp. 227–36. Ankara: Türk Tarih Kurumu Basımevi.

———. 1988. The Early Phrygian Period at Gordion: Toward a Cultural Identity. *Source: Notes in the History of Art* 7.3/4:9–15.

———. 1989. Sculpted Orthostates at Gordion. In *Anatolia and the Ancient Near East. Studies in Honor of Tahsin Özgüç*, ed. Kutlu Emre, Barthel

Hrouda, Machteld J. Mellink, and Nimet Özgüç, pp. 447–54. Ankara: Türk Tarih Kurumu Basımevi.

———. 1992. Work at Gordion in 1990. *Kazı Sonuçları Toplantısı* 13.1(1991): 471–80.

———. 1993. Gordion and the Near East in the Early Phrygian Period. In *Aspects of Art and Iconography: Anatolia and Its Neighbors. Studies in Honor of Nimet Özgüç*, ed. M. Mellink, Edith Porada, and Tahsin Özgüç, pp. 549–55. Ankara: Türk Tarih Kurumu Basımevi.

———. 1994a. *The Early Phrygian Pottery*. The Gordion Excavations (1950–1973) Final Reports Vol. 4. Philadelphia, PA: The University Museum, University of Pennsylvania.

———. 1994b. Aspects of Early Phrygian Architecture at Gordion. In *Anatolian Iron Ages 3. The Proceedings of the Third Anatolian Iron Ages Colloquium held at Van, 6–12 August 1990*, ed. A. Çilingiroğlu and D.H. French, pp. 211–20. British Institute of Archaeology at Ankara Monograph 16.

———. 1994c. Gordion, 1992. *Kazı Sonuçları Toplantısı* 15.1(1993): 467–79.

———. 1995. Midas of Gordion and the Anatolian Kingdom of Phrygia. In *Civilizations of the Ancient Near East* 2, ed. Jack M. Sasson, pp. 1147–59. New York: Hendrickson Publishers.

———. 1996. Gordion Archaeological Activities, 1994. *Kazı Sonuçları Toplantısı* 17.1(1995): 433–52.

———. 2002. Gordion, 2000. *Kazı Sonuçları Toplantısı* 23.2(2001): 219–26.

———. 2005a. Explorations over a Century. In *The Archaeology of Midas and the Phrygians: Recent Work at Gordion*, ed. L. Kealhofer, pp. 10–21. Philadelphia, PA: University of Pennsylvania Museum of Archaeology and Anthropology.

———. 2005b. Gordion, 2003. *Kazı Sonuçları Toplantısı* 26.2(2004): 265–70.

———. 2007. Keith DeVries, 1937–2006. *AJA* 111: 549–51.

———. 2009. Gordion, 2007. *Kazı Sonuçları Toplantısı* 30.3(2008): 139–50.

———. 2010. Gordion, 2008. *Kazı Sonuçları Toplantısı* 31.3(2009): 289–302.

———. 2011a. Gordion, 2009. *Kazı Sonuçları Toplantısı* 32.2(2010): 462–73.

———. 2011b. Anatolia: The First Millennium B.C.E.

in Historical Context. In *Oxford Handbook of Ancient Anatolia*, ed. Sharon Steadman and Greg McMahon, pp. 604–22. Oxford: Oxford University Press.

Sams, G. Kenneth, and R. Brendan Burke. 2008. Gordion, 2006. *Kazı Sonuçları Toplantısı* 29.2(2007): 329–42.

Sams, G. Kenneth, R. Brendan Burke, and Andrew L. Goldman. 2007. Gordion, 2005. *Kazı Sonuçları Toplantısı* 28.2(2006): 365–86.

Sams, G. Kenneth, and Andrew L. Goldman. 2006. Gordion, 2004. *Kazı Sonuçları Toplantısı* 27.2(2005): 43–56.

Sams, G. Kenneth, and İlhan Temizsoy. 2000. *Gordion Museum.* Ankara: Republic of Turkey Ministry of Culture, General Directorate of Monuments and Museums.

Sams, G. Kenneth, and Mary M. Voigt. 1990. Work at Gordion in 1988. *Kazı Sonuçları Toplantısı* 11.2(1989): 77–105.

———. 1991. Work at Gordion in 1989. *Kazı Sonuçları Toplantısı* 12.1(1990): 455–70.

———. 1995. Gordion Archaeological Activities, 1993. *Kazı Sonuçları Toplantısı.* 16.1(1994): 369–92.

———. 1997. Gordion 1995. *Kazı Sonuçları Toplantısı* 18.1(1996): 475–97.

———. 1998. Gordion, 1996. *Kazı Sonuçları Toplantısı* 19.1(1997): 681–701.

———. 1999. Gordion Archaeological Activities, 1997. *Kazı Sonuçları Toplantısı* 20.1(1998): 559–76.

———. 2003. Gordion 2001. *Kazı Sonuçları Toplantısı* 24.2(2002): 139–48.

———. 2004. Gordion, 2002. *Kazı Sonuçları Toplantısı* 25.1(2003): 195–206.

———. 2010. Gordion, 2008. *Kazı Sonuçları Toplantısı* 31.3(2009): 289–302.

———. 2011. In Conclusion. In *The New Chronology of Iron Age Gordion,* ed. C.B. Rose and G. Darbyshire, pp. 155–68. Philadelphia: University of Pennsylvania Museum of Archaeology and Anthropology.

Sapouna-Sakellarakis, Efi. 1978. *Die Fibeln der griechischen Inseln.* Prähistorische Bronzefunde 14.4. Munich: Beck.

Saprykin, Sergei. 1994. *Ancient Farms and Land-Plots on the Khora of Khersonesos Taurike.* Amsterdam: J.C. Gieben.

Şare, Tuna. 2010. An Archaic Ivory Figurine from a Tumulus near Elmali. Cultural Hybridization and a New Anatolian Style. *Hesperia* 79:53–78.

Sass, Benjamin. 2005. *The Alphabet at the Turn of the Millennium: The West Semitic Alphabet ca. 1150–850 BCE: The Antiquity of the Arabian, Greek, and Phrygian Alphabets. Tel Aviv* Occasional Publications no. 4. Tel Aviv.

Schadewaldt, Wolfgang. 1936. Alfred Körte. *Forschungen und Fortschritte* 12:315.

Schaus, Gerald. 1992. West Anatolian Pottery at Gordion. *Anatolian Studies* 42:151–78.

Schefold, Karl. 1968. Der Löwengott von Delphi. In *Festschrift für Gottfried von Lücken,* ed. K. Zimmermann, pp. 769–73. Wissenschaftliche Zeitschrift der Universität Rostock 17. Rostock.

Schiering, W. 1976. Orientalisierende und ostionische Kleinplastik aus Elfenbein: die Herkunft des Delphischen 'Löwengottes.' *Mitteilungen des Deutschen Archäologen-Verbandes e.V.* 7.2:46–49.

———. 2003. Löwenbändiger und Midas-Thron in Delphi. In *Επιτυμβιον Gerhard Neumann. Μουσειο Μπενακη 2ο Παράρτημα,* ed. D. Damaskos, pp. 57–68. Athens: Mouseio Benake.

Schirmer, Wulf, and Winfried Orthmann. 1969. *Die Bebauung am unteren Büyükkale-Nordwesthang in Boğazköy.* Boğazköy-Hattusha VI. Wissenschaftliche Veröffentlichungen des Deutschen Orient-Gesellschaft 81. Berlin: Gebr. Mann.

Schmid, Stephan G. 2000. A Group of Early Hellenistic Pottery from a Well in Eretria. In *Ε΄ επιστημονική συνάντηση για την ελληνιστική κεραμική,* pp. 361–72. Athens: Archaeological Receipts Fund.

Schmidt, Hartwig. 1997. Reconstruction of Ancient Buildings. In *The Conservation of Archaeological Sites in the Mediterranean Region,* ed. M. de la Torre, pp. 41–50. Los Angeles, CA: Getty Conservation Institute.

Schuster, Carl, and Edmund Carpenter. 1986–88. *Materials for the Study of Social Symbolism in Ancient & Tribal Art: A Record of Tradition & Continuity.* New York: Rock Foundation.

———. 1996. *Patterns That Connect: Social Symbolism in Ancient and Tribal Art.* New York: Harry N. Abrams.

Schweingruber, Fritz Hans. 1990. *Anatomy of European Woods.* Stuttgart: Haupt.

Schweingruber, Fritz Hans, Annett Börner and Ernst-

Detlef Schulze. 2006. *Atlas of Woody Plant Stems: Evolution, Structure, and Environmental Modifications.* Berlin: Springer.

Schweppe, Helmut. 1986. *Practical Hints on Dyeing with Natural Dyes.* Washington, DC: Smithsonian Institution. Available at http://www.si.edu/mci/english/learn_more/publications/articles.html (verified June 2012).

———. 1992. *Handbuch der Naturfarbestoffe—Vorkommen—Verwendung—Nachweis.* Landsberg / Lech: Ecomed.

Schwingenstein, Christoph. 1980. Körte, Gustav. In *Neue Deutsche Biographie* 12, pp. 394–95. Berlin: Duncker & Humblot.

———. 1988. Gustav Körte 1852–1917. In *Archäologenbildnisse. Porträts und Kurzbiographien von Klassischen Archäologen deutscher Sprache,* ed. R. Lullies and W. Schiering, p. 102. Mainz: Philipp von Zabern.

Seeher, Jürgen. 2002. *Hattusha Guide. A Day in the Hittite Capital.* İstanbul: Ege Yayınları.

———. 2007. *A Mudbrick City Wall at Hattusa: Diary of a Reconstruction.* İstanbul: Ege Yayınları.

Senff, Reinhard. 2003. Das Aphroditeheiligtum von Milet. In *Neue Forshungen zur Religionsgeschichte Kleinasiens. Elmar Schwertheim zum 60. Geburstag gewidmet,* ed. G. Heedemann and E. Winter, pp. 11–25. Asia Minor Studien 49. Bonn: Habelt.

Sevinç, Nurten. 1996. A New Sarcophagus of Polyxena from the Salvage Excavations at Gümüşçay. *Studia Troica* 6:251–64.

Sezgin, Yusuf. 2004. Clazomenian Transport Amphorae of the Seventh and Sixth Centuries. In *Klazomenai, Teos and Abdera: Metropoleis and Colony,* ed. A. Moustaka, E. Skarlatidou, M. Tzannes, and Y. Ersoy, pp. 169–83. Thessaloniki: 19th Ephorate of Prehistoric and Classical Antiquities of Komotini.

Shackleton, C.M., and F. Prins. 1992. Charcoal Analysis and the "Principle of Least Effort"—A Conceptual Model. *Journal of Archaeological Science* 19(6): 631–37.

Shay, J.M., S.M. Anderson, and C.T. Shay. 1982. Carbonized Seeds and Wood. In *Troy: The Archaeological Geology,* ed. G.F. Rapp and J.A. Gifford, pp. 189–93. Princeton, NJ: Princeton University Press.

Shear, T. Leslie. 1922. A Hoard of Staters of Croesus at Sardes. *Numismatist* 35:349–52.

———. 1926. *Terra-cottas. Part One, Architectural Terra-cottas.* Sardis X. Cambridge: Cambridge University Press.

Sheftel, Phoebe. 1974. The Ivory, Bone and Shell Objects from Gordion, from the Campaigns of 1950 through 1973. Ph.D. diss., University of Pennsylvania, Philadelphia.

Simon, Erika. 1996. Theseus and Athenian Festivals. In *Worshipping Athena. Panathenaia and Parthenon,* ed. J. Neils, pp. 9–26. Wisconsin Studies in Classics. Madison, WI: University of Wisconsin Press.

Simpson, Elizabeth. 1983. Reconstructing an Ancient Table: The "Pagoda" Table from Tumulus MM at Gordion. *Expedition* 25(4): 11–26.

———. 1988. The Phrygian Artistic Intellect. *Source: Notes in the History of Art* 7 (3-4): 24–42.

———. 1990. Midas' Bed and a Royal Phrygian Funeral. *Journal of Field Archaeology* 17:69–87.

———. 1993. A Carved Stretcher from the Big Tumulus at Gordion. In *Aspects of Art and Iconography: Anatolia and Its Neighbors, Studies in Honor of Nimet Özgüç,* ed. Machteld J. Mellink, Edith Porada, and Tahsin Özgüç, pp. 569–72. Ankara: Türk Tarih Kurumu Basımevi.

———. 1995. Furniture in Ancient Western Asia. In *Civilizations of the Ancient Near East, Volume 3,* ed. J.M. Sasson, pp. 1647–71. New York: Scribner's.

———. 1996. Phrygian Furniture from Gordion. In *The Furniture of Western Asia: Ancient and Traditional,* ed. G. Herrmann, pp. 187–209. Mainz: Philipp von Zabern.

———. 1998. Symbols on the Gordion Screens. *Proceedings of the XXXIVième Rencontre Assyriologique Internationale, Istanbul, 1987,* ed. H. Erkanal, V. Donbaz, and A. Uğuroğlu, pp. 629–39. Ankara: Türk Tarih Kurumu Basımevi.

———. 1999. Early Evidence for the Use of the Lathe in Antiquity. In *Meletemata: Studies in Aegean Archaeology Presented to Malcolm H. Wiener,* ed. P.P. Betancourt, V. Karageorghis, R. Laffineur, and W.-D. Niemeier, pp. 781–86. Liège: Université de Liège.

———. 2001. Celebrating Midas: Contents of a Great Phrygian King's Tomb Reveal a Lavish Funerary Banquet. *Archaeology* 54(4): 26–33.

———. 2003. The Conservation of the Wooden Objects from Gordion, Turkey: Methods for the Treatment of Dry Archaeological Wood. In *Art, Biology and Conservation: Biodeterioration and Works of Art*, ed. R.J. Koestler, V. Koestler, A. Elena Charola, and F. Nieto-Fernandez, pp. 359–69. New York: Metropolitan Museum of Art.

———. 2010. *The Gordion Wooden Objects. Volume 1: The Furniture from Tumulus MM*. Culture and History of the Ancient Near East 32. Leiden: Brill.

Simpson, Elizabeth, and Krysia Spirydowicz. 1999. *Gordion Wooden Furniture / Gordion Ahşap Eserler: The Study, Conservation, and Reconstruction of the Furniture and Wooden Objects from Gordion, 1981–1998*. Ankara: Museum of Anatolian Civilizations.

Simpson, Elizabeth, and Robert Payton. 1986. Royal Wooden Furniture from Gordion. *Archaeology* 39(6): 40–47.

Sivan, R. 1997. The Presentation of Archaeological Sites. In *The Conservation of Archaeological Sites in the Mediterranean Region*, ed. M. de la Torre, pp. 51–59. Los Angeles, CA: Getty Conservation Institute.

Sivas, Hakan, and Taciser Tüfekçi Sivas. 2007. *Friglerin Gizemli Uygarliği: The Mysterious Civilization of the Phrygians*. İstanbul: Yapı Kredi Yayınları.

Smart, Tristine Lee, and Ellen S. Hoffman. 1988. Environmental Interpretation of Archaeological Charcoal. In *Current Paleoethnobotany: Analytical Methods and Cultural Interpretations of Archaeological Plant Remains*, ed. Christine A. Hastorf and Virginia S. Popper, pp. 167–205. Chicago: University of Chicago Press.

Solovyov, Sergei L. 1999. *Ancient Berezan. The Architecture, History, and Culture of the First Greek Colony in the Northern Black Sea*. Colloquia Pontica 4. Leiden: Brill.

Spencer, Nigel. 1995. Early Lesbos between East and West: A "Grey Area" of Aegean Archaeology. *BSA* 90:269–306.

Spirydowicz, Krysia. 1996. The Conservation of Ancient Phrygian Furniture from Gordion, Turkey. In *Archaeological Conservation and Its Consequences*, ed. A. Roy and P. Smith, pp. 166–71. London: International Institute for Conservation of Historic and Artistic Works.

———. 2010. Appendix 1: Conservation of the Wooden Furniture from Tumulus MM. In E. Simpson, *The Gordion Wooden Objects. Volume 1: The Furniture from Tumulus MM,* pp. 137–58. Culture and History of the Ancient Near East 32. Leiden: Brill.

Spirydowicz, Krysia, Elizabeth Simpson, Robert Blanchette, Arno Schniewind, Mauray Toutloff, and Alison Murray. 2001. Alvar and Butvar: The Use of Polyvinyl Acetal Resins for the Treatment of the Wooden Artifacts from Gordion, Turkey. *Journal of the American Institute for Conservation* 40(1): 43–57.

Stinson, Philip T. 2008. Lale Tepe: A Remarkable Late Lydian Tumulus in the Hinterland of Sardis. 2, Architecture and Painting. In *Love for Lydia. A Sardis Anniversary Volume Presented to Crawford H. Greenewalt, Jr.*, ed. N.D. Cahill, pp. 25–47. Sardis Report 4. Cambridge, MA: Archaeological Exploration of Sardis.

Storey, Ian C. 2003. *Eupolis. Poet of Old Comedy*. Oxford: Oxford University Press.

Stronach, David. 1959. The Development of the Fibula in the Near East. *Iraq* 21(2): 181–206.

Stubbs, John H. 1995. Protection and Presentation of Excavated Structures. In *Conservation on Archaeological Excavations*, ed. N.P. Stanley-Price, pp. 73–89. Rome: ICCROM.

Tamur, Erman. 2003. *Ankara Keçisi ve Ankara Tiftik Dokumacılığı. Tükenen Bir Zenginliğin ve Çöken Bir Sanayinin Tarihsel Öyküsünden Kesitler*. Ankara: Ankara Ticaret Odası.

Teleaga, Emilian. 2003. Beiträge zur Chronologie der Amphorenstempel und der Amphoren von Heraklea Pontike. *Münstersche Beiträge zur antiken Handelgeschichte* 22:69–113.

Temizsoy, İlhan. 1992. Mamaderesi Tümülüsü Kazısı. *Anadolu Medeniyetleri Müzesi 1991 Yıllığı*:3–28.

———. 1993. Mamaderesi Frig Tümülüsü Kazısı Küçük Buluntular. *Anadolu Medeniyetleri Müzesi 1992 Yıllığı*:110–137.

———. 1994. Mamaderesi Frig Tümülüsü Kazısı Küçük Buluntular II. *Anadolu Medeniyetleri Müzesi 1993 Yıllığı*:5–33.

Tezcan, B. 1981. Yenidoğan, Höyüğü (Tuğrul Höyük) Kazısı 1979. *Kazı Sonuçları Toplantısı* 2(1980): 43–45.

Thierfelder, Andreas. 1980. Körte, Alfred. In *Neue Deutsche Biographie* 12, p. 394. Berlin: Duncker & Humblot.

Thompson, Michael. 1975. Rodney Stuart Young, August 1, 1907–October 25, 1974. *AJA* 79:112.

———. 1981. *Ruins: Their Preservation and Display*. London: British Museum Publications.

Tilley, Christopher. 1994. *A Phenomenology of Landscape*. Oxford: Berg.

Tsatsopoulou-Kaloudi, Polyxeni. 2001. *Mesembria-Zone*. Athens: Archaeological Receipts Fund.

Turan, Nihat. 1984. *Türkiye'nin Av ve Yaban Hayvanları Memeliler*. Ankara: Ongün Kardeşler.

Uçankuş, Hasan Tahsin. 2002. *Ana Tanrıca Kybele'nin ve Kral Midas'ın Ülkesi Phrygia (Kültür Rehberi)*. Ankara: T.C. Kültür Bakanlığı.

Üstay, Ali H. 1990. *Hunting in Turkey*. İstanbul: Bağımsız Basın Ajansı.

Vaag, Lief Erik, Vinnie Nørskov, and John Lund. 2002. *The Maussolleion at Halikarnassos, 7. The Pottery. Ceramic Material and Other Finds from Selected Contexts*. Aarhus: Aarhus University Press.

Vanderpool, Eugene, James R. McCredie, and Arthur Steinberg. 1962. Koroni: A Ptolemaic Camp on the East Coast of Attica. *Hesperia* 31:26–61.

Varinlioğlu, Ender. 1992. The Phrygian inscriptions from Bayandır. *Kadmos* 31:10–20.

Vassileva, Maya. 2001. Further Considerations on the Cult of Kybele. *Anatolian Studies* 51:51–63.

———. 2005a. Phrygia, Troy and Thrace. In *Anatolian Iron Ages 5: The Proceedings of the Fifth Anatolian Iron Ages Colloquium held at Van, 6–10 August 2001*, ed. A. Çilingiroğlu and G. Darbyshire, pp. 227–34. British Institute at Ankara Monograph 31. London: British Institute at Ankara.

———. 2005b. The Belt of the Goddess: Phrygian Tombs versus Greek Sanctuaries. In *Stephanos Archaeologicos in honorem Professoris Ludmili Getov. Studia Archaeologica Universitatis Serdicensis. Suppl. IV*, pp. 91–101. Sofia: St. Kliment Ohridki University Press.

———. 2007. First Millennium B.C. Ritual Bronze Belts in an Anatolian and Balkan Context. *Thrace in the Graeco-Roman World. Proceedings of the 10th International Congress of Thracology, Komotini-Alexandroupolis, 18–23 October 2005*, ed. Athena Iakovidou, pp. 669–79. Athens: Ethniko Idryma Erevnon.

Vita-Finzi, Claudio. 1969. *The Mediterranean Valleys: Geologic Changes in Historic Times*. Cambridge: Cambridge University Press.

Vitruvius. 1914. *Ten Books on Architecture*, trans. M.H. Morgan. Cambridge: Harvard University Press.

Voigt, Mary M. 1994. Excavations at Gordion 1988–89: The Yassıhöyük Stratigraphic Sequence. In *Anatolian Iron Ages 3: The Proceedings of the Third Anatolian Iron Ages Colloquium held at Van, 6–12 August 1990*, ed. A. Çilingiroğlu and D.H. French, pp. 265–93. British Institute of Archaeology at Ankara Monograph 16,

———. 2002. Gordion: The Rise and Fall of an Iron Age Capital. In *Across the Anatolian Plateau: Readings on the Archaeology of Ancient Turkey*, ed. D.C. Hopkins, pp. 187–96. Annual of the American Schools of Oriental Research 57 (2000). Boston, MA.

———. 2003. Celts at Gordion. The Late Hellenistic Settlement. *Expedition* 45(1): 14–19.

———. 2005. Old Problems and New Solutions. Recent Excavations at Gordion. In *The Archaeology of Midas and the Phrygians. Recent Work at Gordion*, ed. Lisa Kealhofer, pp. 22–35. Philadelphia: University of Pennsylvania Museum of Archaeology and Anthropology.

———. 2007. The Middle Phrygian Occupation at Gordion. In *Anatolian Iron Ages 6: The Proceedings of the Sixth Anatolian Iron Ages Colloquium Held at Eskişehir, 16–20 August 2004*, ed. A. Çilingiroğlu and A. Sagona, pp. 311–34. Ancient Near Eastern Studies Supplement Series 20. Leuven: Peeters.

———. 2009. The Chronology of Phrygian Gordion. In *Tree Rings, Kings and Old World Archaeology*, ed. Sturt Manning and Mary Jaye Bruce, pp. 219–37. Ithaca: Cornell University Press.

———. 2011. Gordion: The Changing Political and Economic Roles of a First Millennium B.C.E. City. In *Oxford Handbook of Ancient Anatolia*, ed. Sharon Steadman and Greg McMahon, pp. 1067–94. Oxford: Oxford University Press.

Voigt, Mary, and Robert Henrickson. 2000. Formation of the Phrygian State: The Early Iron Age at Gordion. *Anatolian Studies* 50:37–54.

Voigt, Mary, and T.C. Young, Jr. 1999. From Phrygian Capital to Achaemenid Entrepot: Middle and Late Phrygian Gordion. *Iranica Antiqua* 34:191–242.

Voigt, Mary M., Keith DeVries, Robert C. Henrickson, Mark Lawall, Ben Marsh, Ayşe Gürsan-Salzman, and T. Cuyler Young. 1997. Fieldwork at Gordion: 1993–1995. *Anatolica* 23:1–59.

Völling, Thomas. 1998. Ein phrygischer Gürtel aus Olympia. *Archäologische Anzeiger* 2:243–52.

von der Osten, Hans H. 1937. *The Alishar Hüyük. Seasons of 1930–32. Part III.* Chicago, IL: University of Chicago Press.

von Olfers, Ignaz Franz M. 1859. *Über die lydischen Königsgräber bei Sardes und den Grabhügel des Alyattes nach dem Bericht des K. General-Consuls Spiegelthal zu Smyrna.* Abhandlungen der Königlichen Akademie der Wissenschaften zu Berlin 1858, pp. 537–56. Berlin: Königl. Akademie der Wissenschaften.

von Saldern, Axel. 1959. Glass Finds at Gordion. *Journal of Glass Studies* 1:23–49.

Walsh, John. 1986. The Date of the Athenian Stoa at Delphi. *AJA* 90:319–36.

Wartke, Ralf-B. 2005. *Sam'al: Ein aramäischer Stadtstaat des 10. bis 8. Jhs. v. Chr. und die Geschichte seiner Erforschung.* Mainz: Philipp von Zabern.

Wasowicz, Aleksandra. 1975. *Olbia pontique et son territoire. L'aménagement de l'espace.* Paris: Belleslettres.

Weiser, Andrea, and Dana Lepofsky. 2009. Ancient Land Use and Management of Ebey's Prairie, Whidbey Island, Washington. *Journal of Ethnobiology* 29:184–212.

Wilford, John Noble. 2008. Found: An Ancient Monument to the Soul. *New York Times*, November 17, 2008.

Willcox, George W. 1974. A History of Deforestation as Indicated by Charcoal Analysis of Four Sites in Eastern Anatolia. *Anatolian Studies* 24:117–33.

———. 1979. Preliminary Report: Analysis of Charcoal Remains from Can Hasan III. *Bulletin of the British Institute of Archaeology at Ankara.*

———. 1991. Cafer Höyük (Turqie): Les Charbons De Bois Néolithique. *Cahiers de l'Euphrate* 5-6:139–50.

———. 1999. Charcoal Analysis and Holocene Vegetation History in Southern Syria. *Quaternary Science Reviews* 18(4-5): 711–16.

Williams, Charles K. 1963. "Notes for Architect–Gordion–1963." Unpublished document in the Gordion Archive, University of Pennsylvania Museum of Archaeology and Anthropology, Philadelphia.

Winter, Frederick A. 1988. Phrygian Gordion in the Hellenistic Period. *Source: Notes in the History of Art* 7(3/4): 60–71.

Winterhalder, Bruce, and Carol Goland. 1997. An Evolutionary Ecology Perspective on Diet Choice, Risk, and Plant Domestication. In *People, Plants, and Landscapes: Studies in Paleoethnobotany,* ed. Kristen J. Gremillion, pp. 123–60. Tuscaloosa, AL: University of Alabama Press.

Winterhalder, Bruce, and Eric A. Smith. 1981. *Hunter-Gatherer Foraging Strategies: Ethnographic and Archaeological Analyses.* Chicago, IL: University of Chicago Press.

———. 2000. Analyzing Adaptive Strategies: Human Behavioral Ecology at Twenty-Five. *Evolutionary Anthropology* 9(2): 51–72.

Wittke, Anne-Maria. 2004. *Mušker und Phryger. Ein Beitrag zur Geschichte Anatoliens vom 12. bis zum 7. Jh. v. Chr.* Beihefte zum Tübinger Atlas des Vorderen Orients, Reihe B (Geisteswissenschaften) Nr. 99. Wiesbaden: Dr. Ludwig Reichert Verlag.

Woods, Christopher. 2004. The Sun-god Tablet of Nabû-apla-iddina Revisited. *Journal of Cuneiform Studies* 50:23–103.

Yalçınkaya, Teoman. 2000. Tumulus of Alyattes: An Analysis of a Man-Made Colossal Mound. Unpublished report.

Yağcı, Remzi. 1992. Polatlı-Gordion Kıranharman Köyü Acıkırı Mevkii Kurtarma Kazısı. *II. Müze Kurtarma Kazıları Semineri, 29–30 Nisan 1991:*265–83.

Young, Rodney S. 1950. Excavations at Yassihuyuk-Gordion 1950. *Archaeology* 3:196–201.

———. 1951. Gordion–1950. *University Museum Bulletin* 16(1): 3–20.

———. 1953a. Making History at Gordion. *Archaeology* 6:159–66.

———. 1953b. Progress at Gordion, 1951–1952. *University Museum Bulletin* 17(4): 2–39.

———. 1955. Gordion: Preliminary Report, 1953. *AJA* 59:1–18.

———. 1956. The Campaign of 1955 at Gordion. *AJA* 60:249–66.

———. 1957. Gordion 1956: Preliminary Report. *AJA* 61:319–31.

———. 1958. The Gordion Campaign of 1957. *AJA* 62:139–54.

———. 1960a. Gordion Campaign of 1959. *AJA* 64:227–44.

———. 1960b. Gordion: Phrygian Construction and

Architecture. *Expedition* 2(2): 2–9.

———. 1962a. The 1961 Campaign at Gordion. *AJA* 66:153–68.

———. 1962b. Gordion: Phrygian Construction and Architecture II. *Expedition* 4(4): 2–12.

———. 1963. Gordion on the Royal Road. *Proceedings of the American Philosophical Society* 107:348-64.

———. 1964. The 1963 Campaign at Gordion. *AJA* 68:279–92.

———. 1965. Early Mosaics at Gordion. *Expedition* 7(3):4–13.

———. 1966. The Gordion Campaign of 1965. *AJA* 70:267–78.

———. 1968. The Gordion Campaign of 1967. *AJA* 72:231–42.

———. 1969a. Doodling at Gordion. *Archaeology* 22:270–75.

———. 1969b. Old Phrygian Inscriptions from Gordion: Toward a History of the Phrygian Alphabet. *Hesperia* 38:252–96.

———. 1974. Phrygian Furniture from Gordion. *Ex-pedition* 16(3): 2–13.

———. 1981. *Three Great Early Tumuli*, ed. E.L. Kohler. The Gordion Excavations Final Reports Vol. I. Philadelphia, PA: The University Museum, University of Pennsylvania.

Yourcenar, Marguerite. 1992. Tone and Language in the Historical Novel. In *That Mighty Sculptor, Time*, pp. 27–53. New York: Noonday.

Zeder, Melinda A., and Susan R. Arter. 1994. Changing Patterns of Animal Utilization at Ancient Gordion. *Paléorient* 20.2:105–18.

Zeest, Iraida. 1960. *Keramicheskaya Tara Bospora* (*Ceramic Containers of the Bosporos*). Materialy i issledovaniya po arkheologii SSSR 83. Moscow: Akademii nauk SSSR.

Zettler, Richard, and Lee Horne, eds. 1998. *Treasures from the Royal Tombs at Ur*. Philadelphia, PA: University of Pennsylvania Museum of Archaeology and Anthropology.

Zohary, Michael. 1973. *Geobotanical Foundations of the Middle East*. Stuttgart: G. Fischer.

Contributors

Gunlög Anderson is Professor Emerita of Fine Arts at Wilson College in Chambersburg, Pennsylvania. She received her Ph.D. from Bryn Mawr College, with a dissertation on the Common Cemetery at Gordion. Currently her research focuses on the creative work of women in history, the ancient world, and prehistory.

Mary Ballard is Senior Textiles Conservator in the Museum Conservation Institute at the Smithsonian Institution, where she has worked since 1984. She received her B.A. from Wellesley College, and her M.A. in the History of Art and Conservation from the Institute of Fine Arts, New York University. Prior to joining the Smithsonian, she was textile conservator at the Detroit Institute of Arts. She has published widely on conservation treatments, archaeological textiles, and dyes and pigments.

Brendan Burke is Associate Professor of Greek and Roman Studies at the University of Victoria, British Columbia, Canada. He received his Ph.D. in Archaeology from UCLA in 1998, and has participated in surveys and excavations in Greece since 1994. His primary research interest is cultural interactions between Greece and Anatolia in the Late Bronze and Early Iron Ages, and he is currently co-director of the Eastern Boeotia Archaeological Project.

Gareth Darbyshire is the Gordion Archivist at the Penn Museum. He received his Ph.D. in Archaeology from the University of Wales, Cardiff. His specialties include first millennium BCE Anatolia and Celtic Europe. He has carried out fieldwork in Britain, the Republic of Ireland, and Turkey. He

is preparing a volume in the Gordion series on the ironwork assemblage.

Keith DeVries[†] was Associate Professor Emeritus in the Department of Classical Studies at the University of Pennsylvania and Associate Curator Emeritus in the Mediterranean Section of the University of Pennsylvania Museum of Archaeology and Anthropology. He received his Ph.D. from the University of Pennsylvania, and served as field director of the Gordion Project from 1974 to 1988. He died in 2006.

Crawford H. Greenewalt, Jr.,[†] was professor of Classical Archaeology emeritus (2009) at the University of California at Berkeley and field director (1976–2008) of the Archaeological Exploration of Sardis (co-sponsored by Harvard University Art Museums and Cornell University). He participated in field seasons at Sardis from 1959 through 2007 (inclusive) and excavated at Gordion in 1961, 1962, and 1963; also at Pitane, modern Çandarlı, in 1962, and at Old Smyrna, modern Bayraklı, in 1967.

Mark Lawall is Associate Professor of Classics at the University of Manitoba. He received his B.A. from the College of William and Mary, and his Ph.D. from the University of Michigan. He is a specialist in the study of Greek transport amphoras, and has published studies of amphoras at Ephesos, Gordion, Troy, Athens, the Kyrenia shipwreck, and the Pabuç Burnu shipwreck. Lawall has also published more interpretive articles on the use of data from amphoras in the study of Hellenistic economies, the interpretation of graffiti as evidence for marketing in the Athenian Agora, and various details of amphora chronologies.

Richard F. Liebhart received a B.A. in English in 1971 and a Ph.D. in Classics in 1988, both from the University of North Carolina at Chapel Hill. He has been a Lecturer on archaeology and ancient art in the Classics Department and the Art Department at Chapel Hill since 1990. He spent three years (1980–1983) at the American School of Classical Studies at Athens and worked on excavations in the Athenian Agora and at ancient Corinth. In 1990, he began an architectural study of the tomb chamber of Tumulus MM at Gordion.

Ben Marsh is Professor of Geography and Environmental Studies at Bucknell University, Lewisburg, PA, where he has been on the faculty since 1979. He holds a Ph.D. and an M.S. in Geography from the Pennsylvania State University and a B.A. in Anthropology from the University of California at Santa Cruz. He works as a geomorphologist and geoarchaeologist at several Old World sites and projects. He also works in Pennsylvania on Pleistocene landforms and on human environmental adaptation.

John Marston received his Ph.D. from the Interdepartmental Graduate Program in Archaeology at UCLA in 2010, completing a dissertation on agricultural strategies and land use at Gordion. He is now Assistant Professor of Archaeology at Boston University. He has been a member of the Gordion project since 2002, focusing on the recovery and analysis of paleoethnobotanical remains from the site and ecological survey of the Gordion region. His conference papers on agricultural risk management and sustainability at Gordion won awards from the Society for American Archaeology, the Archaeological Institute of America, and the Society of Ethnobiology at their 2010 annual meetings.

Frank Matero is Professor of Architecture and Historic Preservation at the University of Pennsylvania. He received his B.A. from SUNY Stonybrook, and his M.S. from the program in Historic Preservation at Columbia University. He has consulted on a wide range of conservation projects including the fortifications of Cairo and San Juan (Puerto Rico), the Guggenheim Museum and Trinity Church (New York), the Lincoln and Jefferson Memorials, Ellis Island, and the missions of California and Texas. His archae-

ological site work includes Mesa Verde, Casa Grande, Bandelier, Fort Union and Fort Davis, El Morro, and Indian Key in the United States, Gordion and Çatalhöyük in Turkey, and Chiripa in Bolivia. He has been in charge of site management and preservation at Gordion since 2006.

Naomi F. Miller is Research Project Manager in the Near Eastern Section of the University of Pennsylvania Museum of Archaeology and Anthropology. She received her B.A., M.A., and Ph.D. from the University of Michigan. She has taught at St. Lawrence University and at Washington University, and has conducted field research throughout the Near East, including Iran, Turkey, Syria, and Turkmenistan. Miller has published widely in the field of archaeobotany, and her monograph *Botanical Aspects of Environment and Economy at Gordion* was published by the University of Pennsylvania Museum in 2010.

Gabriel H. Pizzorno received his Ph.D. from the Art and Archaeology of the Mediterranean World Graduate Group at the University of Pennsylvania in 2011. He served as Research Assistant to the Williams Director at the Penn Museum for two years, and is now Research Associate at the Museum. His specialties include the Bronze and Iron Ages in the Near East, landscape archaeology and cartography, and computer applications in archaeology. He has conducted fieldwork in Europe, South America, Turkey, and Iran.

Lynn Roller is Professor of Art History at the University of California, Davis. She received her A.B. and M.A. degrees from Bryn Mawr College, and her Ph.D. from the University of Pennsylvania. A member of the Gordion Excavation Project since 1979, her research interests include Phrygian art, epigraphy, and religion, and the relationships between ancient Anatolian civilizations and the Greek world. She is the author of Gordion Special Studies I: *The Non-Verbal Graffiti, Dipinti, and Stamps,* and Gordion Special Studies IV: *The Incised Drawings of Early Phrygian Gordion.*

C. Brian Rose is James B. Pritchard Professor of Mediterranean Archaeology in the Department of Classical Studies at the University of Pennsylvania, and Curator-in-Charge of the Mediterranean Section of the Penn Museum. He received his B.A. from Haverford College in 1978, and his M.A., M.Phil., and Ph.D. from Columbia University in 1987. Since 1988 he has been head of Post-Bronze Age excavations at Troy, and English language editor of *Studia Troica,* the annual journal of the Troy excavations. He is co-director of the Gordion Excavation Project.

G. Kenneth Sams is Professor of Classical Archaeology at the University of North Carolina at Chapel Hill. He was president of the American Research Institute in Turkey from 1991–2010, and, since 1988, Director of the Gordion Archaeological Project. Sams received his Ph.D. in Classical Archaeology from the University of Pennsylvania. His specialties include Iron Age Anatolia and the Near East, Greek architecture, and the topography of Athens, and he authored a volume in the Gordion series on the early Phrygian pottery.

Elizabeth Simpson is Professor of Ancient Art at the Bard Graduate Center in New York. She received her B.A. and M.A. degrees from the University of Oregon, and her Ph.D. in Classical Archaeology from the University of Pennsylvania. Before coming to the Bard Graduate Center, she was a curator in the Department of Ancient Near Eastern Art at the Metropolitan Museum of Art, and taught at Sarah Lawrence College and Duke University. In 1981, she established the Gordion Furniture Project for the purposes of conservation, research, and publication of the royal wooden furniture from Gordion. As director of the project, she has published extensively on the subjects of Phrygian furniture and ancient woodworking technology.

Maya Vassileva is Professor in the Department of Mediterranean and Eastern Studies of the New Bulgarian University. She received her B.A., M.A., and Ph.D. from the Institute of Thracology, Bulgarian Academy of Sciences, and has been working on the Gordion bronzes for publication since 2000. She was Fulbright visiting scholar at UNC-Chapel Hill, 1999–2000; a fellow at the Metropolitan Museum of Art between 2002 and 2004, and visiting scholar at St. John's College, Oxford, in 2002.

Mary Voigt is Chancellor Professor of Anthropology at the College of William and Mary. She received her B.A. in History and English from Marquette University and her Ph.D. in Anthropology from the University of Pennsylvania. As an archaeologist specializing in the prehistory and early history of the Middle East, she has conducted fieldwork in Iran and Turkey, and has directed fieldwork at Gordion since 1988.

† Deceased

Turkish Summary/Özetler

1. Giriş: Frig Gordiyon'unun Arkeolojisi
C. Brian Rose

Anadolu'daki en önemli yeni keşiflerin bir kısmı Gordiyon'da, yani orta Anadolu'nun büyük bir kısmını iki yüzyıla yakın bir müddet kontrol atlında bulundurmuş, doğusunda ve batısındaki Lidya, Yunan, Asur, Pers ve Geç Hitit ülkesi Tabal gibi devletlerle ve imparatorluklarla etkileşimde bulunmuş olan Frig başkentinde, gerçekleşmiştir. Uzun zamandır, Gordiyon'un topografik gelişiminin iyi anlaşıldığı zannedilirken, geçtiğimiz yıllarda arkeolojik alanın kronolojisi, yeni analizlerin ışığında, MÖ 700 yılında gerçekleştiği varsayılan Kimmer saldırısının, aslında 100 yıl önce gerçekleşen geniş çaplı bir yangın olduğunu ve bu yangının bir ihtimalle bir yeniden yapılımla ilişkili olabileceğini göstermiştir. Dolayısıyla, Orta Anadolu Demir Çağı'nın tarihi ve arkeolojisi hakkındaki yargılarımızın yanı sıra Frig mimarisinin, keramiklerinin ve diğer buluntularının kronolojisi dramatik bir biç,imde değişmiştir. Bu kitap, Nisan 2007'de University of Pennsylvania'da yer almış olan Frig Gordiyon'unun Arkeolojisi hakkındaki bir konferansta sunulan makaleleri içermektedir. İçeriğindeki konular Gordiyon'un altı yüzyıllık tarihini kapsar ve Gordiyon'un ve Gordiyon'la iletişimde olan devlet ve imparatorlukların milattan önceki birinci bin yılda gelişen topografisini inceler.

Haritalama ve Coğrafya

2. Gordion'un Haritalanması
Gabried H. Pizzorno and Gareth Darbyshire

Gordiyon'da altmış yılldır gerçekleştirilen arkeolojik araştırmalar zengin bir bilgi kaynağı olmanın yanı sıra, özellikle de kazı buluntularının mekansal düzeninin kaydedimesinde, bir takım zorluklar çıkartmıştır. Sitenin mekansal temsilindeki eksiklikler, kazı buluntularının analiz ve yayınını devamlı olarak zorlaştırmıştır. Bu sebeple, tüm kazı verilerini birleştiren bir harita bu vakte kadar derlenememiştir ve tüm arkeolojik alanı kapsayan bir koordinat sisteminde antik mimarinin sadece küçük bir kısmının yeri kesin olarak gösterilebilmektedir. Bu makale Gordiyon'daki haritalama çalışmalarının tarihine bir genel bakış sunmakta ve de bu durumun düzeltilmesi için bir strateji önermektedir. Bu yaklaşımın potensiyelini göstermek için höyükte kazılmış olan ana mimari birimlerin aşamalı bir planı taslak olarak bu makaleye eklenmiştir ve türünün ilk örneğidir.

3. Gordiyon Yerleşim Tarihinin Akarsu Çökelmesinden Okunması
Ben Marsh

Gordiyon yakınlarındaki arazilerde gözlenmiş olan geniş çaplı coğrafi hasarlar, arazi kullanımındaki değişim sebebiyle, bilhassa arazinin temizlenmesi ve sürülmesi, koyun otlanması ve kereste ve yakacak odun için ağaç kesimi gibi etkinliklerle başlamıştır. Erezyon yamaçlarda derin oluklar açmış ve toprak ve su kaynaklarına zarar vermiştir. Dere ve nehir vadilerine akmış olan tortu, taşkın yataklarının seviyesinin yükselmesine sebep olup doğal ve kültürel varlıkları 5 metreden derine gömmüştür. Demir Çağı'ndan bu güne, Sakarya Nehri Gordiyon sitadelinin etrafında yer almış olan arazi kullanımının kanıtlarını -binaları, köprüleri, yolları, hisarlarını, sur kapılarını- saklamış yada yok etmiştir. Arazideki bu değişimlerin anlaşılması eski kentin nasıl olduğunun daha iyi anlaşılabilmesi ve arkeoloji için yorumlanabilmesi için gereklidir. Peyzajdaki değişimler, bize, kırsal kaynakların insanların sebep olduğu bozulumunun nasıl, ne zaman ve ne ebatta gerçekleştiğini ve de hasara sebep olan çıkarma aktivitelerinin zamanlamasını ve yoğunluğunu bildirmektedir. Bu bulgu, yerel doğal kaynak tabanının, Sakarya'nın diğer kısımlarına kıyasla yerleşime daha elverişli olduğunu ve bu alanın nehir yatağının geri kalan kısımlarından yaklaşık 2,000 yıl önce iskan edildiğinin göstermektedir. Yerel alanlardaki verimli erken tarımsal yerleşimin şehrin buraya kurulmasında önemli bir etken olmuş olabileceği düşünülmektedir.

4. Frig Gordiyon'unda Ahşabın İşlevsel Kullanımının Karbon Analizi İle Rekonstrüksiyonu

John M. Marston

Ahşap kaynakları, Frig Gordiyon ekonomisinde hem inşaat malzemesi olarak hem de sanayide ve evlerde yakıt olarak önemli bir rol oynamıştır. Kömürleşmiş ahşap kalıntılarının incelenmesi bu malzemenin ne takım işlevlerde kullanıldığının ve bu işlevlerin şehrin günlük hayatı üzerindeki davranışsal etkilerini anlamakta faydalı olmaktadır. Bu bölüm, ahşabın, bir Frig anıtsal yapısının ve bir meskenin inşaasında kullanılımını ve bunun yanı sıra çöplüklerde bulunmuş olan ahşap yakıt kalıntılarının ikincil birikimini yorumlamaktadır. Binalardan elde edilen buluntular, özenle seçilmiş ahşap çeşitlerinin bir takım inşaat işlerinde özel olarak kullanıldığını göstermektedir. Ancak çöplüklerde bulunan yakıt kalıntıları tipik olarak karışık ağaçlardan gelmektedir. Binalar ve çöplükler arasındaki bu farklılık sebiyle, karışık ahşaptan oluşan buluntuların ikincil yığıntı olduğu saptanmaktadır.

Erken Frig Sitadeli

5. Gordiyon ve Frig Keramiklerinin Yeni Kronolojisi

G. Kenneth Sams

Radyokarbon analizleri ile belirlenen yeni Gordiyon kronolojisi sayesinde Erken Frig Sitadeli'nin yıkımının yaklaşık olarak M.Ö. 800 yılında gerçekleştiği saptanmıştır. Yeniden inşa edilmiş Frig sitadelinin altında yatan kil tabakasının oluşumu, bu yeni kronolojiye göre, 8.

yüzyılın büyük bir kısmını almıştır. Yeni sitadele ait önemli bir yığıntı olan Güney Kiler (South Cellar) daha geç bir tarihtense, yeni kronoloji ile yaklaşık olarak 700 yılına tarihlenmektedir. Bu makale, yeni kronolojinin belirli Frig keramik tiplerinin gelişimine nasıl bir düzen verdiğini incelemektedir. Zarif bej üzeri kahverengi (brown on buff) keramik buluntularına tahrip tabakasında ve bundan önceki Erken Frig katmanlarında az olarak rastlanmaktadır. Bu tipin, en çok örneği yeni sitadelden gelmektedir. Hayvan şekilleri içeren küçük ve büyük panolar gözlemlenmiş olsa da bej üzeri kahverengi kapların çoğu figüritif panolar içermemektedir. Bunun yanında, kil tabakasından sonraki katmanlarda, bazı büyük ve kaba kapların, bej üzeri kahverengi kaplara benzer özenli bir şekilde, kapların omuzlarında görülen geniş figüratif sahnelerle ve kapların boyunlarında görülen tek hayvanlı panolarla dekore edilmiş olduğu saptanmıştır. Buna paralel bir duruma parlatılmış simsiyah perdahlı keramiklerde rastlanmaktadır. Bu teknik, Erken Frig Sitadeli'nde çok nadirdir, ama şimdi sırasıyla 780 ve 770 yıllarına tarihlenen K-III ve P tümülüslerinde bol olarak bulunmaktadır. Bu tekniğe her iki defin yerinde değişik tiplerde ve erken Frig Sitadelinde bulunmayan kabartmalar eşlik eder. Kabartmasız veya kabartma süslü parlatılmış siyah keramikler yeni sitadelde kullanılmaya devam edilmiştir. Gordiyon Demir Çağı'nın Yeni Kronolojisi orta Anadolu'da ve ötesinde önem taşımaktadır. Keramik bakımından, mesela, Alişar IV tipi figüratif boyamalar Gordiyon'da 800 yılına denk gelen yıkım tabakasında ve daha önceki Erken Frig sitadelinde bulunmaktadır.

6. Gordiyon Erken Frig Yıkım Tabakasının Bitmemiş Projesi

Mary M. Voigt

Gordion'un temel arkeolojik dizini, Rodney Young tarafından 1950 ve 60'lardaki kazılara dayanılarak hazırlanmıştır. Yakın zamana kadar bu dizinin içindeki ana safhalar statik birimler olarak sunulmakta ve safhalar arasındaki geçişlere önem verilmemekteydi. Bu durum, özellikle Erken Frig Yıkım tabakasından (YHSS 6A) onu takip eden Orta Frig dönemindeki yeniden yapılanma safhasına (YHSS 5) geçiş için geçerlidir. Bu iki safhanın birbirlerinden izole edilmiş olmalarının bir sebebi, Young'un bu devrelerin arasında 150-200 gibi uzun bir zaman olduğunu düşünmesinden kaynaklanmıştır. 1990 yılında Keith DeVries, Rodney Young tarafından tutulmuş olan arazi raporlarlarını kullanarak Erken Frig Yıkım Yangını sırasında inşa edilmekte olan bir grup mimari öğeyi incelemiştir ve bu alana Bitmemiş Proje adını vermiştir. Bu iki olay arasındaki tarihsel açıklık, yeni yapılan kazı çalışmaları ve yıkım ile yeniden yapımın tarihlenmelerindeki büyük değişiklikler sebebiyle kaybolmuştur. Bu bölüm, Rodney Young'un arazi notlarını kullanarak Bitmemiş Proje'nin boyut ve zamanlamasını yeniden ele almakta ve şehrin 9. yüzyıl elit kısmının Orta Frig yeniden yapılanması ile Bitmemiş Proje arasındaki ilişkiye yeni bir bakış açısı getirmektedir.

7. Taşlarda Resimler: Erken Frig Mimarisi Üzerine Kazılmış Çizimler

Lynn E. Roller

Megaron 2'nin duvarlarına kazılmış birtakım resmiyetsiz çizimler Frig sitadelinin M.Ö. 9. yüzyıldaki görsel sanatları ve günlük hayatı hakkında değerli bilgiler vermektedir. Bu çizimlerin bir kısmı acemi sanatkarlar tarafından yapıldığı düşünülen rastgele çizgilerden ve özensiz resimlerden oluşurken, diğerleri sofistike ve kompleks kompozisyonlar sergilemektedir. Bunların bir kısmı güneydoğu Anadolu'nun formal heykelsel programlarının stil ve konularına hakim olduklarını gösterirken, diğerleri Gordiyon çevresindeki günlük hayatı derinlemesine kaydeder. Bu makale, Frig mimarisini gösteren bir grup çizimi incelemektedir. Bir taş blok, mimari eserlerin üç örneğini açıkça göstermektedir ve her biri Megaron 2 gibi Frig megaronlarınının o zamanki önden görünümlerini içerir. Bu çizimlerin dikkatle incelenmesi üç ayrı yapının tasvir edildiğini ve bunların her birisinin gerçek bir Erken Frig yapısına denk geldiğini düşündürmektedir. Bir başka taşın üzerindeki çizim tamamıyla farklı bir konudadır ve basamakların üstünde açılan iki kapıyı içeren bir duvarı ve bunun yanındaki kuleyi gösterir. Beraber olarak incelendiğinde, bu çizimler Gordiyon'un Erken Frig sitadelindeki mimarinin görünümü hakkında önemli bilgiler verir.

8. Gordiyon Sitadelinden Erken Bronz Fibula ve Kemerleri

Maya Vassileva

Bu makale Gordiyon sitadelinde bulunmuş olan erken fibula ve kemerlerle ilgilidir. Fibulalar sitadelde en yoğun olarak bulunan bronz eşyalardır. Yıkım tabakasından 41 fibula çıkmış ve bunların 38'i bronzken sadece 3 tanesi altın, gümüş ve elektrumdur. Dışarıdan gelmiş olan fibulaların tıpa tıp benzerleri bulunamamış olsa da Ege ilhamlı oldukları açıktır. Bronz kemerler Orta Frig tabakalarında ve tümülüslerde bulunmuştur. Beş adet bütün kemer ve kemer parçaları ilk olarak burada yayınlanmaktadır. İthal edilen ve taklit edilen Frig kemerleri Doğu Yunan tapınaklarında votif olarak kullanılmıştır. Bu kemerler Gordiyon'da tapılmış olan Ana Tanrıça kültü ile ilişkili olmalıdır.

Midas ve MM Tümülüsü

9. Frig Mezar Mimarisi: Tümülüs MM'in Kazısının 50. Yıldönümünde Bir Takım Gözlemler

Richard F. Liebhart

1957 yılında Rodney Young tarfından kazılmış olan MM Tümülüsü Gordiyon'daki Tümülüs P gibi Erken ve Orta Frig tümülüsleriyle benzerlikler göstermekle birlikte, yine de Gordiyon etrafındaki 200'den fazla tümülüsün en büyüğü ve özelidir. Gordiyon'da arkeolojik olarak araştılan 44 tümülüsün içinde MM, en büyük tahtadan mezar odasına ve en çok mezar buluntularına ve tek beşik çatıya sahiptir. Mezar odasının inşaası bu makalede mezarın etrafını çevreleyen taş duvarı, moloz yığıntısını, taban temelini, mezar odasının dışını kaplayan ardıç ağaçlarını, sedir taban kirişlerini, çam duvarları ve çatını kirişlerini gösteren yeni kesit ve planlarla tasvirlenmiştir. Ahşap mezar odasının inşaası hakkında yeni bulunmuş olan antik marangozluk düzen hatlarını ve arada bir kullanılmış olan kavelalar gibi yeni kanıtlar sunulmaktadır. Ahşap öğeler üzerinde kalmış sayısız alet izlerinden sürekli olarak keski, balta ve keser gibi düz bıçaklı aletlerin kullanılmış olduğu anlaşılmakta ve bu durum bu anıtta hiçbir testere izine rastlanmamış olamasına tezat etmektedir. 2007 yılında rastlantı sonucu bulunan ve çatı kirişi üzerine yazılmış olan isimler cenaze ziyaretine katılanların isimlerini binanın üzerine konuk defterine gibi yazdıklarını düşündürmektedir. İnşaat buraya defnedilmiş olan kralın ölümünden yıllar önce yapılmış olamaz, ancak iyi organize edilmiş, çok emek isteyen ve bu günün standartlarına göre çok kısa zamanda tamamlanmış bir projedir ve bu sebeple Frig yaratıcılık ve kararlılığını ispat etmektedir. Mezarın inşaasının yeni tarihi olan M.Ö. 740 yılı burada Midas'ın gömülü olamayacağını göstermektedir ancak Midas'ın bu mezarı babası için yaptırmış olması mümkündür.

10. Frig Kraliyet Mobilyası ve Gordiyon'dan Güzel Ahşap Eserler
Elizabeth Simpson

Gordiyon Mobilya Projesi, Tümülüs P, Tümülüs W ve Gordiyon sitadelinde bulunmuş olan mobilyalar ve diğer ahşap eserler üzerine odaklanmıştır. Bu proje daha önce Tümülüs MM'de yapılmış olan ve kakmalı bir masayı, sekiz adet sade masayı, iki adet kakmalı sehpayı, iki tabureyi ve de kralın tabutunu içeren araştırmalarımızı takip etmektedir. Buradan elde edilen bilgiler sitede bulunan bölük pörçük ahşap eserleri anlamıza yardımcı olmuştur. Tümülüs P defni en az 21 parça mobilya ve 49 diğer ahşap eşyayı içermektedir ve bunların arasında kakmaklı bir sehpaya, geometrik desenli ve bronze çivilerle çevrili kaplı oyulmuş tahta bir tabureye, en azından dört masaya, sekizden fazla tabureye, iki ayak taburesine, bir kakmalı yatağa ve bir sandalyeye ve bir tahta rastlanmıştır. Oyulmuş tabaklar, çanaklar, kaşıklar, bir şemsiye parçası, ve şimşir ağacından yapılmış hayvanlardan oluşan oyuncak grubu da bu mezarda bulunmuştur. Tümülüs W'daki mezardan bir sehpa olduğu düşünülen ve ajur oyulmuş ve bronz çivilerle çevrili bir 'screen' ve antik bir tornada yapılmış bir çok tahta tabak çıkmıştır. Sitadelde bulunmuş ve karbonlaşmış örnekler süslü tahta ve fildişi mobilyaların Megaron 3'te yıkım zamanında kullanılmakta olduğunu göstermiştir. Gordiyon'da bulunan muhteşem mobilya ve ahşap eserler kraliyet ustalarının uzmanlığı, Frig tasarımının özel nitelikleri ve Midas'ın şehrinde günlük olarak kullanılmak üzere üretilmiş eşyaların çeşitliliği hakkında bilgi vermekte ve bizler için bu kadar değerli ahşap eserlerin tümülüslerde günümüze kadar sapa sağlam olarak kalmasının ne kadar şanslı olduğunu hatırlatmaktadır.

11. Midas'ın Tekstilleri ve Altın Dokunuşu
Mary W. Ballard

Frigyanın ünü eski zamandan günümüze devam etmektedir: Romalı Pliny 'phrygio'yu tarihçiler için dantelinin başlangıcına bağlamıştır; bugün Frigya şapkası bir çok milletin ulusal armasında bağımsızlık ruhunu ifade etmektedir ve bunun yanı sıra efsaneye göre Midas'ın dokunuşu altındır. Tümülüs MM'de üç çeşit tekstil bulun, incelenmiş ve analiz edilmiştir. En önemlisi, cenaze teskeresinin yanında bulunmuş olan ve kefen olabileceği düşünülen parçaları lif temellerini kaybetmelerine rağmen neredeyse saf bir goethite ile düzgün bir biçimde kaplanmış olduklarından günümüze 'tabby' dokunmuş kumaş olarak gelebilmişlerdir. Bu ince ve pürüzsüz kaplama boyalı pigmentten yapılmamıştır, Frigliler boyamaya benzer bir method geliştirmişler ve bu yöntemle geothide liflere eşit olarak yapışmıştır. Midas'ın altın dokunuşu biyolojinin bir kazası değildi ve iyi hesaplanmış kimya mühendisliği ile yeniden tekrarlanabilir ve analitik onay yapılmıştır. Goethide kalıcıdır (yani solmaz), bakterileri oluşumunu desteklemez, ve ultraviyole ışığı engeller. Frigyalılar o halde teknik olarak üstün bir altın rengini yaratmayı başarmışlardır ve bu bir efsane olmaya layıktır.

12. Tümülüs MM'in Gölgesinde: Gordiyon'un Genel Mezarlığı ve Orta Frig Meskenleri
Gunlög E. Anderson

Gordiyon'daki Genel Mezarlık, 1950'de arkeologların Yassıhöyük köyünün yanındaki kuzeydoğu yamaçlarının batısındaki bir küçük tümülüs grubunu incelemeye başladıkları zamandan beri bilinmektedir. Bu tümülüsler orada daha önce bulunan evlerin ve birkaç yüz kadar toprak gömünün bulunduğu bir halk mezarlığının üzerine inşa edilmiştir ve bu mezarda yatanların tümülüslerin sahipleri kadar statü sahibi olmadıkları açıktır. Bu makale, Genel Mezarlığın daha detaylı bir incelemesini sunmakta ve şimdi burada bulunan mezarlık ile evlerin Orta Frig döneminde, yani 8. yüzyıldan 6. yüzyıla kadar, arada bir rastlanan yıkım ve yeniden yapım işaretlerine rağmen birarada bulunduklarını kanıtlamaktadır. Bu sonuç, evlerde kullanılan çömlekler içerisinde gömülmüş ve ev temellerine yakın olan bebek ve çocuk mezarları ile desteklenmektedir. Bu definler bazen boncuk, bilezik ve biberon içeren minik mezar sunumları ile gömülmüştür. Genel olarak bu mezarlar mütevazdır ve daha önce ellenmemiş mezarların büyük bir kısmında hiçbir hediye yoktur. Bu fakirlik evlere yansımamaktadır, bu evler terkedilmiş ve yıkılmış olmalarına rağmen gene de çanak çömlek ve aletler içerir. Bu sebeple, en azından geçim düzeyinde bir maddi kültürün olduğunu göstermektedir. Bu alanda yaşayanların Frig tümülüs yapımında çalışan bir işçi grubuna dahil olabilecekleri düşünülmektedir.

13. Midas'ın Tahtı? Delfi ve Frigya, Lidya ve Yunanistan'da Güç Politikaları

Keith DeVries and C. Brian Rose

1939 yılında Delfi'de Korint Hazinesi'nin yanında yapılan kazı çalışmalarında bulunan iki votif çukurundan birisinde neredeyse bütün fildişi bir erkek ve aslan heykelciği bulunmuştur. Teknik ve stil bakımından bu heykelciğin Anadolu'dan ve özellikle Frig'den olduğu saptanmıştır. Delfi fildişisi büyük ihtimalle bir tahtın koluna destek olan dikey bir tahtanın ön kısmına aplike edilmiştir. Özenle oyulmuş Frig stili bir mobilya parçasının Delfi'de bulunması, Heredot Tarihinde Delfi'deki Korint Hazinesi'nde bulunan ve Frig kıralı Midas'tan hediye olarak geldiğini söylediği tahtı hatırlartmaktadır. Delfi fildişisinin Midas'ın tahtının bir parçasını oluşturduğu sonucuna varmaya karşı koymak zordur. 5. yüzyıla gelindiğinde, Korint Hazinesi, Frig ve Lidya kıralları'nı da içeren Anadolu kırallar tarafından gönderilen hediyelerin ve özellikle altın, gümüş ve fildişi gibi değerli malzemelerin dikkat çekici bir biçimde sergilendiği bir mekana dönüşmüş gibidir.

Orta ve Geç Frig Sitadeli

14. Gordiyon'da Yeniden İnşa Edilmiş Sitadel: A Binası ve Mozaik Binası Kompleksi

Brendan Burke

Bu makale Gordiyon sitadelinin güneydoğu bölümünde yakın zamanda yapılmış kazı çalışmalarının genel bir özetini sunmakta ve en önemli binalardan ikisinin, A Binası'nın ve Ahameniş Mozaik Binasının tarihlerini anlatmaktadır. Bu yapılar, Erken Frig yıkım tabakasının ardından gelen yeni sitadelin tarihi ve organizasyonu hakkında, Midas'ın zamanından Büyük İskender'e kadar ki döneme ait önemli bilgiler vermektedir. 8. yüzyılda inşa edildiği düşünülen A Binası Gordiyon'daki en büyük binalardan birisidir ve ebatları Erken Frig Teras Binalarına ve Kesik Kil Yapılarına (Clay Cut Buildings) rakiptir. Bu görkemli bina geniş ve renkli yontma taşlarla kaplanmış bir moloz şevinin (glacis) üzerine inşa edilmiştir ve sur kapısıyla beraber etkileyici bir cephe oluşturmaktaydı. A Binası büyük bir değişikliğe uğramış ve Mozaik Binası Geç Frig-Ahameniş döneminde inşa edilirken ilk altı biriminden güneyde kalan ikisini kaybetmiştir. Bu iki kamu binası en azından geç milattan önce 4. yüzyıla kadar kullanılmaya devam etmiştir.

15. Gordiyon'da Pontus Sakinleri? Orta Frig'den Erken Helenistik Döneme kadar Gordiyon'da Çömlekler, İnsanlar ve Ev Planları

Mark L. Lawall

Gordiyon'un Orta Frig'den Erken Helenistik Döneme uzanan amfora buluntularının kaydı geniş Pontus amfora kalıntılarıyla çarpıcı benzerlikler göstermektedir. Gordiyon ve Ereğli (antik Herakleia) arasındaki kuzeysel bir kara yolu büyük ihtimalle bu ticarette önemli bir rol oynamıştır. Erken Helenistik Gordiyon'unun bir mimari öğesi olan taştan yapılmış köşe kutusu başka bir olasılığı da ortaya koyar. Bu çeşit kutular, basitliklerine rağmen çok yaygın değildir ancak Karadeniz'in kıyılarındaki erken Helenistik evlerde sıklıkla bulunmaktadırlar. Erken Helenistik ev yapımının bu detayı Karadeniz'le sadece ticaret yapılmadığını ve Gordiyon'da Pontuslu kişilerin bulunmuş olduğunun mümkün olabileceğini düşündürür.

Gordiyon'da Mimari Koruma

16. Gordiyon'u Hayata Döndürmek: Bir Frig Başkentinin Konservasyon ile Yorum ve Sunumu

Frank Matero

Arkeoloji ve konservasyon, dünya çevresindeki arkeolojik alanların kazı, koruma ve sunumunda önemli bir ortaklık kurmuşlardır. Gordiyon'daki kazı çalışmaları 1950 yılından beri University of Pennsylvania'nın Arkeoloji ve Antropoloji Müzesi tarafından yürütülmektedir. 2006 yılında yeni bir konservasyon programı Penn Müzesi ve University of Pennsylvania'nın Tasarım Okulu'nun Mimari Koruma Laboratuvarları himayesinde başlamıştır. Şimdi ki çalışmalar gecikmiş olan şevlerin stabilizesini, taş duvarların ve binaların korunmasını, ziyaretçiler için bir yürüyüş yolunun ve bilgi levhalarının bulunduğu gözlem istasyonlarının yapımını ve de erken çakıl mozaiklerinin analiz ve korumasını içeren entegre bir programı uygulamaya koymaktadır. Amaç, alanın ve özellikle de mimari kalıntıların yapısal ve görsel okunabilirliğinin, eski Frig inşa tekniklerinin araştırması ve kaydı ile aynı zamanda restore edilmesidir.

17. Doğadan Yararlanarak Gordiyon Sit Alanının ve Peyzajın Korunması

Naomi F. Miller

Açık hava arkeolojik alanlarında bitki örtüsünün yönetimi çevre koşullarının olumsuz etkilerini azaltabilir. Bitkiler aynı zamanda alanın sunumunda estetik ve eğitimsel açıdan da önemli bir rol oynar. Gordiyon bölgesinde\ Frig tümülüsleri tarihi peyzajin en göze çarpan öğesidir ancak sulama ve çift sürü-

mü nedeniyle tehdit altındadırlar. Sitadele gelince, bitki kökleri kazılmış yapılardaki duvarlara zarar vermektedir ve düzensiz büyümeleri alanın planının anlaşılmasını zorlaştırmaktadır. Bu sebeplerle, bitki örtüsünün yönetimi açık alandaki arkeolojik kalıntıların korumasında ve sunumunda kritiktir.

18. Lidyalı Gözüyle Gordion

Crawford H. Greenewalt, Jr.

Bu bölüm Gordion kentini, Frigli arkadaşlarının rehberliğinde Lidya'nın Sart şehrinden 550 yılı civarında gelen bir yolcunun kurmaca ziyareti aracılığı ile bizlere sunuyor. Sart'tan gelip Gordion'a varan o dönemin Lidyalısı, nehir vadisi, dağları ve anıtsal tümülüsleri ile kendi memleketine genel anlamda benzeyen bir peyzajla karşılaşırdı, her ne kadar o tümülüslerin mezar odaları Frigya'da ahşap, Lidya'da taştan yapılmış olsa da. Her iki kentte de muhteşem surlar, kamusal binaların üzerinde çok renkli pişmiş toprak mimari parçalar, ve Matar/Kibele'ye karşı duyulan derin hürmetin izleri görülmekteydi, ancak klasik çağ öncesi tapınakları hem Gordion'da hem de Sart'ta bir bilinmezi temsil ediyordu.

Index

(Ancient authors are listed at the end of the index)

ANATOLIA & THE NEAR EAST in the
EARLY & MIDDLE PHRYGIAN PERIODS

◆ Archaeological Site
● Modern Day City